LIBRARY OF RELIGIOUS BIOGRAPHY

Edited by Mark A. Noll, Nathan O. Hatch,
and Allen C. Guelzo

The LIBRARY OF RELIGIOUS BIOGRAPHY is a series of original biographies on important religious figures throughout American and
British history.

The authors are well-known historians, each a recognized authority in the period of religious history in which his or her subject
lived and worked. Grounded in solid research of both published and
archival sources, these volumes link the lives of their subjects — not always thought of as "religious" persons — to the broader cultural contexts and religious issues that surrounded them. Each volume includes
a bibliographical essay and an index to serve the needs of students,
teachers, and researchers.

Marked by careful scholarship yet free of footnotes and academic
jargon, the books in this series are well-written narratives meant to be
read and *enjoyed* as well as studied.

LIBRARY OF RELIGIOUS BIOGRAPHY

available

Occupy Until I Come

A. T. Pierson and the
Evangelization of the World

Dana L. Robert

William B. Eerdmans Publishing Company
Grand Rapids, Michigan / Cambridge, U.K.

Wm. B. Eerdmans Publishing Co.
255 Jefferson Ave. S.E., Grand Rapids, Michigan 49503 /
P.O. Box 163, Cambridge CB3 9PU U.K.

Printed in the United States of America

08 07 06 05 04 03   7 6 5 4 3 2 1

Library of Congress Cataloging-in-Publication Data

Robert, Dana Lee.
    Occupy until I come: A. T. Pierson and the evangelism of the world /
Dana L. Robert.
        p.   cm. — (Library of religious biography)
    Includes bibliographical references and index.
    ISBN 0-8028-0780-1 (pbk.: alk. paper)
    1. Pierson, Arthur T. (Arthur Tappan), 1837-1911. 2. Presbyterian Church —
United States — Clergy — Biography. 3. Evangelistic work — United States —
History. 4. Missions, American — History. I. Title. II. Series.

BX9225.P52R63   2003
266'.0092 — dc21
[B]

               2003048047

www.eerdmans.com

Contents

Acknowledgments

I want to thank Boston University and the DeFreitas Foundation for making possible the sabbatical during which I wrote this book. Thanks go to Mark Noll, Dick Darr, and Charles Van Hof for reading the manuscript. My gratitude also extends to Bill Hutchison, who offered helpful criticism of the dissertation on which this book is based; and to President Cho of Pyongtaek University, who shares my fascination with A. T. Pierson. I give ongoing thanks to my husband Marthinus, to my sons Samuel and John, and to my parents Charlie and Mary Ellen Robert.

I dedicate this book to Dr. Charles Forman, my mentor, teacher, and friend. Scion of the great Presbyterian missionary family in India and Pakistan, and advocate for Christians in Oceania, Chuck directed my initial research on A. T. Pierson twenty years ago. A superb teacher and gentle spirit, Chuck Forman has been my role model, and I thank him for all his guidance.

Introduction

In 1886, at a summer Bible conference for leaders of the collegiate YMCA, exactly one hundred young men decided to become foreign missionaries. The beginnings of the widespread student enthusiasm for missions, with its watchword "the evangelization of the world in this generation," has gone down in history as the archetypal symbol of a surging American missionary movement. Within thirty years, the United States had displaced the United Kingdom as the leading provider of Protestant missionaries. The numerical dominance of cross-cultural missions by North Americans continued unabated through the twentieth century — a century marked by the geographic expansion of Christianity to cultures of the world that were only dim fantasies to the students of 1886.

In his creation of the student watchword, his mobilization of both denominational and parachurch missions, and his editorship of the leading missions journal of the day, Arthur Tappan Pierson (1837-1911) was the elder statesman of the founding generation of student volunteers and faith missionaries. In fifty books and thousands of articles and speeches, he generated and publicized ideas that became commonplace assumptions of twentieth-century missions, including statistical analysis of the task of world evangelization, the formation of an interdenominational mission council, and the training of an indigenous mission force, to name a few. His ideas were foundational for the twentieth-century Protestant missionary movement, and his voluminous writings were freely copied by subsequent generations.

Yet most people have never heard of A. T. Pierson. The scholarly neglect of his legacy reflects the general ignorance of the so-called "conservative" side of evangelical history, including that of foreign missions. It also reflects his complexity, for his corpus was enormous and wide-ranging. Pierson was famous in his day as a missions promoter, a Bible expositor, a leader in Keswick holiness spirituality, and an urban pastor who cared passionately for the poor. He carried on a transatlantic ministry that made him more famous as a preacher in Scotland and England than in the United States. As a premillennial dispensationalist, he was a founder of the tradition that grew into American fundamentalism by the 1920s. At the same time, his cooperative work for "social Christianity" and his networking on behalf of home and foreign missions also made him a grandfather of the twentieth-century ecumenical movement for church unity. In short, A. T. Pierson's life of holistic activism defied the stereotypes of what is usually implied by the term "conservative evangelical."

While the various pieces of A. T. Pierson's legacy each merit a full study, I have chosen to write a biography that I hope will put his numerous activities and writings into a larger context. The advantage of this approach is that it reveals A. T. Pierson as a leading representative of nineteenth-century, northern, urban evangelicalism. The stages of his life reflected the changing identity of northern evangelicals as they moved from confident dominance during the Civil War period to a sense of defeat in dealing with the changing realities of American society. Immigration and religious pluralism, increasing disparity between rich and poor, and the de-centering of biblical certainty by post-Darwinian science and higher criticism all produced profound intellectual and practical challenges for evangelical Christians in the late nineteenth century. A. T. Pierson faced each of these issues head on. While his friends Dwight L. Moody, A. J. Gordon, J. Hudson Taylor, and George Müller of Bristol have all been remembered as the leading evangelicals of the day, it was A. T. Pierson who crafted the intellectual foundations for his era.

This biographical study explores the relationship between A. T.

Pierson's role in the growing foreign missions movement, and the trajectory of nineteenth-century northern evangelicalism. The ferocity with which Pierson promoted the moral superiority of the Union side during the Civil War continued into urban activism and then into foreign missions, which then captured the popular imagination of a younger generation that came of age during the era of Euro-American imperial expansion. Perhaps the most important reason to attempt a biography of A. T. Pierson was that under his prodding, the meaning of evangelicalism became attached to support for foreign missions. When he started his ministry, support for foreign missions was a minority movement. By the time he died in 1911, foreign missions had become a key marker of evangelical identity. During the twentieth century, evangelical Christianity spread beyond the borders of Europe and North America, and into South America, Africa, and parts of Asia. The universal vision to which A. T. Pierson devoted his life became a vital link between western Protestantism and the spread of evangelical Christianity around the world.

1 Yankee Protestant Beginnings

New York City was overheated and restless in the summer of 1834. Its economic power attracted over 100,000 newcomers during the 1830s and increased its population by one third. With the completion of the Erie Canal in 1825, New York had become the mercantile hub of the Northeast — connected with Europe through transatlantic shipping, and with upstate New York via the Hudson River. From there the Erie Canal headed to the Great Lakes, enabling settlers to travel to Ohio and the Midwest, carve out farms, and ship their agricultural products back to New York City on barges. Eager to make their fortunes in business, young men from older settlements in the Northeast poured into the city. Irish Catholics and Germans disembarked at Ellis Island in increasing numbers, adding volatility to the ethnic mix of Yankee Protestants, Dutch Knickerbockers, Britons, and Jews who already inhabited New York. In 1830, when the advent of horse-drawn streetcars made commuting to businesses on the southern tip of Manhattan possible, the city sprawled north beyond 14th Street. Poor immigrants, freed slaves, and New England farm boys crowded into hastily built housing as they searched for work. It was not surprising that hopes and dreams outran the ability of the city to absorb them all.

But tensions other than ethnic, religious, and economic also played a role in the riots that broke out during the summer of 1834. A group of Presbyterian and Congregationalist businessmen, led by brothers Arthur and Lewis Tappan, and supported by clergymen of the Third Presbytery of New York, had become abolitionists. Based on a radical evangelical Christian faith that asked them to reject all known sins, a group of Protestant New Yorkers, many from old New England families, came to believe that slavery was a sin. Arthur Tappan, the largest silk importer of the era, formed in 1831 a New York committee to oppose slavery. National anti-slavery organizations soon followed. The network of abolitionist activity roused the ire of many. For most Americans, the plight of slaves in the South was less important than the cheap cotton and other agricultural products produced by slave labor. The workingmen who crowded into New York City worried that an influx of freed slaves would make it even harder for them to find jobs. And besides, slavery had only died out in the North within living memory. Most people assumed it would eventually die a natural death in the South as well.

Arthur Tappan was a controversial figure because he used his wealth and power to spread his beliefs. Having moved to New York City from Connecticut, he was seen by the old New Yorkers as an extremist outsider. Exercising the prerogatives of a Christian businessman of the era, he made sure that all his employees attended church and were home nightly by 10:00 P.M. In August 1829 he invited the young and controversial revivalist Charles Finney to preach at his church, the Laight Street Presbyterian. A former lawyer, Finney was known for using "new measures" in his preaching, calling on sinners by name, and "working up" revivals. His preaching of immediate repentance of sin and subsequent growth in grace introduced a kind of perfectionism into Presbyterianism — something that conservatives distrusted, but that encouraged the stark ethical commitments of abolitionists. After Finney's visit, Tappan and other Finney followers founded a new congregation as New York's first "free church," one that did not charge pew rent. The "free church" system ensured that the poor and visitors could be seated during worship services by eliminating the normal practice whereby families who paid the most money got the best seats in the church, while strangers stood in the back. Using his fortune to support free churches, Finney-type revivalism, home missions, tract distribution, the temperance movement against liquor, anti-prostitution, and other causes, by the mid-1830s Arthur Tappan had become infamous as a leader of the abolitionist movement. Not only did Tappan support the end of slavery, but he also supported racial integration as a logical result of abolishing slavery. Southerners considered him so dangerous that they offered bounties of as much as $100,000 for his body.

Anti-abolitionist rioting broke out on July 7, 1834, at the Chatham Street Chapel, the first free church in the city. Arthur and Lewis Tappan had renovated the Chatham Street Theatre into an auditorium-like sanctuary and had called Finney to be its pastor, a post he occupied from 1832 to 1836 when he wasn't touring elsewhere as an evangelist. The converted theater was part of the Tappans' strategy to provide space where poor as well as wealthy New Yorkers could worship. With room for 2500 people, it sat in one of the worst neighborhoods in New York City. The Tappans used the chapel as the headquarters of their evangelistic enterprises and made it available to various anti-slavery, African-American, and other reform-minded groups. But reflecting public opinion, a local newspaper called the chapel a "common focus of pollution" because of the mixed ethnic groups and radical social causes it hosted. On the evening of July 7, a group of black men and women were gathered in the chapel to hear a black preacher. Because of misunderstandings over who was supposed to be using the chapel building that night, a fight broke out that soon attracted a crowd. The crowd of unemployed, recent immigrants, and the generally curious began to riot, fueled most likely by racial prejudice and fear of competition for jobs from free blacks — a widespread reason why most Americans opposed abolitionism in the 1830s. Someone in the crowd spied Lewis Tappan, who was monitoring the situation at his church. Screaming curses, a mob followed him home and stoned his house.

The next evening a crowd again gathered at the Chatham Street Chapel. Hearing a speaker that incited them not only against abolitionism but against the English, who were perceived by Yankees and Irish immigrants alike as oppressors, the crowd broke into a theater on Bowery Street that was managed by an Englishman. Following a scuffle with police, the growing crowd surged along the streets to Lewis Tappan's house where they broke down doors and windows and began tossing his furniture, bedding, and other possessions into the street. When police arrived to quell the mob, it responded by throwing bricks and kindling a bonfire with Tappan's personal property. Not content with destroying Lewis Tappan's house, the next night a mob attacked the Laight Street Church, whose pastor Dr. Samuel Cox was an abolitionist and friend of the Tappans. After breaking the windows, wrecking the church, and cursing "abolitionists and niggers," the mob regrouped at Cox's house, broke it open, and began to sack it. Fortunately the Cox family had left town earlier that day. The night's nasty work ended with a stand-off against police, in which the mobs heaved paving stones in unison from behind barricades in the street.

The fourth day of rioting, July 10, began in the morning once again at Dr. Cox's house, but was quelled by the arrival of a hundred policemen. The mayor called out troops to be ready for further disturbances. At nightfall, crowds gathered in front of Arthur Tappan's store and began stoning it. Tappan's watchmen and clerks tried to resist the mob, but had to flee from its violence. Threats from city officials, combined with police presence, got the mob to move on. But attacks resumed against the Laight Street Presbyterian Church. Another mob attacked the Spring Street Presbyterian Church, also a church with an abolitionist minister and part of the Third Presbytery. Wrecking the windows, ripping out the pulpit and the pews, the crowd piled their booty in the streets as a barricade against the police. Instead of policemen armed with clubs, the 27th Regiment of the National Guards arrived with axes and bayonets, and marched through the barricades, thus dispersing the mob. During the same evening, other mobs attacked the houses of abolitionist clergy, a black church, and diverse locations in the city. The next day the mayor restored calm through a massive show of force and by arresting 150 ringleaders.

Although the abolitionist riots failed to destroy Arthur Tappan's store, in August 1835, residents of Charleston, South Carolina, began boycotting his silk-importing business — a movement that spread across the South. According to Bertram Wyatt-Brown, the boycott was "one of the first organized attempts to bankrupt a national business because of its owner's political and moral convictions." Then in December 1835, the "great fire" burned fifty-two acres of the Manhattan business district, including five to seven hundred buildings, causing damages of eighteen million dollars and destroying Arthur Tappan's silk wholesale house. Bad harvests in 1836 that drove up the price of food, combined with poor financial markets, ushered in the financial Panic of 1837 in which every bank in New York suspended payments, and thousands of businesses failed across the country. This was the world that greeted A. T. Pierson at his birth.

On March 6, 1837, the ninth child of Sallie and Stephen Pierson was born in their apartment above the Chatham Street Chapel. A mere month before his birth, within sight of the chapel a hungry mob ransacked warehouses that reportedly contained flour being hoarded by rich merchants seeking a higher price. The financial panic had driven men to desperate actions as they sought to feed their families. Despite the unenviable risks of living above a controversial building that was nearly wrecked in the riots of 1834, the Pierson family was undoubtedly grateful to Stephen's employer for his patronage. Confidential clerk to Arthur Tappan, Stephen Pierson had risen through the ranks of clerks to become Arthur Tappan's cashier and trusted assistant. When the anti-abolitionist mobs attacked the Tappan store in 1834, he was standing guard with a loaded musket. Besides sharing his hardships, the Piersons also shared Tappan's evangelical Presbyterian religion and anti-slavery commitments. An active member of the notorious Third Presbytery, the home of free churchism and abolitionism, Stephen Pierson was an elder at the Spring Street Church. He had remained with Arthur Tappan through riots and boycotts, fires, threats, belt-tightening, financial panic, and near bankruptcy. In admiration for their patron and friend, Sallie and Stephen named their baby Arthur Tappan Pierson.

Two months after the birth of his namesake, the evangelical abolitionist finally went broke. Selling all his possessions down to his watch to pay his creditors, Arthur Tappan became an employee of his former firm.

A CHILD OF THE THIRD PRESBYTERY

The boy Arthur Tappan Pierson grew up in the New York City of the 1840s. Like many other New Yorkers, his parents were transplanted Yankees descended from old colonial families — part of the new white-collar commercial class, born Protestant and out of state. The first American Pierson, Abraham, was also the first pastor of the oldest church in Newark, New Jersey. He and other strict Puritans had separated from their home community in Branford, Connecticut, moved to New Jersey in 1666, and founded what became a Presbyterian church on theocratic principles. Abraham Pierson believed that those who were not church members should be denied the vote. Grateful townspeople renamed their town Newark after their pastor's birthplace in Newark-on-the-Trent, England. While yet pastor in Branford, Connecticut, Pierson had worked to evangelize the Mohegan and Mohican Indians, preaching to them in their own language and writing a catechism for them. His son, Abraham Pierson, Jr., also a pastor, was a founder and the first president of Yale College, which was founded to combat theological laxity at Harvard. John Pierson, a grandson of Abraham Pierson, was a charter trustee of the college of New Jersey (now Princeton). In the early 1800s, religious commitment remained strong in the Pierson family: Stephen Pierson and his wife Sallie were devout Christians, who raised all ten of their children as evangelical "New Light" Presbyterians. Mrs. Pierson was also descended from one of the founding families of Newark, where she and her husband first met. According to family lore, Arthur Pierson resembled his mother in intelligence and energetic personality.

Like his siblings before him, Arthur attended morning and afternoon Sunday School at Spring Street Presbyterian Church, as well as the regular worship services. There he received his first impressions about the cause to which he would later devote his life — foreign missions. One of his teachers was a young woman preparing for the mission field. At age 7, he joined Spring Street's children's mission band. The Pierson home was marked by the family devotions then typical of an evangelical Presbyterian household — morning and evening worship, memorization of the catechism and Scripture verses, and the Sabbath kept as a day of worship and rest. Throughout his life, Arthur Pierson followed his childhood practice of keeping the Sabbath as God's holy day, with Bible study and worship the only permissible activities. In a family of ten children, there was never much money to go around. After the bankruptcy of Arthur Tappan's business, Arthur Pierson's father worked as an accountant in various business ventures without much financial success. But the family managed to move into their own home further uptown above Canal Street when Arthur was still small. Like other city boys, he played on the streets, chasing fire engines and looking for excitement where he could find it.

Theological controversy was no stranger to the Pierson family. Stephen Pierson was an elder in the Third Presbytery, the group of radical evangelical Presbyterian churches involved in many reforming social causes. The movement to abolish pew rent and to welcome the poor into the churches accompanied strict personal piety — including opposition to liquor and the theater, and firm Sabbath-keeping. Periodic revivals punctuated the life of the Presbytery, which unlike "Old School" Presbyterianism encouraged personal religious experience over strict doctrine. On a national level, the entire Presbyterian denomination split into "Old School" and "New School" factions in 1837, the year of Pierson's birth. Old School churches adhered to narrow interpretations of the Bible, and disliked innovations such as revivalism and grassroots cooperation with Congregationalists. New School churches favored revivalism, broader interpretations of Scripture, and cooperation with Congregationalists in benevolent activities such as tract and Bible distribution, and especially in planting churches throughout the opening West. The Old School accused the New School of doctrinal laxity. In 1837, not only did the denomination split, but the New School faction began building Union Theological Seminary in Washington Square. Most of the support for the new training school for ministers came from the Third Presbytery, which provided seven of the first ten clergymen on its board of directors.

One problem with the combination of revivalism, moralism, and social reform that characterized the Third Presbytery was that members fought among themselves. The whole experiment of abolishing pew rent collapsed around 1840 because without the rent, churches were becoming mired in debt. Also, despite supporting the abolition of slavery, many members of the eleven free churches in New York City still did not want to integrate the pews. It was well enough in theory to talk about ending slavery and welcoming the poor into one's churches, but showing hospitality toward former slaves by sitting next to them in church was another matter. In 1834 when Arthur Tappan sat in the same pew with a mixed-race Presbyterian clergyman, some members of his church threatened to quit. Most churches in America at the time segregated the white and black members, with African-

Americans confined to the balcony. Opposition to slavery did not imply racial equality in most people's minds.

When Arthur Pierson was a little boy, an event occurred in which he was too young to participate, but that later became very important to him. In the summer of 1839, fifty-two African slaves on board the slave ship *Amistad* mutinied and killed the captain and cook. The slaves had just been auctioned on the slave market in Havana, Cuba, and were being shipped to their final destinations. Taking their owners prisoner, the mutineers ordered them to sail to Africa. But at night the owners changed course northward, hoping to land in a southern slave state where the mutineers would be arrested. Finally with provisions exhausted, the leader of the slaves left the ship to find supplies. The entire group was spotted and arrested for piracy off the coast of Long Island. They were taken across Long Island Sound and jailed in New Haven, Connecticut. Arthur Tappan's brother and business partner Lewis, who was living in New Haven at the time, visited the slaves in jail. While arranging for their spiritual instruction, Lewis Tappan began raising funds from sympathetic anti-slavery churches for their legal defense. In a series of trials, the federal court threw out charges of piracy and murder against the slaves, and ordered that as illegal immigrants they should be returned to their homeland.

The case of the Mendi Africans, so-called because of their tribal origins in Nigeria, focused northern churchgoers' attention on the plight of slaves as nothing had done before. The situation of an actual boatload of Africans ending up in Connecticut gripped the public imagination. Creating additional sympathy for the Mendi Africans was their apparent conversion to Christianity while jailed in New Haven. Anti-slavery advocates led by Lewis Tappan hoped to return them to West Africa as missionaries. In the early 1800s, anti-slavery activity and missions to Africa were linked in both the British and American evangelical mind. For mission supporters, converting Africa to Christianity would be the means of its salvation, both spiritually and socially. Christianizing Africa would prevent its people from being enslaved and would begin introducing the stability of western civilization. Mission supporters believed that Christian Africans who learned to read and write would engage in legitimate business and agriculture that would supplant the illegal trade in human beings.

Lewis Tappan and a black pastor in Connecticut, J. W. C. Pennington, began raising money to return the Mendi Africans to Africa as missionaries. The court had freed them, but it provided no means for their return to Africa. Tappan took the Mendi Africans on fundraising tours to churches in New England. In New York City they held their largest rally at the Broadway Tabernacle, an edifice built by Arthur Tappan that was even larger than the Chatham Street Chapel. By singing, speaking, and re-enacting their capture, the Mendi Africans helped raise enough money to outfit a ship for their return. In November 1841 the group held a farewell service at the Broadway Tabernacle. Accompanied by American and African-American missionaries, the Mendi Africans sailed to West Africa as the first mission of the American Missionary Association, a newly constituted, interracial, abolitionist enterprise. Dedicated to founding missions among persons of African descent, both in the United States and overseas, by 1852 the A.M.A. had begun five missions and thirteen stations abroad as well as work among former slaves in the southern United States. All missionaries of the A.M.A. were committed to the principles of abolitionism. Once the North won the Civil War, the A.M.A. sent hundreds of teachers to the South to train the newly freed, illiterate former slaves in basic skills of reading and writing. A.M.A. missionaries were among the most persecuted, despised missionaries of the day because of their close association with African-Americans. White southerners often resented their presence and opposed their educational work.

Arthur Pierson was probably too young to have been aware of the initial public furor over the Mendi Africans. It is likely, however, that his parents contributed money to the Mendi Mission alongside fellow members of the anti-slavery Third Presbytery. Pierson's parents might even have gone to see the recaptives when they performed at the Broadway Tabernacle. In 1848, when Arthur was an impressionable 11-year-old, his cousin George Thompson departed for the Mendi Mission as a missionary. Unable to reach their homeland in Nigeria, the Mendi captives had resettled in Liberia, a country in West Africa founded explicitly by Americans to resettle recaptured slaves. After its founding, the Mendi Mission faced a huge setback because most of the captives threw off their Christianity and returned to their pre-captivity ways. The first American missionaries to the Mendis then died of tropical diseases or lost their interest in the mission, and by 1845 the famous mission verged on collapse. A noted abolitionist, Thompson had

been imprisoned for five years in Missouri for breaking laws supporting slavery. After his release, he was ordained by the American Missionary Association. He worked in Sierra Leone for two years, helping
to put the Mendi Mission back on a firm foundation. After leaving the
mission field in ill health, Thompson remained in the United States as
a missionary recruiter.

Although it is unclear how much the abolitionism of his parents
and cousin directly affected his childhood, as an old man, Pierson
wrote proudly of the abolitionism and missionary work of George
Thompson. To a surprising extent, Pierson's ministry in later life bore
the imprint of a childhood spent in the Third Presbytery of New York
City. Evangelical piety and moralism, free church principles, devotion
to helping the urban poor, and foreign missions all dominated his mature ministry. Although the Emancipation Proclamation and the Union
victory in the Civil War effectively ended his active opposition to slavery, he nevertheless remained committed to the rights of the oppressed. In imitation of the man for whom he was named, the struggle
to take a Christian stance against the easy morality of the "world" was
a thread that ran through the life of Arthur Tappan Pierson.

CONVERSION AND EDUCATION

In 1850, at the age of 13, Arthur Pierson was sent up the Hudson River
to boarding school. As was common in evangelical families, Stephen
Pierson gave his departing son a life motto. It was from Proverbs 3:5-6,
"Trust in the Lord with all thine heart and lean not unto thine own understanding. In all thy ways acknowledge Him and He shall direct thy
paths." The boarding school in which Arthur enrolled had an evangelical orientation, and the principal hoped that each boy would make a
personal commitment to Jesus Christ while there. Accordingly, the
boys were encouraged to attend special revival meetings in the local
Methodist Church in Tarrytown, a nearby town along the river. Methodism in the early 1800s was the fastest-growing branch of Christianity in the United States. By 1850 one-third of churchgoing Americans
were Methodists. With its emphasis on revivalism and gathering converts into small spiritual groups, called "class meetings," Methodism
had a reputation for vigorous piety and personal religious experience.

While attending the revival meetings, Arthur publicly accepted Jesus Christ as his Lord and Savior. Although he had always attended Presbyterian Sunday School, had memorized the Westminster catechism and studied the Bible, he had not previously experienced the emotional power of claiming his own personal salvation through Christ. He later recalled this initial conversion experience:

> One night I was much moved to seek my salvation. When the invitation was given I asked for the prayers of God's people and decided to make a start in serving God by accepting Jesus as my Saviour. On my way back to the school I was forced to ask myself: How am I to act as a Christian before the other boys? We all slept in large rooms with five or six beds and with two boys in each bed. As I went up to where I slept I felt that now or never I must show my colours. If my life were to count, I must give some testimony before my schoolmates.
>
> The boys were not yet in bed and as some others had attended the meeting, the word had preceded me, "Pierson is converted." The boys were waiting to see what I would do. There was not one other Christian in the ward and my own bedfellow was perhaps the most careless, trifling and vicious boy in the school. My first hour of testing had come; much depended on how I would meet it.
>
> As I undressed for bed, I asked God for courage and then when ready to turn in, knelt down beside the bed and silently prayed. The boys were quiet for a moment, then a few began to chuckle, and presently a pillow came flying at my head. I paid no attention to it, though praying was not easy just then — if by prayer is meant consecutive, orderly speaking to God.
>
> My schoolmates were not malicious but only bent on "fun," and when they saw that I did not move, their sense of fair play asserted itself. One of the older boys said: "Let him alone," and silently they all picked up their pillows and got into bed. I was never again disturbed when praying before my fellows.

Arthur Pierson's conversion in Tarrytown was the first of several important personal religious experiences during his lifetime — and not the only one that took place outside of Presbyterian circles. His public experience at the Methodist revival underscores the ecumenical nature of early nineteenth-century evangelicalism: evangelicals could cross denominational lines because they were united in a common experience of Jesus Christ. After his conversion, Arthur for a short time joined a class meeting at the Methodist Church of Tarrytown.

Throughout history, Presbyterians had greatly stressed a learned ministry. In the churches descended from the Protestant reformers, including the Puritan tradition of Pierson's family heritage, the ordained minister was seen primarily as someone educated to read the Bible in its original Hebrew and Greek and interpret it for the congregation. Arthur Pierson may have had a Methodist conversion, but he needed to study the classical languages if he hoped to be ordained as a Presbyterian minister. Accordingly, the following year he transferred to a school in Ossining, New York, about five miles up the Hudson River from Tarrytown. The Ossining School was run by his sister Annie's husband, who was a minister. Prior to the Civil War, Presbyterians had founded more schools and colleges than any other denomination in the United States. With their emotional revivals, Methodists may have outpaced the Presbyterians in planting churches, but in the early nineteenth century, Presbyterians reigned supreme in establishing higher educational facilities across the United States. Many young Presbyterian clerics acted as school teachers on the frontier before settling into a pastorate. While studying in Ossining, Pierson lived with his sister and studied languages, writing, and public speaking so as to prepare himself for a future career in the ministry. He also enjoyed the natural sciences and was teased by other boys for filling his pockets with rocks and other "specimens."

After graduating from the Ossining School, Arthur Pierson returned to New York City to earn money for college. Having graduated from high school at the age of 15, he was too young to be accepted at Columbia, the leading college in his home town. So he joined the thousands of young men who had moved to New York hoping for work. Although Arthur was living with his family, many of the city's other young men were living away from home for the first time. In an era in which cities provided practically nothing by way of family entertainments, sports facilities, or vocational courses, the major leisure occupations were frequenting bars and gambling. Following long, hard hours at factories and businesses unenlightened by minimum wages and labor laws, workers in the New York City of the 1850s gravitated after hours towards bars, cheap theaters, and brothels. Hard liquor was the drink of choice among New Yorkers. No movies, no television, no soft drinks, no gymnasia, no electricity — for the rootless, little to do in New York City except to work and get drunk. With sanitation poor, New York City experienced several cholera epidemics during Arthur's youth that impressed him greatly — especially when none of the members of his church died. For young singles with poor wages, New York City in the 1850s was a brutal place.

The problems of industrialization and urbanization had begun in England a generation earlier than in the United States; while the United States was expanding across the continent, Britain was becoming industrialized. With the most powerful navy in the world, Great Britain kept its factories humming by importing raw materials from its various colonies and then exporting its manufactures abroad. Workers moved off the farms and created industrial zones and slums in cities like Glasgow, Edinburgh, Manchester, Birmingham, and London. In 1844, a young draper's assistant named George Williams decided to organize Christian outreach toward workers in London. Christian life seemed impossible for most young Londoners because they lived in employer-owned housing, worked twelve-hour days, and were hounded by rowdy peers. Williams founded associations of young men for Bible study, evangelistic work, and mutual encouragement. He soon added courses and lectures to meet the young men's desire for higher education. Eventually, recreational activities became part of the program to keep men off the streets and out of trouble. Williams named his organization the Young Men's Christian Association.

In 1852, the YMCA arrived in New York City. On May 28, three hundred young men crowded the lecture room at the Mercer Street Presbyterian Church to learn about the new organization. Having earlier that year joined the Thirteenth Street Presbyterian Church in which his father was then an elder, perhaps Pierson had heard from his minister about the upcoming meeting. At the meeting, leaders of the YMCA described its purpose, and one hundred seventy-three young men joined on the spot. Twelve hundred joined the New York City YMCA in the first year, with Arthur Pierson as one of the charter members. The movement attracted the cream of New York's evangelical youth. The first membership list of the young American "Y" drew its strength from activistic evangelical Presbyterians and Congregationalists like Arthur Pierson. In his case a lifelong commitment to the evangelistic program of the YMCA, beginning at the age of fifteen, eventually took him around the United States and across the ocean in its service. At the sixty-third anniversary of the YMCA in London in 1907, Pierson gave the closing address and reflected on what the movement had meant to him since his adolescence: "Of all the achievements of the Victorian era, none, perhaps, in the moral and religious sphere, eclipse the Y.M.C.A. which I joined in New York over fifty years ago. It helped me at a critical period of life; helped to keep me within moral and religious restraints; turned my attention anew toward the ministry; helped to train me in debate; to bring me into hallowed associations; it helped my heart, conscience and will."

Because of the temptations of city life, Pierson's parents decided that rather than going to Columbia College, he should again return to upstate New York where evangelical religion was strong, and where there were more trees than pubs. In 1853 he therefore matriculated at Hamilton College in Clinton, New York. Clinton was situated in the "burnt-over district," so-called because revivals and religious enthusiasm broke out regularly in that part of New York State. In one dramatic incident, a movement of people waiting for the end of the world spread like wildfire in the area. When the world did not end in 1844, the movement reorganized itself as the Adventists. In 1848, in Hydesville, two sisters claimed to communicate with the spirits of the dead and began holding séances. Spiritualism subsequently broke out across the United States. Mormonism began in Palmyra when a poor laborer named Joe Smith claimed to have found golden plates that contained a new gospel, with North America as the destination for the lost tribes of Israel. Despite all the new religious movements spawned in the "burnt-over district," evangelical "New School" Presbyterianism remained the dominant religious presence. Anti-slavery sentiment was also very strong in the Clinton area. After the Republican Party organized itself in 1854 on an anti-slavery platform, that region of New York State went solidly for the new party.

More than one prominent Presbyterian had attended Hamilton College — Albert Barnes the Bible commentator; H. G. O. Dwight the missionary linguist in Constantinople; and Theodore Dwight Weld, the chief organizer of anti-slavery societies in the Midwest. Weld had been converted by evangelist Charles Finney while a student at Hamilton. Finney himself, the most famous revivalist in ante-bellum America, probably attended Hamilton when it was a Presbyterian preparatory school, before it was chartered as a college. At any rate, Finney was well known as a special friend of Hamilton. Undoubtedly Stephen Pierson had met Finney, since Arthur Tappan had outfitted both the Chatham Chapel and the Broadway Tabernacle for Finney's use in New York City. The Hamilton College tradition thus seemed an excellent choice for a young man from New York's Third Presbytery, who was headed for the ministry.

Arthur took to college life like a duck to water. His enthusiasm and self-confidence were so high that a professor had to pull him aside and caution him that freshmen were better seen than heard. As a student from the big city, he carried an air of precocious self-confidence and wore stylish clothing that impressed boys who had come to college straight off the farms. In addition to his studies, Arthur took every opportunity to give sermons and lectures, and to write articles that he submitted to newspapers and magazines. Gaining a reputation as a poet and essayist, he published over a hundred newspaper and magazine pieces by the time he was 21. By modern standards the poetry was heavy with ornate imagery and overwrought moralism that betrayed Pierson's interests in both classics and in piety. But the young Pierson wrote many charming and creative essays on religion and the natural sciences. He sang in the glee club and earned money for his expenses by playing the organ in a village church. Ever concerned about issues of fairness, he published a humorous seven-part essay series on freshman life in which he poked fun at the "Prez" and hidebound college traditions, but also criticized secret societies and the hazing so popular among Hamilton students. An early photograph shows a wiry teenager who weighed only 124 pounds, with wavy dark hair that fell away from his high forehead.

In academic subjects, Pierson excelled at composition, rhetoric, oratory, and linguistics. His guiding purpose remained intellectual and spiritual preparation for the ministry. Arthur also followed a common practice among evangelicals of the eighteenth and nineteenth centuries by keeping a journal in college in which he recorded not only daily events, but deeper spiritual reflections on his growth in grace. As his son pointed out years later, the remarkable thing was not that he began such a journal, but that he kept it up for sixty years. He recorded the spiritually hopeful conversions of his friends, and the results of his own conversations with them on spiritual topics. In Arthur's junior year at Hamilton, the famous Charles Finney, now president of Oberlin College in Ohio, conducted revival services in the town of Hamilton. The death of a classmate at about the same time created the heightened spiritual atmosphere conducive for a revival at the college, something for which Arthur had been working and praying. Active in the local church, he taught a Bible class and was secretary of a village missionary society. He led many of his pupils to Christ. By 1857 he had adopted a systematic plan of Bible reading whereby he read one chapter a day and three on Sunday, a process that enabled him to read through the Old Testament once and the New Testament twice each year and a half. Strict Sabbath-keeping, journal writing, Bible study, church work, and bringing his friends to Christ — these marks of exemplary evangelical character were all in place by the time Arthur was 20 and graduated from college in 1857.

REVIVAL AND SEMINARY

During 1857-1858, a revival swept over urban areas in the eastern part of the United States. This so-called "Businessman's Revival" began in New York City when a former merchant named Jeremiah Lanphier decided to hold a Wednesday noon prayer meeting for businessmen during their lunch hour. Lanphier was one of the many young men who had migrated to New York in the 1830s, looking to participate in the financial boom. After twenty years of striving in business, Lanphier changed careers and became a city mission worker for the Fulton Street Dutch Reformed Church. Located in the business district, close to Wall Street in lower Manhattan, the Fulton Church seemed an ideal location for Lanphier's experimental outreach to the white collar community. He held the first meeting on September 23, 1857, with six participants. After three weeks, when between thirty and forty attended, Lanphier moved the prayer meeting to a larger space and began daily meetings. Within six months, the noonday prayer meeting had spread throughout cities in the east. By April and May 1858, secular metropolitan presses began covering the "Businessman's Revival," a fact that accelerated its momentum. Stories of the revival sold a lot of newspapers: the revival thrived on news reporting, and newspapers thrived on the revival. The Revival of 1857-58 was thus something of a watershed in the commodification of popular religious piety. Although thousands of religious newspapers and periodicals flourished in the early 1800s, the discovery that religion also sold secular newspapers marked the beginning of an alliance between revivalism and the media that continued into the era of Billy Graham.

The Revival of 1857-58 coincided with Arthur Pierson's return to New York City to attend Union Theological Seminary, the favored training ground for "New School" Presbyterian ministers. Since the year of Pierson's birth, Presbyterianism had been rent by the split between the more conservative, confessional "Old School," and the more revivalistic, ecumenical "New School." Although by the 1850s the increasing theological conservatism of the New School had pushed the two factions closer together than in the 1830s, the New School further split in 1857 between North and South. Some scholars have seen the Revival of 1857-58 as a kind of spiritual preparation by the North for the war against slavery. But in order to maintain the nondenominational unity behind the revival, its organizers forbade discussion of inflammatory political issues like slavery, or whether women could speak in church. The revival itself, therefore, proceeded strictly along personal spiritual lines. Firm rules against political controversy, coupled with strict timetables that guided the length of the testimonies, sustained its pace. Another factor that contributed to its success was a financial panic in 1857. Many of the businessmen who crowded the meetings in lower Manhattan had probably lost their jobs or seen their incomes collapse. In such times, the need for prayer support and spiritual unity intensified.

The new seminarian plunged himself into the revivals. The YMCA of which Arthur was a charter member helped promote and regulate the noon prayer meetings. At the Thirteenth Street Presbyterian Church, easy walking distance north of the seminary on Washington Square where he lived, Pierson led a Bible class of eighty-four, all of whom he helped lead to Christ. The revivals resulted in a membership increase of two hundred forty-five, and Pierson shepherded the new members into a deeper relationship with God. Along with his pastor, he visited seekers and helped in city missions. On Sunday nights, he visited the prisons. Seeking a deepening of his own faith, he began attending inquiry meetings every night. In late March 1858, he experienced the "baptism of the Holy Spirit" and then recorded the value of his own spiritual infilling in his journal:

> I am every night in the meeting for inquiry and feel that the experience is of incalculable value to me. I have just begun to realize the true worth of souls and the true secret of living near to Christ. Now I am constantly and perfectly happy. Christ manifests Himself to me very clearly and closely and I feel that "for me to live is Christ and to die is gain." How sweet it is to do anything for Christ! How strange it is to be permitted to do anything for Him at all. I feel that I have been baptized with the Holy Spirit and am fully resolved never again to pass a day when I cannot feel at its close that I have done something for my Saviour.

Just what did the "baptism of the Holy Spirit" mean for Arthur Pierson in 1858? After all, he was already a "born again" Christian, with a disciplined spiritual life, studying for the ordained ministry. In the theology of his Presbyterian tradition, there had traditionally been little interest in the Holy Spirit. Rather, the work of salvation had been fully accomplished by Christ on the cross for those who were called by him. But a major feature of the Businessman's Revival was that lay people led it, with large-scale participation by Methodists and by women. Although women were typically discouraged from attending the noonday prayer meetings planned for businessmen, they attended other meetings at various times and in many different churches. Just who was holding the evening inquiry meetings at which Pierson received his spirit baptism is unknown. Yet a lay-led, popular spirituality that spread widely during the revival focused on the "baptism of the Holy Spirit."

Methodist lay woman Phoebe Palmer was the acknowledged leader of the search for the spiritual "second blessing," called variously by different terms such as the "experience of perfect love," the "baptism of the Holy Spirit," or "sanctification." She and her physician husband Walter had for decades used the New York home they shared with her sister to conduct a Tuesday afternoon prayer meeting. Through teaching in small groups and at revivals, Palmer brought thousands to a deeper, second religious experience, one that often happened years after their conversion. Her ideas about the "second bless-ing" spread widely during the Revival of 1857-58. Although Presby-terians typically did not embrace such views of sanctification, those from the experiential side of the "New School," such as revivalist Charles Finney, developed a Reformed version of the Methodistic, ex-periential piety. During the revival, Presbyterians and Congregational-ists began using the idea of the baptism of the Holy Spirit to explain their deepened religious feelings of the abiding sense of God's pres-ence. As a young seminarian with his "New School" background and his Methodist conversion experience, it is not surprising that Arthur Pierson was seeking a deeper level of spirituality during the Revival of 1857-58.

Pierson was not the only seminarian at Union to participate in the Businessman's Revival, for it became a defining spiritual experi-ence to a whole generation of men who went on to become the reli-gious establishment of the Northeast after the Civil War. Many of Pierson's generation grew up to become evangelical leaders for whom personal religious experience was the foundation of interdenomina-tional cooperation. Revivalist Dwight L. Moody, born the same year as Pierson, was perhaps the standard bearer of the generation — a YMCA man active in the revival who promoted unity for the sake of evange-lism and missions. Many of Pierson's contemporaries had life-shaping religious experiences in 1857-58, including Moody in Chicago, and John Wanamaker in Philadelphia, who launched a slum Sunday School during the revival and later became a prominent businessman. Pierson's own friend and classmate, George E. Post, felt the call to be a missionary at the same time. Becoming one of the first professors at the Syrian Protestant College, now the American University of Beirut, Post became a well-known "surgeon, botanist, Arabicist, orator, au-thor" and more. Another friend and seminary classmate, D. Stuart Dodge, became the chief benefactor and president of the Board of Trustees of the Syrian College, which was initially a mission project of the American Board, the oldest American foreign-mission sending agency and one supported by many New School Presbyterians during Pierson's youth.

During the financial downturn of the late 1850s, Pierson's father lost his job when his current employer failed. Already on a student budget, Arthur now had need to support himself, which he did by playing the organ at his church, providing private tutoring, and offering public lectures. In the summers he worked as supply preacher, filling vacant pulpits on Sundays. To his immense relief, a well-off uncle named John Gray invited Arthur to live with his family for the final year of his seminary training. Gray was originally from Ireland, and during the revival he hosted a delegation of Irish Protestant clergymen who wanted to observe the revivals and compare them to similar events in Belfast. As Arthur conversed with the visitors from abroad, he developed a desire to hear the great preachers of Victorian Great Britain. That Charles Finney and Phoebe Palmer both departed for Britain to conduct widely acclaimed revivals in 1859 no doubt deepened Pierson's awareness of the transatlantic connections in mid-nineteenth-century evangelicalism.

During his three years at Union Theological Seminary, Arthur Pierson learned many lessons both in and out of school. His personal discipline in Bible reading and the revival's spur to his piety gradually deepened his walk of faith. Learning to take financial risks in confidence that God would supply his needs was an important step of faith he took in seminary. The summer before his senior year, Pierson had earned a hundred dollars from supply preaching, more money than he had ever had at one time. Since his father was unemployed, Arthur needed to use the money to meet his expenses during the school year. When he learned that a seminary classmate from a poor family was down to his last fifty cents and had been unable to find a job, Pierson struggled over whether to keep his hundred dollars.

> The thought kept persistently recurring: I have money and no immediate need and this other child of God has dire need and no money. I consulted my Bible — that ever faithful guide-book — until I was convinced that God taught his children not to hoard earthly treasure, but to use what they have for the relief of the destitute and to trust Him for the supply of future needs. This teaching is unpopular but it is Scriptural and I could not gainsay it. After much thought and prayer I decided to give my friend one-half the money as a loan. I told him that I had no present use for it, and added that if, as my own funds became exhausted, God Himself should supply my need, the loan would become a gift; if not, he could repay it as he was able.

After spending the remaining fifty dollars on his own needs, Arthur received unexpected help from others on four separate occasions, precisely when he needed it. In the end, he forgave the loan and turned it into a gift to his needy friend. These early steps toward living on faith, directly dependent on God to meet his daily needs, were the beginnings of his later support for the "faith missions" movement.

Also outside the classroom, Pierson deepened his knowledge of oratory. As the political atmosphere grew tense, with the impending split between North and South, anti-slavery orators found new audiences in New York City. For Arthur this often meant walking to the Cooper Institute to hear lectures on the public issues of the day, most notably slavery, on the lower east side. Especially exciting speakers were William Lloyd Garrison, the founder of the American Anti-Slavery Society, who edited the incendiary abolitionist magazine *The Liberator;* and anti-slavery orator Wendell Phillips. From Phillips, Pierson learned that a firm moral basis, rather than artistry or drama, was the proper foundation for a moving speech.

Outside the classroom, Arthur Pierson even took the time to learn something about love. While he was attending Hamilton, his parents had moved temporarily to Chicago for work. They entrusted their New York house to a family whose daughter Arthur soon met during a Christmas vacation. His relationship with Sarah Frances Benedict continued during his seminary years. Quiet and patient, Sarah Benedict provided a good balance for the excitable and active Arthur Pierson. Photographs show a woman with a high forehead and large eyes — an attractive face pervaded by a calm spirit. They became engaged despite Arthur's hectic schedule of theological education, evangelistic work, and studying. The fact that she did not complain when he put his work first was a good indicator to Arthur that she would be suitable as the life partner for a future clergyman. A tactful person, Sarah was also helpful to a fiancé and then husband whose stubbornness and tactlessness became legendary. As a temperamental and self-disciplined idealist, Arthur Pierson's firm principles led both to phenomenal accomplishments and an annoying intensity. Sarah Benedict was willing to devote her life to supporting her husband's ambitions and passions, and occasionally to smoothing out the rough edges.

Despite the distractions of New York City in the late 1850s, a blossoming love life, and the start of his pastoral work, Arthur Pierson thrived at Union Theological Seminary. Founded by revivalistic Presbyterians as a place of ecumenical openness and partnership with other denominations in the Reformed tradition, the seminary had five professors and about 125 students while Pierson was there. Among professors who impressed him most was Dr. Thomas H. Skinner, in rhetoric and pastoral theology. Dr. Elias Riggs, the famous missionary to Turkey and Bible translator, nurtured Pierson's understanding of foreign missions. But Professor Riggs made a stronger impact on fellow classmates George Post and D. Stuart Dodge, who went out from seminary to missions in Muslim lands. At this stage of his life, Pierson's literary ambitions were too strong to permit him, or so he thought, to waste his education by going abroad among the less cultured "heathen." Dr. Roswell Hitchcock, professor of church history and future president of Union Seminary, acted as something of a mentor by helping the young theologue find employment and even asking Pierson to become his assistant pastor after ordination. It was Hitchcock whom Pierson asked to participate in his ordination service.

But the professor with the greatest impact on Arthur Pierson was Henry Boynton Smith, professor of church history and systematic theology. Along with Charles Hodge, Horace Bushnell, Edwards A. Park, John Nevin, and Philip Schaff, Smith was one of the leading theologians of his generation. From the beginning of his teaching at Union Seminary in 1850, he was the most influential "New School" theologian of his era. His capacities as bridge-builder and peacemaker made him a leader of the movement after the Civil War to reunite the Old School and New School branches of the church. A former Unitarian, Smith had studied theology and philosophy for three years in Germany, but he rejected the radical German historical research on the life of Jesus. Instead of using biblical higher criticism to discover a supposedly earthly Jesus, Smith maintained his faith in the Bible as traditionally interpreted by the Reformed tradition of Protestantism. To him, the Bible remained a divine book, the Word of God. A man of broad interest and sympathies, Smith was nevertheless a biblical inerrantist committed to the plenary inspiration of the Bible: all parts of the Bible are divinely inspired, the object of such inspiration being "the communication of truth in an infallible manner, so that, when rightly interpreted, no error is conveyed."

Smith's ecumenism, combined with his doctrine of biblical infallibility, profoundly shaped Arthur Pierson. Smith's teachings reinforced both Pierson's tolerance of other evangelical denominations and his unwavering seriousness toward every word in the Bible. Smith and the students he trained revitalized the cooperative, ecumenical aspect of the New School tradition. This tradition had declined somewhat in the 1840s and 1850s after the split with the Old School, when the New School became more withdrawn and less activistic. Henry B. Smith tried to reactivate the outreach of the New School by basing it on as high a view of Scripture as maintained by Charles Hodge and the Old School seminary at Princeton, New Jersey.

But biblical inerrancy was not on Arthur Pierson's mind when he was finally licensed to preach on April 3, 1860. He graduated from seminary in May and was ordained as an evangelist in the Third Presbytery of New York City. The designation "evangelist" was unusual because most Presbyterians were ordained as pastors of particular churches. It is likely that Pierson was ordained as evangelist because of his great promise and his already considerable experience in bringing people to a personal decision for Christ, but also because he lacked a call from a specific church upon graduation. Nonetheless, the designation "evangelist" was appropriately prophetic of the new minister's future nomadic lifestyle. At the ordination service at Thirteenth Street Presbyterian, his pastor preached the sermon on the progressive unfolding of revelation in the Bible. Because Dr. Roswell Hitchcock of Union Seminary was prevented by illness from attending the service, his substitute Dr. Walter Clarke asked the trial questions of Pierson, gave the ordaining prayer, and delivered the charge. Then on July 12, Arthur Pierson and Sarah Benedict were married.

Twenty-three years old, graduated, ordained, and married, Arthur Pierson felt ready for full-time ministry. Raised in the ethically charged piety of the Third Presbytery, converted and spiritually deepened in revivals, and disciplined through participation in evangelistic outreach and rigorous formal education, the young theologue possessed a firm foundation for his ministerial vocation. All he needed was a church willing to provide him housing and a steady income. On their honeymoon, the newlyweds learned that Arthur had received calls not to one, but two different churches. Now all they had to do was decide which offer to take. In the summer of 1860, the future looked bright.

2 Early Ministry: From Authoritarianism to Activism

With the zeal of his Puritan ancestors, the self-assurance of his abolitionist heritage, and the self-righteousness of a recent seminary graduate, 23-year-old Arthur Pierson accepted a unanimous call to serve as the pastor of the First Congregational Church of Binghamton, New York. It was not strange that a Congregational church would call as minister a Presbyterian, since under the old Plan of Union, from 1801 the two denominations had established a program of cooperative church planting. Although the Plan of Union had been dissolved, Yankee evangelicals in both denominations still shared similar perspectives on theology and ethics. In addition, the Binghamton church's willingness to call a newly married, recent seminary graduate probably reflected its poor financial condition and an inability to afford a more experienced minister. The young pastor faced big challenges in his first congregation: it was divided into factions, labored under severe financial problems, and was badly located next to a more successful and well-established Presbyterian church. Binghamton itself, an upstate New York city of ten thousand inhabitants, lay squarely in the revival belt of the early nineteenth century. By the 1860s, however, revivalistic energy had given way to spiritual languor. Arthur Pierson entered this scene eager to save the world, fresh from the spiritual high of the Businessman's Revival and his own ordination.

The idealistic young preacher was installed on Wednesday, September 5, 1860. The installation of a pastor was a solemn affair in the mid-nineteenth century, particularly for congregations that hired their ministers after an often lengthy search process. The evening service gives a glimpse into the religious world in which Pierson moved. It opened with the reading of council minutes pronouncing the candidate satisfactory. Following prayer, Scripture readings, and a choral anthem, the Reverend Professor Benjamin N. Martin of the University of New York preached from Ezekiel 3:17-19, encouraging Pierson to speak the gospel of warning and judgment despite pressure to take things easy. The formal prayer of installation, charge to the pastor, and extension of the right hand of fellowship followed. After completion of the ceremonies, the Congregational minister from the neighboring town Elmira, the Reverend Thomas K. Beecher, stood to speak. In tones described by the local newspaper as typically "Beecherian," he charged the congregation not to find fault with their new pastor, but to give him a chance. He also told them not to expect the pastor's wife to "take the lead in everything." Beecher was something of a local celebrity as the brother of the famous writer Harriet Beecher Stowe, whose anti-slavery classic *Uncle Tom's Cabin* had only recently been published. A long-term, experienced pastor himself, the son and brother of famous ministers, Thomas Beecher encouraged the people to let their newlywed minister have his privacy, and to live out the truths they heard him speak. Newspaper accounts of the installation reported that the congregation was suitably impressed by the service of two and a half hours.

The Sunday following this auspicious installation, Pierson eagerly mounted the pulpit to address his expectant listeners. Congregational churches, descendants of the Puritan tradition, typically built a high pulpit as the focal point at the front of the sanctuary. Plain, almost severe, wooden churches dominated by a prominent pulpit underscored the centrality of preaching in the life of Congregational churches. The new preacher's first sermon set a serious tone and high expectations for his ministry. Preaching on 1 Corinthians 2:2, "I determined not to know anything among you save Jesus Christ and Him crucified," the young theologue laid out the doctrines of Christ as incarnate Son of God, as crucified Savior, and as the one who meets the deepest human needs. In the evening service, he preached on John 13:20, "Verily, verily, I say unto you, he that receiveth whomsoever I send, receiveth me." Having laid out an exalted view of Jesus Christ in the morning service, in the evening service he similarly endorsed a high view of the ministry by arguing that the minister is an ambassador of Christ. The congregation was to treat the minister as a person of dignity in his position as spiritual leader. Although a fallible human, Pierson proclaimed, the minister "is professionally a student of spiritual things and on these subjects it ought to be presumed that he is right until it can be shown that he is wrong. . . . Otherwise measures over which a pastor has studied long and earnestly may be defeated by the crude and ignorant opposition of some layman." Thus in his first day on the job, the eager young minister laid out both his theological platform and his view of the minister's authoritative role in the community. His first sermon at the First Congregational Church, Binghamton, pegged him as an intense young man who took himself very seriously. He had not yet learned the lesson that marks mature ministry, namely, it is better to establish a relationship with the congregation before preaching to them about clerical authority.

CALVINIST AND PIETIST

The ease with which young Pierson claimed the mantle of "ambassador of Christ" seems peculiar to our more egalitarian age. His presumption of authority in spiritual matters would not have struck the old-timers in his congregation as odd, however, for nineteenth-century Presbyterians and Congregationalists were heirs to the Reformed tradition of the "learned ministry." During the Protestant Reformation in the sixteenth century, many of its most important leaders were scholars, including John Calvin, the father of the Reformed tradition. The heart of the Protestant Reformation was rediscovering the importance of the Bible. Rather than relying on the inherited doctrines and customs of the Roman Catholic Church, Protestants believed that the Bible contained within it all that was necessary for salvation, namely, the idea of God's grace for those saved by Jesus Christ from sin and damnation. Early Protestant leaders in England, Germany, and France were scholars who translated the Bible into the languages of the people so that they could read about God's plan of salvation for themselves. Those in the Calvinistic tradition, in particular the English Puritans who founded New England in the early 1600s, believed that the Bible provided the model for daily life. All practices in the church and community must conform as closely to biblical norms as possible. Given the importance of understanding the Bible properly, the New England Puritans were led by some of the best-educated, university-trained men of their day. The chief task of the Puritan minister was to study and interpret the Bible for the local community. Puritan clergymen not only delivered sermons on Sundays and theology lectures midweek, but they also gave biblical addresses on important public occasions, such as election days. The minister was a leader in the entire community, not only the church. Preparation for ministry therefore required the best liberal arts education possible, including years of studying Greek and Hebrew, the original languages of the Bible.

In preaching his first sermons, Pierson placed himself in this Reformed tradition of the learned ministry. Like his Puritan forebears, he viewed the minister as one divinely called by God and who studied long and hard so as to interpret the Bible, the Word of God, for his congregation. Pierson's assumption of leadership stemmed from his unwavering belief that the chief work of ministry was to preach the Word of God. The ministerial task was a public one, and the relevance of the Bible extended beyond the personal needs of his parishioners to social issues affecting the larger community. Although Pierson believed that all Christians should read and interpret the Bible for themselves, believers needed the guidance and assistance of "professionals" who understood its original languages.

Yet at the same time as he embraced the model of learned ministry, Pierson was a product of American revivalism. Early in his Binghamton pastorate, he decided never to preach on anything that he had not personally experienced or practiced himself. His own life was punctuated by spiritual peaks, starting with his conversion as a schoolchild, and then especially his experience of the Holy Spirit during the revivals of 1857-58. He wanted his sermons to strike the hearts of the hearers. His goal as minister was to convert his own congregation by bringing them to a personal experience of Christ who had called them and saved them individually from their sins. In addition to conducting worship services in Binghamton, he held regular small-group prayer meetings and youth meetings at which he worked to bring people to the point of conversion, a moment of explicit faith in Jesus Christ. As a product of revivals himself, he longed for others to gain the spiritual power and emotional certainty that characterized evangelicalism in the early 1800s.

According to George Marsden, leading historian of American fundamentalism, the paradoxical fusion of Calvinism and pietism, of intellectualism and emotionalism, was a chief characteristic of Puritanism that was carried through the nineteenth century in "New School" Presbyterianism and then into twentieth-century fundamentalism. This creative tension between learning and piety was evident during Arthur Pierson's Binghamton pastorate, and it would characterize his entire ministry. Rather than choosing either intellect or emotion, he balanced disciplined, exhaustive Bible study with a pietistic search for religious experience.

CRISIS OF FAITH AND THE "EVIDENCES OF CHRISTIANITY"

But Pierson's fame as both Bible teacher and spiritual leader was not yet assured in his first pastoral charge. Not everyone in his new congregation wished to be instructed and converted by an earnest yet inexperienced 23-year-old. Claiming the authority of "ambassador of Christ" was probably the first of several strategic pastoral blunders committed by the young minister. According to a later biography by his son, "As the uncompromising character of the pastor became known, enemies began to test the strength of his armour. He found himself the target for a fusillade from infidels who sent him pamphlets and books by the score in their efforts to find a joint in his harness." As the new minister was confronted by questions he could not answer, heady self-confidence gave way to crushing doubt, and a crisis of faith in the basic doctrines of Christianity that apparently lasted some months. He even began to doubt the "inspiration of the Bible" and the certainty of his own salvation in Christ. As the difficulties of his pastoral appointment grew painfully evident, Pierson sank into depression. He realized that despite his own experiences, he was preaching a faith inherited from his parents rather than one constructed from his own soul-searching and Bible study.

To deal with the spiritual crisis and doubts that threatened to overwhelm him, Arthur Pierson began studying the "evidences of Christianity." Coming from a devout evangelical family, he had probably not been confronted previously by the popular skepticism about biblical authority that had entered American consciousness with the eighteenth-century Enlightenment. His self-confident sermons irritated the "village atheists" of the congregation, who barraged him with critical questions about the truthfulness of the Bible. Since he had staked his own ministerial authority on the Bible, he interpreted the people's doubts about biblical integrity as attacks on his own ministry.

Among the many features of the eighteenth-century Enlightenment was the idea that all truth was provable through scientific observation rather than inherited tradition. The Enlightenment produced ideas that underlay American independence, namely the "rights of man," democracy, and the concept of government as a contract between the people and their rulers. As part of attacking inherited authority, the Enlightenment had also defined as "facts" only those things that could be proven through rational observation. The Enlightenment therefore encouraged modern science, in which the truth of something was proven by empirical evidence. Carried to extremes, however, this reasoning proved a problem. Christian doctrines that were regarded as true because of their supernaturalism, such as the existence of God and the truth of the Bible, were now questioned because they lacked empirical proof. By definition, what was supernatural could not be "scientific." Only the natural, the observable, and the provable could pass the standards of rationality upheld by extreme partisans of the Enlightenment.

As public intellectuals, clergymen in the Puritan tradition were the mediators of scientific, Enlightenment thought to the people in the pews. Through their education and rationality, they had long held the front line against "superstitious" popular religious practices such as astrology or predictions of the future through supernatural "signs and wonders." In the early 1800s, therefore, one of the major tasks keeping American theologians busy was a "scientific" defense of Christianity. Assuming that all truth could be scientifically proven placed a premium on the search for the "evidences" of Christianity. Theologians believed with confidence that Christianity was a provable, rational religion, unlike other faiths with their presumed superstitions, wild creation stories, and unethical practices. Classes in apologetics, or evidentiary defenses of the Christian faith, were common at theological seminaries. Major theologians like Archibald Alexander of Princeton Seminary and Andrews Norton of Harvard Divinity School wrote tomes on biblical evidences. One way the "evidences" worked was by finding analogies between the natural world and the characteristics of God. For example, Christian naturalists found parallels to the Resurrection in its analogy to caterpillars emerging from the chrysalis as butterflies. Another way of using the "evidences" was to offer geological proofs consistent with the Genesis account of creation. By the 1840s, lectures on the various "evidences" of Christianity were widely popular. Congregationalist and Presbyterian missionaries among non-Christian religions also tried to prove the truth of Christianity by showing its compatibility with the modern, scientific worldview.

In the early 1860s, when Arthur Pierson began his study of the "evidences of Christianity," he did so with the assumption that there was no conflict between science and faith. From the rock-collecting days of his boyhood, he had been interested in the natural sciences. He enjoyed writing popular essays on the sciences, and on scientists such as the German naturalist and explorer Baron von Humboldt, and the French mathematician and philosopher Blaise Pascal. In 1857-58, he wrote a six-part series for the *Clinton Courier* titled "A Visit to the Sea." Elaborating on different aspects of ocean life, he recommended that people buy an aquarium tank and set up their own "aqua vivarium," with a perfectly balanced, self-sustaining combination of fish and plants. God's existence would be confirmed if people studied his creation carefully. "We heard a lady of great intelligence say that she could not see how one could be a Christian and not have a microscope. And there is a great deal of truth conveyed in this seemingly extravagant remark. — How can we love God as we ought without studying the works of His hand? He who said under divine inspiration, 'add to faith, virtue,' said also, 'add to virtue, KNOWLEDGE!'" With a view of science keyed to observation of the natural world, Arthur Pierson believed similar direct study of the Bible would reveal its truth.

Confronted in Binghamton with skeptics' doubts about the truthfulness of the Bible, Arthur Pierson set about systematically studying the biblical prophecies according to scientific principles of observation and classification. Along with other theologians whose philosophical principles were forged before the Civil War, he was a firm adherent of "Baconianism," an American school of Scottish common sense philosophy. Scottish common sense philosophy dominated the ministerial training for Presbyterians and Congregationalists, especially after its effective promotion by John Witherspoon, the Scottish-born minister who became president of Princeton College in 1768. The principles of Scottish realism were that "philosophy depends on scientific observation," and moral judgments could arise from "self-evident intuitions." Baconianism took its name from the inductive approach of Sir Francis Bacon, the seventeenth-century lawyer and philosopher, who argued that knowledge of the natural world should be based on the "common sense" accumulation and classification of data acquired through observation, rather than on trusting the authority of the ancient philosophers. According to Protestants who used the Baconian method, the Bible was a clear, historical statement of facts easily understood by the methods of "common sense." Theologians, especially Presbyterians like Charles Hodge, professor of theology at Princeton Seminary from 1840 to 1877, developed their views of biblical inspiration in a Baconian fashion. Baconianism reinforced American Enlightenment belief in the virtues of the common man, the self-evidence of truth and human morality, and the futility of abstract metaphysics.

As he struggled to prove the truths of the Bible, Arthur Pierson wrote an article, "Aristotle and Bacon," that outlined his first formal position on the Scriptures. Arguing that Aristotelian and Baconian methods were two alternative systems of science, Pierson rejected Aristotelianism as speculative and deductive, "leading downward from a supposed law or conjectural theory, to the phenomena whose explanation is desired." Baconian philosophy, by contrast, sought the "practical improvement of the happiness of man." Its system was inductive, "leading upward from particular facts or phenomena to some general law, by which they may be explained." Bacon's method was to analyze and classify facts until a correct hypothesis explaining the facts could be proven. Benjamin Franklin's experiments with electricity were an oft-cited example of the inductive method.

Pierson argued that the Baconian method came from the Protestant Reformation, especially from Martin Luther who had applied "inductive" methods to Bible study. The proper method of Bible study was not the Roman Catholic, Aristotelian way of twisting Scripture to preconceived dogmas, the way of "deduction." Rather, "inductive" Bible study consisted of investigating "the facts as to what the Bible teaches, and comparing spiritual things with spiritual thus ascertain[ing] what is truth." Studying the Bible must begin with the texts, "which are as the phenomena, from which a true philosophy will discover its laws of interpretations." Not only did Baconianism apply to Bible study, but it also guided the Christian education of children. The role of the teacher was to present the truth to the child, who would observe the "facts" of salvation and hope to be saved. Knowledge was the way to faith, and faith was empirical proof of having correct knowledge.

In his first real crisis of faith, Pierson resolved his doubts about the truth of the Scriptures through inductive study of the Bible. As he studied the evidences of Christianity and wrestled with the biblical witness that undergirded his beliefs, he experienced a breakthrough in which he became firmly convinced that the Bible was the Word of God. Although Pierson still saw apparent contradictions in the text, he learned to recognize that the explanations for biblical discrepancies might not come until later in life or in the hereafter. God's truth was one, whether the form was scientific or biblical. But the believer must wait for the Spirit of God to reveal God's mysteries. As stated in the Proverb given to Arthur by his father as a life motto, he must not rely only on his own understanding. Pierson reflected while writing in his journal after a period of doubt, "My gloom lasted for days, but was then dispersed by a most marked communication of the Holy Spirit, conducting me to a full assurance of faith. It was an uncommon experience of the grace of God."

Arthur Pierson's crisis of faith during his first pastorate was not the only one he would experience, but it was probably the most serious because it was so early in his career that it caused him to question the entire basis of his faith. Only a few years later, his reading of Charles Darwin's works on evolution would cause him to sharpen his view of the relationship between science and the Bible, and to craft exegetical tools that led him out of the pastoral ministry into a career as Bible expositor. But the resolution of this early crisis firmly entrenched him in a lifelong, "Baconian" commitment to inductive Bible study. Pierson's clarity about his epistemology — his principles of knowledge — was such that historian George Marsden uses him as a primary example of how common sense realism led to the development of fundamentalist biblical exegesis in the late nineteenth century. What must not be overlooked is that the resolution to Arthur Pierson's first and most serious crisis of faith was emotional and spiritual, not only intellectual. Although he diligently applied his reason to the problem of doubt, it was a cathartic experience of the Holy Spirit that finally resolved the crisis. Just as he had experienced childhood conversion in a Methodist revival, and had embraced deeper religious faith during the Businessman's Revival of 1857-58, it was a spiritual experience that calmed the churnings of rationalistic doubt. In fact, he took his personal religious experience as proof that his understanding of Scripture was true. Writing on "Spiritual Emotion" in the early 1870s, Pierson affirmed that knowledge begets emotion, and that the brain is the way to the heart. Systematic reflection promotes religious emotion, as deep spirituality has a basic rationality. In the mold of eighteenth-century theologian Jonathan Edwards, Arthur Pierson recognized the interdependence of his mind and his heart, and in the final analysis refused to tear them asunder. The deep spirituality of Pierson's intellect belies the stereotype of evangelicalism as a form of dry rationalism, and it underscores his continuity with the New School of Charles Finney, the Beecher family, and nineteenth-century revivalism.

Even as Pierson was working through his intellectual and spiritual doubts, life in his Binghamton church was proving difficult. The problem was factionalism, with two groups of parishioners even refusing to sit on the same side of the church as each other. Despite his best efforts, they refused to be reconciled. In frustration, Pierson began preaching sermons against the sins in the congregation. In one sermon, "Iniquitous Solemnities," he preached about those who attended church services out of unrighteous motives — visibly pious but secretly sinful. The negative reaction to the sermon was so great that a fellow clergyman had to intervene with the congregation and defend Pierson's courage in "speaking the truth."

Another of the evils against which he preached was the tendency of the church to cultivate the rich and neglect the poor. The system by which most churches supported themselves in the nineteenth century was that of pew rents, whereby the richest members of the church who could afford to pay the most were rewarded with the best seats in the church for themselves and their families. Everyone knew from the seating arrangement who were the rich power brokers in the congregation. The pew rent system made it difficult for the poor or for visitors to worship in the church, as they had nowhere to sit or were relegated to bad seats. Having grown up in the experimental "free church" Third Presbytery, Pierson now learned of the evils of the pew rent system first hand. As he recalled many years later,

> The church of which I was then pastor was comparatively poor; my congregation had few men of means, and even my small salary was not easy to raise. The building was small, unattractive, badly located. . . . I found myself preaching to a congregation where everything was done to gather and retain families that added nothing to our spiritual power and influence, and all others were neglected. The prayer-meetings were almost deserted; Christian activity sank to its lowest ebb. The poor who were rich in faith were pushed aside, or crowded out to make room for the worldly and even wicked who had more means. And so, whenever I lifted my voice against abounding sins, or spoke against worldliness and wickedness with point and power, I was openly threatened with the withdrawal of some who paid the highest pew rents, or it was quietly whispered to me by my trustees that it would not do to alienate those from whom my support was mainly drawn. God did not leave me to cowardice and silence; but gave place to others, who, with less money, brought what is far more precious, spiritual health and strength and help. But though the Lord may graciously nerve His servant to disregard threats, the tendency of such a system is to shut one's mouth, and intimidate the minister of Christ.

Arthur Pierson's challenging experiences in his first pastorate were all too common for earnest young ministers. His elitist assumption of authority based on his education rather than gaining the sympathy of his congregation, his inability to solve interpersonal disputes that predated his arrival, his condemnatory attitude toward the human weaknesses of his parishioners, and his crisis of faith when confronted with skepticism — all these factors constituted a baptism by fire into the realities of ordained ministry. In addition, personal difficulties were compounded by the severe poverty in which his family lived. His elderly parents, with father seriously ill and paralyzed, came to live with him. Sarah Pierson bore two little girls in quick succession. But the church went months without paying the promised salary, leaving the Piersons unable to pay their medical bills, rent, and food. They subsisted on oatmeal, potatoes, and pea soup. Arthur was embarrassed at having to beg for money from the very people over whom he regarded himself a leader. But the Piersons' troubles in the Binghamton church did not arise solely because of Arthur's inexperience in the ministry, for his first pastorate coincided with the greatest social trauma of nineteenth-century America — the Civil War.

THE CIVIL WAR: AMERICA'S MISSION TO THE WORLD

Barely three months after Pierson's installation, on December 20, 1860, South Carolina seceded from the Union because of the election of Abraham Lincoln, presidential candidate of the newly organized anti-slavery Republican Party. The long-festering sore of slavery broke open as one southern state after another followed its lead by withdrawing from the Union and joining the Confederate States of America. The country plunged into anxiety and confusion, as government officials disagreed on how to handle the constitutional crisis. Was the sacredness of the Union worth any compromise with the South? Did the regional disagreements mean it was better to let the South go peacefully rather than retain a nation divided over such a basic issue as slavery? After all, had not the largest churches of the nation — Methodist, Baptist, and Presbyterian — been divided over the issue of slavery since the 1840s? How could the victory of the Republican Party on an anti-slavery platform be respected while maintaining the peace? Most Americans opposed war as an unthinkable last resort. Lincoln's assumption of the presidency on March 4, 1861, did little to resolve the crisis.

The nightmare of indecision became the certainty of war when on April 12, 1861, President Jefferson Davis of the Confederacy demanded the surrender of Fort Sumter, a federal garrison in the Charleston, South Carolina, harbor. Federal troops had consolidated forces there within firing range of Charleston. After brief resistance, they capitulated. Overnight, Northern opinion coalesced in opposition to the Confederacy. When President Lincoln called for 75,000 volunteers to quell the rebellion, young men eagerly stepped forward. The addition of the upper South to the seven states of the lower South solidified the Confederacy, and the two sides prepared for war. For most white Northerners, the beginning of the Civil War was not about slavery, but about the preservation of the Union. The secession of the South forced a fight to maintain the territorial unity of the United States, not necessarily to free blacks from bondage.

Historian James Moorhead argues that the fall of Fort Sumter infused moral significance into rhetoric about saving the Union, for since the time of the American Revolution, many American Christians had commonly believed that democracy was part of the progress toward God's kingdom foretold in the Bible. Once the Union was threatened by violence from the slaveholding states, Northern clergy easily equated the Union with God's coming kingdom, arrayed against the evil Confederacy. In ministers' eyes, the struggle between North and South represented the cosmic battle between good and evil, between democracy and slavery. The Southern secession violated America's divine mission to spread democracy and freedom around the world; the Confederacy was clearly evil and needed to be resisted at all costs. Just as the eighteenth-century Congregational clergy had seen the Revolutionary War as part of the cosmic struggle between good and evil, so did nineteenth-century Congregational clergy in the Northeast see the coming Civil War as a cosmic confrontation.

Ministers from anti-slavery traditions were the first to seize upon the idea of Civil War as a great moral struggle. Abolitionists saw the coming war as the showdown with slavery for which they had been waiting all along. Coming from an abolitionist family to whom slavery had long been regarded as a sin, Arthur Pierson supported the possibility of Civil War as a great moral crusade — a virtual form of home and foreign missions. Reading the "signs of the times," clergymen like Pierson saw the hand of God at work in the unfolding events. In continuity with the Puritans who believed the New World was to shine like "a city on a hill" and dispense the light of truth to the rest of the world, Pierson and other activistic clergy, especially those of the New School, interpreted the outbreak of war as part of God's plan both to cleanse the soul of America and spread true liberty and true religion around

the globe. The Businessman's Revival of 1857-58 came to be seen in retrospect as the spiritual preparation for the crusade.

Early in 1861, as the nation waited with bated breath to see if war
could be averted, Pierson's political stance was controversial in
Binghamton. Not all of his parishioners were comfortable hearing sermons about "politics." Not only were many people opposed to going
to war with the South, but they were not convinced that ending slavery was worth bloodshed and the sacrifice of their children in armed
conflict. Would not slavery end gradually in the South, just as it had
ended in the North? As he preached against slavery and in favor of
war early in 1861, Arthur Pierson found himself the object of criticism
in his church. Then volunteers across the country began mobilizing for
battle in response to President Lincoln's call. Young men from Broome
County, in which Binghamton was located, eagerly signed up for military service. As the nation waited to see if a twenty-day armistice
would cool off the heated passions in North and South, Companies A
and B of the Broome County volunteers prepared to depart for the
front. Still a newcomer in Binghamton, Pierson opened his church for a
farewell service on May 5, 1861. In a building that seated three hundred people, the soldiers and well-wishers packed the pews, leaving
many standing and hundreds turned away for lack of room. The volunteers had received Bibles given them by the Broome County Bible
Society to wear next to their hearts. The young minister gave what
would become the most famous sermon he preached in his three years
in Binghamton, "The Duty of Civil War."

The fortunate few who obtained seats stood as the choir sang the
"Star Spangled Banner" for the opening of the service. Ascending the
pulpit, Pierson read the text, Judges 20:28, "Shall I yet again go out to
battle against the children of Benjamin, my brother, or shall I cease?
And the Lord said go up!" Comparing the occasion to the beginning of
the Revolutionary War, he solemnly stated, "Since that day when the
old liberty bell in Philadelphia rang out its wild peal to announce that
the 'Declaration of Independence' was signed, the country has seen no
day such as this. . . . It is sufficient to say, we are undoubtedly on the
eve of civil war. The chief magistrate has granted twenty days for rebels to disperse and lay down their arms, and that armistice closes to-
morrow; but thousands have yet failed to comply with its terms and
must meet conflict." After alluding to the biblical example of Israel at

37

war, Pierson defended the morality of war as compatible with Old Testament teachings and as justified on the grounds of self-defense. With violence clearly opposed to the teachings in the New Testament, how could a Christian nation justify armed conflict? Christians should not fight for revenge, he argued, but the corporate body of Christians should defend itself from attack or from creeping evil. In the case of the firing on Fort Sumter and the secession of the Southern states, the nation should defend its unity by fighting the aggressors, even though, like the children of Benjamin, they were brethren. Truth was sometimes advanced by resistance rather than by "patient suffering."

While recognizing that brother killing brother would be the most painful aspect of the conflict, Pierson argued that the unchecked growth of evil and moral ruin was even worse. Civil War was necessary because peace with slavery was an even more horrible alternative.

> War is dreadful; civil war is awful; fraternal war is horrible; no sane man can dispute it. — But there are some things even worse; a forever divided nation nominally one is worse; perpetuated and increasing evils are worse; civil anarchy or despotism is worse; a shattered republic is worse; a demoralized nation is worse; a vitiated social sentiment is worse; inevitable moral ruin is worse!

In the years leading up to the outbreak of hostilities, the North had repeatedly appeased the South for the sake of peace. Slaveholders were allowed to be equal citizens, and gag rules in Congress had long suppressed the discussion of slavery. As were most anti-slavery Americans, Pierson was still uncertain how to accomplish the immediate abolition of slavery without "ruining the nation," presumably by releasing a flood of freed African-American slaves into general society. Calling himself a "moderate" rather than "extremist," Pierson nevertheless called slavery wrong and "a great evil." He believed that slavery must be contained by force if necessary until God providentially made clear the way to abolition. Although secession was the "stalk," slavery was the "root" of the war. In a reference to the Dred Scott Decision of 1857, in which the Supreme Court annulled the agreement that had prohibited slavery from western territories, Pierson insisted that slavery must not be admitted into the free states and must be stopped by war.

In the end, Pierson justified the coming Civil War because of the sacred mission of the United States. If the government falls, "it buries underneath its ruins the liberties of mankind." Not only was the United States the great beacon of Liberty to the world, but it was the source of true Religion as well. "When the Pilgrim Fathers reared this noble lighthouse on these western shores and lifted the Bible as the lantern in that lighthouse, we had hope that sending out its holy rays it would glance across the mountains and down into the valleys of our own land, flooding all with a mystery of glory, and thence leaping even across Atlantic and Pacific seas, strike the shores of the old world and illume the darkness of heathen lands. If that lighthouse fall, who can tell how seriously the cause of the world's spiritual illumination is to be for centuries retarded in its advance." Pierson continued, referring to the eager young volunteers packing the pews, many of whom were undoubtedly his own age, "I was thinking tonight that we have here in these young men a living contribution to Home and Foreign Missions. For every drop of life-blood spilt in this struggle to save our nation from ruin, is a sacrifice offered to the cause of evangelization on our own borders and throughout the world." The sacred significance of the coming war was because "the battle is God's. In the name of our God we will set up our banners."

For Arthur Pierson, a Yankee born and bred, the sons of the Puritans had a mission to evangelize the world by fighting against slavery. War against the South was a form of mission. As someone who always looked for God's hand in the "signs of the times," Pierson found divine significance in the coincidence that the first blood spilled both in the Revolutionary and Civil War was on April 19, and in both cases the dead were from the same township in Massachusetts. As participants in God's war, the young recruits of Broome County must not be motivated by greed or by vengeance. Rather, they must believe that in the words of President Lincoln, "right makes might." Duty must be done, and ultimate victory was certain. Pierson challenged the troops, "As you go forth to rescue from worse than heathen desecration the temple of our liberties and faith, . . . let your battle cry be, 'It is the will of God.'" And whether they lived or died, he concluded, one day all would be reunited in the company of the redeemed in heaven.

Arthur Pierson's view of mission in his mid-twenties was dominated by his generation's experience of the Civil War. As a married man with children, a clergyman, and sole support of his elderly parents, it was out of the question that he enlist himself. But certain of the righteousness of the North's position, especially after slavery was abolished by the Emancipation Proclamation on January 1, 1863, he fought the Civil War on the home front as an apologist for the moral superiority of the North. As the war dragged on, he wrote and organized on behalf of the Christian Commission, a voluntary organization that came into existence to care for the religious and physical needs of Union soldiers. It distributed tracts and other literature to soldiers, assisted military chaplains, and helped families communicate with their loved ones on the front. Over five thousand volunteers enrolled in the Commission, which also raised money and collected medical supplies and clothing for the soldiers.

The financial sacrifices required to pay for the war fell heavily on the civilian population. Sending the Broome County volunteers was only the first of many hardships for the people of Binghamton. For the first two years of the Civil War, the Union reeled from one defeat to another. Despite superior economic resources and a larger population, the Northern generals seemed unable to counter the superior military skills and spirited troops of the Confederacy. The North realized that its perceived moral superiority did not instantly translate into military victory. More soldiers, more money, and more sacrifices by grieving families were required to defeat the Rebels. By late 1862, Pierson's salary had evaporated completely. His spiritual maturity had steadily deepened, but his pitiful financial condition only multiplied the discouragement he felt about his ministry. He realized that the church could no longer afford to pay a minister, and therefore drastic measures were necessary. His parishioners disagreed over the best solution to their financial crisis. Some wished to dissolve the church, while others wished to push on. Pierson supported a third option — that of moving the church across the Chenango River and away from competition with the more successful Presbyterian church next door. In the midst of the controversy, Arthur Pierson resigned his charge on January 4, 1863, on the condition that the congregation sell its property and move across the river. The money they would save by not trying to support him would go into establishing themselves in a new location. Praising him for the good relationship and work he had cultivated with the congregation, the church council regretfully accepted his resignation. At age 25, with a growing family to support and Union troops in disarray, the Reverend Arthur Pierson was unemployed.

MISSION RENEWED: THE
WATERFORD YEARS, 1863-1869

The year 1863 was a turning point for both the Pierson family and the Union cause. In the summer, Arthur's paralyzed father died, leaving his widowed mother to make her home with him for her remaining thirty-two years. His older brother Joseph, a fellow minister and role model who had performed the wedding of Arthur and Sarah, died also. Arthur worked as summer supply preacher in the Congregational Church of Norwalk, Connecticut, thereby requiring the family to relocate. But following the untimely death of their pastor, the Presbyterian Church of Waterford, New York, unanimously voted to call Pierson to its pulpit in August. This upturn in the Pierson family fortunes mirrored the turning of the Civil War toward Union victory. After suffering massive defeats by the Confederacy for the first two years, the Union regained its morale with the issuance of the Emancipation Proclamation. The clarification of the moral issue of slavery seemed to reinvigorate the Union cause, and the numerically superior Yankee forces began overwhelming the Confederacy, beginning with the Battle of Gettysburg in July 1863. Hope blossomed. As Union victory began to seem possible, the Pierson family — Arthur, Sarah, Arthur's mother, and the two little girls — moved to a parsonage near Troy, New York, with fruit trees and a yard that ran down to the banks of the Hudson River. Now the Pierson children would be able to grow up in the lovely small town of Waterford. The Presbyterian church was healthy and vigorous, and Arthur Pierson could return to the denomination in which he held his ordination credentials.

The hallmark of Pierson's pastorate in Waterford, New York, was "Christian Action," the name of the installation sermon preached by a visiting professor on October 6, 1863. The biography by Pierson's son records of the Waterford pastorate that "Mr. Pierson brought to his work all the enthusiasm of a young man of twenty-six — and a minister's second charge usually benefits much by his first experience." Pierson's nervous energy and intensity became legendary; he was

41

noted as "a wide-awake speaker who did not believe in following the old beaten track made by our fathers to the neglect of more modern methods and ideas." His reputation rested on a single-minded power of concentration — the secret to his large literary output, but also the cause of an absent-mindedness that made him habitually oblivious to the people around him. Preaching, pastoral visitation, Sunday School work, and prayer meetings occupied his time — as well as a growing family. Two more Pierson children were born in Waterford. As his skill in Bible study grew, his reputation as a Bible teacher spread. On Sunday afternoons he taught a Bible class with up to two hundred persons present, attracted by his teaching method of encouraging informal discussion on the texts. By holding special prayer meetings for the outpouring of the Holy Spirit, Pierson was able to launch a three-week preaching revival that resulted in thirty-two persons coming to Christ. Two years later, prayer meetings among the youth resulted in a Sunday School revival and the conversion of thirty-eight young people. During the seven years of Pierson's ministry in Waterford, 111 people joined the church and the sanctuary required remodeling to twice its original size. Clearly A. T. Pierson was a minister on the move.

The "Christian Action" of Pierson's Waterford years emanated from his commitment to America's mission. Arthur Pierson had supported the Civil War from the beginning as a moral crusade against slavery. He welcomed the Confederacy's surrender to General Grant at Appomattox on April 9, 1865, as a divine victory for freedom. Equating the laws of God with human rights, he saw the Union victory as resting on biblical principles of justice. Arthur Pierson shared the optimism of Northern clergy at the end of the Civil War, as he confidently anticipated a steady improvement in morality as a result of defeating the slave power. He gave voice to his faith in moral progress in an article, "The Law of Growth." Arguing that every sphere of life has stages of progress, "under the influence of Christ, the world is orbing toward perfection." The exhilaration of Union victory, he believed, was only the beginning of Christian progress toward a more moral society.

Scholars have termed the kind of optimism expressed by Pierson and other Northern clergy during and after the Civil War to be an expression of "postmillennialism." For the North, Union victory resulted from Christian action toward human progress. Clergy believed that the world would steadily progress toward a time of perfection; human history would culminate in the coming of God's kingdom. The millennium, a thousand-year time of peace foretold in the Book of Revelation, would occur steadily and gradually in the course of human history. Although Arthur Pierson shared many of the attitudes characterized by an optimistic postmillennialism, such as belief in the final perfection of human history under the rule of Christ, his theology of human sin made him stop short of the extreme triumphalism stereotypical of Northern victors. Along with prominent Congregationalist theologian Horace Bushnell, Pierson compared the blood spilled by the soldiers to the sacrifice of Jesus Christ on the cross. The death of so many in the cosmic struggle for freedom and morality was an atonement for the sin of the corporate body, the entire country. Rather than seeing the spilled blood as punishment for the sins of the South, Pierson coupled the losses experienced by North and South alike with the need for reconciliation, and the speedy end to sectional animosities. Now that the sacrifice was complete, and the bloodiest war in American history was over, it was time to be reconciled.

In an article he wrote supporting "Decoration Day," the precursor to Memorial Day, on which women put flowers on the graves of Yankee and Confederate soldiers alike, Arthur Pierson drew upon biblical precedents for reconciliation between warring parties over the graves of the dead. "I cannot but remember how the alienated brethren Isaac and Ishmael, and also Esau and Jacob, met, mingling their offices of love over a father's grave. And in presence of these wounds, let all sectional animosities be forgotten — all fraternal alienations reconciled. Let us bury in these graves the sword of strife." In disagreement with those who called the decoration of Confederate graves an act of treason, Pierson rather interpreted the spilled blood of the soldiers as a call to mission — a crusade for unity, morality, and a virtuous society. "Our blood-bought heritage brings a heritage of duty. Other foes are to be fought, other wars to be waged. A host, a legion of evils, threatens our peace and prosperity. Four millions of freedmen, emancipated by the war, appeal to us for education, and evangelization. . . . Public sentiment, public virtue, must be brought to a higher plane. Against intemperance, licentiousness, profanity, desecration of the Sabbath, political corruption, disobedience to parents, rationalism, materialism,

43

and godlessness, we must proclaim war to the last extremity. The land which so much money, blood and tears has brought to Freedom, we must now aim to introduce to a higher estate of liberty. Vain for us to garland these graves, and then make these sacrifices of no avail. Our truest tribute to the dead is to make the land they saved, a nobler heritage to the living!"

The war's end, for Arthur Pierson, was a renewed call for a mission to American society. The Civil War had not only released four million uneducated and needy blacks from slavery, but it had also spawned the evils of political corruption, personal vice, and galloping materialism. After the war, the South sank into poverty from which it would not recover until the mid-twentieth century. But for the North, the spur given to industry by the winning war machine was creating new wealth and the beginning of great disparities between rich and poor. Although Arthur Pierson greeted the end of the war with optimism, at an intuitive level he grasped that somehow the war was only the prelude to the problems of modern America — a postwar landscape of industrial conflicts, urban poverty, and the decline of Protestant values relative to the burgeoning immigrant population. The war against slavery had ended, but the battle for Christian civilization was only beginning.

During the late 1860s, Arthur Pierson began grappling with the enormity of the mission to America, a theme that would motivate his increasing social activism in the 1870s. But his years in Waterford also awakened in him the passion for foreign missions that came to dominate his life. The Waterford Presbyterian Church had a strong missionary vision and supported its own missionary in Siam, Dr. Samuel R. House. A medical doctor, House had first gone to Siam in 1847. Pierson was mildly interested in foreign missions before he arrived in Waterford. His cousin George Thompson had been a missionary under the abolitionist American Missionary Association in Sierra Leone, and his seminary classmate George Post had gone to Syria. The emancipation of the slaves had also piqued his interest in their evangelization and education. But it was the commitment to foreign missions by his parishioners that forced him to begin studying the historical and theological issues for himself. As a conscientious young pastor, he felt he must either lead his people in their mission interest, or else resign his pastorate. His recollections of his awakening to missionary commitment are worth quoting at length. Speaking at the centenary celebration of the Waterford church in 1904, he recalled,

> I owe much of my own enthusiasm for missions to my six years in this church. It was most active and aggressive in this department of service. It had its own missionary in the field and kept in living contact with him by correspondence, gifts, and prayer. . . . I found myself to be lacking in my knowledge of missionary history and biography and set myself to gather new facts through the study of missions, the trials and the triumphs. Thus I began to see more clearly, on the one hand, the awful spiritual destitution of the world and on the other hand the perfect adaptation of the Gospel to human need. I began to feel more and more my previous ignorance and lamentable indifference, while the conviction took deep root that the interest and zeal of a congregation cannot ordinarily be expected to rise above the pastor's level.

As he read the biographies of missionaries, and studied how the world was opening to the Christian message in the middle of the nineteenth century, Pierson gave a series of lectures on the prominent mission fields of the day — Hawaii, Burma, the South Pacific, and Madagascar. Each of these locations was experiencing large-scale movements of tribal peoples to Christianity. In his lecture series, Pierson explored how the acceptance of the gospel was transforming the lives and cultures of whole ethnic groups. Taboos and idolatries were broken, wars ended, people were learning to read, Christian ethics were taking root, and the Bible — the Word of God — was being translated by missionaries who had left their homes for a lifetime of hardship in foreign lands. After lecturing on current mission fields, Pierson gave a lecture series comparing the various religions of the world to Christianity, and pointing out the deficiencies of each. As he gathered all the facts he could find about modern missions, Pierson began collecting data that would one day result in hundreds of books and articles on the "miracles of missions," the theory of missions, missionary biography, and the various types of missionary work. "Glimpses of the past and present condition of each of the heathen nations enabled me to marshall into array that grand host of facts which students of missionary history have found to constitute the resistless logic of missions and the overwhelming argument for a deeper devotion to the world's enlightenment. No man can study these subjects without his own missionary spirit burning with a fervour before unknown." Arthur Pierson brought the same systematic approach to mission studies as he brought to Bible study — studying, collecting, and organizing "facts" until the total picture emerged with persuasive clarity, and the force of logic awakened his emotional commitment to the missionary cause.

The period of Arthur Pierson's awakening to foreign missions was a low point for American missionary efforts. The sending of foreign missionaries from the United States had begun in 1812, when the first group of Congregationalist missionaries sailed to India from Massachusetts. Within a few years, American missionaries opened work in Burma and Hawaii. Although missions were seen by many as a foolhardy and expensive venture, New School Presbyterians were generally favorable to the idea and had cooperated with the Congregationalists in supporting the ecumenical American Board. Before 1870, only two thousand missionaries had gone from American churches, and one-tenth of these went to American Indians. The mortality rate in places like southeast Asia and western Africa was shockingly high. Before it became a world power, the United States did not have the political clout to persuade colonial powers like England, or xenophobic nations like China, to accept its missionaries. Neither did American evangelicals typically have the economic resources required to support many missionaries abroad. By the mid-nineteenth century, American missionary successes were few. Sizable numbers of conversions were largely confined to a few groups that did not practice world religions, like Polynesians in Hawaii and the Karens of Burma. The Civil War had dealt a blow to American missions by cutting off many missionaries, especially Southerners, from their home base of financial and moral support. Organization of denominational missionary societies among women had not yet occurred, and so missionary work among women and children was limited to what missionary wives could do with their own limited resources.

Yet the nineteenth century has been remembered, in the words of mission historian Kenneth Scott Latourette, as the "Great Century" of Protestant missions. Protestant missionary interest grew steadily with the opening of China, Japan, Korea, the Philippines, and Latin American countries to Protestant missions during the latter part of the century. By recognizing the importance of missions in the 1860s, Arthur Pierson was unwittingly poising himself to stir up the wave of missionary enthusiasm that would begin sweeping American shores in the 1880s and 1890s. By the time the attention of American churches turned whole-heartedly toward foreign missions, A. T. Pierson had become the master of missionary facts, the promotional speaker *par excellence*, the senior statesman for the student missionary movement of the century's end. His awakening to missions in the small town of Waterford, New York, was a vital step in stoking the missionary flames that swept American and British Protestant churches during the peak of the "Great Century."

The study of foreign missions challenged Pierson's parochial vision of church life. Another challenge to his Yankee superiority and staid Presbyterian worship style was his first visit to Europe. Accompanied by the wealthy friend who had sponsored the trip, he sailed on the steamship *Cuba* from Boston in July 1866. He wrote hundreds of pages to his family describing his impressions. It goes without saying that Pierson's first trip abroad was important to his intellectual growth and enhanced his effectiveness as a preacher. But its major significance for the development of his life and career was his exposure in England to Victorian Christianity — to the great Nonconformist preachers of the day. Pierson "made the tour" of the foremost Protestant pulpits, hearing such luminaries as Alexander Maclaren of Manchester and Newman Hall of London. Historians have documented the high degree of cross-fertilization between British and American Protestantism in creation of a transatlantic evangelical culture during the nineteenth century. Symbolic of Pierson's future intimate relationship with British evangelicalism was the completion of the first transatlantic telegraph cable while he was sailing across the ocean for the first time. By the early 1870s, Pierson was making frequent references in his sermons to the devotional writings, sermons, and biographies of prominent nineteenth-century British evangelicals. He also broadened his reading habits to include religious periodicals from Britain that reported on the work of Baptist, Presbyterian, and Congregationalist mission leaders.

The high point of Pierson's tour of British pulpits came on Sunday, August 19, 1866, when he joined the milling crowd of thou-

47

sands waiting to enter the Metropolitan Tabernacle. As home to the largest Baptist congregation in the world, the Metropolitan Tabernacle had been opened in 1861 to accommodate the followers of Charles Haddon Spurgeon, one of the greatest preachers in the history of Protestantism. Arthur Pierson was immediately impressed with the open floor plan of the new building, a stark contrast to the square, gated, formal pews of the ordinary Presbyterian or Congregational church. Resembling an "opera house," the Metropolitan Tabernacle was one of the first Protestant churches built like an auditorium to make ordinary urbanites feel at home in an informal, non-churchlike setting. It was a prototype for what became the urban gospel tabernacle movement — a late nineteenth-century combination of church architecture, revival preaching, and gospel hymnody designed to draw the unchurched working classes. As a pastor dependent upon the hated pew rent system, Pierson was impressed that the design of the church allowed visitors to relax. It reminded him of the "free churches" of his childhood, like the Broadway Tabernacle built for Charles Finney in New York City.

Even more impressive than the Metropolitan Tabernacle was its famous preacher — the great Spurgeon, founder of a preachers' college and orphanage, and eventual author of fifty volumes of collected sermons. Spurgeon's sermons became so popular in Victorian England that he once went on vacation to a remote location and heard one of his own sermons being preached by the minister of the small church. Pierson wrote to his family, "We had been seated but a few moments when the preacher walked forward and raised his hand to invoke divine blessing. A more unclerical looking man you could scarcely imagine as occupying a metropolitan pulpit. But when he began to speak the physical was forgotten in the intellectual and spiritual. I have known many people who were good-looking until they opened their mouths; Mr. Spurgeon becomes good-looking when he opens his."

In addition to being impressed by Spurgeon's plain appearance, Pierson was struck by his manner of lining out psalms and hymns for the congregation to sing. This old-fashioned way of singing without instruments, in which the congregation echoed the line right after the song leader, was the traditional Protestant method of psalm singing at the time of the Reformation and had long ago given way to unison singing from a song book in American Presbyterian churches. "One part of the audience follows another, out of time, like a duck dragging a lame leg. Nevertheless I never heard such singing. It was like a great wave of praise surging up against the pillars of the throne of God. No matter how refined your ear, all offenses against the laws of art were forgotten in the impression of music in which there was such devotion. In comparison with it, all the splendid swell of the grandest organ, all the finished culture of the costliest quartette are a parody on worship."

In Pierson's eye, the simple spirituality of the old-fashioned singing style complemented the same qualities in Spurgeon's prayers and sermon. Powerful praise and intercessory prayer preceded the reading of the Scripture, which lasted half an hour with commentary designed to explain the meaning to the humble listeners. "Before he came to the sermon we had received a blessing. Everything had been conducted as though it was intended to bring God near. There was no hurrying over preliminaries, as though to sing, to read the Word, to pray were mere forms by which the sermon is approached. Each part of the service was itself a sermon and produced definite spiritual impressions and results. The sermon was preaching indeed, — it was the text expanded. One could not have said in this case that while 'the text was the gate to the Lord's garden the preacher, instead of going in, only got on it and swung to and fro.'" As a young preacher with high literary ambitions, Pierson was startled by Spurgeon's straightforward commentary on the Bible text as a homiletical method designed to reach unchurched urban dwellers. He concluded in a letter to his family, "Whatever may be the secret, Mr. Spurgeon has practically solved the problem: how to bring the multitude to the house of God. He is a prince among preachers. He is not a mere machine for talking or marrying, baptizing and burying people. He evidently aims to bring God's thoughts down to the minds and hearts and consciences of men. Nothing impressed me more than his simplicity and his entire freedom from all artificiality or affectation. He bends every power and purpose to reach and mould men for newness of life. How puerile some of the criticisms of this great man seem. He is the most effective preacher of the century and I rejoice to see a man who dares to know only the grand theme of 'Jesus Christ and Him crucified' have such a place filled with thousands of hearers."

Pierson's visit to the Metropolitan Tabernacle occurred at a formative stage of his own ministry. Charles Haddon Spurgeon was only three years older than he was, and yet he was attracting thousands of urban dwellers in a city where spiritual apathy was the norm among the working class. Both men had promising careers ahead of them as preachers, Bible expositors, and evangelical controversialists. Although he probably did not meet Spurgeon during that first trip to London, it was the beginning of a long relationship that would take surprising twists and turns.

In the year after his trip to Europe, Arthur Pierson turned 30. He had come a long way since that first day in Binghamton when he imposed his clerical authority from the pulpit. In Waterford, he had successfully shepherded two major revivals through dedicated use of prayer meetings, Sunday Schools, afternoon Bible study, and waiting upon the Holy Spirit. In Binghamton, he presided over a faction-ridden congregation that failed economically and had to relocate; in Waterford, he energized church growth and oversaw a $17,000 expansion of the church facilities. In Binghamton he antagonized people by preaching about "politics" and publicly identified their sins. In Waterford he saw that his people were passionately interested in missions, and so he studied mission history and theology and helped them expand their commitment. In Binghamton, he struggled through a crisis of faith, whereas in Waterford he tapped new resources that inspired his preaching, systematized his church administration, and expanded his horizons. As his reputation grew in the late 1860s, he began receiving invitations to candidate for positions in Boston, New York, Brooklyn, Chicago, and other locations. Clearly a small-town ministry was too limited a venue for such a promising preacher — it was time for the fish to swim in a bigger pond.

In January 1869, Pierson decided to accept the invitation to become the minister at the Fort Street Presbyterian Church of Detroit, Michigan. The leading Protestant church in a growing metropolis of 80,000 souls, the church's membership included the cream of Michigan society — wealthy railroad magnates, leading politicians, and even a United States Senator and a future Secretary of War. After sleepless nights and prayer, Pierson wrote his wife, "If I have any confidence in the leadings of the most marked providences of my life, I must give an unequivocal acceptance . . . now I have no doubt as to my duty, for I believe that here I can accomplish twice as much for my Saviour. . . . Pray that I may not think of mere prominence of position but may really be so absorbed in His work that I shall be content with the lowliest sphere that I may serve Him more truly and efficiently. I am conscious that I need to sanctify ambition rather than to crucify it." With regret for the loss of village community, but ambitious for the larger possibilities of the city, Arthur Pierson never pastored in a small town again.

3 Evangelical Identity in Postwar America

Whatever sadness the Pierson family felt about leaving their riverside manse with its apple trees must have turned to awe when Arthur was installed as pastor of the Fort Street Presbyterian Church on May 5, 1869. With its 230-foot limestone spire supported by flying buttresses, the gothic church was one of the "sights" in Detroit, a growing midwestern city. The leading industrial metropolis of Michigan, Detroit's population of 80,000 doubled between 1870 and 1880. The first missionary in 1801 to the frontier outpost that became Detroit had been a Presbyterian, and the denomination continued setting the social pace by founding schools and bringing "civilization" to the area across the Great Lakes from Canada. Completed in 1855, the elegant, carpeted sanctuary seated 800. Although recent difficulties had caused the membership to decline to less than 300 members, the socially prominent congregation started their new pastor at a generous salary of $3000 a year. They bet that a young, dynamic preacher could carry their church to even greater heights. Fort Street Church's gamble paid off, because by 1880 A. T. Pierson's ministry had tripled the church membership. Under Pierson's leadership, Fort Street Presbyterian solidified its position as the leading church of the city, and the most dynamic Presbyterian church in the state.

52

A. T. Pierson's reputation as a powerful preacher attracted so many to the church that within two years, the sanctuary had to be enlarged. By 1880, he was the highest-paid minister in Detroit, with an annual salary of $4500. Average attendance on Sunday morning was 850, and pew rent income brought in $9000 a year, well above the running expenses of the church. A local newspaper described the earnest young preacher as

> one of Julius Caesar's lean men, tall, sharp of visage, with dark hair and beard. His face is pale but eager and his eye penetrating. He has not a powerful voice but uses it admirably. He is slow and emphatic in speech, enunciating clearly so as to be easily heard. He dresses simply and his behaviour before a congregation is absolutely unaffected. There is no bravado about his sermons but much bravery, for he often teaches unpalatable truths. The thought of delivering some of his discourses would be enough to throw not a few prophets of the Lord into a cold perspiration. John Knox — of the grim visage and lion heart — would find a fellow in this mighty man of valour.

The "prince among preachers," a title awarded him by his growing reputation, held Sunday morning and evening as well as midweek services. He organized prayer meetings and youth groups, a mission band, and monthly prayer for missions. New women's and men's foreign missionary societies flourished under his hand, and a men's group began supporting its own missionary. Giving for both outreach and the local church budget doubled in Pierson's first five years. Large numbers of articles poured from his pen, and his sermons were printed and distributed throughout the region. The Pierson family grew along with their father's reputation. Three more children were added to the four born in New York, making a total of five girls and two boys.

Perhaps A. T. Pierson's most important accomplishment in Detroit was helping to shape evangelical identity for the post–Civil War generation of Protestant clergy and churchgoers. His thirties corresponded to the decade of the 1870s, an era of major changes in American culture. The same year he moved to Detroit, 1869, the Central Pacific Railroad constructed from the East met the Union Pacific Railroad extended from the West. The joining of the two railroads at Promontory, Utah, completed a transcontinental transportation system that opened the final frontiers of the "Wild West" to thousands of immigrants, farmers, and eastern urbanites seeking land and a new start in life. From 1870 to 1900, eleven million immigrants poured into the United States, attracted by the economic opportunity born of seemingly endless open space. Cities like Detroit drew immigrants to plentiful jobs in construction and industry. Situated in the country's industrial heartland, Detroit in 1870 was a hot spot where the transplanted traditions of the East Coast rubbed against the needs of an expanding western population, and where the Protestant establishment of the founding families clashed with the working-class Catholicism of many new immigrants. As old-stock Protestant Americans moved into middle-class, managerial positions made possible by economic expansion, issues of materialism and irreligion also confronted the churches. The challenges A. T. Pierson faced in Detroit during the 1870s were a microcosm of the challenges facing America. Urban ministry gave him a platform from which to address the spiritual and social problems of the country. And struggles with the challenges of postwar, urban America sharpened and affirmed his self-conscious identity as an evangelical.

BUILDING A MISSIONAL CHURCH:
FORT STREET AND MIDWESTERN PRESBYTERIANISM

Arthur Pierson tackled his new charge with his characteristic energy and zeal, his enthusiasm guided into productive channels by nearly a decade of pastoral experience. The immediate task at hand confronting the new pastor was to put the church on a sound spiritual and financial basis. Because of conflicts with the previous minister, the number of families paying pew rent had dropped to a dangerous low of eighty-two. Helping the Fort Street Church to grow was thus Pierson's number-one priority on a list of goals he wrote in his journal. The list of "Things to be accomplished with divine help" began with increasing the size of the congregation. Second on the list was reorganizing the Sunday School. Other goals included building up the evening service, visiting all the church members, organizing the youth, introducing systematic outreach, starting a mission church and Sunday School, strengthening prayer meetings, reviving the missionary commitment of the congregation, founding a Bible class for teachers, improving worship and congregational singing, praying for revival, and promoting Christian union in Detroit. Although "church growth theory" would not be formalized for another hundred years, in retrospect it appears that Pierson's approach to ministry instinctively followed many of the techniques conducive to church growth. He possessed a well-located building with a congregation open to change, situated amidst an expanding population base. He multiplied the number of small groups that new members could join, adding Sunday School classes, Bible classes, prayer groups, missionary societies, youth groups, and women's groups. He combined biblical preaching with extensive pastoral visitation. Carrying a notebook to his pastoral visits, he wrote down the names, birthdays, interests, talents, and problems of each person he visited. This practice helped him relate to all the church members with sensitivity, as well as pray for them personally. One socially prominent member of the congregation who had criticized Pierson's preaching as too severe was nevertheless won over to Christian commitment after Pierson repeatedly visited him during his final illness.

One of the principles of modern church growth theory is that ordinary lay people are the "bridges of God" to reaching other people with the gospel. The most effective way to grow a church is to have new members immediately reach out to their family and friends, and to involve new members in small-group activities that reinforce their commitment to others in the church. New members are the most effective agents of evangelism because they are "bridges" to whole new networks of people, and they are usually enthusiastic about their new identities as church members. A. T. Pierson's jottings in his diary show that he practiced from experience what ministers a century later would learn in church growth seminars. One Monday a young man visited him in his study, having heard Pierson preach the day before on "The wages of sin is death, but the gift of God is eternal life through Jesus Christ our Lord." Feeling the pressure of his own inadequacies and sinfulness, he sought out the preacher the next day and asked how to obtain eternal life. After weeping with the young man and asking him if he would accept Jesus Christ as his "only hope of eternal life,"

Pierson knelt with him as the stranger prayed and gave himself to God. At that point in the encounter, Pierson could have sent the man away, feeling satisfied with a good day's work in the ministry of empathetic soul saving. Instead, the minister would not let the man leave his office before he promised to tell others of the Savior he had found. The young man went straight to a prayer meeting and testified to his newfound joy in Christ, and then home to tell his wife. Through the testimony of the new believer, his wife joined the church. The pastor directed them into a small group, a mission class.

Arthur Pierson promoted a mission-minded church by stimulating the members to take an open attitude toward outsiders, and to pray for revival and renewal. Rather than governing the church as a dictatorship, he started a church council in which leading members met to make decisions regarding the goals and programs of the congregation. Something began happening at Fort Street Church nearly every day of the week. As new people were drawn into the congregation, they were directed immediately into activities that fit their personalities and abilities. By emphasizing that outreach was among the normal responsibilities of a church member, Pierson cultivated a growth-oriented congregation. Less than two years after Pierson became pastor to the Fort Street Church, expanding the seating capacity of the sanctuary became necessary. At a cost of $35,000, the sanctuary was enlarged to seat two hundred additional people. Black walnut pews, frescos, carpets, and cushions completed the elegant interior.

Pierson cultivated a high profile among other clergymen in Detroit. He joined the Detroit Ministerial Union composed of pastors of evangelical churches — primarily Presbyterian, Methodist, and Congregationalist. Founded in 1850, the Union provided weekly fellowship for Detroit clergy and it sponsored joint church services. Some of the other ministers in the fellowship group became his closest friends and confidants. As he had done in Waterford, Pierson began a weekly Bible study on Monday evenings for anyone who was interested. His growing reputation as a Bible teacher drew people from a wide area. The success of the Bible study was so great that he transformed it into a Saturday night Teacher's Institute for all the Sunday School teachers in Detroit. In 1872 at its fifth national convention, the American Sunday School Union put into place a uniform, international program of lessons, so that children around the world would be studying the same Bible texts each Sunday and could systematically progress in their understanding of the Scriptures. Pierson provided a valuable service to the area churches by teaching the uniform Bible lesson to Sunday School teachers in preparation for the next day's classes. The Sunday School was a major form of outreach for evangelical churches in the late 1800s, and a number of prominent churches grew out of the Sunday Schools that were founded among the unreached city dwellers. Sunday Schools not only taught the Bible, but they often taught reading, the English language, and even citizenship skills to immigrants and the poor. For years, Pierson taught a Sunday School Bible class at the Detroit YMCA. Just as in New York City, Boston, and other major cities, the YMCA functioned in the late 1800s almost as a nondenominational arm of the churches devoted to outreach among young men. As a loyal member since his teenage years, Pierson led a fundraising drive to provide a building and gymnasium for the Detroit Association.

As part of his plan to reach beyond the doors of the church, and even beyond the local community, Pierson introduced systematic giving for outreach, or "benevolences," as good causes were called in the nineteenth century. According to the Fort Street "Church Manual" of 1872, benevolent giving was "for one object: the spread of the Gospel." Pew rent sustained the running expenses of the church, but members filled out pledge cards in January that indicated the minimum they could give for benevolences during the year. In addition to collections taken for foreign missions at the regular missions prayer meeting, the "monthly concert of prayer," January was foreign missions month at Fort Street Church. Members could pledge to finance Presbyterian missions in Japan, China, Siam, Laos, India, Colombia, Brazil, Liberia, and other locations. February pledges supported the Fort Street Sunday School. Collections for March through July funded various Presbyterian boards such as publications, church building programs, and theological education for ministers. August contributions aided the poor, September was ministerial relief month for poor and retired clergy, and October funds went to the Bible society. In addition to November collections for home missions, for $250 a member could support one home missionary to the "Great West." In December, Christmas generosity raised funds for the education and relief of the freed slaves in the South.

57

The outreach program of the Fort Street Church reflected that the western half of the United States was still in a pioneer stage and in many places lacked the institutions of settled society such as schools, churches, and housing for community workers. The building of churches and parsonages, children's education, support of the ministry, the purchase of Bibles and tracts, and sustenance for the poor were major challenges facing the established churches in the late 1800s. Since a long economic depression occurred in the 1870s, a period decades before the federal government instituted such safety nets as social security or workmen's compensation, churches were stretched to the limit trying to meet the spiritual and physical needs of the growing American population. Because of their high educational requirements for ordination, Presbyterian churches in particular faced clergy shortages after the Civil War. The number of ministers who could be highly educated were inadequate to meet the needs of the expanding population. Hence the collection of money for ministerial education and salary relief for clergy in poor areas were also substantial priorities for relatively prosperous congregations like Fort Street Presbyterian.

SHAPING MICHIGAN PRESBYTERIANISM

Following the Civil War, churches throughout the United States underwent a period of denominational institution building, mostly along regional lines. The Methodists and Baptists, both of which had suffered church divisions over slavery, resumed building and strengthening their regional churches. The Episcopal Church, following a "national" ideal whereby churches were organized according to national divisions, had split only during the war itself and quickly reunited. Congregationalists were mostly a northern denomination all along, but concerns that more churches founded under the Plan of Union had become Presbyterian than Congregationalist caused the Congregationalists to end the Plan of Union in 1852. After the war, the Congregational Church found itself in sole control of what previously had been ecumenical agencies, such as the American Board of Commissioners for Foreign Missions, and the American Home Missionary Society. Denominations fractured along racial lines, as the primarily northern African Methodist Episcopal Church began recruiting members in the South; and the southern Methodist Church released many of its black members to found the racially separate Colored Methodist Episcopal Church. All of the denominations coming out of the Civil War entered an expanded phase of denominational organization, church planting, and mission work.

Six months after Pierson's installation as pastor in Detroit, the northern New School and the northern Old School branches of Presbyterianism voted to reunite, thereby founding the Presbyterian Church in the United States of America (PCUSA) in 1870. Since Presbyterians had first split over slavery in the year of Pierson's birth, Arthur Pierson had grown up entirely in the more revivalistic and smaller "New School." Both the Waterford and Fort Street churches were affiliated with the New School. The Old School, on the other hand, was suspicious of so-called "enthusiasm," or overly emotional religious experience, and it felt that doctrinal unity was a more important foundation for denominational identity than shared religious experience. With their more negative view about human capabilities to change society, the Old School had also contained a large number of Southerners and people who felt powerless or unwilling to challenge the slave system. But as the Civil War loomed, sectional differences began overriding the differences between the two schools of thought. The Old School split between pro-slavery and anti-slavery factions in 1861, thereby eliminating one of the areas of disagreement between northern Old and New Schoolers.

From the side of the New School, the original split in the church had left them weakened. As mid-century approached, the optimism about cooperation with Congregationalists in church planting and mission work had collapsed amidst worries about denominational identity: How could Presbyterian identity be maintained in an increasingly pluralistic context? Which Presbyterian distinctives remained valuable in the overwhelmingly revivalistic orientation of American Protestantism? Probably the most significant factor behind the decision to reunite the Old and New Schools was the Civil War itself. The shared experience of being on the same side during the war was a tremendous boost to unity between church factions. The things that had divided the New and Old Schools in 1837 seemed unimportant to the generation who had just survived the Civil War.

For young ministers like A. T. Pierson, the 1870s were an exciting time to be a Presbyterian. The formation of the new denomination, with its reinvigorated Yankee denominational consciousness, carried forward the energy of evangelical cooperation that had played such a prominent role in prosecuting the recent war against slavery. In 1872 Pierson helped found the Presbyterian Alliance of Detroit, a small group of self-supporting churches that attempted to strengthen the struggling Presbyterian churches, missions, and schools in Detroit. In 1877 the Fort Street Church began a mission in the northwestern part of Detroit that resulted in the establishment of Trumbull Avenue Church in 1881. Along with local voluntary activity, the new denomination crafted structures that coordinated and strengthened the missional outreach of the churches. The new Presbyterian Church USA founded boards of publication, home missions, and foreign missions. Under the denominational boards, Presbyterians cooperated on projects such as city evangelization. They reached out to particular ethnic groups, such as the 150,000 Chinese immigrants who poured into the United States to work on railroads between 1848 and 1875. Since the end of the Civil War, Presbyterians had been concerned about the education of the freedmen in the South. Whether in the rural South, urban centers, or the new West, the expanding American population needed Bibles and Christian literature. The shortage of clergy underscored the need for theological seminaries west of the Mississippi, along with funds to pay for the education of indigent but promising ministerial candidates. As the mission to America reinforced denominational identity, new denominational structures mirrored the needs of the expanding American population following the Civil War. Much of the monthly giving for benevolences that Pierson instituted at Fort Street Church went into the coffers of the new Presbyterian enterprises. Funds for home missions, foreign missions, church construction, ministerial education, publications, freedmen, and ministerial relief were all channeled through denominational units.

Along with founding centralized agencies, the creation of the Presbyterian Church USA breathed new life into the normal Presbyterian structures. Baptist and Congregationalist congregations were traditionally laws unto themselves, while Methodists, Episcopalians, and Catholics maintained denominational unity under the control of their respective bishops. The Presbyterian system lay somewhere between congregational independence and episcopal authority. Instead of relying on bishops, Presbyterians developed a system of "judicatories," or governing councils consisting of ministers and laity. At the local level, each congregation had a Session, and each local group of Presbyterian churches worked together in the Presbytery. The Synod was the statewide administrative body of the church. Elected lay and clergy delegates from the presbyteries attended the national General Assembly, held annually at different locations. As pastor of the leading church in Detroit, Arthur Pierson threw himself into Presbyterian governance at every level. He attended the annual meetings of the Synod of Michigan from the Detroit Presbytery every year from 1870 to 1882 with the exception of 1876. His reputation as a preacher grew quickly, for after only two years in Detroit, he was chosen to be "primate speaker" at Synod. He became chairman, or moderator, of the Synod of Michigan in 1875. From 1871 to 1873, he was a delegate to the General Assembly, the highest governing body of the church. In 1872, he chaired the Committee of Arrangements for the General Assembly, which was held at the Fort Street Church. Holding the General Assembly in his church was both a huge honor and responsibility for the up-and-coming pastor.

SUPPORTING HIGHER EDUCATION

A. T. Pierson made substantial contributions to the Synod of Michigan in the area of education. Postwar denominational organization was absolutely crucial to the spread of higher education in the United States. By the 1870s, the Presbyterians had founded more schools for higher education than any other church in the United States. Consistent with their emphasis on the importance of an educated clergy, Presbyterians supported advanced institutions across the Midwest. A Presbyterian minister was founder and first president of the University of Michigan. The Synod of Michigan contributed substantially to women's higher education in Michigan by founding Michigan Female Seminary in Kalamazoo, a school for the higher education of girls. Michigan Female Seminary was founded as "The Mount Holyoke of Michigan," modeled on what became the first college for women in the United States, Mt. Holyoke Female Seminary in western Massachusetts.

Founded in 1837 by Mary Lyon, Mount Holyoke was the major producer of women missionaries and pioneer schoolteachers in the mid-nineteenth century. Keeping tuition low so that ordinary girls could afford to attend, Mt. Holyoke was known for requiring the students to do housework themselves, and for the intensely revivalistic piety that brought most of the early students to make a personal decision for Jesus Christ. Imitating Mount Holyoke, Michigan Female Seminary required an hour a day of household labor of its students, and it cultivated the kind of piety that would lead women into Christian service. In 1873, the Synod appointed A. T. Pierson to be a trustee of the Kalamazoo Seminary, a post he held for ten years.

Pierson had from his Binghamton years encouraged women to pray in public at prayer meetings. Perhaps his experience of women's spiritual leadership in the Businessman's Revival of 1858 had convinced him of the role women could play in leading people to Christ. In the Fort Street Church, he supported women's prayer groups and the founding of a branch of the Woman's Foreign Missionary Society, part of an emerging movement in Protestant churches for women to have their own missionary societies that would send unmarried women as missionaries. Encouraging women to testify in public and to have their own missionary society was a progressive, if not bold, stance for a Presbyterian minister to take in the mid-nineteenth century. While frontier "sects" like the Christian Connection, Adventists, and Methodists had let women preach to mixed groups in the early 1800s, the stodgy Presbyterians were part of the conservative, East Coast establishment that long opposed the ministry of women. The tradition of the educated ministry served to exclude both women and lower-class men from leadership roles in the Presbyterian churches. Even the founding of women's mission societies was controversial. When in 1877 Pierson represented the General Assembly as fraternal delegate to the National Council of Congregational Churches, he heard a paper by a Congregationalist minister directed against separate women's mission societies. In a report on the National Council written for *The New York Observer*, Pierson criticized the speaker and publicly defended the right of women to organize their own mission societies. Appointment as trustee of the Michigan Female Seminary was made because Arthur Pierson believed in the college-level education of women as a means of fitting them for leadership roles in Christian society. That he had five daughters gave him a vested interest in female education.

But not everyone supported women's higher education, and Michigan Female Seminary faced constant financial worry. Disaster struck in 1880 when the mortgagee foreclosed on the school, encumbered with $18,000 in debt. When Pierson complained that the seminary property was worth far more than its indebtedness, the Presbytery of Detroit appointed him to canvass the state for funds to clear the debt. Taking a four-week leave of absence from the church, Pierson circled the state, giving lectures on the educational and missionary vision of Mary Lyon. While canvassing for funds, he also solicited donations of badly needed books and equipment, as well as additional money for furniture and a grand piano. Within three months, he had raised enough money to pay off the mortgage, and made himself liable for the rest of the seminary's debts. He eventually took a personal loss of $205 on the school's debts in 1882.

Olivet College also benefited from Pierson's commitment to higher education. Olivet began in 1844 as an intentional Christian colony of thirty-nine persons on the Michigan frontier. Founded by the Reverend John Jay Shipherd, who also founded Oberlin College as a frontier colony, Olivet was part of the manual labor movement, an idealistic venture by radical evangelical egalitarians who believed in providing equal educational opportunities for the poor and middle classes. Students were expected to do the physical work of running the college facilities in efforts to keep tuition low so that the poor could afford to attend, and to promote radical equality among the students — male and female, black and white. A combination of intense piety and social reform characterized the manual labor movement, which can be seen in retrospect as part of a broader impulse toward utopian experimental communities in the 1840s. Because of its abolitionism, the college was denied a state charter in 1845. Its founders concluded, "Poverty is our endowment. Our principal object is to do good to the poor, and it may be that we need to be poor ourselves to accomplish this object." Olivet colony was only able to begin its liberal arts college in 1858, once public opinion had swung against slavery.

Unlike elite East Coast colleges like Yale, Harvard, and Princeton, part of the progressive nature of midwestern schools like Olivet and Oberlin was the admittance of women. Olivet's first three graduates in

1863 were women. Olivet's president appealed to the Synod of Michigan for financial help in the 1860s and 1870s. Arthur Pierson and several other clergy visited Olivet in 1870 and approved it as worthy of synodal support, especially in light of the fact that the Synod of Michigan had no coeducational, liberal arts college of its own. In 1871, Olivet accepted a faculty member recommended by the Synod and became nondenominational, having previously been largely under Congregational sponsorship. The relationship between Olivet and the Synod of Michigan continued until 1886 when the Synod felt wealthy enough to found its own liberal arts school, Alma College.

An indirect recipient of Arthur Pierson's commitment to Presbyterian higher education was the University of Michigan. Outraged at hearing at Synod of the low spiritual and moral state of the students at the university, Pierson stood and made a speech on the need for missionary work among college students. The commotion resulted in founding the Tappan Presbyterian Association as a campus ministry to care for the spiritual needs of the Presbyterian students at the University of Michigan, Ann Arbor. Named after the first president of the university, the Tappan Association was one of the first denominational campus ministries established in the United States.

As far as ministerial training was concerned, Arthur Pierson's most important role in higher education began in 1871, when he attended the annual General Assembly of the Presbyterian Church USA. Representing the Presbytery of Detroit, he was appointed to the Committee on Theological Seminaries and to the Board of Directors of the Theological Seminary of the Northwest, located in Chicago. The seminary experienced dramatic increases in enrollment and faculty during Pierson's fourteen years on the Board. In 1886, money contributed by Cyrus McCormick, inventor of the mechanical reaper, caused its name to be changed to McCormick Theological Seminary. Although he supported theological education for clergy while a young minister in Detroit, years later Pierson turned down an offer of the chair of systematic theology at McCormick with the words, "I confess that I do not feel in sympathy with the method of teaching theology from its polemic or controversial side rather than from its Biblical and practical side. In my opinion, students should be taught not so much how to throw up defenses as how to win souls and build up believers." While his commitment to theological education never waned, Pierson's interest in denominational higher education shifted to lay Bible training in his mature years.

In 1874, in recognition of his stature as preacher, Bible study leader, and supporter of Presbyterian higher education in the Midwest, Knox College in Galesburg, Illinois, awarded Pierson an honorary Doctorate of Divinity. Founded in 1837 as a manual labor school by the Reverend George Washington Gale, Knox College had also been part of the radical egalitarian movement of anti-slavery evangelicals in the 1830s and 1840s. Reverend Gale, in fact, was revivalist Charles Finney's pastor before moving west to found Knox College. The minister who most influenced Finney's development, Gale had tutored him in Presbyterian theology and showed him how to preach and pray for people in revivals. In 1845, radical abolitionist orator Jonathan Blanchard became president of Knox College. A Sabbatarian who refused to travel on Sunday, opposed all liquor, and demanded that slavery be abolished, Blanchard made Knox College and Galesburg a hotbed of anti-slavery agitation. In 1860, Blanchard left Knox College to become president of Wheaton College, which in the twentieth century became the preeminent evangelical college in America.

In their early decades, manual labor schools Olivet, Oberlin, and Knox College were part of the network of Congregationalist and New School Presbyterian radicalism that cut a swath from New England, through upstate New York, across to the Old Northwest of Ohio, Illinois, and Michigan. Presbyterians like Gale, Finney, Shipherd, Blanchard, Lyman Beecher, and Arthur Tappan combined abolitionism with moral strictness, undergirded by personal encounters with the saving power of Jesus Christ. Although Arthur Tappan Pierson lived a generation later than the ante-bellum New School abolitionists, his reception of an honorary doctorate from Knox College was consistent with what he considered to be his own spiritual heritage. Although the postwar issues were different, Pierson lived out the same ethical rigidity and uncompromising spiritual discipline that had characterized his abolitionist fathers in the faith. He proudly added the Knox College "D.D." behind his name, and was henceforth known to the public as Dr. A. T. Pierson.

PROMOTING FOREIGN MISSIONS

Pierson's interest in Presbyterian education operated hand-in-glove with his concern for evangelization. Reminiscent of the anti-slavery activists, he was confident that right knowledge and Christian conversion would lead to a Christian social order. Since the civilization of Michigan and even of the world depended on a symbiotic relationship between education and evangelization, missions became a top priority in Pierson's denominational commitment. In 1873, the Synod of Michigan appointed him to give a speech on foreign missions. In 1877, they appointed him to a special committee to incorporate home and foreign mission conferences into the life of the Synod. He gained a berth in 1878 on the standing committee on foreign missions, and in 1880 became its chairman, serving until 1882. By the late 1870s, the Presbytery of Detroit was giving thousands of dollars annually to Presbyterian missions whereas none of the other presbyteries gave more than a few hundred. And of the Detroit money, Fort Street Church gave a large percentage, reflecting the leadership of its missionary-minded pastor.

The Presbyterian Board of Foreign Missions was one of the first agencies founded by the reunited church in 1870. Its founding required promotional work across the nation so as to raise awareness of its existence and to call for support of Presbyterian missionaries abroad. Just as ministers at home worked to lead people to Christ, found schools and churches, provide Bibles, and train men for ministerial leadership, so did the church's foreign missionaries. Reaching the unreached and providing them with the tools for advancing Christian society were crucial tasks both at home and abroad. Most Presbyterians saw the need for home missions as self-evident, for they could see the unchurched poor firsthand. Most people knew someone who had moved to newer parts of the United States where schools and churches were lacking. But in the 1870s, making the case for foreign missions was a lot tougher than for home missions. While European powers vied for world domination, Americans were more interested in developing the United States. With the denominational mission boards just getting off the ground, some synods conducted their own promotion and fundraising for support of "their" missionaries. The Synod of Michigan launched its Synodical Foreign Missionary Conference at Ypsilanti in January 1871, the first of what became an annual event. Pierson attended as a new pastor, and wrote several articles praising the convention and comparing it to the grand annual meetings of the American Board of Commissioners for Foreign Missions, which had been the joint Congregationalist-Presbyterian mission board supported by the New School of his youth.

The Synodical Foreign Missionary Conference of 1871 was also the venue for Pierson's first public missionary address, entitled "The Christian Law of Unselfishness." While exhibiting little of the passion of his later speeches on missions, it was significant because it was Pierson's first mission statement delivered beyond the walls of his own church. He delivered it to a packed house on the afternoon of the second day of the conference, as the opening commentary on the theme "The Cause of Foreign Missions as Related to the Growth and Development of the Individual Christian Life." Pierson granted that it was difficult to interest most Christians in foreign missions because missions didn't "pay." There was no financial return and little result visible to ordinary Americans. Home missions, on the other hand, could scarcely "be distinguished from patriotism or even self-protection. No alternative is left us but to evangelize our borders. The Gospel acts as the dikes in Holland, if nothing more, keeping back the tide of infidelity and irreligion from submerging us. Men who have no sympathy with Christ, invest in Home missions as a measure of national development. They build churches, as they do schools, as a pecuniary investment." But foreign missions, on the other hand, required genuine unselfishness and self-abnegation. The results of foreign missions were not evident to the average churchgoer. Yet, he continued, foreign missions were most in line with the spirit of Christ because they involved self-sacrifice, with no thought to receiving benefits in return. One thousand million were dying without Christ. If those dying without knowing Jesus Christ were to walk by at a rate of sixty a minute, it would take thirty-three years! "All these multitudes can offer you no recompense for bidding them to this Gospel feast. . . . You may never get back one dollar expended in their evangelization, or ever see any adequate result of the effort made to bring them to Christ." In conclusion, Pierson solemnly intoned, because foreign missions appeal to "unselfish benevolence, they are closely related to the development of the Christian life."

Pierson's insistence in "The Christian Law of Unselfishness" —

that foreign missions were unselfish and spiritual, rather than worldly and profitable — was not a new argument. His appeal to "disinterested benevolence" echoed an idea popular among the followers of Jonathan Edwards who had launched the American Board in the early 1800s. What was new about Pierson's talk was not his basic theology, but his use of a numerical calculation to illustrate the necessity of missions — how many millions of people were walking into damnation without Christ! Who could fail to be convinced of the spiritual necessity for foreign missions given Pierson's merging of classic American mission theology with a modern "scientific" numerical analysis of the unsaved hordes? Pierson's first public missionary address linked the mission theology of his youth with the number-crunching, factual approach of his later mature missionary thought. His fascination with numerical approaches to world evangelization was just beginning to take shape in his mind in 1871. Decades later, he commented that around 1870, he had read a paragraph by British Baptist mission leader Joseph Angus in which Angus called for raising 50,000 missionaries to preach the gospel to the unevangelized within twenty-five years. This article set Pierson to thinking, and by 1877, he had formulated his first concrete plan for evangelizing the world. In 1871, Pierson's ideas for a rational, statistical approach to world evangelization began fermenting in the context of working to inculcate missions-consciousness into Michigan Presbyterianism.

During the 1870s, A. T. Pierson's evangelical and practical ministry interests took denominational form. After his move to Detroit, which coincided with the founding of the Presbyterian Church USA, his own spiritual growth was intertwined with that of a growing denomination. His Presbyterian identity reflected post-bellum optimism about human cooperation in building new institutions — schools, church agencies, small groups, mission societies — to meet the needs of both church and society, in his Detroit neighborhood and around the world.

EVANGELICAL IDENTITY AND THE GIANT ANAKIM

The roots of nineteenth-century American evangelicalism lay, to a large extent, in revivalism. As new settlements emerged across the American frontier, churches used revivals as social gatherings and as safe spaces in which people could be led into personal experiences of saving faith. The individual acceptance of God's forgiveness through Jesus Christ drew people to seek fellowship in the churches, and church people cooperated in founding schools and other institutions that created stable communities. By the mid-nineteenth century, evangelicalism was in the mainstream of the American way of life. Whether Baptist, Methodist, Presbyterian, or one of the smaller pietistic denominations, evangelical churches periodically held preaching revivals to renew spiritual commitments and to draw the youth into full church membership. Large revivals even swept through the encampments of soldiers during the Civil War. The victory of the North after the Civil War seemed to many northern evangelicals a sign that God was blessing them and their beliefs. The victory over slavery marked a triumph for democracy over despotism, and for the kingdom of God over the kingdom of Satan.

But all that glittered was not gold. Despite the rebuilding of denominations that occurred after the Civil War, evangelical Protestantism found itself at a crossroads. The Civil War provided a huge impetus to northern industry. With the growth of unregulated industry, immigrants and rural people — the new lower classes — crowded into the cities. Cities became more congested, poor, and visibly "foreign." From 1870 to 1890, the urban proportion of the American population grew from one-fifth to one-third. Increased access to education by the middle classes spread new ideas, such as the theory promoted by Charles Darwin that people had evolved from apes rather than created by God as described in the book of Genesis. Middle-class American Protestants began improving their economic position with broader access to education and to mass-produced consumer goods, but materialism and religious skepticism traveled in hand with the middle-class consumer culture. Increased wealth and improved transportation also began the suburbanization of Protestantism, as middle-class Protestants moved away from the older city centers. On the spiritual front, the ultimate symbol of changing times was the new higher criticism of the Bible coming from Germany and taking hold in theological seminaries, though not without acrimonious denominational debates. Evangelical Christianity began facing problems of identity and status it could not have imagined in the old days of organizing churches and social institutions in rural settlements. The problems of the "Gilded

Age," as Mark Twain labeled the late nineteenth century, threw down the gauntlet to evangelical assumptions about Protestantism's dominant role in American society. Simply put, Catholics were outnumbering Protestants, new urban values were overriding old rural ones, and non-English speakers were streaming into America in unprecedented numbers. To make sense to a new generation, evangelicalism had to reframe its identity.

Urban clergy of the late nineteenth century stood on the front lines of a battle to make evangelicalism relevant in a changing America. It was in the cities that the changes in American life and culture were most apparent. It was urban clergy who stumbled over the foreign-born poor as they walked the crowded and dirty streets to their offices. It was ministers in urban, middle-class congregations who were finding that the old truths of sin, self-denial, and submission to Christ were being rejected by newly rich congregants caught up in conspicuous consumption. As part of the educated elite in the days when only a small percentage of Americans attended college, urban ministers had to study and interpret for their communities what the new scientific theory of evolution implied for the biblical accounts of creation. The challenge of mediating between science and religion was made more acute as higher criticism undercut the widely accepted truth-claims of the Bible, and also threatened the old "Christian evidences."

As Arthur Pierson faced in Detroit the same issues that troubled his fellow clergy in Cincinnati, Rochester, Chicago, and other industrializing cities, he did so as part of a network of self-styled "evangelicals." While being just as interested in social problems as their more theologically liberal colleagues, urban evangelicals reaffirmed the role of individual conversion in meeting the social needs of the day. Since they valued personal religious experience so highly, they sought fellowship with like-minded brethren across the denominational spectrum for the purposes of Bible study and addressing social problems. Pierson's concern for unity among Protestants in Detroit, one of the early priorities he listed on his set of goals for his ministry at Fort Street Church, was because he believed in a basic evangelical consensus that cut across denominational divisions. In the late nineteenth century, northern evangelicalism and ecumenism were inseparable concerns; they continued the momentum begun by the evangelical cooperation during the war.

In a three-part article probably written in 1873, "The Unity of the Church," Pierson noted that evangelical clergy shared interests in "practical union," including opening their pulpits and the Lord's table to "evangelical Christians" of other denominations. Comparing the different denominations to different households in God's family, he noted that being one in Christ was not a matter of "organic union" but of unity in fundamentals. Unity through Christ was invisible, but its evidence was being manifested in new organizations for Christian cooperation. Citing Jesus' prayer that his disciples might all be one (John 17:20-23), Pierson noted that the chief result of Christian unity would be the conversion of the world. Employing an example from science, he indicated that as atoms were attracted to each other, the larger the units, the greater the attraction for other atoms. Churches acting together against evil would help secure Christ's kingdom.

The most significant Protestant organization for "practical union" in the late nineteenth century was the Evangelical Alliance, first organized in London in 1846 as a visible witness to the unity evangelicals felt in Jesus Christ. The eight hundred British, European, and American delegates agreed on a statement of common doctrine, that while not the sum total of Christian belief, denoted the shared self-understanding of evangelical Christians that ignored denominational distinctives. The basics of evangelical belief included the divine inspiration and authority of the Bible; the right to private judgment in biblical interpretation; the Trinity; the depravity of human nature; Jesus' incarnation, atonement, and intercession for sinful humanity; justification by faith alone; the work of the Holy Spirit in the believer; and a few other points about the sacraments and final judgment. While the essentials were not meant to be a creed considered binding on churches, they were the yardstick by which individual members could measure if they belonged to the group. In 1873, the International Evangelical Alliance held its meeting in New York City. Highly successful, the meeting was the first major ecumenical meeting held on American soil, with 15,000 persons in attendance from Europe and the United States.

While the American branch of the Evangelical Alliance was mostly a fellowship group before the Civil War, its reinvigoration in 1866 marked it as an organization poised to tackle the social problems of the United States. New School Presbyterians were a core group of constituents, and two of the Union Seminary professors with whom Pierson had studied were among its leaders. The Reverend Thomas Skinner, a founder of Union Theological Seminary, was a member of the Board of Counselors for the American branch of the Alliance. Henry B. Smith, Pierson's professor of theology, was chairman of the Executive Committee of the American Alliance from 1866 to 1870. William E. Dodge, Sr., a prominent New York businessman, was the first president of the revived Alliance in 1866; and his son William E. Dodge, Jr., one of Pierson's fellow New York YMCA charter members, served as president from 1885 to 1898. So when in 1873 A. T. Pierson attended the International Conference of the Evangelical Alliance in New York City, he was among old friends who shared his concern for Christian unity.

The constituency of the American Evangelical Alliance was urban, educated, and represented the intellectual elite — urban pastors, editors of religious journals, college presidents, denominational leaders, and prominent businessmen who felt an urgent need to apply evangelical solutions to the problems at the cutting edge of American social change. Issues emanating from major cities set its agenda — immigration, materialism, liberty of conscience, changes in the relationship of science and religion, and other problems of "modernity." The historian of the Evangelical Alliance notes that although its membership never numbered more than a few hundred, the prominence of its members brought the American Alliance "into contact with that vast inter-locking directorate of evangelical voluntary societies, publications, church boards, and assemblies which enabled the Alliance to reflect the general evangelical opinions of the time." As traditional Protestant American culture seemed threatened, the Evangelical Alliance brought together Protestant leaders who needed mutual support.

The Evangelical Alliance was the generative source of what became powerful currents toward Protestant unity by the end of the century. During the meeting in 1873, the Presbyterian members formulated a plan to found an international Presbyterian Alliance that met four years later as the first international body bringing together Presbyterian and Reformed churches. Similarly, Methodists meeting in the mid-1870s decided to begin an international Methodist body, whose founders credited the Evangelical Alliance with facilitating the openness that made it possible. Episcopal participants in the Alliance pushed for an international Anglican body. Experiences of fellowship in the Evangelical Alliance thus generated the energy and trust that pulled American Protestant leaders toward denominational cooperation at global levels. Its focus on addressing urban social problems in the 1880s and 1890s provided the precedent for the Federal Council of Churches in 1908, into which the American Alliance merged. The international Evangelical Alliance was also the founding organization of what became in 1951 the World Evangelical Fellowship.

In 1877, the American Evangelical Alliance chose Detroit as the site of its second biennial meeting. The decision to meet in Detroit undoubtedly owed something to the energy and perseverance of Arthur Pierson, who was chosen to give the closing address. One of the younger members, he was a bridge between the East Coast roots of the organization, and the evolving realities of industrial cities in the Great Lakes region. During the 1870s and early 1880s, Arthur Pierson outlined all of his sermons in a notebook. Combined with his articles in the popular press, the sermon outlines were consistent with the stands taken by the Evangelical Alliance of the USA during that period. Sermons and articles show Pierson's driving obsession with the preservation of equality and democracy for all Americans, including freed slaves, American Indians, and Chinese immigrants. Maintenance of a democratic social order depended on the extension of evangelical Christianity to the American populace. The "social Christianity" espoused by Pierson never wavered from the central importance of conversion as the chief means of solving the pressing social issues of the day.

The sermon that best demonstrated Pierson's fusion of evangelical and social concerns was based on Numbers 13:27-28: "We came to the land to which you sent us; it flows with milk and honey, and this is its fruit. Yet the people who dwell in the land are strong, and the cities are fortified and very large; and besides, we saw the descendants of Anak there." The Anakim were the race of giants encountered by Joshua as the Hebrews fought their way through the Promised Land. Pierson compared the Giant Anakim to America's social problems. Depending on the occasion, he identified a variety of issues as Anakim, each of them consistent with the priorities of the Evangelical Alliance. That the descendants of Anak lived in the cities added to Protestant perceptions of American cities as places of evil and danger.

In sermon #1118, Pierson identified five Anakim, or "questions needing a solution" — those relating to the Indians, Mormons, Chinese, freedmen, and "anti-Republicanism," as Pierson termed Southern racialism. The American Indians and the Chinese represented two persecuted ethnic groups within America, groups that were being denied the democratic privileges to which all Americans were entitled. Pierson decried how the Indians had been lied to through broken treaties that seized their land. Chinese immigrants, though frugal and temperate, were "kicked and cuffed" and threatened by extra taxes and anti-immigrant legislation. When in 1882, the U.S. government passed the first Chinese Exclusion Act, it was clergy like Pierson, who had a knowledge of Presbyterian missions to the Chinese, who spoke against the injustice of legislation denying them the privileges of citizenship. Pierson condemned the neglect of the freed slaves after the Civil War as another example of broken promises by the American people toward the marginalized. With the end of Reconstruction in 1877, the South began reasserting white supremacy by denying African-Americans political equality and making it nearly impossible for them to vote. Although he commended Mormons for their temperance and orderliness, Pierson, like most Christians of his generation, considered Mormonism a blight on the continent because it permitted polygamy. He perceived the answer to the problems of the Indians, Chinese, Mormons, former slaves, and anti-democratic white Southerners to be knowledge of the gospel. The church must evangelize the groups on the margins of North American society for freedom and democracy to reign in the United States. Pierson's view of what was marginal in post-bellum America was colored by his own identity as a white, Northern evangelical — a self-conscious guardian of true American values.

Another way that Pierson formulated the "Giant Anakim" was as evils "demanding removal." Similar to the blight of slavery, the American Republic was threatened by intemperance, Romanism, materialism, and socialism. Other dangers to American society about which Pierson preached in his sermons included gambling, anti-Sabbath sentiment, crime, public education without the Bible, atheism, extremes of wealth, caste lines (classism), trade monopolies, and most especially the neglect of the poor by the church. Pierson's list of Giant Anakim contained a curious mixture of what by contemporary standards appear to be public and private concerns. But for northern evangelicals in the nineteenth century, private motivations and goals were inseparable from public results. To believe in the Bible and in a personal relationship with Christ resulted in one being a virtuous citizen, who upheld "Republican" institutions and supported equality for all. Infidelity, or nonbelief, was just as dangerous to democracy as Marxism, which Pierson condemned as a violent leveling of all distinctions in society. Marx's theories led to the bullet rather than the ballot. Rationalism and materialism Pierson denounced as spiritual dangers that subverted the Christian faith, and by implication American values.

Of all the issues that Pierson defined as dangerous to American democracy, the ones that worried him most in the 1870s and 1880s were intemperance, Romanism, atheism, and a whole gamut of issues relating to the growing class distinctions in American society — extremes of wealth, urban poverty, and the violence between labor and capital that accompanied rapid industrialization. Some of these issues carried over from his youth, while others emerged during the Gilded Age. Along with the evils of slavery and lack of place for the poor in church, intemperance was the social issue that carried over from Pierson's childhood. When asked in 1893 if he had become an abstainer from alcohol, Pierson replied, "No, I have never been anything else." Following the Revolutionary War, the United States had been cut off from its supply of European beer and maltsters. Hard liquor made from corn became a frontier currency, and American consumption of hard liquor skyrocketed. During the early nineteenth century, the growing churches in new settlements enforced teetotalism as an antidote to the fightings, killings, and rapes that were part of frontier violence. Even back in the "civilized" East, evangelicals jumped on the water wagon. The Methodists had always been a temperance church. Around 1811, Congregational leader Lyman Beecher was shocked when a newly ordained minister was so drunk he fell off his horse. Beecher began a lively campaign against the social dangers of alcohol. When Charles Finney held his successful revivals in the 1830s, converts renounced liquor as one of their "known" sins. Abolitionist Presbyterians and Congregationalists supported the temperance movement not only because of liquor's deleterious effect on society, but because rum was a unit of exchange in the slave trade.

As a young minister, Arthur Pierson named temperance as the

next great crusade to be undertaken after the successful war against slavery.

> Of all the fatal forces, Satan marshals into line,
> What hosts can be more deadly than the countless
> bands of "Wine!" . . .
> It fills our homes with widow's wailing and
> with orphans' moans,
> It fills the world with agonizing shrieks and dying groans;
> Enchanted cup, O dash it down! touch not, taste not the wine:
> Though diamonds deck the chalice, it is marked
> with Satan's sign!

> Let us, a mighty Temperance league, unite with heart and hand,
> to drive this Legion of the Devil from this goodly land! . . .
> So shall our homes be blest with peace, with harmony and love,
> And God shall rain his blessings down like showers
> from above. . . .

> In love to Man, wherever found throughout the living world,
> Let every Demon, from his throne, by moral might, be hurled!
> Let every chain be broken, every soul on earth set free,
> till men shall live in brotherhood and eye to eye shall see!
> Till Eden's flowers shall spread the fragrance of a living bloom,
> And God shall plant the tree of life where Death once
> built his tomb.

The kingdom of God as foretold in the book of Revelation would come on earth with the defeat of demons, starting with alcoholic beverages. Pierson's temperance poem traveled throughout Waterford as the "New Year's Greeting" from the *Waterford Sentinel* in 1867.

The analogy between drinking and slavery was continued in a twelve-part essay series, "Letters on Temperance," that Pierson published in the *Watchword and Patriot* in 1871-72. Calling temperance the last great crisis following the war against slavery, Pierson targeted drinking as a moral ruin that caused a nation to decay from within, just as slavery was a moral cancer within. Alcohol enslaved the body, mind, and soul, destroying human reason, self-respect, and will. Because God made humankind in his image, drinking alcohol was unbiblical. Along with smoking tobacco and eating rich foods, it was bad for the body. Just as anti-slavery radicals and other utopians of the 1840s had experimented with health reform, eating "Graham bread," whole grains, and fruit, so Pierson throughout his ministry opposed liquor — along with smoking and eating fatty meats, rich gravies, lard-laden pies, and heavy puddings.

The temperance movement gained new energy after the Civil War when massive immigration brought German beer, Irish whisky, and European wine into the United States. In 1873, Protestant women in Hillsboro, Ohio, launched a national movement when they invaded bars, dropped to their knees in prayer, and refused to move until the bar owners signed the temperance pledge. The "Woman's Crusade" swept through the Midwest, and before it ended 912 communities in thirty-one states and territories had experienced its protests. With one bar per every fifty males over age 15 in working-class areas, combined with women's lack of legal rights over children or property in cases of abusive men or divorce, temperance became the premier church-women's social crusade after 1873. Similar to the scourge of illegal drugs in minority communities a century later, the liquor trade, which gained huge political power on the local and statewide levels, was opposed by progressive Protestants in the late 1800s. Arthur Pierson considered "wine-bibbing" to be a cause of crime, poverty, and insanity. Alcoholism was a hereditary danger that damned to misery one's offspring as well as oneself.

The tendency of Protestant middle classes to adopt wine-drinking as they moved up the social ladder also alarmed teetotaling clergy like Arthur Pierson. In a sermon based on Proverbs 20:1, "The Folly and Wickedness of Wine-Bibbing," Pierson called drinking a sin against God that demanded repentance and reform. The ascetic vows of John the Baptist and the Nazarites provided him with biblical parallels to the modern temperance pledge. After the Methodist minister from Vineland, New Jersey, T. B. Welch, discovered that pasteurizing grape juice kept it from fermenting into wine, Protestant ministers gained access to a reliable source of grape juice that they could substitute for communion wine year-round. During the 1870s, Pierson's Detroit years, Protestant churches throughout the Northeast began switching from communion wine to Welch's grape juice, a movement promoted around the country by evangelical clergy and women connected with the newly formed Woman's Christian Temperance Union. Temperance sentiment also resulted in public water fountains becoming part of the metropolitan landscape. By the end of the nineteenth century, the pro-temperance position had become a mainstay of Protestant, Republican politics.

The temperance movement of the late nineteenth century was a distinctively middle-class approach to the challenges presented by ethnic diversity and industrialization. It focused on a combination of moral suasion toward individuals, and social control of hard-drinking urban masses. In 1869 it spawned a Prohibitionist political party that was supported by many evangelical clergy and WCTU women, including some of Pierson's closest friends. Pierson organized temperance societies in the church, and he supported the idea of legal Prohibition of liquor. In "The Church and the Crisis in Cities," an article he wrote in 1906, Pierson linked alcoholism with the boring jobs held by urban industrial workers. Their foreign origin and their poverty led them to drink to escape their misery. The church, he said, must evangelize and assimilate the poor workers to the American way of life. Although conversion to Jesus Christ was the ultimate solution to intemperance for individuals, Pierson also believed in political and social solutions like Prohibition, high taxes on liquor, and organizing temperance societies from the local to national levels. As in the struggle against slavery, northern evangelicals believed that biblical morality would dovetail with legislative solutions in a seamless approach toward social crises.

Another cause dear to the hearts of Evangelical Alliance clergy in the late nineteenth century was "Romanism," defined by Pierson as a "religio-political system, a sort of Christianized paganism," or a "system of priestcraft" that perpetuated pagan practices in the name of Christianity. Pierson claimed that the pope was like a feudal slaveholder whose adherents were vassals. Anti-Catholicism had a long history in North America, as the Puritan settlers who populated New England in the 1600s were fleeing from "Roman" tendencies in the Anglican Church. Because the British established church was Protestant while the French and Spanish monarchies enforced Catholicism, Roman Catholicism was an enemy of English-speaking America in the colonial era. As both political and religious rulers, the popes called for the overthrow of the "heretical" British monarchy because it had broken from the Catholic Church under Henry VIII. During the 1830s, "nativist" violence broke out in eastern cities as Yankee Protestant workers felt that their jobs were being threatened by the thousands of Irish Catholic immigrants willing to work for less pay. Evangelical clergy like Lyman Beecher also feared Catholicism and urged that Protestant churches blanket the West with churches and schools before it could be overrun by Catholics with anti-democratic tendencies. Anti-Catholic sentiment advanced through Northeastern politics in the 1850s until the issue of slavery diverted attention from it.

The issue of Romanism took on new urgency in 1869, when Pope Pius IX convened the Vatican Council, a meeting in Rome of all Catholic bishops. The pope had long been a powerful force in European politics, and through the papal states the pope was the virtual monarch of much of Italy. As Italian revolutionaries moved to liberate Italy from papal rule, the Vatican Council voted for Papal Infallibility, declaring that the pope was infallible in speaking in matters of doctrine. From an American Protestant perspective, the pope's claim of infallibility combined with his political power was a threat both to biblical truth-claims and to democracy. The papacy had long called for the overthrow of Protestant governments. The 1864 *Syllabus of Errors* had condemned religious liberty and the separation of church and state, and affirmed the right of the Catholic Church to stand above all governments. Clearly the papacy did not understand the idea of religious freedom in the nineteenth century. American Protestant clergy were scandalized by the pope's claiming to take the place of the Bible as the source of divine authority, and by his open condemnation of democracy. Because of Catholic immigration, the Roman Catholic Church had become the largest church in the United States. Since the United States was the bastion of democracy in a still largely monarchial, autocratic world, Protestant clergy were worried that Catholic immigrants would subvert American democracy on the order of the pope. With a democratic constitution less than a century old, the United States needed to be protected from Romanism as a "religio-political system."

Arthur Pierson supported religious tolerance toward Catholicism as a belief system, and supported the right of the Catholic Church to exist as an ecclesiastical institution. But he firmly opposed papal claims to infallibility and to political power. In his first few years at

Fort Street Presbyterian, he wrote a series of articles on prominent figures of the Protestant Reformation, including John Hus, the Bohemian
burned at the stake by the Catholic Church in 1415; Martin Luther, the
leader of the Protestant Reformation in Germany; and John Knox, the
founder of Presbyterianism in Scotland. Each Reformer fought such
perversions of Christianity as "clerical avarice, auricular confession,
idolatry of images, prayers to the Virgin and saints, and masses for the
dead." Pierson's chief criticism of Catholic doctrine was that it in-
serted the papal system as the authority between the individual and
God. Unlike Protestantism in which the individual relied directly on
God through reading the Bible, "Romanism puts the church between
the soul and Christ, as the channel of salvation, the interpreter of the
Word, and the mediator at the throne."

Another event that galvanized Protestant clergy against
Romanism occurred in the 1880s, when Catholic bishops in New York
City began agitating for state support of parochial schools. Failing in
their attempts to get public funds for private schools, Catholics began
bringing lawsuits against public school systems to get the Bible removed from public schools. The combination of papal pronounce-
ments against democracy with forced removal of the Bible from New
York schools outraged evangelical clergy, and Pierson responded with
his harshest words against Catholicism:

> But to the Romish church *as a political power,* teaching the construc-
> tive treason of allegiance to a foreign temporal sovereign . . . to the
> Romish church *as a Jesuitical cabal,* manoeuvering to get possession
> of common schools, public institutions and state funds; to the
> Romish church *as a persecuting despotism,* making it a crime for men
> to think, to read, to talk, to obey conscience or to encourage prog-
> ress, we are opposed, and against *that* we proclaim eternal war.

Pierson vigorously upheld the need for using the Bible in public
schools so that Catholic children could read it and learn to think for
themselves. The duty of American Protestantism was to educate the
Catholic for individual mental freedom and for modern life.

Upholding Protestant free choice as the source of democracy,
Pierson believed with his fellow evangelicals that divine destiny had
made the United States a Protestant country. In an article "America:

Our Heritage, Our Opportunity," he advocated home missions and as-similation of Catholic immigrants to Protestantism as a solution for the anti-democratic tendencies of Romanism.

> God unveiled the continent when a reformed church was ready to occupy it, and from it as a center radiate in missionary endeavor. He diverted Columbus by a flight of parakeets and the drift of floating wood and weed, from the mainland of North America to the Bahamas and South America, and so prevented Papacy from here getting a foothold. In the border wars He gave victory to the Protestants. In the Civil War He preserved the unity of the repub-lic, and all this for a purpose.

In the sweep of history, Pierson saw the hand of God preserving the United States for Protestantism so that it could be the radiating center of world evangelization. God allowed the invention of the compass and the printing press when he did so that Protestants could come to America, disseminating the Scriptures in their wake. Freedom to read the Bible in one's own language was not only the essence of Protestant-ism, but was the beginning of belief in human equality and democracy.

Pierson's confidence in the Protestant destiny of North America was shared by other American members of the Evangelical Alliance. The Second Biennial Conference of the United States Evangelical Alli-ance met in Detroit at First Presbyterian Church from October 30 to November 2, 1877. The conference demonstrated the intimate connec-tion in the minds of evangelicals between emerging social problems in the cities and the threat of Romanism. After two days of preaching on evangelical unity and urban evangelization, the final day of the conference was devoted to "Romanism and Rationalism as Related to Modern Thought and Literature." The participants responded so fa-vorably to a paper on the tyranny of absolutism that the conference spent two sessions on it. As leading minister in Detroit, Arthur Pierson had the honor of giving the closing address. In it he empha-sized the essential unity of all evangelical believers in Christ Jesus and their common alliance in prayer, in work, and in war. His parting comment was for Christians to be aware of the "leaven of Pharisees and Sadducees — Romanism, Ritualism, and Rationalism." Later con-ferences of the American Evangelical Alliance in 1887 and 1889 similarly linked Catholicism with the cause of America's urban social problems because it identified the poverty of the urban immigrants with a Catholic "priestcraft" that oppressed workers by stifling their democratic possibilities.

Historians have often portrayed the pro-temperance, anti-Romanist tendencies of the Evangelical Alliance in the 1870s and 1880s as a movement to exert social control over the poor. While such assumptions have some truth, they represent only part of the picture. While a college-educated, prominent minister like A. T. Pierson might believe in using public schools to oppose Romanism among the urban poor, he even more vehemently attacked rationalism and ritualism, which were characteristics of upper-class Protestantism during the Gilded Age. Along with the increase of urban poverty in the Gilded Age came a rising standard of living among the new "white collar" classes, who typically were the churchgoing, Yankee descendants of colonial families. Urban clergy were dealing not only with the poverty they found in the streets, but the new wealth they faced sitting in the rented church pews Sunday after Sunday. After the dust settled from the Civil War, the newly prosperous began enjoying a middle-class "Victorian" lifestyle, complete with wallpaper and household furnishings selected from catalogues, formal parlors seen as necessities in city houses, and clothing that reflected one's social status. Along with personal consumption came pressure from congregations to build bigger and finer churches, replete with stone towers and steeples, carpeting, stained-glass windows, hardwood pews, and fine organs. The grandchildren of people who had been content with clapboard churches and rough-hewn benches thought it a sign of social progress to enjoy stained-glass sanctuaries, paid choirs with organ accompaniment, and fancy crosses or lighted candles gracing their altars. The popularity of the "high church" movement in Episcopalianism exerted upward pressure for elegance in wealthy congregations of other denominations. "Ritualism" was not confined to "Romanism": it was a danger to evangelical Protestantism as well. As Pierson's temperance poem attested, the bejeweled chalice was also a sign from Satan.

Yet the descendant of Anak that most distressed A. T. Pierson was the neglect of the poor by an increasingly prosperous church. As he stated in his report on the Detroit meeting of the Evangelical Alliance, "population tends to the *cities,* and hence the evangelization of the cities is of the highest moment . . . the tendency of all religions is to grow away from the common people as they acquire prestige and culture; and yet all real power resides with the people." An image Pierson frequently used to describe society was a pyramid. If the base were unstable, poor, and outcast, the whole pyramid would tumble. All classes were mutually dependent, and society would avenge the weakest if they were neglected. In using a pyramid as his model for society, Pierson was showing his basic agreement with the analysis of social problems by urban clergy who crafted an emerging "social gospel" movement. During the 1870s and 1880s there was broad agreement among the clergy, who began addressing the social needs of urban America. Shared experience as urban pastors was part of what drew clergy to meetings of the Evangelical Alliance. Theological differences widened by the end of the century, but in the two decades following the Civil War, divisions between "liberals" and "conservatives" were secondary to the common task of making Protestantism relevant to the changing urban context. While pioneer "social gospel" clergy like Washington Gladden began experimenting with structural and political solutions to urban problems, evangelical clergy like A. T. Pierson retained their basic faith in evangelistic solutions. But Pierson shared the speaker's platform with his contemporary Gladden, a noted theological liberal and critic of free enterprise who served churches in Springfield, Massachusetts, and Columbus, Ohio.

The single event that most frightened urban clergy into analysis of the social and economic structures that underlay the industrial expansion of the Gilded Age was the national railroad crisis of 1877. Rapid overexpansion of railroads by rich businessmen eager to corner the transportation market had caused a financial panic in 1873. The mild depression dragged on; immigrants and workers survived six lean years, with growing resentment against the apparent omnipotence of the railroad companies. In the summer of 1877, the Baltimore and Ohio announced another wage cut, thereby provoking wildcat strikes from Philadelphia to San Francisco. In the cities, crowds rioted and looted businesses. Federal troops marched into cities to control them. This "first national holiday of the slums" was America's first national strike. With no income tax, no social security or unemployment pay, no government regulations on working conditions or safety standards, widespread child labor, and long working hours with no minimum wage, the strike revealed the growing divide between rich and poor, and the polarization of capital and labor. It also demonstrated that city slums were powder kegs of discontent. Although even the most progressive clergy condemned the violence of the strike, it forced them to analyze the social costs of unregulated capitalism.

As pastor in a wealthy Presbyterian church that counted railroad barons among its members, yet a minister with a heart for the urban poor, A. T. Pierson was passionately interested in the strike. He wrote a set of articles on it for the *New York Observer,* one of the leading religious papers of the day. The first article demonstrated the shock Pierson felt at street violence as a "relic of barbarism." He affirmed his faith in the self-regulation of supply and demand. Believing that prices would rise and fall in balance with the fluctuation in wages, he therefore condemned workers who squandered their pay and who then insisted they were underpaid. In affirming the basic principles of capitalism, he was in agreement with the majority of clergy. At the same time, he favored a uniform management of the railroads so as to prevent the cutthroat competition that had caused the depression in the first place, and destroyed the steady wage.

In his second article on the railroad strike, however, Pierson accused greedy capitalists of helping to cause it. He argued for an equalization of wages between labor and management. He encouraged profit-sharing of capital with labor and urged special emergency funds for disablement or death. Pierson supported unions in theory, but he hoped they would become outdated "by a radical reform in the management of our railway corporations, so that from the engineers to the switchmen, every man shall feel that the Railway Company is his true 'brotherhood.'" He called for regulation of competition between railways so that proper prices and profits could be secured to provide decent wages for workers. As a Christian, Pierson asked employers to conduct their businesses on religious grounds, providing libraries for workers and obeying the Lord's day by not requiring work on the Sabbath. He believed that "morally and spiritually, to improve the character and condition of the working-classes is to lay the very cornerstone even of financial prosperity. . . . Any business that is not conducted with respect to religious restraints demoralizes the conscience of the employees." Pierson closed the articles with his belief that society is organic, is one whole, and the health of the total society is determined by the well-being of those on the bottom.

By the late 1870s, A. T. Pierson was advocating a combination of government regulation, appeal to the Christian consciences of employers, and the evangelization of workers as the way to improve the lives of the poor. His constellation of views rested on his belief that individual, evangelical Christian faith caused concrete, beneficial results for society as a whole. Successful democracy relied on improving both the "character and conditions" for working Americans. His solutions to the social crises of the Gilded Age were not a matter of merely "controlling" the poor. The Giant Anakim were also found among the wealthy and powerful of his own status-conscious congregation. Church neglect of the poor was an issue that struck at both rich and poor, to the right and to the left, at the ritualists and the Romanists. An active member of the Evangelical Alliance in the 1870s and 1880s, Pierson was part of the generation that was reshaping evangelicalism to meet the needs of an urban America. By struggling together against the Giant Anakim, late nineteenth-century, northern middle-class evangelicals reaffirmed their identity. The war against slavery was only the beginning of their mission to America. As they fought the social problems of the Gilded Age, they rediscovered themselves.

RECONVERSION AND ITS CONSEQUENCES

The unending problems of the urban poor in Detroit brought A. T. Pierson to the greatest identity crisis of his ministry. The crowded, poverty-stricken, unevangelized city forced him to doubt the casual optimism of his faith — that right knowledge would lead to conversion, conversion to Christian action, and Christian action to Christian civilization. In Detroit, the postmillennial certainty of the war years gave way to doubt. No matter how hard he worked, he seemed unable to reach the unevangelized poor.

Rather than blaming social conditions or cultural differences for his lack of results among the poor, Pierson blamed himself. In his frustration over his apparent lack of evangelistic power, he doubted if he were saved. As he confessed to the 25th International Convention of the YMCA's held in Milwaukee, Wisconsin, in 1883,

> I am ashamed to say that from 1860 to 1875 I preached the gospel *without knowing myself to be a saved man.* . . . The fact is, though it is a most humiliating confession, that during all those years I was making an idol of literary culture and popular applause. I was ensnared by the ambition to be a great pulpit orator and shine; and so I was preaching elaborate literary essays, and had few souls converted.

He blamed the lack of conversions on his own lack of faith and his overly "literary" theology. Depression and job pressure began damaging his health. In a letter to his daughter Helen written in 1890, Pierson recalled that he had loose bowels for ten years in Detroit.

What A. T. Pierson experienced as a spiritual crisis had all the markings of a midlife vocational crisis. As for feeling he was not truly converted, the evidence shows he had already experienced at least three major encounters with God's grace — once as a child at boarding school, again in the Businessman's Revival, and finally his conviction of biblical truth in Binghamton. After a few years at Fort Street Church, Arthur Pierson had built it into one of the leading Presbyterian churches in the Midwest. He was a powerful figure in midwestern Presbyterianism and was active in ecumenical ventures like the Evangelical Alliance and the Detroit Ministerial Alliance. His fame as a preacher meant that he filled the expanded sanctuary without difficulty; his published sermons were read by many. His family life was cheerful and solid — with a good marital relationship, his mother in good health, and an orderly but lively house full of children. He made a decent salary and had accomplished all he had set out to do when he moved to Detroit. Nearing age 40, he had reached the top of his profession and was in demand as a lecturer and essayist. At some point during his Detroit years, he turned down an offer from a New York City pulpit at a salary of $10,000 a year. So why was he depressed?

The very context in which he ministered increased his discontent. Fort Street Church was the epitome of success, with its cultured congregation and elegant building. Yet as an evangelical with a heart for the poor, Pierson was feeling trapped by the upper-class expectations that surrounded him. He wanted to save souls, and to solve the social problems of the city while doing it. As a man who believed that one's relationship with God had direct consequences in daily life, he decided that the fault must be his. In Pierson's tradition of piety that went back to the Puritans, if a person were truly saved, there would be fruits to show for it. Perhaps the lack of fruits in evangelism meant that he was not really saved.

The catalyst for Pierson's reconversion was a seven-week revival conducted by Major D. W. Whittle of Chicago and his singing partner Philip Paul Bliss. Whittle was a Civil War officer and businessman befriended by Dwight L. Moody, who in the early 1870s was on his way to becoming the leading American revivalist of the late nineteenth century. In 1873, Moody went to England and began a two-year revival whose success catapulted him to fame on both sides of the Atlantic. At the same time, Moody convinced Major Whittle to go into full-time evangelistic work, which he did in 1874. Detroit was one of the first stops for the new revival team. Arriving as virtual unknowns, Whittle and Bliss took Detroit by storm. Daily services and prayer meetings ran from October 6 to November 19, 1874. Crowds of twelve to fifteen hundred persons attended the main preaching events, with hundreds seeking prayer in inquiry rooms afterward. Services began at 9:00 A.M., with exhortations, prayers, and sermons led by the evangelical clergy of Detroit, including Baptists, Methodists, Presbyterians, and Congregationalists. Immensely successful, the Detroit revivals culminated in the "ordination" of Whittle by the evangelical pastors of Detroit. The local newspaper reported that although the evangelical pastors knew the ecumenical ordination service was not strictly legal, "we cannot but feel that this unanimous approbation of these representatives of various denominations should have all the practical force of a more formal act, in serving to commend him both to the cordial confidence and co-operation of Christian pastors and churches of every name."

Pierson's dissatisfaction with his own ministry grew because the unlettered evangelist had more power with the masses than he did, despite his superior literary talents. Consequently, when Whittle and Bliss came, he "gladly sat at their feet, as a learner." From Whittle and Bliss, Pierson learned that simple gospel preaching was more effective in reaching the uneducated for Christ than literary style. Pierson was also deeply influenced by the effectiveness of Bliss's singing. Whittle was one of the first modern evangelists to have a regular song leader as partner; Bliss's gospel choruses and revivalistic hymns seemed to "soften up" the crowd and put them in the mood for receiving spiritual truths.

Known as "the gospel singer," Bliss was a pioneer in collecting simple choruses that he published in the ground-breaking hymnal *Gospel Hymns*. His most enduring hymn was probably "Let the Lower Lights Be Burning," also known as the sailor's hymn because of its metaphor of preventing shipwreck by keeping the lights on shore. Just as he had been impressed with the simple, lined-out singing at Spurgeon's Tabernacle in the 1860s, Pierson realized that popular congregational singing could be a valuable part of worship, and could more effectively reach the poor than old-world, formal hymns. He put his talent for poetry to use by writing lyrics for several of Bliss's revival tunes. For a month, the evangelists lived with the Piersons, and Arthur was impressed by their spirituality and peace of mind. Before he left Detroit, Whittle said to him, "Brother Pierson, Bliss and I are firmly convinced that God would mightily use you if you were wholly consecrated to Him. We have agreed to pray for you daily that you may be fully surrendered."

Whittle's parting words increased the pressure for spiritual perfection that Pierson felt. He daily rose an hour or two before breakfast to have uninterrupted time for Bible study and prayer in a tower room that he outfitted at the church. As he immersed himself in the Scriptures, he began thinking of them as a guide for daily life. As the Bible filled his mind, he began composing simpler, more direct biblical sermons rather than the literary-style essays on popular themes that had been so successful with the cultured crowd. He made extensive notes on the Bible, analyzing its language and imagery, and cross-checking verses with similar ideas elsewhere in the text. He wrote,

> For myself I feel constrained to bear witness that no amount of study of commentaries or any other human product has been of such help as the spiritual, devotional study of the Scriptures (if possible in the original tongues). The case and number of a noun, the mood and tense of a verb, the relation of clauses and words to each other may throw new light on a passage. Above all prayer and the supreme regard for the mind of the Spirit will lead to a receptive attitude of mind and comparative indifference to mere literary standards.

In November 1875, Pierson experienced a spiritual breakthrough when he realized that his ambition stood between himself and God, and he prayed for God to remove it from him. In January 1876, as Pierson prepared a sermon on 1 John 5:4, the words of the text struck him hard, "For whatever is born of God overcomes the world; and this is the victory that overcomes the world, our faith." Feeling that he needed to overcome worldliness and not be guided by human approbation, Pierson struggled to renounce "literary culture and applause." Confiding in his journal, he wrote:

> I began to pray aloud in private and found this a great help to my realization of the presence of God, and I learned what real prayer meant. Then I was impressed with the necessity for honesty, absolute candour with God in asking what I really wanted, and what I was willing to give up everything else to obtain. I saw that my life had been full of self-seeking and idolatry, such as I had never realized. Next I felt the need of present faith in the sure Word of God which promises answer to such prayer. God gave me this assurance in the preparation of a special sermon to my people. Finally I saw that I must give up every ambition and every idol, and must place myself unreservedly in the hands of God. It was a terrible battle, but at last I said, with all my heart, "Lord, let me be nothing, but use me if Thou wilt to save souls and to glorify Thee."
>
> From that day I was conscious of the presence of the Holy Spirit in my life and work in a way that I had before never known. The text, 1 John v. 4, "I have overcome the world," was revealed to me in a new light and instead of depending upon my energy and ability to overcome the world, I saw that God must do it and all the glory was to be His, not mine.

He turned to a new biography of Charles Finney and decided to model his own ministry on that of the revivalist, a great saver of souls.

The literary ambition and applause that Pierson was rejecting were exemplified for him in the Fort Street Presbyterian Church — the gothic towers, rented pews that shut out the poor, and wealthy congregation. Men such as the Honorable Zachariah Chandler, who had been a U.S. Senator, a founder of the Republican Party, and Secretary of the Interior under President Grant, were members of his congregation. The church building itself seemed insulated from life in the streets and from real need in the city of Detroit. Pierson regretted that he had helped to remodel the church to its present elegant form only a few years before. Finney's leadership in the free church movement of New York City during the 1830s inspired him, and he determined to speak against the prosperity of complacent church life. He decided to preach plainer sermons more easily understood by the uneducated. His accusations against Fort Street Church were accusations against himself and his own complicity in a worldly church.

An essay he wrote in Detroit in support of the Presbyterian mission board, "Selfishness, the Sin of the Church," clearly expressed what Arthur Pierson was trying to say to his congregation by January 1876. Although he preached numerous sermons on the failure of the church to evangelize the masses, the essay allowed full expression of his passion, perhaps saying in print what he dared not say so baldly from his pulpit:

> Go into our churches. Are they meant for the evangelization of the masses? No! With architectural elegance, artistic decoration, expensive furnishing, costly choirs, they are built for the wealthy, aristocratic, cultivated *few*. If the people at large desired to come, there is not room; were there room, they would not feel at home. The real secret purpose in the construction of most of our church buildings is to provide luxurious accommodation and artistic entertainment for a select class, where they may recline in damask pews, feast their eyes on architectural symmetry and artistic beauty, feast their ears on operatic music, and feast their cultured, intellectual taste on eloquent, poetic, philosophic and rhetorical essays or orations. The idea of building a church for the people, where the unevangelized masses may hear the gospel, without money and without price, — the idea of going out into the highways and hedges to compel them to come in, — now few Christian churches have any practical conception of duty or privilege in this direction! What a marked contrast to the primitive church where all were together and had things in common, and none said of his possessions, "they are my own!"

Pierson followed this paragraph with an exhortation to systematic giving of benevolences for the poor, destitute, and unevangelized. A century before ecumenical mission documents were connecting the poor with the unsaved, and realizing that they were the same people, A. T. Pierson was drawing lines between physical and spiritual poverty. He used the primitive communism of the early church as an argument for stewardship: all money really belonged to God and was not the private property of the rich men who made it.

Pierson began a lecture series on the life of Charles Finney to convince the Fort Street congregation to open itself to the urban poor of Detroit, and to abolish pew rents and other attitudes that discouraged strangers from attending. On Friday evening, March 24, 1876, the pastor led a prayer meeting of sixty or seventy parishioners who had braved hail and a snowstorm to come to the sanctuary. He unburdened his heart to his people about the lack of power and selfishness in the church. He told them how tradition, formality, and fashion were blocking them from reaching the poor. Those gathered responded sympathetically, and they worked through a series of Bible passages on answers to prayer. Then, in an unprecedented action, they knelt on the floor and asked God to remove any obstacle that stood between Fort Street Church and ministry to the poor.

After the congregation rose from its knees, a few people noticed smoke in the room, but there was no trace of fire. Assuming that smoke from the chimney had backed into the room, the people went home. At 6:00 the next morning, the huge church suddenly burst into flames and was quickly consumed, with its immense steeple falling across the road. A faulty stove pipe had ignited the plaster between the walls and had spread quietly until the explosion. The only items recovered from the church were the communion service, housed in a closet away from the flames, and all the manuscripts of Pierson's sermons and Bible notes. The manuscripts were in the tower room in a desk. The tower conducted the fire straight up like a chimney, and no trace of the desk was found. Although Pierson's entire library was destroyed, his life's work in sermon notes was recovered from the tower, soaked in water.

The fire and the saving of his Bible notes were messages from God. Convinced of the righteousness of his cause, Pierson went the same day to hire Whitney's Opera House in which to hold services. The opera house had just been completed in 1875 on the northwest corner of Shelby and Fort streets. It seated fourteen hundred people and was a center of night life in Detroit. Pierson also went straightaway and purchased three hundred copies of *Gospel Hymns*, which had been published the year before as a collaboration between P. P. Bliss and Ira Sankey, who was revivalist Dwight Moody's song leader. The day after the fire being Sunday, Pierson had no time to prepare a sermon. He chose a text for extemporaneous delivery — 1 Corinthians 3:13, "The fire shall try every man's work, of what sort it is." At the Sunday night service he preached on the life of Charles Finney from memory, since his manuscript on the study table had been burned up. From that day on, Pierson never again preached a sermon from manuscript.

Arthur Pierson believed that the fire was God's dramatic answer to his prayers for guidance. With his mid-life vocational crisis resolved, he felt the inner peace of knowing he was converted and in full compliance with God's will. From now on, instead of being a minister with a heart for mission, he would be a missionary engaged in urban ministry. With the Bible as his guide, and *Gospel Hymns* under his arm, his calling from God was to evangelize the unreached.

4 Saving Souls in the City

The fire at Fort Street Church not only burned down a building but seared Arthur Pierson's soul. No more compromises to worldly success! No more doubts about the direction of his ministry! Convincing the church trustees not to designate seats for church members, Pierson opened Whitney's Opera House to all who wanted to attend, with no distinction between rich and poor. Discarding his Presbyterian formality, he launched into extemporaneous sermons, introduced gospel hymn-singing and a voluntary choir, and invited inquirers to come forward during the service to be prayed over. Soon the Detroit newspapers were talking about the "great revival." Services at the Opera House were packed from the start, with as many as a thousand people turned away in the evenings for lack of room. Hundreds of inquirers requested prayer. During the sixteen months of revival, more people were converted than in Pierson's previous sixteen years of ministry. Two hundred ninety-four people joined Fort Street Church on confession of faith during the services.

The whole focus of Pierson's ministry changed in response to God's voice speaking through the fire. The preservation of his Bible notes told Pierson that God wanted him to preach plain, biblical sermons instead of literary creations. The local paper described the first service at the Opera House, as the curious public packed the hall:

> As the people began to fill the house from pit to top gallery, two theatre men who dropped in out of curiosity remarked that such an audience would bring a good sum at fifty cents a head. When the audience joined in singing, "Praise God from whom all blessings flow," it made the house ring as it never had rung before even for the grandest opera chorus. Some of the people, who were more accustomed to the opera than to church, were so impressed by the singing that they began to applaud. A hushed stillness pervaded the vast audience during the prayer and they listened sympathetically to the sermon on "The Ordeal of Fire." Two actors who came in at the stage door to look for their baggage stood behind the flies, with hats in hand, listening with rapt attention to the man who stood where they had performed the evening before.

According to his hearers, Dr. Pierson gave "one of the most startling, plain spoken discourses a nineteenth century audience ever listened to." As the revival unfolded, Arthur Pierson felt himself the instrument of God, and that God was anointing him for a new ministry, the shape of which was not yet clear.

By conducting worship in an opera house, with its stage and theatrical seating, Arthur Pierson was able to adopt the new, less formal "gospel style" that was becoming a feature of urban revivalism in the late 1800s. Gospel tabernacles or their imitators opened in New York City, Boston, and other large cities in the late 1800s, as evangelical ministers like A. T. Pierson felt the need to return to the revivalistic roots that predated denominational Protestantism's rise into middle-class prosperity. The "tabernacle style" of building encouraged more informality and congregational participation, and rolicking gospel hymnody encouraged even timid singers to belt out their praises to the Lord. A series of popular gospel hymnals that contained new hymns by Fanny Crosby, William Doane, Ira Sankey, and others, launched a revival of congregational singing that spread across the country. Even though Pierson's innovations were related to his personal experience, he was part of a larger movement toward the renewal of popular worship. In addition to the regular worship services, he led two prayer meetings and two Bible studies a week.

Since his major goal was to reach the urban masses with the gospel, Pierson focused his sermons on the simple gospel message of repentance from sin, the new birth in Christ, and eternal salvation. Preaching a classic Protestant gospel, he stated that the Bible is "the true word of God," the "one rule of Doctrine and Duty." Another rudiment of faith for Pierson was the incarnation — God had come to earth in the human form of Jesus. In the doctrine of the atonement, Jesus paid the price for human sin through his death. Pierson frequently preached sermons on the Christian life, especially on obedience to God's commands through the power of the Holy Spirit. In his messages, the new birth required living a new life — one of service, self-sacrifice, renunciation of power and riches, and devotion to reaching the poor and the unsaved. He stated in his second week at the opera house, "When Christian people are not willing to sacrifice their tastes for art, architecture, music and oratory in the house of God, they do not reach the masses. A kid glove is often a non-conductor between man and man." He emphasized the Christian life so much that Christian biography became his favorite means of illustrating the practical truths of Christianity. Never one to skirt controversy, he preached biblical messages of sin and judgment as well.

During their sixteen months in Whitney's Opera House, the congregation of the Fort Street Church grew in faith and opened themselves to the city in a way that had not been possible before. Detroit experienced revival. And Arthur Pierson experienced a kind of fulfillment that had eluded him previously — finally God was using him to save many souls.

MANY INFALLIBLE PROOFS

Some of the inquirers who spoke to the pastor after opera house services were not certain God existed, or else nourished secret doubts about biblical truth-claims. Some professed themselves to be followers of Robert Ingersoll, the "great agnostic." A prominent lawyer and Republican politician from Illinois, Ingersoll was one of the most popular speakers in the late 1870s and 1880s, receiving as much as $3500 a night for a single evening's performance. Speaking with a lawyer's logic on humanistic philosophy and scientific rationalism, he popularized the higher criticism of the Bible. Ingersoll asked entertaining "village atheist" questions that pitted modern science against the truth-claims of the Bible, and he set up the Christian believer as a straw man of ignorant buffoonery. He was anathema to evangelical Christians, especially after 1879 when he published his best-seller, *Some Mistakes of Moses.* Much as lawyer Clarence Darrow would humiliate biblical fundamentalists at the Scopes trial over evolution in 1925, Robert Ingersoll sowed seeds of doubt and "infidelity" wherever he appeared on the lecture circuit.

The essence of Pierson's opera house ministry was personal encounters with seekers concerned for their souls. After one sermon on "Abiding in Christ," the preacher issued the usual invitation for interested parties to meet him in the inquiry room. A 30-year-old man, with a clouded and furrowed face, met the minister and confessed that he was a follower of Robert Ingersoll. In answer to Pierson's queries, he admitted that he did not believe in the Bible as the book of God, in Jesus Christ as son of God, or even in God. An unhappy law student, he was drawn by hearing the organ and remained for the sermon: "I heard nothing but simple congregational singing, but curiosity led me to remain and hear what you had to say, and one thing impressed me, — that you have faith in somebody or something, and you are happy in believing. My envy of you brings me in here." Praying to God for guidance, Pierson put his arm around the young man and guided him to two Bible texts: John 5:39, "Search the Scriptures; for in them ye think ye have eternal life and they are they which testify of Me and ye will not come unto Me that ye may have life," and Matthew 6:6, "Enter into thy closet, and when thou hast shut thy door, pray to thy Father which is in secret, and thy Father which seeth in secret Himself shall reward thee."

Even though the man did not believe in either God or the Bible, Pierson assured him that God would not ignore a genuine effort to find him. After sharing several more Bible texts that guided the seeker toward Jesus Christ as his "personal Saviour," Pierson prayed with the man and sent him on his way. Two weeks later, the man returned to the church. Having followed the preacher's prescription for Bible study, he returned in joy to celebrate having found God and Christ. In Arthur Pierson's words, "As he read and prayed and sought for light, light was given; he humbly tried to follow every ray and to walk in the light, and the path became clearer and plainer and the light fuller and brighter, until his eyes rested in faith upon Jesus."

Although during the revival Dr. Pierson dealt with doubters on a one-to-one basis, the greater challenge was to counteract Ingersoll's influence on the broader society. Ingersoll's writings and dramatic presentations had a sensational impact because he tapped into the deeper insecurities of the Gilded Age, an era of rapid social change and shifts in worldview that undercut the "old-fashioned" simple faith in the Bible as God's truth. Ironically, at the same time that northern, middle-class families were purchasing large "picture Bibles" for display in their parlors, actual belief in the Bible's truth was declining. The "great agnostic" arrived in Detroit and spoke to sellout crowds at Whitney's Opera House. Ingersoll caused such an uproar that even the secular press called for a champion of biblical orthodoxy to rebut him. As the leading Bible teacher and preacher in Detroit, Pierson challenged "the mistakes of Moses" with a course of lectures on the "proofs" of Christianity. He repeated them by popular demand in 1883. They appeared as one of his first books (c. 1880), *Many Infallible Proofs: The Evidences of Christianity*. Thousands thronged to hear Pierson refute Ingersoll. His book *Many Infallible Proofs* went through multiple editions and became one of the classic late nineteenth-century Protestant rational defenses of the trustworthiness of the Bible, being reprinted well into the twentieth century and translated into Spanish and other languages.

Questions of science and religion had fascinated Pierson from his youth, with his logical frame of mind and his insatiable intellectual curiosity. By the late 1870s, however, the ground had shifted from under the comfortable equilibrium he had reached in Binghamton between the claims of science and the claims of the Bible. With popularizers like Ingersoll, Charles Darwin's theories of evolution and human descent from apes had succeeded in reaching ordinary Americans. Set forth in his books *Origin of Species by Means of Natural Selection* (1859) and *Descent of Man* (1871), Charles Darwin's theories of human evolution challenged the whole "Baconian" foundation of inductive science. Instead of seeing in geological evidence God's individual acts of creation, scientists used a hypothesis, evolution, to explain how organisms changed over time. Instead of believing the Bible as the Word of God, scientific inquiry asked whether Jesus really lived, whether a big fish swallowed Jonah, whether Joshua made the sun stand still, where the sons of Adam and Eve got their wives, whether Moses wrote the first five books of the Bible, and so on. With historicism being the order of the day, people in the Gilded Age were fascinated by big theories of historical change — whether it be Marxism as an explanation for economic history, or evolution as the cause of biological developments. Modern science shattered supernatural explanations as sources of truth — anything that happened outside the realm of normal history or the principles of natural law could not be "true" in the scientific sense. Historians of the late nineteenth century have indicated that supernaturalism and the Bible seemed as dead orthodoxy when measured against the inventive power of humanity that could harness steam and soon tame electricity. Christian morality seemed irrelevant in the face of "the survival of the fittest" and human descent from apes.

Arthur Pierson brought the full force of his intellect and the results of decades of meticulous Bible study into the task of refuting the skepticism of Ingersoll, and with him, the whole challenge that science brought to faith in the late nineteenth century. He filled twenty-five notebooks with his daily Bible study, as well as the margins of fifteen Bagster's study Bibles. He read the works of Darwin, geologists, and skeptical philosophers like David Hume and August Comte; he worked through the problems of the age in dialogue with the Bible. After exhaustive study, Pierson concluded there was no conflict between modern science and the Bible, because "the object of the Bible is not to teach science, but moral and spiritual truth. Scientific facts and truths may be discovered by the intellect and industry of man; and hence no revelation of them is needed. But our origin and destiny, our relations to God, the way of peace and purity, the link between the here and the hereafter — the highest wisdom of man has only guessed at these things: and here comes the need that God shall speak."

The first thing that Pierson did to assuage the anxieties of his listeners was to give them permission to doubt. He urged them to throw away their fears of applying the intellect to issues of faith. Pierson believed that since God was one, truth was one. Believers need not fear that science would somehow undercut religious truth. Maintaining that "honest doubt" should be honored, Pierson urged that as a person grew from childlike intuition into adult reason, he should study the "evidences of Christianity." As God was the author of reason, so was faith based on intellectual understanding. "A faith not firmly founded upon good evidence deserves not the name of faith, for the basis of all true faith or trust is belief which is the assent of the mind, or understanding, to truth supported by adequate proofs." Blind faith, in fact, only begat bigotry and religious persecution.

Although truth was unified, scientific and moral truths were directed toward different ends. In a series of journal articles on "Religion and Science," Pierson ridiculed ministers who tried to fight Darwin and Huxley on scientific grounds, for ministers would be bested by scientific experts on scientific turf. Rather, clergy should stick to spiritual grounds in which their expertise was clearly superior to that of the scientists. Clergy should not be Davids fighting Goliath in Saul's armor. Because the Bible had not been written as a scientific textbook, its reliability could not be doubted just because its poetic and figurative language did not precisely fit "modern" scientific categories. Joshua would have looked ridiculous if he had told the earth to stop rotating on its axis when all the people believed the sun moved across the sky. Rather, he spoke in the idiom of his age when he commanded the sun to stand still. In his lectures refuting Ingersoll, Pierson applied literary criticism to biblical language, demonstrating how many of the so-called "mistakes of Moses" were in fact consistent with scientific knowledge if one consulted the Greek and Hebrew words. The idea of "firmament," for example, did not mean a solid sphere in which the stars were fixed. Rather, he argued that the Hebrew word *rakiya*, translated as firmament, meant an expanse. To say that the world was created in seven "days," using the Hebrew word *yom*, was to say that God created the world in seven seasons, or periods of time. The brilliance of biblical language, according to Pierson, was that its flexibility allowed it to encompass the growing range of human knowledge. "God might lead inspired men to use such language, that, without revealing scientific facts in advance, it might accurately accommodate itself to them, when discovered. The language might be so elastic and flexible as to contract itself to the narrowness of ignorance, and yet expand itself to the dimensions of knowledge, like the rubber bandage, so invaluable in modern surgery, which stretches about an inflamed and swollen limb, yet shrinks as the swelling abates."

One way in which Pierson tried to halt the spiritual panic begun by theories of the gradual evolution of the earth was by shrewdly distinguishing between proven facts and theories. In a "common sense" argument, he limited the domain of science to proven facts, thereby excluding unproven hypotheses. After all, just because Darwin saw a bear swim in the sea and catch insects like a whale did not mean that the bear would evolve necessarily into a whale. The first observation was the fact, and the second, that a bear would become a whale, was mere theory. And why should Christians discard their religious beliefs about God creating the world to adopt theories of geology, evolution, and anthropology upon which scientists did not even agree? Much of modern science was guesswork and speculation, and hypotheses should not be taken as "facts" until proven.

Pierson limited strictly the realm of science to the physical world by denying its moral or social superiority over religion. In his 1883 preaching series on Christian evidences, he dared anyone to find a scientific theory that could transform human character as could the Bible:

> I studied natural philosophy, astronomy, botany, geology, read novels and histories and poems, works on law and medicine and philosophy; but I never found these books restraining lust, curbing sensual appetites, inspiring noble aims, exposing sinful propensities, moving me to be a truer son, better husband, kinder father. But somehow from the day I began systematically to read the Bible, I began to be sensible of a new power at work in my mind and heart.

His strict limitations on the sphere of science eventually permitted him to speculate that evolution was possibly God's way of working in the physical universe. The order of creation from lower to higher animals, the idea of separating the dry land from the sea — the accounts of creation in the book of Genesis were consistent with current scientific theories. But Pierson refused to apply geological and biological evolution to areas that lay outside its boundaries — such as human character, racial differences, or social structure.

Pierson's efforts to limit science were a brilliant attempt to reconcile the categories of the Enlightenment with traditional belief. His intelligent defense of the flexibility of biblical language, his emphasis on the deeper purposes of the Bible itself, and his refusal to let scientific "facts" take over the whole realm of morality and interpersonal relationships all are positions that resonate with late twentieth-century philosophical defenses of Christianity. Yet another part of his argument seems more consistent with his reputation as a father of fundamentalism, namely, his clinging to early nineteenth-century "Baconian" and "common sense" definitions of science that also permitted belief in the supernatural as scientific. On the basis of common sense, or Baconianism, Pierson attacked higher criticism of the Bible as unscientific. Common sense regarding the beauty of the world pointed to a Creator, not to a mechanical view of creation. That witnesses wrote down in the Bible that Jesus performed miracles proved that miracles existed. The religious experiences of believers proved the truth of the Bible. The first "infallible proof" of the Bible's truth was in fact the visible impact it had on the spiritual state and life of the believer. Personal transformation by Jesus Christ was a "scientific" validation of the Bible.

As an inductive logician, Pierson refused to go outside the Bible for critical theories of its origin or meaning. He therefore "proved" the truth of the Bible by demonstrating the fulfillment of prophecy in the Scriptures. He pointed out Old Testament references that predicted the coming of Jesus, and he argued that Jesus himself predicted the destruction of Jerusalem. Because he took the text as true historical reporting and as internally coherent, Pierson refused to consider that Gospel writers could have deliberately manipulated the facts of Jesus' life to fit Old Testament predictions. Because he dated the earliest Gospels to before A.D. 70, he did not speculate that they could have been written after the destruction of Jerusalem. Jesus' miracles were a refutation of skeptics like Hume who did not believe miracles were possible. People who did not believe miracles were possible would never believe proofs of their existence, and so they were not reading the Bible with an open mind. Even biblical language was prophetic of future scientific discoveries. For example, when morning stars sing together in Job 38, Pierson interpreted the "music of the spheres" as a prediction of the scientific fact that light travels in vibrations, though too shrill for the ear to hear.

Pierson argued for biblical truth in the "organic unity" or internal coherence of doctrines in the Bible. He believed in the progress of revelation in the Scriptures, with more and more revealed about God through the centuries. In the creation of the biblical canon, that the early church had approved and placed the books of the Bible in a particular order, Pierson found a divine development of biblical theology from Genesis to Revelation. By 1883, in his second set of lectures on Christian evidences, Pierson was on the verge of developing a complete theory of biblical unity. He felt that he held the key, but had not yet unlocked the door. "After twenty-five years daily study of this one book in the original tongues, I can already see that each book fills a place in the great plan; what further study may disclose as to the extent of the sphere which each fills, I cannot now say." Although he searched constantly for the perfect system by which to interpret the Bible according to God's will, Pierson by his forties had nevertheless become comfortable with the idea of mystery in the Bible, and waiting on God's time to unlock its secrets.

For Pierson, the greatest Christian evidence for biblical truth was the person and power of Jesus Christ. Jesus' perfection of teaching and character pointed to the mystery of the incarnation, the ultimate proof of God's reality. His death on the cross showed the superiority of a new law of self-sacrifice. Proof of biblical truth lay in Jesus Christ and the benefits of salvation and sanctification through him. The experience of Jesus' power in the life of the believer was the most basic "infallible proof":

> There are simple-minded believers who know nothing of the proofs from prophecy and miracle, who do know that God is faithful to his promises, and see the miracle of the new heart and changed life actually wrought in themselves. Christ is a living Saviour by that most infallible proof — what He has done and is doing for them. He opened their blind eyes to see their sin and need, and his beauty and love; he cleansed the leprosy of their guilt, cured the palsy of their helplessness and the fever of their raging passion, and cast out the demon from their hearts.

The ultimate "scientific proof" of Christianity, both of its general truth and its application by the believer, was one's personal experience of Jesus Christ.

Faith or reason? Religious experience or biblical doctrines? Religion or science? Many of Pierson's intellectual contemporaries and fellow urban clergymen were beginning to reject the supernatural in favor of new definitions of science in the 1880s. Yet from his platform at the opera house, Arthur Pierson combated the skepticism of the Ingersoll age by refusing to separate the emotional and intellectual sides of Christianity. Through an evangelical experience of the "new birth," seekers could appropriate for themselves the trustworthiness of the Bible. Conversely, through studying the Bible, the Word of God, seekers would find a personal relationship with Jesus Christ. The "fire that tries every man's work" reaffirmed that the Holy Spirit would supernaturally intervene in the life of the believer. Through his "common sense" defense of evangelical faith, A. T. Pierson threw a lifeline to thousands of honest doubters who nevertheless longed for religious certainty.

FROM POSTMILLENNIALISM TO PREMILLENNIALISM

Judging his ministry from 1860 to 1875 as unconverted, Arthur Pierson solved his mid-life spiritual crisis by a renewed conversion experience. The Holy Spirit solved his vocational crisis by opening a ministry to the masses through the destruction of the Fort Street Church. His intellectual crisis was solved by finding proofs for Christianity which did not contradict the conclusions of modern science that obsessed the intellectuals of his generation. And in 1879, by becoming a premillennialist, he resolved the conflict between his optimistic ideology of the steady progress of Christian civilization, and the harsh urban realities of crime, poverty, and industrial strife. He did not realize at the time that the trajectory from postmillennialism to premillennialism was an increasingly convincing option for other urban, evangelical clergy of his generation — men like A. B. Simpson, A. J. Gordon, Dwight Moody, and James H. Brookes — who would one day become his close companions in the search to reconcile biblical prophecies with modern life.

In May 1878, barely two years after the fire, Dr. Pierson traveled with friends by train to San Francisco. Tired from his exertions at the opera house, he took the trip in order to rest and to give a few speeches. While enjoying the beautiful city on the Pacific coast, he heard that George Müller of Bristol, England, was speaking across the bay in Oakland. Since his trip to England in 1866, Arthur Pierson had admired George Müller, who ran a large orphanage complex in Bristol on the "faith" method. Like Hudson Taylor, founder of the China Inland Mission, Müller had made it a spiritual principle never to ask for funds. A Prussian by birth, much influenced by pietist A. H. Francke, Müller and his wife forsook a set salary and gave away all money but the absolute minimum they needed to live. In 1832, they moved to Bristol and opened their orphanages. By 1870, Müller was supporting five orphanages of approximately two thousand orphans, all on the faith principle of trusting to God for all support. At age 65, Müller began seventeen years of touring to spread his principles of faith, church, and Scripture.

Having followed Müller's ministry for twenty years but never having met him, Pierson was seriously tempted to travel to Oakland in violation of his firm convictions against traveling on the Sabbath. One of the chief symbols of evangelical commitment since the days of the Puritans had been keeping the Sabbath as the Lord's day. Evangelicals followed the biblical commands not to work or travel on the Sabbath. A typical evangelical household spent the day going to church, engaging in spiritual reading, and spending time with one's family. Disappointed but keeping to his principles, Pierson refused to travel on Sunday.

But virtue was rewarded. When taking the train back to Detroit, Pierson discovered in Ogden, Utah, that Mr. and Mrs. Müller had laid over on the Sabbath. Because they had refused to travel on Sunday, they boarded Pierson's train, and the three traveled together to Chicago. While in Chicago, Pierson heard Müller speak and invited him to visit the Fort Street Church the next time he was in the United States. During his next tour of America in January 1879, Müller visited the Piersons and spoke four times at his church.

Pierson and Müller felt a strong kinship for each other, despite Müller being thirty-two years older. Both were men of prayer and diligent students of the Bible. They spent precious hours over a ten-day period studying the sacred Scriptures together. But they soon discovered that on a key point their interpretations differed. Arthur Pierson had been a postmillennialist all his life. He had always believed that the Bible taught that Jesus would return after the millennium, after a thousand years of peace and prosperity brought about by human effort and benevolent Christian civilization. Postmillennialism had inspired many northern pastors during the Civil War and given them the conviction that the war against slavery was part of bringing in the kingdom of God. After the war, Pierson's postmillennial confidence had kept him engaged in social struggles for the millennium — attacks on the alcohol powers, efforts to convert and assist the urban poor, support for schools, denominational agencies, and other institutions of Christian civilization. His involvement in social justice issues grew out of his postmillennial convictions that working hand-in-hand with God's purposes on earth, humanity would effectively solve the problems of modern society.

But George Müller was a premillennialist. As Arthur Pierson argued for the virtues of postmillennialism, Müller silenced his arguments with the statement, "My beloved brother . . . not one of them is based upon the word of God." Then he took Pierson step by step through the biblical evidence for a premillennial interpretation of God's kingdom. Society would not progress gradually toward the kingdom of God on earth. Rather, with Satan in control, events on earth would worsen until Jesus returned in person. Only after Jesus' return would the millennium begin. Rather than improving naturally through human effort, the world would only be cleansed and purified through a supernatural act of God — the return of Jesus Christ.

The premillennial principles of Scripture interpretation taught by George Müller were the product of a group called the Plymouth Brethren. The Brethren's founder, the former Church of Ireland priest John Nelson Darby, believed that the church on earth was apostate or evil, and that all believers should separate from ecclesiastical systems to wait for Christ's imminent return. The Plymouth Brethren began spreading their views to the United States and Canada in the 1870s and 1880s through the efforts of "missionaries" like George Müller. Believing that God's Word was self-explanatory and needed no explanation — in its way also a Baconian approach to Scripture — the Plymouth Brethren instituted the practice of "Bible readings," a substitution for the sermon, in which the leader read a string of Bible verses and commented upon them. In their worship, the Plymouth Brethren celebrated the Lord's Supper as a lay-led, simple, democratic meal. They had their greatest impact in America on northern Presbyterian and Baptist leaders, who were searching for systems of Bible interpretation that would be both faithful to the Word and would answer some of the objections of higher criticism, as well as make sense of the apparent failure of Christian churches to transform society in the late nineteenth century.

The discussions between Müller and Pierson revealed some differences that could not be bridged despite Pierson's acceptance of the premillennial system of biblical interpretation. The Plymouth Brethren believed in the "ruin of the church," that the visible, denominational churches on earth were totally corrupt and should be renounced. But what made sense to Darby in the context of European established churches, biased against dissenters, did not make sense in the American context, in which people joined evangelical churches out of their own free will. Arthur Pierson was fully involved in denominational activities, and was working to build up Presbyterianism at local, state, and national levels. In the 1870s, he saw no contradiction between evangelical principles and the building of denominations that encompassed evangelical believers. When Arthur Pierson explained to George Müller the urgency he felt about his church activities, about the movement for free pews and simple worship, and the evangelization of the masses, Müller told him that God had given him light and would hold him responsible for its use. Pierson should follow his own conscience under God's will. If that meant remaining involved in denominational and social justice ministries, then it was Pierson's decision.

In addition to premillennial Bible interpretation, the thing that most attracted Pierson to George Müller's views was his practice of relying upon prayer rather than a stated salary. Pierson had years before come to the position of requesting that his salary be withheld so that pew rent would no longer be needed. Although the churches he served had refused his request, Pierson's spiritual views on money were the same as Müller's. The instinctual closeness the men felt for each other was such that they covenanted to pray for each other daily for the rest of their lives. They did so until George Müller died in 1898.

The premillennial interpretation of Scripture made sense to Arthur Pierson biblically, and also experientially. Not only did the system provide a key that unlocked many aspects of Scripture that had seemed hidden to him, but its view that the kingdom of God would only begin with the supernatural return of Jesus Christ resonated with

Pierson's increasing frustration about the state of the world. The Civil War had not ended evil on earth. No matter how hard he tried, no matter how anxious, exhausted, and discouraged he became from overwork, the kingdom of God seemed no nearer than it had been twenty years before. Labor strikes, urban unrest and anarchy, materialism, increased skepticism and infidelity, the growing strength of Romanism and the decline of biblical Protestantism — all these seemed to indicate a world getting worse and not better. Now in his forties, Pierson was facing also the limitations of his own energy. He was losing the optimism of his youth and taking on the realism of middle age. No matter how well he preached, not everyone was going to become a Christian. The vision of a Christian America was not being fulfilled.

At the same time, Pierson disagreed with the Plymouth Brethren on their pessimistic view of the church. God was continuing to work through faithful Christians in the churches. Refusing to work for God on earth would be to shirk one's duty. To throw up one's hands and wait passively for the return of the Lord was not biblical, even though the public stereotype of premillennialism emphasized its passivity and fatalism. In Jesus' parable of the household servants, the master told his servant to "occupy until I come." Believers were required to keep working for the kingdom, even if they were unable to bring it about on their own. The imminence of Jesus' coming meant there was little time to do what was needed on earth, so believers had better keep moving.

Arthur Pierson did not give up his Christian activism once he became a premillennialist. While believing in the Second Coming, he tried to follow Christ's implicit command in the parable to "occupy until I come." But his change in views toward biblical interpretation eventually opened a divide between himself and some of his oldest ministerial acquaintances. Not only was belief in the Second Coming at odds with the naturalistic, modernist theologies being adopted by educated clergy, but it went against the contemporary spirit of progress that characterized liberal theologies. As the United States grew richer and more powerful in the world, many middle-class Americans saw the "signs of the times" in the increased prosperity, comfort, and power of their generation. But from A. T. Pierson's vantage point in urban ministry, he saw the dark side of human nature. In 1879, becoming a premillennialist was a lonely position to hold, as it seemed to flow against the secularizing and scientific spirit of the age. Years later in

107

the biography he wrote of Müller, Pierson reflected upon the isolation that grew because of his adoption of premillennialism:

> It need not be said that to carry out conviction into action is a costly sacrifice. . . . But he who will fly as an eagle goes into the higher levels where cloudless day abides, and live in the sunshine of God, must consent to live a comparatively lonely life. No bird is so solitary as the eagle. . . . But the life that is lived unto God, however it forfeits human companionship, knows divine fellowship. . . . Whosoever will promptly follow whatever light God gives, without regard to human opinion, custom, tradition, or approbation, will learn the deep meaning of these words: "Then shall we know, if we follow on to know the Lord."

Although he suffered public misunderstandings and broken relationships because of his theological convictions, looking for the Lord's return became the inspirational focus of A. T. Pierson's mature years.

TRUTH AND ITS CONSEQUENCES

Arthur Pierson's chief goal in the latter half of his Detroit ministry — whether in its post or premillennial phase — was to preach to the working classes of the city. After sixteen marvelous months at the Whitney Opera House, the congregation completed a new Fort Street Church that was virtually identical to the edifice that had burned. Sixty thousand dollars of the insurance money plus thirty thousand dollars raised by the congregation paid for the building, which was re-dedicated on June 10, 1877. Even the church china, with a picture of the church on it, had been replaced. The 1877 *History and Directory of the Churches of Detroit* called the new building one of the "most elegantly furnished and perfectly ventilated churches in the country." All the meeting rooms were carpeted. Pastor Pierson was unhappy that the church had been rebuilt, rented pews and all. He had begged the church session not to build a glamorous building that would discourage the ordinary people from attending. Although they did not follow their minister's advice, the session compromised by permitting free pews during the evening services.

The months at the opera house had changed the congregation in some respects. They welcomed strangers to the church and conducted missionary work in Detroit that resulted in starting several new churches. Pierson continued preaching in the extemporaneous style he had assumed at the opera house, but gradually the church growth stopped. The church choir began singing elaborate anthems again, despite Pierson's opinion that "God never intended thirty or forty people to stand in a choir and do the singing for all the people." Having developed a deep aversion to ritualism or liturgy in church services, Pierson refused to go back to Presbyterian formality without a fight. The gap between Pierson's evangelistic sermons and the cultured music program continued to grow.

Dr. Pierson attributed the decline of conversions to the worldliness of the new Fort Street Church — its rented pews, fancy building, and formal style of worship. He believed that ostentatious wealth, no matter how friendly, hampered spiritual growth. He began preaching more and more sermons on the worldliness of the church, many of which appeared in the *Detroit Post and Tribune* or the "Fort St. Presbyterian Pulpit," a ten cent periodical begun to meet the demand for Pierson's sermons. He proclaimed against paid choirs and choral anthems. He harangued worldly trustees who were legally recognized as the church government because they paid pew rent. Pierson abhorred this practice because it "put the conduct of the kingdom of Jesus Christ in this world in the hands and under the control of men who, by their own confession, have not the spirit of God." Preaching on the early church, he showed that its apostolic power was based on its simple worship style, communal fellowship, free pews, no rigid priestly caste, and no paid choirs. In a sermon, "Limiting God by Unbelief," preached on December 28, 1879, Pierson asked that Fort Street Church conduct itself along the lines of George Müller's philosophy by depending upon prayer and voluntary contributions for its support. He asked the congregation to make the pews free and to set up a branch church so that the poor would have somewhere to worship. In sermon after sermon, Pierson asked for these changes, reminding the congregation of the spiritual power that had been theirs in the sixteen months at the opera house. He requested in January 1880 that his salary be paid from voluntary contributions rather than from pew rent, thus taking the chance that it would not be paid.

In March 1880, Pierson printed a lengthy open letter, "The Pillar of Fire, to the Brethren in the Minstry [sic] of Christ." In it, he testified to the worldliness with which he had begun his ministry and his subsequent transformation under Whittle and Bliss and the study of 1 John. He wrote of his need for a wider area of service, of the providential burning of the church after the prayer meeting, and of the spirit-filled months at the opera house. Pierson reaffirmed his love for the people of Fort Street Church and his refusal to leave them, despite a conviction that the pillar of cloud had been moving in another direction than the congregation. Pierson had thrown himself into the work at the new building, holding "after meetings" and "inquiry meetings" and taking no vacation in 1877 so that the revival might continue. Yet the conversions declined, and the poor people left Fort Street Church.

In "The Pillar of Fire," Pierson laid down the "Bible principles" of the church, stating that it existed to save souls. The more destitute the souls, the greater the responsibility of the church. The indifference of the church caused it to forfeit its "claim to God's blessing." He related how a brush with death by drowning in July 1877 forced him to realize that he would be better off alone following God than continuing to compromise his convictions. Pierson concluded "The Pillar of Fire" with the story of a New York rector who served food to the street people, thus drawing the hungry to Christ. He called for Fort Street Church to establish an Industrial Home for Boys to feed, clothe, train, and employ homeless boys. Not surprisingly, as his demands for change continued unabated, the church officers began objecting to his opinions. His frank views and haranguing of the congregation angered people and caused a stalemate.

At the same time he was urging his congregation to reopen itself to the poor, Arthur Pierson began stirring up Christians in Michigan. On February 19, 1880, he preached before the Christian Conference of the State of Michigan. In his sermon, "A Higher Type of Piety the Great Demand of Our Day," on Christian morality and the responsibilities of the church to society, he questioned whether it were ever proper for a disciple to accumulate money, arguing that the great need of the church was renewed spiritual life and consecration for God's work of evangelization. He wrote a paper for the Synod of Michigan on "Free Churches," presented in 1882. The paper called for free churches in accordance with the practices of the early church — with no stated salary for clergy, only voluntary donations. The synodal committee assigned to consider Pierson's paper reported favorably on the ideological grounding of his proposals, but rejected the idea of voluntary salaries as unrealistic. The committee urged that a new, scriptural system of church support be investigated, but that "it is scriptural and wise both because of the ignorance and selfishness of men, to suffer the existence of that which in principle we condemn." To both his congregation and the wider church in Michigan, Dr. Pierson insisted that the purpose of the church on earth was "to rescue unsaved souls." Everything in the church should be directed toward saving the lost, and building up the believers.

With his reputation as a leading preacher, A. T. Pierson kept receiving calls to other churches at large salaries. One church that would not take no for an answer was the Second Presbyterian Church of Indianapolis. Located in the capital of Indiana, the Second Presbyterian Church had been founded in 1838 by withdrawal from First Presbyterian over the Old School-New School controversy that split the denomination. Their first pastor had been the young Henry Ward Beecher, son of Lyman Beecher, brother of Harriet Beecher Stowe and Thomas Beecher, and by the 1860s one of the most famous preachers in America. Forty years later, the proud and socially prominent Second Presbyterian Church had not forgotten that the foremost preacher in America had been their first minister. They pursued A. T. Pierson according to a list of attributes they drew up for their ideal preacher, including personal appearance, pulpit manner, delivery, voice, intellectualism, spirituality, magnetism, and age. The nature of their list of qualifications was such that a local paper commented it was as if the church were judging a prize pig at a county fair. Second Presbyterian issued a unanimous call to their "prize winner" Pierson in June 1882.

In his lengthy letter of refusal, Dr. Pierson replied,

I am in no sense "in the market." God put me in Detroit and has kept me here by marked providential signs. I would go anywhere at any cost if I could clearly see His blessed hand leading, but I have made up my mind never to take one step of my own towards a change of field. . . . I have fought here a thirteen years' battle against worldliness in the church, against having worldly men in the Board of Trustees, worldly singers in the choir, and worldly

111

spirit in the church management. I have stood for a free church, for the pure Gospel and for a deep Christian experience. God has given the victory — at least in large measure — for fully three-fourths of the church are with me.

There is only one reason why I think it possible that I may leave Detroit and that is that I have substantially completed the work for which God sent me here. . . . If I go elsewhere it will be only that I may reach more souls. If Indianapolis can assure me freer access to the unsaved and an earnest prayerful church to cooperate with me in the effort to evangelize the neglected thousands, all I can say is "Here am I, Lord, send me."

Detecting a possible chink in Pierson's armor, the Second Presbyterian Church repeated its call. Finally persuading him to visit Indianapolis, the people greeted him with enthusiasm and assured him that they would comply with his wishes to become a great evangelistic center for the unchurched in the city. Despite being impressed with the spirit of the people, he pondered over the invitation for six weeks. Then he wrote another letter of refusal because the sanctuary of the church could barely seat its membership. It would be impossible to bring new people into the church if there was no room for them. Not even the Sunday School could fit into the sanctuary, if the church members were there. To impress upon Second Presbyterian the gravity of his viewpoint, Pierson sent them the sermons and letters that had offended people in Detroit — papers showing his desire to eliminate pew rent, abolish choirs, eliminate "worldly" trustees, and to run his whole ministry with evangelism as its top priority. Instead of being offended by the letters and sermons, the people at Second Presbyterian held a congregational meeting and appointed a committee to draw up plans for enlarging the church. The committee also planned to rent an opera house while the renovations were taking place.

After much prayer and agony of spirit at the idea of leaving dear friends and the family home, Pierson accepted the call from Second Presbyterian Church. Believing that the church's actions had signaled its agreement with his vision of the church, he and his family moved to Indianapolis in the fall of 1882. The large parsonage stood next door to the imposing edifice, with its grand steeple and arched doorways. There was plenty of room for Sarah and Arthur's seven children, and for Pierson's elderly mother. A salary of $5000 per year would allow the family to live in comfort.

From his first sermon, however, Dr. Pierson offended the people of Second Presbyterian. It was as if he had forgotten all the hard lessons learned in Binghamton about the necessity of getting to know his congregation before judging them. While his parishioners in Detroit had come to know and love him over the years, and accepted his reprimands for their weaknesses, the people in Indianapolis were still strangers. As Pierson waded in against certain popular amusements, and even chastised church officers he found playing cards, he quickly began making enemies. Not everyone wanted a strict, puritanical "John Knox" as their preacher.

Some of the people appreciated his plain speaking, his calling members to live a higher Christian life, and his biblical sermons. Pierson began weekly meetings for the promotion of "holiness," the deepening of people's piety so that they would increasingly rely on God and reduce the power of sin in their lives. The meetings grew so large that they turned into a city-wide prayer and Bible study that had to be held at the YMCA hall. He repeated his lecture series on "Christian Evidences" with great success in the community. In October 1882 he spoke at the Christian Conference of the State of Indiana. Over the winter, the church rented the Grand Opera House for Sunday evening services, and Pierson began reaching crowds of people who would not have attended the church itself. He addressed the 25th International Convention of the YMCA's in Milwaukee, Wisconsin, in May 1883. His ecumenical reputation also endeared him to other ministers in Indianapolis, and he made close friends, including Henry C. Mabie, future home secretary of the American Baptist Missionary Union.

But on April 20, 1883, after a night of agonized prayer, Arthur Pierson resigned his position a mere six months after moving to Indianapolis. What precipitated his sudden action was the failure of the Board of Elders to enlarge the church as promised in their job offer. Although Pierson had offended the old guard by attacking their personal habits, his revivalistic preaching and high standards were attracting new people to the church. He wanted to begin constructing the larger sanctuary on faith that the Lord would make it necessary. The Board of Elders, being successful businessmen rather than visionary preachers, wanted to wait until the enlargement was absolutely necessary before beginning an expansion. Impatient with the delay, Pierson resigned with no prospects for employment in sight. The resignation threatened to split the church. Pierson supporters from another congregation offered to open a "gospel tabernacle" according to Pierson's evangelistic vision of no pew rents, congregational singing of gospel hymns rather than a paid choir, expository rather than literary preaching, and outreach to the poor.

A. T. Pierson was torn as to what steps to take next. He had given up an income of $5000 plus housing a year, with no solid prospects in sight. He had no savings, as he had given away his money as he made it, trusting in the Lord to provide. Should he accept the offer to found a ministry that would compete with Second Presbyterian? Some of the leading people in Indianapolis were behind the idea of founding a gospel tabernacle with him at the helm. Such a possibility might mean leaving the Presbyterian Church, but it would be the fulfillment of a dream. Should he become an itinerant evangelist, living on faith? Should he seek another job in a large Presbyterian church? In depression and confusion, he retreated alone from Indianapolis to think. Letters poured in with competing visions of his future. Pierson's closest friend from Detroit advised him against starting an independent, non-denominational ministry because it would wear him out and be opposed by both the churches and the devil. He also cautioned that the wrong decision would increase Pierson's restlessness and make him even more enemies. Yet another letter-writer advised him against starting an itinerant evangelistic ministry because he did not have the kind of popular personality needed for free-lance evangelism. Pierson was too intellectual, and more suited for a teaching ministry than itinerant evangelism among the unchurched. Another friend from New York City offered him a temporary preaching position for July and August if he needed the work.

God seemed strangely silent in Pierson's confusion. He prayed for days without receiving guidance from the Lord. He was emotionally at a breaking point, unable to sleep, and feared a nervous breakdown. Then finally he heard God's voice one night after rising at midnight to pray. "God has answered," he confided on paper the next day. "God showed me that in all this movement I had been willful and stubborn, however conscientious. I had been heedless of consequences. I spent the night in prayer beseeching God to enable me to give up my own will, and He did. I then made an entire surrender of this darling project and covenanted with God not to take another step without his manifest leading." It became clear to Pierson that he had been following his own will, and not God's. If the tabernacle movement succeeded, it would suck away support from Second Presbyterian and would weaken the other churches in Indianapolis. For a man who had spent his career devoted to practical unity, it was wrong to divide the church of God.

After a month of reflection, Pierson decided against accepting the offer from the competing congregation, as it would have split Second Presbyterian. Feeling the relief of being in line with God's will, Pierson wrote to Indianapolis and declined the call to start the gospel tabernacle. He knew that saying no would turn many people against him, for his supporters had gone out on a limb for him. As Pierson's health nearly broke from the strain, he spent the summer coming to terms with his own pig-headedness and arrogance. He had caused his own problems in Indianapolis. He had not exercised the patience of waiting for his congregation to trust him. As he said in a letter to a church member a few years later, "I was full of a certain sort of enthusiasm and I fear it gave much heat to my nature. I was not calm and could not be content to gain the confidence and cooperation of the people by slow degrees. But I learned many a lesson that is daily blessed to me."

Pierson also belatedly realized that he had resigned unnecessarily from his church in Detroit. If he had only been more patient, and tried to lead people instead of driving them, he would have been more successful in his plans. He also began to suspect that perhaps his gifts lay more with helping to strengthen the spirituality of Christians, bringing them to a higher and deeper level of piety, rather than converting the unsaved. Perhaps the purpose for which God took him to Indianapolis was to teach him a lesson about himself — about his spiritual pride and impatience and willfulness. Although he had experienced some success in Indianapolis with saving souls, the main result of his Indianapolis ministry was in coming to terms with the sad state of his own.

5 From Ministry to Missions

During 1882 and 1883, at the age of 45, A. T. Pierson rebelled against inauthenticity in his life. His "mid-life crisis" consisted of an intense restlessness at being confined to a vision of ministry he no longer supported. He had tired of doing the bidding of church committees and prominent parishioners whose faith he found wanting. Part of his interest in evangelizing the urban masses stemmed from the fact that he enjoyed the challenge. He longed to make a difference — to God, to the unsaved of the cities, and to the world. His restlessness drove him to resign from a highly successful pulpit in Detroit where he was respected and where his family was happy, but that no longer provided him the challenges he needed. He moved to Indianapolis in hopes of greater contact with the poor, but he soon found that he had jumped from the frying pan into the fire. Unable to stand the status quo — a wealthy congregation with social-climbing members and worldly trustees — he precipitously resigned. More than anything in the world, regardless of the consequences, he yearned to be faithful to God's call.

During the mid to late 1880s, Pierson maintained an uneasy balancing act between the traditional pastor he had been for twenty-five years, and the visionary mission crusader he was becoming. Starting in 1885, his work on behalf of foreign missions mushroomed until it took precedence over his other interests. Always a prolific writer, in 1886 he produced what became a best-selling book that spread his reputation as a missions promoter throughout North America. By the end of the decade, his efforts to follow God's guidance had resulted in the expansion of his influence from a regional to a national sphere.

BETHANY CHURCH AND SUNDAY SCHOOL

In the spring of 1883, Pierson's sermons began reflecting an undercurrent of millennial urgency, the expectation of Jesus' return at any moment. Although eschatology, the study of the "end times," was not standard fare in Presbyterian churches, it is clear from published sermons that tension was building within Pierson over his desire to promote premillennial themes — the need for believers to separate from the world, the Bible as prophecy, and proofs of the supernatural. In one of his final sermons published in Indianapolis, Pierson pleaded for purity in the church: "Most earnestly therefore do we plead in God's name for practical separation between the godly and ungodly. . . . Mixture is always weakness." Clearly here was a man who had reached the end of his patience, and was no longer willing to compromise his principles for the sake of a secure pulpit.

Arthur Pierson's determination to follow God's leading despite its impact on his family and friends was due to his resolve to live according to the steadily strengthening theological principles that he had first embraced in 1879. Influenced by the British Plymouth Brethren, he was one of a pioneer group of American Christian leaders who adopted premillennialism in the 1870s and 1880s. In the summer of 1882, Pierson attended a Bible retreat on Mackinac Island, Michigan. Known as the Believers' Meeting for Bible Study, the annual event had begun in 1875 as an informal fellowship for pastors who had come to believe in the premillennial Second Coming of Jesus Christ. Some scholars assert that as the first group of its kind in America, it launched a widespread Bible study movement that was the predecessor to modern fundamentalism. While in transition between Detroit and Indianapolis, A. T. Pierson attended the Believers' Meeting, and with great emotion stood and announced that he had become a be-

liever in the imminent and literal Second Coming of Jesus Christ. Recalled Arno Gaebelein, editor of a millenarian magazine and founder
of missions to the Jews, "perhaps the most marked feature of the conference of 1882 was the glowing public announcement by Dr. Arthur T.
Pierson, who was greatly admired and beloved by the brethren, that,
having become thoroughly convinced of our Lord's personal and
premillennial return, he would maintain and proclaim it as the truth of
God. And so he did." With his reputation as a Bible expositor preced-
ing him, he was a "big catch," and soon became a leader in the group.

Undoubtedly Arthur Pierson's fellow participants in the Believers' Meeting sympathized with his plight the next year in Indianapolis. Many in the growing network of premillennialists were of
Pierson's age group and had experienced from a similar vantage point
the Businessman's Revival, the Civil War, and challenges of urban
ministry in the 1870s. As they studied the Bible together, prayed, and
shared their problems with each other, the Believers' Meeting became
a support group and anchor for its participants.

In May 1883, Pierson spoke at the 25th International Convention
of Young Men's Christian Associations held in Milwaukee, Wiscon-
sin, on "Qualifications of Heart and Life Needed in Work for Young
Men." Whether he became aware of Pierson's unstable situation at the
YMCA meeting, or through Presbyterian contacts, in June 1883 Pres-
byterian John Wanamaker persuaded him to visit Bethany Church in
Philadelphia. Founder of the famous department stores that pio-
neered modern methods of marketing and pricing, secretary of the
Christian Commission during the Civil War, and future Postmaster
General of the United States, John Wanamaker had become a devout
Christian at age 18. The next year, in 1858, he became secretary of the
Philadelphia branch of the YMCA, one of the first men in the United
States to hold a full-time paid secretaryship. In his capacity as YMCA
secretary, during the Businessman's Revival of that winter he opened
a mission Sunday School below South Street in the Schuylkill River
area. The south side of town was full of ash heaps, swampy landfills,
and brick piles patrolled by a gang, the "Schuylkill Rangers."
Throwing rotten eggs, bricks, and snowballs at the poor children, the
street gang broke up Wanamaker's first three attempts to hold a
Sunday School. As news of the persecution spread, Irish volunteer
firemen to whom Wanamaker had ministered during the winter re-

vivals spread the word that nobody should mess with him and the women teachers helping him. From twenty-seven children at the first meeting, the number of Sunday School scholars increased to over three hundred by July 8, 1858. By the following January, the school had advanced from meeting in a tent to a simple wood-frame chapel. Wanamaker named it the Bethany Sunday School, commemorating Mary and Martha's home where Jesus rested, and recalling Luke 24:50: "And he led them out as far as Bethany, and he lifted up his hands, and blessed them." In September 1865, twenty persons organized Bethany Presbyterian Church to accompany the flourishing Sunday School. By the end of the year, the Sunday School had nine hundred members and the church had one hundred seven.

A. T. Pierson had long known of Bethany Church's unique history, but he had heard that the Sunday School was like a circus, and he had never seen it in action. Wanamaker held all the power in the working-class church, as he was the only ordained elder. With his growing department store empire, he also had a reputation for getting his own way. But by June 1883, Pierson was in a more open frame of mind and eager for new challenges. After his visit to the "city of brotherly love," then the third largest metropolis in the United States, he was still not sure if he was the man for the pastorate. Pierson wrote to Wanamaker and laid out requirements for any church he might take — "My desire is to take a small church and mould it to my mind. To have a Sunday-school with Bible models, maps, etc., instead of a library with passing fiction; an undenominational sort of church, with a font for immersion of those who believe in that form of baptism." Pierson shared his premillennial views and his plan to have altar calls with inquiry meetings after the services. Wanamaker's response expressed full agreement between Pierson's views and everything Bethany stood for:

> I believe through and through in your plan for a broad Bible church. Strange, isn't it, that builded into Bethany, covered up until wanted, is a baptismal pool waiting for the man wise and brave enough to use it! For years we have taught our scholars to bring their Bibles to Sunday-school. We have no Sunday-school library. We discarded it ten years ago, disgusted with the silly fiction it was distributing, so that the way is clear for any new plan. Your "after

meeting" thought has been one of the plans in our hearts for some time. And I have always held the view of our Lord's Second Coming with you and take comfort in the blessed hope that His day may dawn at any moment.

After receiving a call to become Bethany's pastor, Pierson traveled to the Believers' Meeting for Bible Study, held that year for the first time at Niagara-on-the Lake, while he sought God's guidance. After a month of reflection, he wrote to Bethany accepting their offer. But he refused to take the offered salary of $5000 a year, which had matched his previous one. Feeling that it would put him too far above the lives of the humble parishioners, and wanting to be rid of pew rent once and for all, he accepted an annual salary of $3000 a year to be raised by free will offerings. In October 1883, the Pierson family moved into a modest brownstone in a borderline area on Spruce Street, several blocks north of the Sunday School and east of the Schuylkill River. With a salary reduction and modest living quarters, A. T. Pierson took a stand against the growing materialism and prosperity of the mainline churches in the 1880s. Presbyterianism, in particular, had become a church of the educated elite and well-to-do. Arthur Pierson associated "materialism" with "godlessness," and he viewed the world more and more through the lenses of class conflict. By accepting the job at Bethany, he was also making a de facto decision to focus on a teaching ministry. For the challenge there was not to get the masses into the church, but to teach and empower them in both their spiritual and physical lives. The membership at Bethany stood roughly at fifteen hundred for the church, and twenty-five hundred at the Sunday School, with space for holding five thousand people at once. Thus the church had many more members than either the Fort Street or Second Presbyterian Churches.

With the trust of Bethany's powerful founder, A. T. Pierson set about shaping it into his vision of the ideal church — a topic on which he had preached many times in Detroit. The ideal church would be "evangelical in faith," accepting the Bible as its rule; "evangelistic," obeying the Great Commission, Jesus' command to take the Good News to all people; "educative," reforming the individual in service to the home, community, and world. The ideal church would also refuse the "spirit of caste" and not favor the rich over the poor by charging pew rent. In his sermon "The Two-Fold Mission of the Church," based on Isaiah 62:6-7, he preached that the church exists in the world for two ends, "to show the beauty of holiness," and to be "the source of direct work for souls." In fulfilling its mission, the true church would encompass four ideals for Christian life: As a home, the church exercises the social virtues of hospitality, sociability, and democracy. As a workplace, the church is a center for evangelization and Christian work. The church is a school, training members in Christian knowledge. As a center for worship, the church exercises its faith in God through the Word, music, art, and prayer.

The practical result of Pierson's missional view of the church was that he shaped Bethany into what by the 1890s would be called an "institutional church" — a large city church whose doors remained open day and night, providing humanitarian services, including educational, recreational, and spiritual opportunities for the poor. The institutional church movement grew in the late 1800s among British and American urban clergy with social consciences, men who sought to make the church relevant to life in the city. Pierson preached against a disturbing trend of the Gilded Age: wealthy churches moving uptown or into suburbia to escape their responsibilities toward the urban poor. As wealthier members moved into new neighborhoods and took their churches with them, the city cores were left decimated by poverty and crime. Highly critical of this abdication of responsibility by the middle and upper classes, clergy involved in the emerging social gospel movement believed in transforming church structures to meet round-the-clock needs of the urban poor, rather than succumbing to the temptation to climb the social ladder and escape into suburbia. Pierson praised the work of early leaders in the "institutional church" movement, men like Stephen H. Tyng of Trinity Episcopal Church in lower Manhattan, and Norman McLeod of Farony Church in Glasgow, Scotland.

Notable "institutional church" activities begun by Pierson at Bethany included sewing schools, the Penny Savings Bank, and an aid society. He organized a children's temperance organization called the "White Ribbon Army," which quickly enrolled five hundred members. Other activities he sponsored included prayer meetings, ladies' aid societies, a men's literary society, youth groups, children's societies, and missionary societies. In 1884, he organized an Evangelist Band to engage in city outreach and to provide communal support for moral and temperate living. The Evangelist Band was close to Pierson's heart, but he was unable to manage it personally because of his heavy responsibilities as sole pastor to several thousand people. Neither did the church have the money to hire an assistant pastor. Praying to God for relief, Pierson was delighted when in 1885 a young businessman from Indianapolis, Thomas C. Horton, agreed to become assistant pastor. Pierson had led Horton into Christian service during his brief ministry at Second Presbyterian Church. Horton agreed to supervise the Evangelist Band, and he was hired and ordained at Bethany Church. The younger man also believed in the Second Coming, and as assistant pastor was like an apprentice to Pierson in city mission work. The Evangelist Band organized a mission in the southwestern part of the city. Erecting a tent and building furniture themselves, the young men of Bethany held a Sunday School and religious services that had attracted 538 converts within three months. Their activity culminated in the founding of the John Chambers Memorial Church, named after the Presbyterian minister who had brought John Wanamaker to Christ in the late 1850s.

When he arrived in Philadelphia, A. T. Pierson found Bethany occupying a ten-year-old complex of buildings on the corner of 22nd and Bainbridge streets, not far below South Street where Wanamaker had begun the Sunday School. The presence of the church had stabilized the area, as a working-class neighborhood of modest houses replaced the slums. The members had built the church at great personal sacrifice, with children even collecting bones and rags to earn money for its construction. But a heavy debt weighed it down, thereby presenting Pierson with his first big challenge. Another difference he quickly discovered between Bethany and the wealthier churches he had served in the Midwest was that the working people of Bethany had little free time to attend meetings or provide lay leadership.

Pierson immediately democratized Bethany's autocratic structure by founding a church council to manage the affairs of the church. With his high view of the Holy Spirit, he believed that all Christians had spiritual gifts to exercise. As he preached sermons to prepare the people of Bethany for their expanded leadership roles, he emphasized that every disciple of Christ was ordained by God for individual work, fed by one's spiritual gifts. In a threefold model of the Christian life that he used frequently, Pierson emphasized first salvation for the believer, then sanctification of the believer, and finally service by the believer. To direct the service of the believers, he expanded the Deacons' Board from one to twelve members, who were responsible for home visitation to the sick and outreach to the needy. Pierson surveyed his congregation and made an incredible two thousand pastoral calls in his first year, but thereafter he relied on the expanded Deacons' Board to help meet the physical and emotional needs of church members.

The histories of Bethany covering Pierson's years there praise him as one of the greatest Bible teachers of the century. One of the first steps he took toward getting the lay people more involved in the church was to organize a class for Sunday School teachers that prepared them for the Sunday lessons. The class became so popular that it regularly drew over a thousand participants. As in Detroit, the demand for Pierson's teacher preparation program grew so high that it was moved to the YMCA auditorium, and expanded to include all the Sunday School teachers in the city. John Wanamaker brought his skills as salesman and marketer into the Sunday School; part of its popularity was because of his use of special invitations, certificates, and Bible cards that made each scholar feel special. John Wanamaker had in 1871 purchased the *Sunday School Times*, the main national publication for Sunday School teachers, and he published *The Scholar's Quarterly* for students. With Pierson supplying the Bible training, and Wanamaker supporting the infrastructure, they together promoted a dynamic educational ministry as top priority at Bethany.

In 1881, Wanamaker founded a night college so that unskilled day-laborers, many of them immigrants, could study and improve themselves in hopes of getting better jobs. When Pierson came two years later, he added a religious studies department to the secular branch, and taught the religion courses himself. The educational work at Bethany College, later called Wanamaker Institute, remained one of Pierson's major priorities at Bethany. An important component of an institutional church, the "college" helped working people with no other access to educational resources. In 1884, Bethany College offered courses in German, Bookkeeping, Mechanical Drawing, Dressmaking, Elocution, and Church History. Tuition for members of Bethany Church was only twenty-five cents a term.

John Wanamaker was open to innovation in worship and had pioneered new worship features even before Pierson's arrival, most notably supplying printed programs for worship that included the hymns. Pierson was able to put his long-frustrated ideas on worship into practice at Bethany. Although Bethany was a Presbyterian church, it took on the innovative worship style of the nondenominational gospel tabernacle movement. Within a few months, he had persuaded the church to abolish its choir in favor of congregational singing. The change was not hard to make because the Bethany congregation already liked the new gospel hymns. The revivalist team of Moody and Sankey had preached and sung their gospel songs at Bethany during the highly successful Philadelphia revival of 1875-76. Wanamaker had been a big supporter of the Moody-Sankey revival and had even donated a railroad car for its use. Bethany's Sunday School song-leader in the 1880s was John R. Sweney, composer of such popular favorites as "Beulah Land," "Tell Me the Story of Jesus," and "Will There Be Any Stars in My Crown?" With its orchestra, and singing led by Professor Sweney, the music at Bethany Church was one of its most crowd-pleasing features. Pierson continued his tradition of writing hymns that he had begun when Whittle and Bliss had visited him in 1874. Some of them appeared in the famous set of hymnals published by Bliss and Sankey, and then by Ira Sankey alone after Bliss's tragic death in a train wreck. *Gospel Hymns* was the most successful hymnal series in Victorian America. In 1894, Pierson and his friend A. J. Gordon edited and published *The Coronation Hymnal*, which contained many of the gospel hymns Pierson wrote while at Bethany Church.

One of A. T. Pierson's greatest contributions to life at Bethany Church was paying off the crushing church debt. He set the church on a firm financial basis that led to even greater involvement in social programs under its succeeding pastor, J. Wilbur Chapman. At its twentieth anniversary celebration, Pierson announced a plan of systematic giving that included even the poorest members. After four years of ten cents a week donated by members, plus the help of a few wealthier ones, the church lifted a debt of $45,000. The congregation celebrated with a mock funeral and burned the mortgage. By April 1889, church membership stood at 1495 and the Sabbath school at 2560, and its debts were paid. Boasting a healthy range of activities and social services, with a vibrant worship life, Bethany Church was the apex of Pierson's pastoral ministry. Church members knew him as "Brother Pierson," a title that reflected his egalitarian, lay-oriented ideals.

SOCIAL CHRISTIANITY

From the mid-1880s to the end of the decade, A. T. Pierson thrived at the nerve center of overlapping networks of Christian activists who were shaping major trends in American Protestantism. Perhaps most remarkable was his endless energy for writing, speaking, preaching, traveling, and praying — in an era when he wrote everything in long-hand, traveled by train or horse-drawn carriage, and preached without microphones. What is fascinating about the scope of Pierson's activities is that he embodied in one person what subsequent generations have seen as separate, competing interests. In his concern for the urban poor, he participated in predecessor organizations of the "social gospel," the movement to change society in ways that promoted economic and social justice for the poor. Yet in his commitment to the Bible as the divine rule for life and human history, he shaped a theological movement that anticipated twentieth-century fundamentalism.

The 1880s were the height of an ecumenical and evangelical consensus about the role of the church in the world. People who would eventually be remembered as either "liberals" or "conservatives" were still working together in the 1880s. Shared practical activism and inter-denominational cooperation from the ground up dominated the thinking of progressive clergy of varied theological views and different denominational traditions. The public split between "social" and "individual" methods of Christian work lay in the future. Arthur Pierson's generation, forged in the crucible of civil war, still clung to hopes that American Protestantism could embody a broad consensus.

Since his Detroit pastorate, Arthur Pierson had been active in a network of ecumenical associations for Christian unity, a practice he continued at Bethany. Behind the practical interest in church cooperation was a desire to reach the poor for Christ. Growing from the work of the Christian Commission during the Civil War, the American Christian Commission was a hands-on organization that gathered church workers by holding frequent local, state, and national conventions. These conferences brought together ordinary church members with experts in urban missions. The "Christian Conventions" began identifying practical ways to reach the urban poor through district visitation, outdoor preaching, work among the homeless, and humanitarian work done through the churches. During the 1860s and 1870s, along with the YMCA, the Christian Commission was facilitating the most practical and effective work among the urban lower classes of any Christian organization in America. After the Detroit revivals, Pierson became a sought-after speaker in various Christian conferences and YMCA gatherings. For instance, he spoke at the Michigan State Christian Conference in 1880.

Continuous with his interest in Christian conventions, it was natural, therefore, that Pierson was a founding member of the Convention of Christian Workers in Chicago in 1886. The Convention of Christian Workers became an annual event, as workers in city missions met to pursue a practical agenda of helping local churches with their urban outreach programs. One of its methods was to set up field education sites for theology students, thereby connecting the students with active Christian workers in the city. It advised churches on organizing outreach in poor and unevangelized neighborhoods, including mobilizing women workers for city mission work. It became a source of information and clearinghouse for city mission societies, as well as founding the Boys' Club movement. The Convention of Christian Workers attracted both ordinary people and the leading "social Christians" of the day. By the end of the century, it had over 2500 members.

While the Convention of Christian Workers was a practical network of city missionaries and de facto social workers, the intellectual center of social Christianity in the 1880s was the Evangelical Alliance, in which A. T. Pierson had been active since 1873. Founded to unify Protestants around a common evangelical theology and Christian action, the Alliance functioned primarily as a fellowship group in the 1870s. But in 1886, it appointed the Reverend Josiah Strong to the new post of general secretary. Strong's widely acclaimed book of 1885, *Our Country*, analyzed American society to identify urgent problems of industrialization and urbanization. The immensely popular book told comfortable Americans what they did not want to hear: rural Protestant values were collapsing under the weight of new social realities and massive immigration. The price of developing capitalism was extremes of wealth and poverty that left many Americans underfed, unchurched, and predisposed to violent crime. Pierson read and took voluminous notes on Strong's *Our Country*, and his sermons for a time reflected the kinds of analysis and illustrations used in the book.

In 1886, Pierson was one of 150 church leaders who gathered in New York with ambitious new plans for the Evangelical Alliance. The conference compared the situation in American cities to that of Europe, with widespread crime, unemployment, and class division. The 1886 gathering appointed Strong as general secretary and arranged for a national conference to be held the next year to analyze the problems besetting urban America. Under Strong's leadership, the Evangelical Alliance convened three national conferences to discuss the relationship between Christianity and social problems. The first two, in 1887 and 1889, analyzed the problems in American civilization. The 1893 conference discussed possible solutions and steps to be taken by churches combating the social crises. The December 1887 conference in the nation's capital lasted three days with twelve to fifteen hundred delegates. Entitled "National Perils and Opportunities," it included speeches on such topics as immigration, the misuse of wealth, saloons and alcoholism, labor and capital, and the threat to democracy posed by allegiance to the pope. The large attendance at the meeting was probably spurred by the shocking Haymarket Riots in Chicago in May 1886. In the most violent conflicts between labor and capital since the railroad strike of 1877, as labor unions agitated for an eight-hour day, someone threw a dynamite bomb that killed seven policemen and injured sixty other people.

As city mission worker and head of a thriving urban church, Arthur Pierson delivered a trenchant analysis of classism in the church in an address, "Estrangement of the Masses from the Church." Despite his stated opposition to Marxism, Pierson argued that the lower classes were hostile to mainstream Protestantism because it had become associated with the upper classes. Because the upper and lower classes were living in separate neighborhoods, there was no longer a sense of community between them. The poor were marginalized in dangerous occupations and grew up without even a common education. "The fact is that Society has long stood by, while Labor, blinded and bound, has gone the rounds grinding in the mill of capital." If the poor continue to be neglected by the churches, Pierson warned, they will eventually be avenged by society, for all classes of people together form the society: "We cannot afford to neglect the condition of the common people, for the condition of the common people is the condition of the commonwealth."

In his speech, Pierson indicted the church for perpetuating class distinctions by linking itself with aristocracy. Churches move out of neighborhoods when they decline; expensive buildings perpetuate a "caste spirit"; church organization is based on rule by the rich rather than democracy; and the system of pew rental alienates the masses. Even charity is administered through a "kid glove" by churches that found schools for the poor called "ragged schools" and cheap "mission chapels for the poor." These distancing mechanisms were not really true charity, for the true Christian should live in the midst of the poor in solidarity with their poverty — not merely build chapels for them.

In 1887, Pierson could speak courageously in the plain language of class conflict because he himself had made the wrenching transition to downward mobility by moving from the fancy manse in Indianapolis to the simple townhouse in Philadelphia. His salary remained frozen at the level at which he had begun his ministry in Detroit. His indictment of materialism and wealth in the churches was an indictment of his earlier compromises with "worldly" trustees, pew rents, fancy buildings, formal worship, and the like. Although Pierson was a generation older than those who eventually founded "settlement houses," cooperative living arrangements among the poor, the whole tenor of his speech pointed in that direction. Even though the term "institutional church" was not coined until the 1890s, Pierson's description of his experiences at Bethany made it clear that social Christianity was inseparable from spiritual work:

> The Providence of God has thrown me into contact, in the last few years, with a church for the people, that I went to because it was a church for the people. From the time the fires are lighted on the first of October, till they go out on the first of May, that building is open from Monday night to Saturday night, for everything which, in the way of secular instruction, entertainment, amusement and uplifting, can draw the people. We have 1,800 church members, and from four to five thousand people pass in and out from Sunday to Sunday.

THE PHILADELPHIA PRESBYTERY

In addition to being involved in the network of socially concerned Christians in the Evangelical Alliance, A. T. Pierson also circulated in Presbyterian circles during the 1880s. Upon moving to Philadelphia as senior pastor of a large church, he was immediately voted into leadership positions by his fellow clergy. Less than a year after arriving in Philadelphia, Pierson was elected moderator of the Presbytery of Philadelphia for two six-month terms. He also became chairman of the Foreign Missions Committee, a post he retained until 1889. In that capacity, he wrote reports for the synod and maintained an active round of speaking engagements in Presbyterian settings. In January 1884, the famous professor of theology who was himself a former missionary to India, A. A. Hodge, invited him to visit nearby Princeton Theological Seminary, the flagship theological training institution for Presbyterian ministers. With his extensive ministerial experience and powerful gifts of reasoning, Pierson discovered an ability to inspire students. With his analytical mind and emotion-packed delivery, he was in many respects the thinking man's evangelist. He spoke at Princeton College, a Presbyterian school, in 1886 on the Annual Day of Prayer for Colleges. One of the teenagers who answered his altar call and attended the after meeting for inquirers was a freshman football player from a small town in Pennsylvania named Robert Speer. Dating his decision to give his life to Christian service that day, Speer grew up to become one of the most important American church leaders of the early twentieth century — head of the Presbyterian Board of Foreign Missions. Pierson's address on missions at nearby New Brunswick Seminary, the theological school of the Reformed Church, led student Samuel Zwemer to become a missionary who served in Arabia and Egypt for thirty-eight years before becoming professor at Princeton Seminary.

Part of Pierson's ability to lead young men like T. C. Horton, Robert Speer, and Samuel Zwemer into Christian work may be attributed to his own guilty feelings at not becoming a missionary himself. In an article he published in 1882 entitled "The Progress of Missions," he confessed how in seminary he and his friends had talked themselves out of becoming foreign missionaries by such arguments as "let the rude, rough uncultured men bear the Gospel to the brutal pagans; we who have refinement, accomplishment, urbane culture, will remain at home," for "the home field offers the amplest yield in honors, salaries, and temporal rewards." But over the years, Pierson realized that his early arguments against becoming a foreign missionary were worldly and selfish; he set out to redeem his youthful refusal to consider missionary service. Pierson's remorse that he had wasted his time in "literary pursuits" among the upper classes, and had neglected evangelism at home and abroad, led him to re-examine the Presbyterian requirements for the ministry. Requiring Greek and Hebrew for ordination may have guaranteed the intellectual superiority of Presbyterian clergy, but it hampered church growth because it restricted its own leadership to the cultured few. Instead of ordaining men because of their spiritual qualifications, the Presbyterian Church was turning out educated men with upper-class pretensions. He ought to know, for he had been one himself.

In 1885, Pierson presented a paper to the Presbytery of Philadelphia on "The Problem of Missions and Its Solution," which put forward concrete suggestions based on "25 years of study and prayer." The subject of the paper was how to deal with the lack of candidates for missionary service. The official mission boards of the church never seemed to have enough men to be appointed to foreign fields. One suggestion he put forward was that the presbytery call for an ecumenical missions council to map out the world, and assign denominations areas of responsibility. Pierson also made the explosive suggestion that less educated men be sent as missionaries rather than relying on seminary-trained clergy. Under the current system requiring a college degree, Greek and Hebrew, and seminary courses, the preparation time for Presbyterian missionaries was five to ten years. Perhaps the entire educational system for clergy was a more "burdensome yoke than a harness for efficient work." Calling himself a "conservative Presbyterian," Pierson listed famous missionaries who agreed with him, including Elias Riggs of Constantinople, Henry Jessup of Syria, John Nevius of China, and John Scudder of India. He cited with approval the method pioneered by John Nevius of sending out, under the supervision of the missionary, relatively uneducated native converts as lay evangelists.

Another radical proposal contained in Pierson's paper was that the presbytery ordain a number of uneducated people as missionaries, who under Pierson's leadership would go in a missionary colony to a new mission field, sponsored by Bethany Church. Bethany had already raised a thousand dollars toward the colony, which would be modeled on the settlements of former slaves in Liberia. Pierson may also have had in mind the intentional communities that had founded Olivet, Oberlin, and other "manual labor" abolitionist colleges in the Midwest. He knew that American mission colonies, including skilled tradesmen and teachers, had proven successful in planting Christianity in Hawaii and other parts of the South Pacific earlier in the century. The idea of missionary colonies abroad was continuous with Pierson's idea of living among the poor in America's cities. Bethany's colonists would be skilled in a wide variety of trades so that they could provide industrial training as well as a model for the Christian home. Rather than wasting time studying Greek, Hebrew, and advanced subjects, it would be more effective if the colonists could study the languages of the people to whom they were called. But Pierson believed they needed to be ordained by the presbytery despite not meeting the standard qualifications for ordination.

The Presbytery of Philadelphia was one of the oldest and most conservative presbyteries in the United States. It was due to Pierson's stature that it even considered his paper at all, for his central plea to lower ordination requirements had been the cause of more than one church split in the early nineteenth century. Any talk of lowering standards was practically heretical in the Presbyterian context. After several sessions discussing it, the presbytery requested that the paper be printed and submitted to a committee for consideration. The committee report read on February 1, 1886, was sympathetic to the spirit of the paper, recognizing Pierson's personal calling to increased zeal in the area of foreign missions. The report recommended that the "revolutionary" proposal of sending spirit-filled but uneducated workers should be considered by the full Presbyterian Church. It appointed another committee to pursue the matter with the secretaries of the Foreign Mission Board.

The presbytery took no action on Pierson's proposal for a locally supported Christian colony, or for an ecumenical missionary council. But his plan to evangelize the world via Christian colonies received favorable press in *The Missionary Review of the World*, a new periodical edited by the Reverend Royal G. Wilder, a former Presbyterian missionary with years of service in India. *The Missionary Review* printed the report of the presbytery next to a letter by a prominent English mission supporter that favored cooperative efforts to evangelize the world. The journal applauded the presbytery's decision to appeal to the church to change ordination standards for missionaries, but it questioned whether it would not be better to send more laymen overseas than to lower the standards for ordination.

The suggestions that Pierson made to the presbytery seemed wildly radical in 1885. In reality, they represented the cutting edge of what was about to explode beyond recognition, namely, the American missionary movement. What seems laughable in retrospect is that A. T. Pierson bothered to present his ideas before a presbytery, the local unit of his denomination. It was the last report he would ever bother to send through a Presbyterian committee, for his ideas had outgrown the capacity of a single denomination. Within a decade, all of the visionary things for which he petitioned in 1885 had come true, though not in the form he expected. In 1889, Secretary F. F. Ellinwood of the Presbyterian Foreign Mission Board refused a suggestion that ordination standards be lowered for Presbyterian missionaries. Yet even as Pierson and Bethany Church were chafing at the educational bottleneck that kept unschooled missionaries from reaching the mission field, mission-minded pastors in both Britain and North America were launching training programs in their own churches to equip thousands of laity as both home and foreign missionaries — informal programs that developed into nondenominational Bible and missionary training schools. Within a few years, the mission societies of American and British Protestantism would hold the first interdenominational ecumenical missionary conference in world history — the beginning of the modern ecumenical movement. By the early 1890s, a massive student movement would surge forward, filling all the available assignments under the denominational missionary societies, and spilling over into the founding of independent, nondenominational "faith missions" to reach the world's unevangelized millions. The idea of a "Bethany" style, lay-staffed mission supported by a local church would not seem absurd at all.

THE NIAGARA NETWORK

Besides his activism in circles for city missions, social Christianity, and Presbyterian affairs, A. T. Pierson also belonged to what at first was almost an "underground" network of premillennialists. As premillennialism was a controversial doctrine in the 1880s, many of its advocates avoided preaching it from the pulpit so as not to alienate their church members over a "nonessential" doctrine on which most Christians did not agree. In a sermon preached in 1883 on the essentials of the Christian faith, Pierson defended the unity of evangelical doctrine around a few basic principles: the incarnation of God in Christ, justification by faith in him, the resurrection of the dead, and so forth. "But since it is not essential that in all things we should see alike, since unanimity does not demand uniformity, the Spirit allows divergence on matters not rudimental." The preacher, Pierson believed, should focus on the shared beliefs of evangelical believers, and avoid the debatable nonessentials. But likewise he should uphold at all costs the interrelated core beliefs of the Christian faith, and allow no compromises with them.

Because premillennialism was not a doctrine upon which evangelical believers agreed in the 1880s, Pierson, like other premillennialists in established denominations, kept his views on the Second Coming out of his preaching and writing aimed for a broad audience. He therefore especially looked forward to the annual Believers' Meetings for Bible Study. They were where Pierson could be fed spiritually, relax, and be with like-minded friends, and he attended them whenever his schedule permitted. Historian Ernest Sandeen remarks that premillennialism, also called millenarianism, became "a spiritual home, a community" for its "true initiates." Practicing the "Bible reading" method of exposition, the group shared theological views on the pervasive sinfulness of humanity, the Second Coming, salvation by faith in Christ, the infallibility of the Bible, the promotion of holiness piety, and a dislike of ritualism. From 1883 the group was known as the Niagara Conference. Avid Bible scholars, the group consisted mostly of Presbyterians and Baptists whose Calvinistic theological backgrounds predisposed them to look for a system of biblical interpretation that would make sense of all of Scripture. Scholars of American fundamentalism have attributed its rise and organizational beginnings to the Niagara conferences, which were held for a week or two every summer until 1897.

It is possible that William Erdman, his old friend and classmate from both Hamilton College and Union Seminary, first invited Arthur Pierson to the Believers' Bible Study. Both William Erdman and his brother Albert were regular members. Other premillennial stalwarts whom Pierson got to know at Niagara included James H. Brookes, a Presbyterian pastor in St. Louis and organizer of the group. Henry M. Parsons, Presbyterian pastor in Toronto, attended nearly all the conferences and became a good friend. Nathaniel West was an English Presbyterian who, like Pierson, served several churches in the Midwest. Former Presbyterian missionary William G. Moorehead was professor of New Testament and then president of United Presbyterian Seminary in Xenia, Ohio. The network of men with whom Pierson had the most in common were born in the mid-1830s and shared his support for the YMCA, inductive Bible study, urban ministry, ecumenical evangelicalism, foreign missions, and premillennialism. Men in the Niagara network became some of his closest confidants in the 1880s. The man who by the late 1880s had become like a brother to him was an occasional participant — A. J. Gordon, pastor of the Clarendon Baptist Church in Boston.

The participants in the Niagara meetings decided to hold several conferences on biblical prophecy at which they could hash out the finer points of their emerging theological system. There was a lot of disagreement about how to interpret some of the difficult passages of Scripture. The first prophetic conference was in 1878, before Pierson had become a premillennialist. But he was a key speaker at the second American Prophetic Conference in Chicago in 1886, and the third one in Allegheny, Pennsylvania, in 1895. He also spoke at the International Prophetic Conference in Boston in 1901. In cooperation with a sympathetic committee of Philadelphia clergymen, Pierson organized his own Niagara-type conference at Chambers Church, the mission church planted by Bethany's Evangelist Band. Held on November 15-18, 1887, it was called the Bible Inspiration Conference, one of the most significant conferences of its type in the late 1800s. At the 1887 and 1895 meetings, Pierson gave addresses on the Bible and the Second Coming of Jesus Christ. He also edited the proceedings of the 1887 conference.

A. T. Pierson was not the gatekeeper of the movement. That role was played by James Brookes, who tended toward a simplistic biblical literalism and was willing to disfellowship others over their different interpretations of the Second Coming. Because of his travel schedule, neither was "Brother Pierson" able to attend every year. But his influence was wide because of his deep knowledge of the Bible, grounded as it was in a minimum of an hour daily study before breakfast. According to Pierson's son Delavan, his father had a powerful prayer life, and kept a record of all his prayer requests correlated with relevant Bible verses, including God's answer to each one. A regular "prayer warrior," Arthur Pierson was widely admired both for his knowledge and his devotion. He often led textual studies and reflections at the Niagara meetings. As in his university and seminary visits, he influenced young men who came to learn from the teachers at the Niagara conferences. His address at the 1886 American Prophetic Conference caused the young Presbyterian Henry W. Frost, a graduate of Princeton College, to devote his life to foreign missions. A few years later, Frost became the founding North American director of the China Inland Mission, the most important Anglo-American faith mission of the late nineteenth century.

The most important presentation Pierson gave at a Niagara-related meeting was his paper at the second American Prophetic Conference of 1886, entitled "Our Lord's Second Coming a Motive to World-Wide Evangelization," later published in pamphlet form by John Wanamaker. This paper laid the groundwork for the vital connection between premillennial biblical exegesis and the cause of foreign missions. It also showed how radically Pierson's views were changing from the heady triumphalism of his youthful confidence in Christian civilization. He delivered the "brilliant and scholarly" address on the first day of the Chicago conference; he was "interrupted often by approving applause." Recalled Dr. Moorehead, "Some of us will never forget his addresses on 'The Lord's Second Coming a Motive to World-Wide Evangelization' and 'The Comings of Our Lord as the Doctrinal and Practical Centre of the Bible.' He spoke without notes and used the blackboard to illustrate the chief points. He pictured to the eye the three great dispensations: The Altar of Sacrifice to represent the Mosaic Age, The Lord's Table to indicate the Christian or Gospel Age, and the Throne and Crown to represent the Millennial Reign." The powerful address, amply illustrated and outlined on a blackboard, as were Pierson's weekly Bible lessons to

Sunday School teachers, was one of the first systematic presentations of premillennial motivations for mission.

Pierson outlined how "the blessed hope of our Lord's Coming, when unhampered and unhindered in its normal action, makes every true believer fruitful in the seed of propagation, fits and prompts him to sow the seed, and himself become the seed, of the kingdom." "The imminence of our Lord's coming quickens activity." Since believers did not know when Jesus would come, yet were certain he would, they must work hard to prepare for his return by doing his work. Pierson believed that losing sight of Jesus' Second Coming would lead to indolence and to controversy over minor issues.

The Lord's coming excited missionary zeal, Pierson believed, because it meant that workers would soon be rewarded for their service and stewardship. The Christian hope helped believers separate themselves from worldliness, for they knew they had no time to accumulate possessions. Belief in the Second Coming, as well as foreign missions, improved human character by making only the eternal of first importance.

"Our Lord's coming inspires missionary labor with a hope that is not disappointed." Waiting for Christ's return inspired evangelism because it did not depend on the conversion of the world to succeed. Pierson believed that the Great Commission commanded Jesus' followers to proclaim the gospel to the world, not to convert everyone or to bring in Christian civilization. Rather, the purpose of missions was to gather out Christians from all the nations, not to christianize the nations themselves. Hope of the Lord's Second Coming was realistic because it matched the facts of evangelism: not all people would accept Christianity. Here Pierson drew upon his own discouraging personal experiences after years in urban ministry: If one hoped that the world would get better and better through the spread of the gospel and that the world would become Christian, he or she would be disappointed. Although Christians were a shrinking minority in a growing world population, premillennialism nevertheless inspired activity because regardless of the failures of Christian missions, they were being obedient to God's command. A crucial part of Pierson's argument was that Jesus would return once the world had been evangelized, though not necessarily converted.

The new premillennial movement was being criticized by postmillennial theologians who argued that it "cut the nerve" of missions by assuming a fatalistic stance toward world events. As a former postmillennialist who had previously believed in the earthly march of progress toward God's kingdom, Pierson argued vigorously that looking expectantly for Jesus' coming encouraged missions because it emphasized the duty of Christians over the results: "Thus, while premillennialism is charged with cutting the nerves and sinew of Foreign Missions, it in fact supplies their perpetual incentive and inspiration in teaching us that duty is ours; results God's."

Pierson's paper reflected apparently contradictory optimism and pessimism about the possibility of world evangelization. At one level, missions were doomed to failure because empirical facts of life in the late nineteenth century indicated that the world was not being, and could not be, converted to Christianity. At another level, this apparent failure was actually a realistic position consistent with the biblical witness. Strenuous efforts to evangelize the world were part of Christian duty and hope for Jesus' return, and they would be rewarded in the end. A key text in the argument was Matthew 24:14, "And this gospel of the kingdom shall be preached in all the world for a witness unto all nations; and then shall the end come."

Pierson spent many pages in the printed version of the Chicago paper proving the realism of the premillennial position about the world and the sentimentality of beliefs in eternal human progress. The Bible showed that human beings were incapable of upholding God's covenant, and the latter times would be marked by spiritual decline and the parallel development of wheat and tares amid a gigantic, godless civilization. "However faithfully we sow the seed of the kingdom, Satan's agents outstrip us in sowing tares. . . . Every cast of the gospel net encloses but a few fish out of the world-sea, and even these include both the evil and the good, and so it will be until the end." Pierson derided the notion that the millennium was occurring through evolution and human progress. Protestant church members comprised only a fraction of the world's population, and population increase was outstripping the number of conversions. Even the Protestants are "divided into five hundred sects, and this number of their strength includes also all the thieves, ex-convicts, the debased, besotted, the speckled and streaked in Christendom." The church, Pierson argued, was leavened by worldly pleasure, materialism, and skepticism, and had lost spiritual power.

The evils of American civilization itself disproved the idea of a progressive millennium:

> Gigantic as it [American civilization] is in invention, discovery, enterprise, achievement, it is gigantically worldly . . . monstrously God-denying and God-defying. This "Christian civilization" has indeed produced giants in these days . . . but they often use their intellect, knowledge and fame, only to break down . . . all Christian faith. Philosophy now blooms into a refined and poetic pantheism, or a gross, blank materialism, or a subtle rationalism, or an absurd agnosticism. Science constructs its systems of evolution and leaves out a personal God, spontaneous generation becomes the only Creator, natural law the only determining power, and natural selection the only Providence. . . . Government is rendered helpless by the destructive forces which science has put into the hands of the ignorant and lawless. The ballot and the bullet alike become weak in competition with dynamite, and war becomes impossible until men are ready for mutual extermination. . . . If the reign of law be, as many think, the great hindrance which prevents the development of the man of sin, we are on the verge of the final catastrophe; for the reign of lawlessness seems now at hand!

Pierson's pessimistic view of American society concluded that there would be no age of peace launched by the triumphs of modern technology. The United States would not be "the little child" that "leads" the rest of the nations into the peaceable kingdom.

Before the age of peace foretold in Revelation could occur, Christ must first return to eliminate evil. The purpose of missions, according to Pierson's premillennial thought, was not to convert the world, but evangelize it and gather the believers out of all nations in obedience to Scripture so that Christ would return. Believers must work hard since there was work to do. Discouragement only occurs when a worker believes that western civilization is somehow Christian and therefore despairs when confronted by the power of evil in the modern world.

> But he who is working upon a biblical basis can bear to see the rose-colored cloud of poetic sentiment dissipated, and the bald, bare peaks of fact stand out unveiled. He is God's servant. The

plan of the campaign, the map of the field of conflict, the weapons of warfare, the strategy of the march, he leaves with the general-in-chief. Into the very thickest of the fight, surrounded by the smoke of battle, dimly seeing even his scattered fellow-soldiers, it is enough for him that he is obeying marching orders, that the white plume of his leader still moves before him, and the clarion peal echoes all along the lines, "Go ye, disciple all nations!"

For Arthur T. Pierson, participation in the Niagara fellowship allowed him full scope for his frankest statements on the relationship between the world of the late nineteenth century and biblical prophecy. For the most part, as he doggedly persevered in parish ministry, he kept these views to himself. In his most popular writings, he rarely alluded to his belief in Jesus' Second Coming, for he feared it would distract other Christians from the core message of the gospel. Yet his views of the Second Coming became a lens through which he interpreted world events and the church's role in them. Clearly by 1886, when speaking before both the Evangelical Alliance and the Prophetic Conference, he had rejected the optimism of his youth, and beliefs in the congruence of God's kingdom with American civilization. Yet the death of optimism did not mean the end of activism. On the contrary, the "realism" of preparing for Christ's Second Coming meant that believers must work harder than ever. World evangelization must become the top priority for believers, rather than one priority among many. For only after the completion of world evangelization would Jesus return.

In a sermon he delivered to his Bethany congregation, Pierson shared with them Jesus' parable of the household servants. The master left, entrusting the care of the house to the servants with the words, "Occupy until I come." To occupy until Jesus returned meant to go into all the world, carrying the light of the gospel into the dusty garrets of the poor. The church was not a lighthouse, drawing all people to itself, but a ship on the move to "rescue the perishing." Mission to the poor in Philadelphia and mission to the world were the same, inseparable task in God's eyes. For the Master said, "Occupy until I come."

THE CRISIS OF MISSIONS

In 1886, Dr. A. T. Pierson burst upon the North American scene with his first full-length book about missions. Capturing the spirit of the age, and awakening Americans to the needs and possibilities in the world beyond their shores, *The Crisis of Missions* did for foreign missions what Josiah Strong's *Our Country* had done for urban missions the year before. While *Our Country* awakened American Protestants to the demographic realities and changing needs in American cities, *The Crisis of Missions* put the problems and possibilities of world evangelization into bold focus. It introduced American Protestantism to the changing prospects for world Christianity in the imperial age, and challenged them not to let the opportunities pass without taking action. Positive response to the book was immediate. *The Congregationalist* called it "one of the most important books to the cause of Foreign Missions, and through them, to Home Missions also, which has ever been written. It should be in every library and household. It should be read, studied, taken to heart, and prayed over." The book had a wide circulation in Great Britain and was translated into French and Dutch.

The appearance of *The Crisis of Missions* so soon after Strong's *Our Country* raises the issue of the relationship between home missions and foreign missions for Dr. Pierson. After all, his mature ministry had been spent actively engaged in urban mission work. Yet his ongoing support for foreign missions at the same time indicates that they were interrelated: city, home, and foreign missions were merely different contexts for the same task, namely the evangelization of the world. With so many foreigners moving into the United States, home missions could even be seen as parallel to foreign missions. The growing lack of homogeneity in American society meant that only home missions could restore the country's unity of purpose and destiny: "Nothing *short of Christianity* can either *save* our Land or *fulfil* the *Purpose of God*," he stated in a sermon on the meaning of America. Yet Pierson remarked, in the sermon "Are We in Danger of Practical Apostasy from Christ in the Matter of Foreign Missions?," that God seemed to be opening the world to the Christian gospel. The definition of foreign missions was "the Church seeking the lost." And the "lost" outside the United States were needier than those within. For at least in the United States there were Bibles, whereas foreigners had nothing.

By the mid-1880s, the balance in A. T. Pierson's mind between home and foreign missions was shifting in favor of foreign missions for two major reasons: the foreign field was needier, and the Lord was providentially opening the world to the Christian presence. *The Crisis of Missions* opened by challenging the reader to follow the Great Commission as a divine command: "Go into all the world and preach the gospel to every creature." Pierson pointed out how God was leading the believers of the nineteenth century by a pillar of cloud and fire, just as he had led the ancient Israelites across the desert:

> Changes more rapid and radical and revolutionary than in any preceding age are taking place before our very eyes. God is moving with great strides in His march toward the final goal. . . . The fullness of time has come, and the end seems at hand, which is also the beginning of the last and greatest age.

Only a few years earlier, wrote Pierson, China and Japan's ports were sealed, India was controlled by an empire hostile to missions, Africa was impenetrable, Muslims were forbidden on pain of death to convert, and Roman Catholics were forbidden to read the Bible. Women were secluded without rights or access to outsiders, and the word "Christian" was a stench to those who had opium and liquor forced down their throats, and slaves taken by so-called Christians. But recently, Pierson believed, God had overcome hundreds of barriers to open the world to Christianity.

Pierson marched the reader through each part of the world, showing how the barriers to the gospel had been dropping over the last few years — all as part of God's great plan for history: "God has unquestionably gone before His church to open doors great and effectual for the entrance of the gospel. This implies a corresponding movement within His church to train and prepare an elect, select band of warriors and workers to carry the gospel through those open doors." While foreign missions had previously been the work of a faithful few, Pierson now called for a great movement of Christians to go through the open doors, under God's guidance, and build upon the foundations already laid.

Even as Pierson saw God's hand in the Bible, he saw the Holy Spirit shaping history. In the actions of powerful nations, God was opening the world to Christian missions. After the Sepoy Rebellion in India in 1857, for example, the negative attitude of the British government toward Christian missions changed. It now became clear that Indian missions struck at the caste system and helped to educate women. Christianity was forbidden in Japan until Admiral Perry opened its ports in 1854, after which Japan quickly modernized itself and gave Protestantism a hearing. Korea was opened by treaty in 1882, and in 1884 the first Presbyterian missionaries entered. The explorer David Livingstone died in Africa in 1873. Since then, missions dared to enter the interior of the "Dark Continent"; and in 1884, the nations of the world set aside the Congo Free State to help suppress slavery.

Recent events demonstrated that obstacles to Christianity around the world were disappearing. The churches of England, Scotland, and America were supporting missions after having opposed them earlier. Miraculously, Pierson exclaimed, native conversions were occurring in unexpected places. Women were awakening to the degradation of their sisters around the world and were rushing to help them. The crisis of missions in 1886 was the present "combination of grand opportunity and great responsibility." Christians must move quickly to take advantage of the circumstances, or the nations would turn elsewhere for the knowledge they seek. The Christian must throw off apathy and respond to God's providence while there is still time.

Pierson called for the spirit of missions to help revitalize the churches who sent missionaries. For as famous missionaries like Alexander Duff of India had often observed, "the Church that is no longer evangelistic will soon cease to be evangelical." The best means of strengthening the churches at home was to move aggressively into foreign missions. More people should volunteer, and more people at home should be "living links" between the home churches and the work abroad. Pierson assumed that home missions led to foreign missions, and foreign missions led to home missions, as both were part of an inseparable whole. To meet the crisis of missions, Pierson advocated global organization and a world council of missions to mobilize the resources of Protestantism, to map out the world field, and to distribute resources equitably. Pierson concluded the book by calling for an international revival of piety and prayer to make it all possible.

The Crisis of Missions jolted its readers into taking seriously the biblical claim of world missions upon their lives. Before Jonathan

Goforth and Donald MacGillivray went as the first Canadian Presbyterian missionaries to China in 1888, they read it. MacGillivray recalled, "It was Dr. Pierson's *Crisis of Missions* that so tremendously stirred up Jonathan Goforth and myself before we ever came to China. So inspiring did we find the book that we gave away hundreds of copies in Canada and I think that book chiefly responsible for the great revival of missionary interest which took place about that time." Goforth went on to lead the famous Shanghai Revival, a turning point in the development of Chinese Christianity. With its multiple editions, *The Crisis of Missions* continued inspiring people to enter mission work well into the twentieth century. Bishop Stephen Neill, author of a hundred books on missions and other theological topics in the mid-twentieth century, recalled reading it while a boy in Scotland. Appearing as it did during the period when European nations, either by persuasion or by force, were opening large parts of Asia and Africa to trade, the book captured the crusading optimism of the age by linking developments in global politics to God's providential control of human history.

The brilliance of *The Crisis of Missions* was that it operated on multiple levels, simultaneously carrying on several kinds of discourse with different constituencies. To casual readers both in northern Europe and the United States, it introduced a moral justification for the recent increased involvement in the affairs of other countries by western powers. For evangelical Protestants, who like Pierson felt that western culture was losing its moorings and drifting into worldliness and religious skepticism, it called them back to the heritage that linked American destiny to the spread of Protestantism. It promised to help revive the struggling home churches by pointing them in new directions beyond themselves, and assuring them that God was still in charge. For young people interested in missions, it provided a biblically and historically based mandate for immediate involvement in a vital, new social movement. And for premillennialists, it spoke the secret language of the "end times." The miraculous changes in world affairs hinted of prophecies fulfilled, and the implied Second Coming of Jesus Christ. To all groups, it gave marching orders for action — typically American, optimistic, progressive activism. But this time instead of Yankees marching to free the slaves, Protestant Christians could unite to free the world from sin and darkness.

For A. T. Pierson, *The Crisis of Missions* represented both continuity and discontinuity with his earlier commitments to evangelical Protestantism as the chief vehicle for making the United States a more moral and better place. The spirit of activism and confidence, and the reading of the signs of the times as markers of God's work in the world, continued from his youth. But the venue was shifting from urban America to the non-Christian world. With his underlying pessimism about whether American civilization was truly Christian, it was unclear in 1886 whether foreign missions more represented an expansion of Pierson's concern to evangelize America, or a retreat from his earlier confidence about the role of the church in American society. Were foreign missions a natural development of Pierson's social activism, or were they a welcome diversion from his generation's sense of failure about the worldliness of mainstream Protestantism? Taken as a whole, Pierson's writings in the late 1880s represented both trends. The multiple levels on which *The Crisis of Missions* operated were indicative of new complexities for evangelicalism's public role.

With *The Crisis of Missions*, Arthur Pierson finally unleashed the restless dynamo that had been churning within him for a decade. The success of the book launched his career as the greatest promoter and the most prolific writer about foreign missions in the late nineteenth century.

6 The Evangelization of the World in This Generation

A s A. T. Pierson was finishing *The Crisis of Missions* in July 1886, he received an urgent telegram from evangelist Dwight L. Moody, requesting that he come to Northfield, Massachusetts, to "help out" with a summer Bible school Moody was holding for leaders of the collegiate YMCA. Two hundred fifty young men from ninety colleges had traveled to Northfield for a month-long Bible conference. They went at the request of Dwight Moody, the famous urban revivalist in America and Britain, who since the 1870s had toured London, Philadelphia, New York, Chicago, Boston, and other large cities. Although his city-wide crusades were the greatest success stories of late nineteenth-century evangelism, Moody's long-term involvement in the YMCA meant that he remained committed to the education of youth. In 1879 he took his evangelistic work in a new direction by opening a school for girls in his family home at Northfield, in the lush Connecticut River valley, with its rolling hills, farms, and forests. Purchasing additional land, in 1881 he opened the Mount Hermon School for boys. With a vision of helping deepen the spirituality of lay people through Bible study, in 1880 he also began holding summer conferences in the peaceful surroundings. Moody's turn toward education reflected his realization that there was a serious lack of biblically trained lay workers in the evangelistic enterprises of the church. According to his biographer, it was also probable that Moody intuited that popular interest in large revival meetings was waning in the 1880s, and he needed to build a more lasting approach toward evangelism.

With his charismatic personality and fame as a revivalist, Moody gathered followers. In contrast to A. T. Pierson, Dwight Moody was uneducated, having begun his working life as a shoe salesman. But Pierson and Moody shared a lot — a passion for urban evangelism, early commitment to the YMCA, and generational affinities. They were even born the same year. They probably had first met through William Erdman, Pierson's college friend and Moody's pastor in Chicago during the early 1870s. Pierson admired Moody's work, and was perhaps even jealous of the sway Moody's powerful preaching held over the masses. For his part, Moody felt insecure around intellectuals like Pierson. Over the life of their friendship, they engaged in some public disagreements, and Pierson felt hurt by Moody more than once. But in the summer of 1886, faced with a group of college men for a month, Moody was desperate for assistance. Although he had held several summer conferences for lay workers since 1880, only arm-twisting by the head of the inter-collegiate YMCA had persuaded him to invite college students in 1886.

Uncertain of his own abilities to sustain their intellectual interest, Moody put out a call to Pierson and a few others to help him with the students. Seeing the telegram as a call from God, the Pierson family packed up and left Philadelphia for Northfield. They arrived to find Dwight Moody in his element, holding daily prayer meetings with the students at 6:00 A.M. and competing with them in afternoon races, games, and sports. Despite the "education gap," Moody's magnetic personality gave him great success with collegians. He urged them to be the starting point for the evangelization of college students throughout the United States.

Pierson's official purpose at the 1886 Mount Hermon conference was to give Bible lectures on "The Bible and Prophecy." All the speakers that summer believed in the premillennial Second Coming of Jesus Christ, a view shared by their host. Pierson already knew James H. Brookes and William G. Moorehead from the Niagara Bible conferences. At Northfield in 1886 he also spent time with the man who soon became his closest friend, the Reverend Adoniram Judson Gordon, pastor of the Clarendon Street Baptist Church in Boston. Gordon's church had actively participated in Moody's Boston revivals in the 1870s. Both believers in the Second Coming, Pierson and Gordon were stirring orators and writers, seekers of holiness, passionate promoters of foreign missions, and urban pastors with a holistic vision. Their theological views were conservative but pragmatic and inclusive like Moody's, rather than doctrinaire and literalistic like those of J. H. Brookes. Arthur and Judson were immediately drawn to each other when they first met in 1885. They became "regulars" at Moody's various Northfield conferences over the years, and have been somewhat condescendingly characterized by historians as two of "Moody's lieutenants."

Moody's summer conference for collegiate YMCA leaders was the beginning of a long history of summer conferences for college "Y" members. But the 1886 meeting in Northfield has gone down in history not because of its meaning to the YMCA, but because it launched the late nineteenth-century North American student movement for foreign missions. Interest in foreign missions was mushrooming in the 1880s among the younger generation, partly because of the larger role being played by the United States in world affairs. After all, it was Americans who were opening Japan, Korea, and soon the Philippines to western, Protestant influence. Seminary students founded the Inter-Seminary Missionary Alliance to cultivate missions interest among ministerial candidates. Student interest in missions also grew in Great Britain in the 1880s, with a veritable explosion of missionary candidates at Cambridge University. Before the 1880s, English foreign missionaries tended to come from working-class backgrounds. But the infusion of hundreds of idealistic, college-educated men into British missions substantially changed the profile and expectations of the missionary movement as the twentieth century neared, and gave it a cachet it previously lacked.

Arthur T. Pierson, with his emotional yet rational approach to foreign missions, became a father figure to the new student missionary movements in both North America and the United Kingdom. His intellectualism and "scientific" presentation of the world's need for Christ, combined with the emotional power of a great preacher, and faith in the movement of the Holy Spirit in world events, gave him special appeal among college students. The greatest student mission movement in American history began when a Princeton student named Robert P. Wilder approached Pierson with a request: "Dr. Pierson, there are ten or twelve of us who have decided to devote our lives to God as foreign missionaries. We have been meeting every day to pray that others may see the vision and we want you to give us a missionary address." Young Wilder had grown up in India where his father, Royal Wilder, was a Presbyterian missionary. As founding editor of *The Missionary Review of the World*, Royal Wilder had praised the mission scheme laid out by Pierson before the Presbytery of Philadelphia and had shown interest in his work by publishing his reflections. Robert Wilder undoubtedly knew of Dr. Pierson's growing reputation as mission promoter through his father. Since the conference schedule was already fixed, the mission enthusiasts arranged for an extra evening session to hear him speak.

Despite lacking his usual visual aids, Pierson drew a map of the world on the blackboard and demonstrated a strategy for world evangelization, showing how God was moving through world events to open it to Christian penetration. Recalled John Mott, who was attending the conference as YMCA leader from Cornell University, "On the evening of July 16, a special mass meeting was held at which Rev. Dr. A. T. Pierson gave a thrilling address on missions. He supported, by the most convincing arguments, the proposition that 'all should go and go to all.' This was the keynote which set many men to thinking and praying." Pierson's appeal led several students to decide to become foreign missionaries. Tension mounted as men prayed in small groups and struggled with the missionary call upon their consciences.

On the evening of July 24, the students held the "meeting of ten nations," during which the sons of missionaries and students of seven nationalities gave their testimonies. As reported in *The Missionary Review*, one speaker was a Lakota Indian who appealed for American rights, American citizenship, and American education for his people. Another YMCA officer from Siam, then a student at Williams College, spoke of his country as open to the gospel, "ready and waiting for you, young men, to come and reap her harvest of souls for Christ." Dr. Pierson broke in and indicated that his church in Detroit had paid for the young man's tuition as part of its mission giving. At the end of each speech, the student speakers appealed for more missionary volunteers. The next day, YMCA leaders began discussing the organization of mission bands in colleges, the systematic study of the mission field, and establishment of missionary libraries for student use. By a week later, one hundred of the college students had decided to devote their lives to foreign missions.

The Mt. Hermon 100 were a link with the tradition of students who began American foreign missions at the Haystack Prayer Meeting at Williams College in 1810. That the famous missionary prayer meeting was also held in western Massachusetts added to the drama of the Northfield Conference. They were also inspired by news of the Cambridge Band, seven Cambridge University students who in 1884 decided to become China missionaries and who visited the universities of Great Britain promoting missions. In imitation, the Mount Hermon 100 elected a committee to tour American colleges enlisting further student support for missions. During 1886-87, Robert Wilder and John Forman of Princeton visited 167 institutions in Canada and the United States with the result that 2200 students signed a volunteer declaration, "I am willing and desirous, God permitting, to become a foreign missionary." Six hundred others became missionary volunteers in 1887-88, despite the absence of a visiting delegation like that of 1886-87.

The commitment of the Mount Hermon 100 changed the course of the history of Christianity. The number of potential missionaries went from a trickle to thousands within a few years. In 1888, with organizational assistance from the YMCA, fifty missionary volunteers met at Northfield and founded the Student Volunteer Movement for Foreign Missions. Bands of student volunteers, who prayed and studied together, formed in colleges across America. John Mott, one of the original Mount Hermon 100, became head of the movement at the request of the YMCA. As the enthusiasm of the student volunteers spread to the United Kingdom, to Scandinavia, and by the 1890s to other parts of Europe and to mission fields around the world, an international student Christian movement was born. From the World's Student Christian Federation came the leaders of twentieth-century world Protestantism, and the eventual founders of the World Council of Churches. As for missionary service, by 1911 over five thousand Student Volunteers had made it to the mission field from the United States. While the Student Volunteer Movement was not itself a mission agency, it channeled the major life decisions of educated young people into the missionary movement. Serving in every kind of mission agency, the student volunteers by their sheer number and capabilities propelled missions from being an afterthought of Protestant churches to the leading form of global outreach in the twentieth century. The Student Volunteer Movement even provided an inspiration for the founding of American Catholic foreign missions in the early twentieth century, and the organization of the Catholic Students' Mission Crusade.

But in 1886, the remarkable history of the Student Volunteer Movement was just beginning to unfold. While the SVM vision evolved over the generations of students who participated in the movement, its earliest identity strongly reflected the influence of A. T. Pierson. Not only was he spiritual father of the movement, but he popularized what became its motto or "watchword," "the evangelization of the world in this generation." And according to Robert Wilder, "The Student Volunteer Movement did not so much produce the Watchword, as the Watchword — or rather the thought behind it — helped to bring into being the Student Volunteer Movement."

THE VOLUNTEER WATCHWORD
AND SYSTEMATIC WORLD EVANGELIZATION

The watchword "the evangelization of the world in this generation" was the guiding philosophy of the early student missionary movement. It summed up the activistic optimism of the pre–World War I generation in North America. While criticized by some older mission strategists as too "American" and unrealistic, it nevertheless captured the idealism of the burgeoning mission movement in the age of empire. As Great Britain, and to a lesser extent the United States, saw their political influence growing around the world, many Christians saw in the imperial expansion of Protestant nations a God-given opportunity to spread Christianity. The "crisis of missions," about which Pierson wrote so eloquently, was an unprecedented divine opportunity for the evangelization of the world. Missions needed to take advantage of the divinely appointed moment in God's plan for world history. While "the evangelization of the world in this generation" did not see itself as political, it nevertheless reflected the spirit of the age. It implied missionary activity in a way that reflected youthful American traits — a pragmatic, entrepreneurial approach to challenges both material and spiritual.

While A. T. Pierson was widely acknowledged to be the author of the watchword, he himself denied that he had originated it. Nevertheless, he defined it and popularized it through his speeches and writings, especially through articles in *The Missionary Review of the World*. In an article printed in 1891, he explained that around 1870 he had read a paragraph by British Baptist mission leader Joseph Angus of London that called for raising 50,000 missionaries to preach the gospel to the unevangelized within twenty-five years. As Pierson mulled over Angus's plan, he began drawing up his own plans for systematic world evangelization. By 1877, Pierson calculated that if one in every hundred Christians would become a missionary, and if all Protestants would give a dollar a year, then 300,000 missionaries and thirty million dollars a year would be available for world evangelization. The original idea behind "the evangelization of the world in this generation" was thus a concrete plan for systematic organization that would see the world evangelized around the year 1900.

After he became a premillennialist, Pierson's commitment to world evangelization increased, for he perceived through biblical prophecy that Jesus' return hinged upon the successful evangelization of the world, as in Matthew 24:14, "This gospel of the kingdom shall be preached in all the world for a witness unto all nations; and then shall the end come." The wedding of premillennial hopes and a numerical scheme made the idea even more compelling, and Pierson began actively promoting his vision during the mid-1880s.

The first public discussion of Pierson's plan for world evangelization occurred in 1885, one year before the Mount Hermon 100. After a hiatus of three years while he conducted revivals abroad, in 1885 Dwight Moody held a Northfield Conference for Christian workers. It was A. T. Pierson's first experience of a Northfield Conference, and he found that sitting at the feet of the great revivalist was a powerful spiritual experience. He wrote,

The power of God pervaded the assembly from first to last. At times His presence seemed almost visible. Mr. Moody rang out the motto: "My soul wait thou only upon God for my expectation is from Him," and from that moment all eyes seemed turned upward in expectation. Think of it! No program — yet hundreds of believers hanging with deep interest on the lips of speakers. The leader simply looked to God from day to day for guidance and called on such speakers as he felt led to select. At the close Mr. Moody said to me: "I have attended hundreds of conventions but never one like this for power." The Spirit's presence was felt in prayer, in song, in speaking, in hearing; not a break nor a blunder nor an inharmonious note nor an infelicitous speech.

For ten days, the conference of Christian workers considered the responsibility of foreign missions, while participants prayed about "the common salvation, the blessed hope, and the duty of witnessing to a lost world." August 11 was made a day of prayer for missions, and Pierson was asked to give a missionary address. In a speech that thrilled the hearers and brought Moody to his feet in approval, Pierson called for a rapid increase in the number of missionaries — not only the ordained and educated few, but men and women from all walks of life who would receive special short courses in Bible and missionary preparation. Echoing the plan he had recently put forth before the Presbytery of Philadelphia, Pierson called for a worldwide, ecumenical council to summon the evangelical churches of the world. Much as ministers divided cities into sections for systematic evangelization, Pierson suggested that the proposed council divide the world into sections for noncompetitive, efficient evangelization in the shortest time possible. A call should be sent to evangelical Christians around the world to unite in a world council for planning the immediate evangelization of the world.

Overwhelming support greeted Pierson's motion. Moody appointed an ecumenical committee with Pierson as chairman to draw up a call for a world council. Members of the committee included mission-minded pastors A. J. Gordon of Boston (Baptist), L. W. Munhall of Indianapolis (Methodist), and George Pentecost of Brooklyn (Presbyterian); Baptist China missionary William Ashmore; Emma Dryer, soon to found the Moody Bible Institute; and Dwight Moody himself. Also assigned to the committee was young J. E. K. Studd of London (Anglican), one of the key promoters of foreign missions among university students in England. Studd was in the United States at Moody's request, speaking to students on behalf of missions. The committee formulated "An Appeal to Disciples Everywhere." By invoking the memory of Jonathan Edwards's systematic prayers for missions, eighteenth-century "concerts of prayer," and pioneer missionary William Carey's work in India, the committee placed its appeal squarely in the mainstream of Anglo-American, evangelical piety. Recalling the pillar of fire and cloud that led the Israelites through the wilderness, it saw God forging ahead, opening the world to missionary penetration:

> The ports and portals of Pagan, Moslem, and even Papal lands are now unsealed, and the last of the hermit nations welcomes the missionary. Results of missionary labor in the Hawaiian and Fiji Islands, in Madagascar, in Japan, probably have no parallel even in apostolic days; while even Pentecost is surpassed by the ingathering of ten thousand converts in one mission station in India within sixty days, in the year 1878. The missionary bands had scarce compassed the walls and sounded the gospel trumpet, when those walls fell, and we have but to march straight on and take possession of Satan's strongholds.

Yet despite God answering prayer and opening the doors to the nations, Christians were not taking advantage of the present opportunities. If only ten million Christians would systematically reach one hundred others with the gospel message in the next fifteen years, entreated the committee, then the world could be evangelized by the year 1900. Two things were needed: "first, the immediate occupation and evangelization of every destitute district of the earth's population; and, secondly, a new effusion of the spirit in answer to united prayer."

The committee called for the meeting of "a great council of evangelical believers" to strategize for the systematic evangelization of the world. The cooperation of evangelical Christians across their sectarian differences would create a marvelous "spectacle" and witness to the world. "What we are to do for the salvation of the lost must be done quickly; for the generation is passing away, and we with it. Obedient to our marching orders, let us 'go into all the world, and preach the gospel to every creature,' while from our very hearts we pray, 'Thy .

kingdom come.'" Besides immediate distribution of the appeal, Pierson printed it the next year as an appendix to his book *The Crisis of Missions.*

The committee appeal from the Northfield Conference of 1885 contained within it Pierson's ideas behind the phrase, "the evangelization of the world in this generation." It called for immediate and systematic world evangelization as part of God's providential plan for the coming of his kingdom. Although the Second Coming was not mentioned explicitly, reference to the "blessed hope" made the appeal attractive to persons of varied opinions on end-time events. The appeal gave specific figures for a concrete plan that would evangelize the world by the year 1900. It defined "generation" as those currently alive, who logically could only be reached by their own generation.

One of the secrets of the watchword's motivating power for young people was its simple definition of "evangelization." Rather than missions being seen as a complicated matter requiring lengthy preparation, the erection of supporting institutions like schools and hospitals, the years of training a native ministry, and fighting immoral social customs over many generations, evangelization meant the preaching of the gospel to all. Rapid dissemination of the gospel was only possible if the definition of evangelization was "doable." Young people could visualize themselves as part of God's unfolding plan for the world, with a hope that it could be accomplished in their own lifetime. Rather than missionary success being measured by how many people converted or accepted the gospel message, Pierson's plan assumed that communicating the gospel was enough. The rejection or acceptance of the message was left up to the hearer and was not part of the responsibility of the missionary. At stake was not the conversion of the world, but the faithfulness of the church to Christ's mandate.

In 1888, the newly founded Student Volunteer Movement for Foreign Missions adopted as their official watchword "the evangelization of the world in this generation." Although Pierson dropped the numerical scheme for evangelizing the world as early as 1895, the idea endured that each generation was uniquely responsible for the salvation of those living during its own lifetime. As early as 1888, A. T. Pierson himself gave speeches interpreting the watchword as a call to the current generation, rather than a numerical plan or prophecy for the Second Coming. The watchword was phenomenally successful because it could be used in many settings, with different levels of meaning by persons of different theological and ecclesial persuasions . . . and the youth loved it.

The Student Volunteer Movement began holding quadrennial conventions, large meetings every few years, so that every college student could have the opportunity to attend one during his or her undergraduate years. A. T. Pierson was a speaker at the first two International Student Conventions, held in 1891 and 1894. Many commitments to missions were made during the conventions. By 1894, 624 student volunteers were in the mission field under the aegis of various denominational boards. In 1895, retired President McCosh of Princeton praised the SVM as the greatest missionary revival since the first century A.D. The student volunteers infused the American missionary movement with new blood and with young, enthusiastic, well-educated foreign missionaries.

As a symbol of radical commitment and immediacy in missions, the watchword was carried across the ocean by Robert Wilder, John Mott, and A. T. Pierson himself. In 1896, the Student Volunteer Missionary Union, a British counterpart to the Student Volunteer Movement, held its first international convention in Liverpool. At the meeting, the British students adopted the watchword as their own. The 1896 conference gave Norwegian, French, Swiss, German, and Dutch students an opportunity to organize their own volunteer organizations, and the students from the Continent took home with them the volunteer watchword. In a "Memorial to the Church of Christ in Britain," British students explained what they meant by the watchword: "Simply that the good news of salvation was intended by God to be made known to the 1500 millions of the present human family, and that the responsibility for this gigantic undertaking lies on all who have been redeemed by his Son." Appealing for greater consecration to missions, the British student movement requested that British churches make "the evangelization of the world in this generation" their official mission policy.

The SVM watchword continued inspiring student movements into the 1920s, when changing theologies of mission caused it to fall from favor. It was reinvoked in the 1960s by the Inter-Varsity Christian Fellowship and the Evangelical Foreign Missions Association, an umbrella agency uniting the work of many evangelistic missions. As a motivating force and a call to systematic organization for world missions, until the 1970s the watchword was the single most important phrase expressive of American evangelical missionary commitment besides the Great Commission itself. With his fingers on the pulse of the student generation and his eyes on God's providential workings through the spirit of the age, A. T. Pierson helped launch the greatest wave of missionary enthusiasm in American history.

PROMOTING MISSIONS THROUGH
THE MISSIONARY REVIEW OF THE WORLD

After the euphoria of the two Northfield conferences in 1885 and 1886, A. T. Pierson must have had a hard time returning to his normal pastoral duties at Bethany Presbyterian Church. With the publication of *The Crisis of Missions* in 1886, invitations to speak on behalf of foreign missions multiplied. He began speaking at student-related meetings, for example the annual conferences of the Inter-Seminary Missionary Alliance, the organization for theological students committed to foreign missions. In 1887, he published *Evangelistic Work in Principle and Practice*, the capstone of his reflections on years in urban ministry. While Pierson did not lose his interest in urban missions — which he argued in his books were inseparable from foreign missions — he nevertheless felt called by God to broader responsibility in promoting the foreign missions movement. It was also clear that his long-term interest in uniting evangelicals in "life and work" was surpassing his denominational loyalties. By 1887, A. T. Pierson was consumed by a series of events bigger than himself. He had been instrumental in unleashing torrential energy for foreign missions among college youth. As interest in foreign missions spread among young evangelicals, they began approaching him privately for advice and support. He counseled a whole younger generation of would-be missionaries, many of whom were not content to pursue their dreams in the context of traditional denominational structures. The new urgency towards missions was churning up a tidal wave of evangelical, nondenominational parachurch activity.

While the private reasons behind some of Pierson's difficult personal decisions cannot be reconstructed with certainty, there are hints that allow ample room for speculation about some of his motivations after 1886. Before settling into the role of missions promoter and senior advisor to young missionaries, Arthur Pierson needed to resolve his own sense of guilt about his failure to become a missionary himself. How could he preach "all should go, and go to all" without personally devoting himself to the mission field? His proposal for a mission colony from Bethany Church had fallen flat in the presbytery. Then in 1887, he asked to go as a missionary directly under the Presbyterian Board. But at 50, with a wife and seven children, the idea was not realistic. Being unable to fulfill his dream of foreign mission service personally, Pierson devoted the prime of his professional life to stirring missionary commitment among others. In retrospect, 1886-87 also represented a point of no return as his mental world expanded beyond the limitations of local Presbyterian ministry, and he set his compass on distant goals that required sailing into uncharted waters.

Because he believed as strongly as he did in God's providence, Arthur Pierson came to see God's leading in the unfolding events of the late 1880s — despite his personal disappointments. In 1887, Royal Wilder's health failed. As a frequent contributor to Wilder's *Missionary Review of the World*, Pierson was asked to step in as co-editor along with the Reverend J. M. Sherwood. Although overworked at Bethany Church, Pierson undertook the editorship as a call from God. Writing in an editorial, he said, "We undertook the work because we heard a loud call of God and saw a great need of man. Now it has been clearly demonstrated that just such a review of universal missions is an imperative need of our day; and that in seeking to supply this need we were simply falling into our place in a divine plan." The day Pierson signed the agreement to become editor, Royal Wilder died. Ten years old, *The Missionary Review* was one of the few general-interest mission periodicals of the day. Although some individual denominations supported their own mission journals, and women's missionary societies did the same, *The Missionary Review* was becoming the American voice of a nondenominational movement in missions.

Another event that helped Arthur Pierson reconcile himself to his role as promoter of missions rather than missionary himself was the marriage of his daughter Helen to Frederick Curtis, a member of Bethany Church, in December 1887. Fred and Helen were accepted under the Presbyterian Board of Missions as missionaries to Japan, and

Curtis was ordained evangelist by the Presbytery of Philadelphia. As a force of modernization, missions to Japan were having a big impact on the samurai "warrior" class, and they needed educational missionaries in the late 1880s. Despite his personal disappointments, Pierson was exceedingly proud of his daughter and son-in-law. He poured out his heart to them on the eve of their departure in 1888, promising that every evening the family would worship and pray for them, asking God to strengthen them and give them access to the Japanese. The proud father closed his letter by asking that Helen and Fred represent him on the mission field. In their work, he could begin his life anew: "Give me the privilege of teaching and preaching through you, and may God grant that it may be many many years and very very successfully." With Helen's decision to become a missionary, Pierson could turn himself even more enthusiastically to his promotional work in *The Missionary Review*. What he was doing for the support of missions, he was now doing for the sake of his own flesh and blood. His heartfelt desire, repeated publicly in his speeches, was that all seven of his children would grow up to be missionaries.

Under Pierson and Sherwood, and then under Pierson alone after Sherwood's death in 1890, *The Missionary Review of the World* became the foremost American missions periodical of the era, covering both popular and technical missions information. Pierson and Sherwood expanded Wilder's periodical to eighty pages monthly. They covered the news from the world's mission fields by employing a series of paid correspondents, some of whom were the most prominent missionaries of the age. Articles of general interest poured in from around the world — reports of revivals, political developments affecting missions, and emerging trends. Pierson wrote most of the feature articles and the editorial section. The journal contained a literary department composed of book reviews of the latest in mission studies and translations from German missions periodicals. A particularly valuable feature of *The Missionary Review* reflected Pierson's conviction that "facts are the fire with which to feed the missionary flame": a monthly statistical analysis of the mission field. Each month concentrated on a different mission field so that the entire world would be covered in one year. In echoes of his "Baconian" approach to biblical studies, Pierson commented, "No greater need exists than that of the *universal diffusion of information* as to the facts of past and present missionary history. To know those facts, to be informed and to keep informed and fully informed, as to the march of God and His hosts in all the earth, is, in effect, to quicken the pulse of the whole Church of Christ."

Under A. T. Pierson's leadership, *The Missionary Review* announced that it would be "Undenominational, International, Independent, and Aggressive." Its stated purpose was "the informing of disciples, and the quickening of our whole church-life, the promotion of an intelligent interest in the work of missions everywhere and the inspiring of an unreserved consecration to the work." It quickly became the mouthpiece of ecumenical evangelicalism, covering the work of non-denominational groups such as the Student Volunteer Movement, the Evangelical Alliance, and the YMCA as well as the work of denominational mission boards for a broader audience. Student volunteers recommended it for subscription as the most informative missionary magazine of the day, and it was studied by the student missionary bands springing up in colleges and seminaries across the country. In his feature articles, Pierson called attention to the work of new missions and movements, including the China Inland Mission, the work of Brahmin widow Pandita Ramabai among child widows in India, women's mission work, and more. Pierson or his correspondents covered the major conferences of ecumenical groups like the Evangelical Alliance as well.

Arthur Pierson now had a sturdy platform from which to promote immediate, systematic world evangelization. At 50, he was at the peak of his intellectual development. Ordinary limitations of sect, denomination, education, gender, and geography were no longer barriers to the grand vision that animated him, "the evangelization of the world in this generation." He was a man possessed by a God-given passion. Under his editorship, *The Missionary Review* immediately stirred controversy. For slow-moving traditionalists, the new student mission movement seemed as radical as abolitionism had once seemed to those who thought slavery would die a gradual death. Pierson was recapturing his youthful idealism through the student volunteers, and he soon found himself defending them against accusations of youthful hot-headedness. He wrote in May 1887,

> After long and patient waiting, God is taking the matter out of the hands of those who are older, more conservative, over-cautious,

and who lack the daring of a courageous faith, and Himself leading on the younger men of our generation to take up the great
work of evangelizing the world. To the young men who flamed
with enthusiasm for the country, we owe the successful issue of the
late war for the Union. To the young men, under God, the world
may yet be indebted for the universal proclamation of the Gospel.
Let us stand still and see the salvation of God.

For all his emphasis on the importance of "facts," it was better in
Pierson's view to be zealous without knowledge, than to have knowledge without zeal.

Ironically, the group that most opposed *The Missionary Review* in
its early years were conservative Presbyterians. Pierson and Sherwood
felt that their attempt to raise the standards for missionary literature
were being praised and supported by all the evangelical denominations except their own Presbyterian Church. Perhaps remnants of the
Old School/New School split meant that Presbyterian confessionalists
distrusted the activism and enthusiasm of Pierson's new approach to
missions. The spectacle of thousands of college students throwing
themselves into missionary activity raised alarms among doctrinal
conservatives who worried about the consequences of youthful energy
and apparently hasty schemes of evangelization. Pioneer Presbyterian
missionary John Nevius of China was one of those who disapproved
of the student mission movement at first, and especially of the implicit
millenarian urgency of "the evangelization of the world in this generation."

As a shaker and a mover in Presbyterian circles, Pierson had also
begun to make enemies. His intensity and single-mindedness irritated
people who did not agree with him. It is probable that denominational
executives in the Presbyterian Board of Missions were beginning to see
him as something of a loose cannon. The movements he was espousing
were helping to create a parachurch and nondenominational culture
that threatened to outflank denominational structures. They dis-
avowed his suggestion to lower educational standards for missionaries
as "revolutionary." Premillennial theology was not accepted as biblical
either by traditional conservatives or by liberals whose theology sought
to replace eternal damnation for nonbelievers with "brotherly love."
Even though Pierson kept his views on the Second Coming out of *The*

Missionary Review for the sake of unity on evangelical essentials, Presbyterian leaders were undoubtedly wary of Pierson's participation in the Niagara Bible conferences, biblical prophecy conferences, Moody's Northfield conferences, and writings on premillennialism — not to mention the various schemes for mission support he had floated before denominational mission committees.

During the summer of 1887, the Pierson family returned to beautiful Northfield for Arthur to speak at Dwight Moody's "Summer School for College Students." The Moody and Pierson families grew even closer as Moody's son William and Pierson's son Delavan became good friends. With 450 college students in attendance in 1887, the student conference tradition was taking firm hold at Northfield. Moody brought in well-known professors from theological seminaries in a program more inclusive than the previous year's crop of premillennial speakers. Discussions among "experts" included a conversation on preparation for overseas evangelistic work among Moody, Pierson, and popular lecturer Joseph Cook of Boston. The question of whether long preparatory studies were necessary for missionaries occupied the conference, or whether the urgency of world evangelization required emergency measures. While everyone admitted that "trained men" were necessary, Moody and Pierson felt the situation also required "irregulars," or rank-and-file Christians willing to undertake the burden of world missions. Said Moody during one of the conference discussions, "We want some men to stand between the laity and the ministers — I don't know what you would call them — gap men. We want men to stand in the gap." It was the support of such un-Presbyterian measures as "gap men" that made traditionalists uncomfortable with A. T. Pierson and his *Missionary Review.*

THE CENTENARY CONFERENCE AND
SCOTTISH MISSIONARY TOUR OF 1888

Besides recruiting new sources of missionaries, the biggest cause initially promoted by *The Missionary Review* under Pierson's editorship was a world missions conference in which Protestant mission supporters from around the world could meet and plan out their strategy of world evangelization. The idea of a world conference of missions was not new. It had first been suggested in the early 1800s by William Carey, the "father of Protestant missions." Writing from India, Carey believed that a world conference of missionaries should meet in Cape Town, South Africa, every ten years, to coordinate mission work among Protestants. Although Carey's idea was not put into effect, small British or American mission conferences were held in 1854, 1860, and 1878. By the late 1800s, momentum toward the world conference idea was building among missionaries, who had also begun holding nondenominational field conferences like the meeting of China missionaries in Shanghai in 1877. As Christian minorities swimming in a sea of non-Christians, missionaries in Asia recognized that they needed to work together rather than import historically western theological and organizational differences into struggling new churches. In the United States, the ecumenical vision was also growing in strength as the Evangelical Alliance reached new heights of interest among a broad spectrum of Protestants. Pierson attended and spoke at its national conference held in Washington, D.C., in December 1887. If evangelical Christians could meet to tackle the social problems of America's cities, why not meet to strategize about the problems facing mission work around the globe?

Pierson had first published an appeal for a world council of missions in 1881. His articles in *The Missionary Review* calling for a world conference of evangelical mission-minded Christians were endorsed by a letter to the editor in January 1887 from Robert Arthington of Leeds, an ardent English premillennialist and the leading financial backer of British Baptist and Congregationalist missions. Arthington's letter showed that the sentiment in favor of a world evangelical conference was shared by mission enthusiasts across the North Atlantic. While Pierson was promoting the idea of a world conference in the United States, fifty-two British missionary societies were issuing a call for an ecumenical mission meeting "to stimulate and encourage all evangelistic agencies, in pressing forward, in obedience to the last command of the risen Saviour, 'Go ye therefore, and make disciples of all nations.'" Upon learning of the British plans to hold a "Centenary Conference on the Protestant Missions of the World" in June 1888, Pierson began promoting the British proposal as consistent with his dreams for a permanent world council of missions. The London Conference would be the first meeting of its kind: an ecumenical gathering to consider missionary comity (the division of the world by mission societies); the home side of foreign missions including literature, exhibits, maps, and prayer meetings; the role of education and of native agency in missions; and mission methods. As someone with a strong aesthetic sensibility, a writer of poetry who loved to draw, Pierson had long encouraged the collection of missionary artifacts into an exhibit to document the progress of missions. The forthcoming world council thus held the promise of fulfilling more than one of his dreams.

The American Bible Society and the Presbyterian Board of Foreign Missions helped the British to secure American attendance at the Centenary Conference. To his great delight, A. T. Pierson was invited to attend as "delegate-at-large." He wrote in his diary, "My thought and prayer of years have been centering upon the world-wide work of missions and the need for a world council to map out the field and to plan to occupy every part of it. It was laid on my heart in Detroit, and I voiced it there. Again at Northfield, it met with cordial response. This council is now called to meet in London next June and I am asked to go." As the first substantial ecumenical conference that included both British and Americans, the organizers tried to be inclusive and drew delegates widely from the missionary activists of the day, including denominational executives, leaders in parachurch agencies like the Evangelical Alliance and the Woman's Christian Temperance Union, representatives from independent missions and women's missionary societies, and of course practicing missionaries. Sixteen hundred men and women from 139 mission societies made their way to London for the conference. Two hundred nineteen of the delegates were from North America.

Along with support for student volunteers and "gap men," A. T. Pierson supported a strong role for women in mission and ministry. His very first article written for *The Missionary Review* had been on how recruitment of women as missionaries would solve "the missionary problem" of a shortage of personnel. During the 1870s, the idea of separate women's denominational missionary societies had swept through the women in Congregational, Methodist, Presbyterian, Baptist, and other churches. Pierson supported this still-controversial "women's missionary movement." In his pastorates, he had founded women's prayer meetings and encouraged the organization of women's missionary societies. With one daughter on the mission field, and four more to go, the proud father had a personal reason for supporting women missionaries. His wife Sarah received appointment to the Centenary Conference as a representative from the Woman's Foreign Missionary Society of the Presbyterian Church, and the couple eagerly anticipated their cruise together. They planned to take a European tour with Judson and Maria Gordon after the conference ended. Maria Gordon had received appointment to the meeting from the American branch of the WCTU. The international WCTU supported its own "temperance" missionaries who worked closely with missionary women around the world for the elimination of alcoholic beverages and other social evils. The May 1888 issue of *The Missionary Review*, the last issue to appear before their departure, carried a feature article by Pierson on the leadership of women in missions. Arguing that the time was at hand for women to exercise their God-given capacity for missionary service, he lamented that denominations had neglected and ignored women's leadership. Women missionaries, student volunteers, "gap men," and a world mission council with a continuation committee were all part of Pierson's vision for systematic world evangelization.

The Piersons sailed from New York on May 26 on the six-thousand-ton steamship *Umbria*. They were delighted to find fellow delegates on board, including Dr. Josiah Strong, head of the Evangelical Alliance and author of *Our Country*, the plea for home missions that paralleled Pierson's *Crisis of Missions*. Another passenger was Dr. Young J. Allen, superintendent of Southern Methodist missions in China and editor of the *Globe Magazine*, an important Chinese-language news publication. The conference delegates arranged missionary services on board the *Umbria*. They arrived in London in time for the opening of the council on June 9. It was held at Exeter Hall, the center of evangelical England and for twenty years or more the headquarters of the London YMCA. With its auditorium for three thousand people, it was also the center of London's musical world until supplanted by the Royal Albert Hall. Lord Aberdeen presided. In attendance were some of the greatest evangelical leaders from Europe, Britain, and America. Probably the delegate who attracted the greatest excitement was the elderly Bishop Samuel Adjayi Crowther, the first consecrated African bishop in the Church of England, translator of the Bible into Yoruba, and the initiator of the missions for the Church Missionary Society in the Niger Delta. Crowther embodied the mid-century vision of Henry Venn of the CMS to plant "native" churches as the goal of missions.

In his capacity as journalist, Arthur Pierson sent back glowing reports of the conference for immediate publication in *The Missionary Review*. Thousands thronged the venue that had been planned for hundreds. As he stood gazing at the "battle-scarred missionaries," the writers and Bible translators, the women's representatives, missionary pastors, and a few "native" Christians, Pierson said to himself, "This is indeed the grandest ecumenical council ever assembled since the first council in Jerusalem! What a fitting commemoration with which to mark the completion of the first century of modern missions; what a fitting inauguration with which to introduce the new century of evangelism!" In addition to plenary speeches and discussions, simultaneous section meetings split people into interest groups. Popular topics considered by the speakers included non-Christian religions, Roman Catholic missions, and commerce and Christian missions. Eyewitnesses gave reports on missions around the world. Experts held a series of private meetings to discuss a broad range of concerns within the missionary movement. On Sundays, delegates fanned out across the city, visiting and speaking at local churches.

Dr. Pierson gave the closing address on the second day of the conference. Following a series of brief surveys of each mission field, he gave a magisterial "general survey" of missions around the world that garnered wide attention in the British religious press and marked him as one of the men to watch at the conference. Missions should start with Jerusalem and radiate outward, he thundered, spreading from there to all the peoples of the world. After surveying the progress of missions, he urged that colonies of missionaries be sent "to plant Christian homes amid the dark places of the earth." Individual consecration, combined with the supernatural power of God, would make it possible "to publish the Gospel to all living people before the end of the present century!" He concluded his speech by drawing an analogy between a church united in mission, and a military action: "Let us sound the imperial clarion of advance; let us move together, and turn the staggering wings of our adversary, pierce his centre, capture his cannon, and plant the flag of Christ upon the parapet of every stronghold of the devil!"

Pierson's military language exemplified why the Centenary Conference of 1888 has gone down in history as representing a merger of imperialist triumphalism with missionary outreach. Occurring at the height of British imperialism and talk of the Anglo-Saxon responsibility to civilize the world, the conference thrilled its participants because it represented new heights of British and American Protestant unity in a great world crusade. The Centenary Conference was an important step in the eventual creation of the International Missionary Council and then the World Council of Churches. But historian Clifton Phillips notes that "perhaps nowhere was the association between Christian mission and imperial expansion expressed more unabashedly than in the official report of the great international missionary conference held in London in June, 1888." The themes of Christianization, commerce, and civilization were unapologetically interwoven in such discussion topics as "Christianity, Commerce, and Education." The editor of the conference proceedings underscored self-conscious Anglo-American racial unity when he claimed that God was "giving success as the colonisers and conquerors of the world" to the "race" that was sending out the majority of missionaries. Speakers emphasized that the missionary movement was a giant crusade for world Christian domination. Pierson's argument that Christian colonies should be as well funded and supported as political ones showed that colonialism was providing something of a model for the evangelization of the world.

Yet the naïve enthusiasm of the historical moment is not the only explanation for the militaristic language and "culture Christianity" that shone through the proceedings. To A. T. Pierson and A. J. Gordon, who were widely agreed to be the best of the North American speakers at the conference, the fervor they brought to a world missionary crusade owed as much to their formation as part of the Civil War generation as to current British imperialism. In their speeches and writings on the conference, both men drew upon imagery from the Civil War to describe the mission of the church. As a young man, Arthur Pierson had believed that the war against the slave powers represented the triumph of Christian civilization. But despite the military victory, the reality of evil was made manifest in the challenge to Protestant values after the war, as new, non-Protestant immigrants poured into the cities and social problems worsened and grew in complexity. The missionary movement now seemed poised to complete what the Civil War had failed to accomplish — though by spreading the gospel so that Jesus would return. For both Pierson and Gordon, the missionary movement of the high imperial age was a deepening and broadening of their Yankee anti-slavery crusade. Support for world evangelization was a logical outgrowth of previous evangelical actions against slavery, alcohol, and other evils both personal and social. The metaphors of war came from deep within A. T. Pierson's "New School Presbyterian," Yankee, abolitionist soul. War against Satan and the evil forces of the world would of necessity take political form, and be prosecuted by supernatural means within human events. God's truth was marching on.

More than ever before, the conference gave A. T. Pierson a sense of the importance of Christian unity, and the triviality of nationality or denominational affiliation. He wrote in *The Missionary Review* that the conference had driven thoughts of his own particular identity out of his head. In the presence of God and the perils of the enemy, he could affirm only "that we have one Lord, one faith, one baptism, one common cause, hope, and home. . . . A man who, in such a presence, magnifies his denomination is only a fossilized ecclesiastic — a mere mummy." The result of such magnificent Christian unity, for Pierson, was the necessity of continued cooperation for the sake of world mission. He urged in *The Missionary Review* the creation of a permanent "interdenominational and international missionary committee" to which could be referred issues of comity, the occupation of new mission fields, and other questions needing efficient resolution. On the issue of creating a permanent missionary council, Pierson agreed with German Lutheran mission theorist Gustav Warneck. Although Warneck was soon to lead the attack on the Anglo-American triumphalism and haste that he perceived in the slogan "the evangelization of the world in this generation," he and Pierson were ahead of their time in pushing for a world council in their respective spheres of influence. Warneck's paper on the subject of a permanent missionary council was read at the conference in his absence, although it is unclear whether Pierson heard it.

The frustration of the Centenary Conference for A. T. Pierson and other evangelical activists was that it involved only words. Since delegates to the conference had no legislative authority from their churches, they could not put into place a permanent committee for solving the many problems raised about mission strategy, comity, and so forth. They also could not vote on ethical issues that impacted missions. Yet speakers continued to press for action. In his first speech, J. Hudson Taylor, founder of the China Inland Mission, the archetypal "faith mission," railed against the opium trade as destroying the Chinese and counteracting the good works of missions. British merchants in collusion with the government were dumping opium on an unwilling China in exchange for Chinese goods — actions protected by the infamous "unequal treaties" imposed on China at mid-century. Delegate "Mother" Mary Ninde, of the American Methodist women's missionary society, stood and moved that the conference take action against the alcohol powers. Just as opium was devastating China, liquor was a scourge in Africa. Since many of the women delegates were active in the WCTU, they had hoped for a conference resolution on temperance. The missionary crusade might be in full swing, but the West was also exporting its worst vices through imposing opium on China, dumping rum and liquor in Africa, and legalizing prostitution in British colonies for servicing Her Majesty's troops. These cancerous sins needed to be excised from the mission field for the world to be able to hear the gospel message from western lips.

On the final day of the Centenary Conference, the British called upon "our two eloquent American brethren," Drs. Pierson and Gordon, to give the closing words. Afterward, a small group of evangelicals held a rump caucus on July 20 to vote against the opium and liquor traffic, censuring especially Britain and Germany, and registering their disapproval of licensed prostitution. Those who attended the after meeting included J. Hudson Taylor of China; George Post of Syria, Pierson's old seminary classmate; A. J. Gordon; H. Grattan Guinness, evangelical faith mission leader in Britain; and A. T. Pierson. An active social agenda remained a priority for the most evangelistic delegates to the conference.

What is interesting in retrospect is that the evangelicals who criticized the morals of the British and German governments were largely premillennialists who did not believe in the inevitable onward march toward human progress. Despite their military rhetoric and simplistic confusion of western hegemony and missionary expansion, they were critical of aspects of the western global expansion. Clearly their belief in the Second Coming did not keep them from being openly critical of western governments, or of ignoring social issues in the juggernaut of world evangelization. Occupying the world for Christ, while waiting for his return, also meant judging the corporate sins of the West. Evangelicals like Pierson, who had only a few months before attended the Evangelical Alliance conference on urban problems, were highly negative about certain aspects of western culture, especially the materialism and "worldliness" that arose in middle-class Protestantism after the Civil War. Under Pierson's editorship, over the years *The Missionary Review* grew increasingly critical of the colonialist enterprise. While the Centenary Conference of 1888 may have epitomized Anglo-American triumphalism and racial superiority, the after meeting of evangelicals to pass resolutions against the German and British governments showed that other currents were running beneath the surface.

After the conference, the Piersons and Gordons began their sightseeing. But the high visibility of Arthur and Judson put them in great demand as speakers on behalf of foreign missions at the churches and institutions of their newfound friends. The evangelical periodical, *The Christian*, reported on their whereabouts and published a number of their speeches. The Pierson and Gordon team took British evangelicalism by storm. One of their most important contacts was with Henry Grattan Guinness, who though grandson of the wealthy Irish brewer, had studied theology and become an independent evangelist. In 1872, he and his wife Fanny founded Harley College, a missionary training institute for missionaries located in East London. An ardent premillennialist, writer on biblical prophecy, and founder of both the Livingstone Inland Mission and a Congo mission that evolved into the Regions Beyond Missionary Union, Guinness had given a powerful speech at the conference that Pierson secured to print in *The Missionary Review*. On June 22, the Piersons and Gordons attended a farewell service for missionaries from Harley House, and each gave an address. Another American conference delegate spoke as well — Methodist businessman William E. Blackstone, author of the best-selling classic of 1878, *Jesus Is Coming*.

The meeting of Guinness, Blackstone, Pierson, and Gordon at Harley House brought together several important new movements. Of immediate concern, of course, was world evangelization. All four men devoted their mature years to the missionary movement. Gordon was soon to be elected head of the American Baptist Missionary Union. He had previously convinced the American Baptists to adopt Guinness's Livingstone Inland Mission as an official mission in 1884. Blackstone and Guinness were both founders of faith missions and ardent supporters of Zionism, a position that grew from their premillennial reading of biblical prophecies. Blackstone had founded the Chicago Hebrew Mission for the evangelization of the Jews, and in 1890 he sponsored the first Jewish-Christian conference calling for the establishment of a Jewish state in Palestine. Despite his advocacy of "Messianic Judaism," converted Jews who maintained their Jewish culture, he was years later designated an official "Father of Zionism" by the State of Israel. Harley College provided a model for running a missionary training institution that would soon be taken up by Gordon and Pierson; and Blackstone funded at least three missionary training schools — the Chicago Training School (for Methodist women), Moody Bible Institute, and the Bible Institute of Los Angeles. Pierson, Gordon, Guinness, and Blackstone shared interests in premillennial prophecy and Bible study, faith missions and world evangelization, and the preparation of lay people for missionary service. The intersection of these four men in 1888 signified the coalescence of an international premillennial movement.

From June 27 to 29, the Piersons and Gordons attended the thirty-third Mildmay Conference, a center of evangelical Anglicanism. Mildmay conferences had been started by William Pennefather, Vicar of St. Jude's Mildmay. After his death in 1873, his widow had continued her husband's work, including support for missions, schools, hospitals, deaconess training and residence halls, and the annual conferences on spiritual life that attracted thousands of Christian workers. The great hall at Mildmay held three thousand persons for prayer, singing, and spiritual sustenance. Both men addressed the conference, with Pierson giving one of the closing addresses. The Americans were thrilled to meet the cream of European evangelicalism at Mildmay — men they had long admired such as Pastor Monod of Paris; Horatio Bonar of Scotland, the hymn writer; Prebendary Webb-Peploe of London; Adolph Saphir, the Jewish-Christian Bible commentator; Hudson Taylor of the China Inland Mission; F. B. Meyer, the spiritual writer and Baptist preacher; and others. Of particular interest to Sarah Pierson and Maria Gordon were the Mildmay deaconesses, consecrated Protestant women who worked in the slums of London, wore uniforms, and lived communally in deaconess homes. The revival of the ancient order of deaconesses had begun in mid-nineteenth-century Germany and spread to England and the United States. While Lutheran women led the movement in Germany, and Methodist deaconesses were just beginning in the United States, the Anglican Mildmay deaconesses were the leaders of the movement in the United Kingdom. In addition to home mission work, some deaconesses also became foreign missionaries. The consecration of women for deaconess work added to Pierson's perception that women were key to answering the problem of inadequate missionary personnel, and he supported the deaconess movement in his writings. The paper he read on June 18 at the Centenary Conference, in fact, included a section on the importance of women in shaping human character. Behind careers in missions lay consecrated women at the center of family life.

On July 3, Dr. Pierson attended the Pan-Presbyterian Alliance meeting in London, to which he was one of three hundred delegates. Stimulated by the example of the Evangelical Alliance, the Pan-Presbyterian Alliance was the beginning of what would become the World Alliance of Reformed Churches. Pierson delivered a major address on July 4 on his two favorite issues: the crisis of missions and the crisis of the cities. The inseparability of the two crises was evident in the address. The only solution to each was cooperation among all believers for what Pierson called "life and work." His phrase "life and work" anticipated the slogan around which church unity movements would cohere in the 1920s. Whether rich or poor, Christians must worship and work together without class interest. The best men must be sent "to the garrets and cellars" to bring rich and poor into one congregation. Patronizing "mission chapels" to the poor must be avoided for the sake of Christian unity across class divisions.

Following the meeting of the Pan-Presbyterian Alliance, the Piersons and Gordons finally departed for Rome. But carefree sightseeing was not to be part of the schedule, because there they received an urgent invitation from Scottish ministers in Edinburgh to hold a missionary meeting for university students about to disperse for summer vacation. Seeing the hand of God in their invitation, the couples returned to Scotland for three days of ecumenical meetings at the Synod Hall of the United Presbyterians, the largest hall in Edinburgh. At a gathering at the Mission House of the Church of Scotland on July 17, leaders of the churches of Scotland asked Pierson and Gordon to conduct an extended missionary recruitment campaign in Scotland. The call was confirmed at a meeting of over two thousand people on July 22, when an interdenominational committee from the Established Church, the Free Church, the United Presbyterian, and the Wesleyan churches praised the Americans for their assistance in spearheading a revival of missionary enthusiasm and of rekindling their "drooping faith." Scottish churches agreed to collect money and pay what was necessary for the American brethren to conduct an extended tour among them. The committee wrote to the Clarendon Street and Bethany churches asking that their pastors be spared from their pastoral work as long as possible. Scottish pastors would supply their pulpits, if necessary.

Scottish interest in missions had begun in the late 1700s and had developed into a distinctive intellectual tradition stemming from the "Scottish Enlightenment." While famous Scottish missionaries like David Livingstone had come from humble backgrounds, Scottish missions were famous for promoting education as a means of evangelization. Scottish missionaries were also famous for their use of scientific classifications in their study of both the natural world and religious systems. After all, it was Scottish Presbyterians who had first introduced "common sense philosophy" into American intellectual life. Alexander Duff, a founder of higher education in India; William and John Muir, scholars of Islam and Hinduism respectively; James Legge, pioneer Sinologist; and James Stewart, principal of Lovedale, the leading source of higher education for black South Africans, were all representative of the nineteenth-century Scottish intellectual approach to missions. As an educated Presbyterian, Arthur Pierson shared the Scottish enthusiasm for factual data and rational analysis in theology and biblical studies.

But by 1888, missionary enthusiasm among Scottish university students had waned. Scottish mission advocates saw in Pierson and Gordon the possibility of reviving the fading missionary tradition in Scottish churches. It helped, also, that Gordon was of Scottish blood, and was able to joke about his ancestors emigrating from Scotland two hundred years before, as well as the strict Calvinism of his own father. Pierson was a Presbyterian with a reputation for intellectual discourse that had already proved effective among American university students, of whom over 2000 had volunteered for missionary service since the Mount Hermon 100 of 1886. The Moody-Sankey revivals of 1875-76 in Scotland were still fresh in the memories of churchmen, and it certainly inspired confidence that Pierson and Gordon were confidants of Dwight L. Moody.

Accepting the challenge of the Scottish churches, the team worked for a week in Edinburgh among university students before heading across Scotland. Everywhere they went large crowds greeted them. Local people met them at the train station at each stop and hosted them. At each meeting, Pierson first instructed the people by outlining the history, progress, and rationale for missionary effort. Gordon followed by presenting the practical effects of missions, the grace and wonders given through the gift of the Holy Spirit. As the Scots said of the crusade, "Dr. Pierson inspired us; Dr. Gordon fed us." Pierson saw the purpose of the mission tour to put the "facts" before people and so convince them of the importance of missions. Presentation of factual data would refute skepticism and lead to Christian action. Just as Pierson had refuted the agnostic Robert Ingersoll with the scientific "evidences of Christianity" and "infallible proofs" from the Bible, so he combated nay-sayers and skeptics about the hopes for missions. Pierson's uniting of home and foreign missions as part of one goal also appealed to the Scottish experience. Slums surrounded three of the four Scottish universities from which most missionaries came. Thus experience in slum rescue work sparked comparisons between the "heathen" at home and the "heathen" abroad.

The Scottish missionary tour was not without its critics. Not all British Protestants appreciated the evangelical immediacy promoted by the energetic Americans. High churchmen had refused to participate in the Centenary Conference in the first place, and those with Anglo-Catholic leanings were always suspicious of anything smacking of "enthusiasm." One critic of the conference wrote in the journal The Nineteenth Century that evangelistic, western-style missions were less effective in India than the approach taken by monastics, who lived in poverty as "holy men" among the people. The critic also noted that the emerging field of the history of religions was opening new, more sympathetic approaches to the non-Christian religions than allowed by militant evangelistic campaigns based on assuming eternal damnation for nonbelievers. The article implied a difference between the sincerity and humility of actual missionaries, and the overblown "cant" and "tirades" by missionary promoters. Criticisms from another angle indicated that missions had worked long and hard already with very little to show for it. Why should new energy be put into a cause so clearly difficult and basically unsuccessful? Dr. Pierson found himself not only giving promotional addresses, but responding to critics of missions in *The Times* and the *British Weekly*.

In part, the Americans' missionary crusade was a temperance crusade. A. T. Pierson had always abstained from hard drink and had supported the temperance cause by voice and pen. The Gordons were strongly involved in temperance politics, with A. J. Gordon supporting the Prohibition Party, a third party in American politics that proposed to outlaw the sale of alcoholic beverages and give women the vote. With Mrs. Gordon present as a delegate from the American WCTU, the Piersons and Gordons also found themselves addressing temperance meetings among the churches. Maria Gordon was a preacher in her own right, and she willingly addressed the mixed crowds of men and women in support of abstinence from liquor by individuals, coupled with the prohibition of alcohol by the state. She urged the women to be braver about giving their testimony and taking a public role in the churches, reminding them of what the gospel had done to elevate the role of women in Christian lands. Mrs. Pierson was more reserved and only occasionally addressed women's meetings. But all four of the Americans enjoyed the sightseeing they squeezed in, including the island monastery of Iona from which St. Columba had evangelized Scotland in the sixth century, and various castles and famous sights.

After several weeks in Scotland holding meetings in Aberdeen, Glasgow, Edinburgh, and other locations, the Gordons steamed home for Boston on August 9. Although pressured to stay on, Judson could not neglect his church any longer, and his wife insisted that he return in time to rest before beginning a new season of preaching. But the Piersons remained, with Arthur visiting twenty-one places by August 24 and addressing 35,000 people. The Piersons took time out to attend the World's Conference of the YMCA in Stockholm, August 15-20, where Dr. Pierson gave an address. They traveled in Europe while waiting to see if Bethany Church would permit them to remain longer. But pressing needs at the church and at home called them to return in late September.

On the evening of September 28, well-wishers held a farewell meeting for the Piersons in Hope Hall, Liverpool, that was attended by "representatives of all sections of evangelical Protestants." Dr. Pierson gave one final fact-filled and emotional address in support of missions. He described the "cruelties of heathenism" and the "triumphs of missions," urging people to heed the Scriptures and take personal responsibility that "all should go, and go to all." Being a woman or being a lay person was no reason not to become a missionary, for all persons were called to the great task. All forces of "modern civilisation" such as steam, the telegraph, the printing press, and the wealth of modern society should be put to work for the evangelization of the world. It may be that "before this generation passes away, the whole world may have heard the Gospel message." On September 29, the Piersons steamed out of Liverpool, once again on the *Umbria*. In his pocket were urgent invitations from across the British Isles to give missionary addresses. Dr. Pierson promised to return as soon as he could.

After the exhilaration of the Centenary Conference and the Scottish mission tour, return to normal life seemed impossible. Pierson had shared his grand vision for immediate world evangelization with thousands of people. He had met like-minded believers like Grattan Guinness and others who exemplified a life totally devoted to missions. He had experienced fellowship with people across the denominational spectrum and felt liberated from denominational structures. He was in demand as a popular speaker by churches throughout the British Isles. His stature had increased from being a national to an international figure. He was a key player in the emerging Euro-American network devoted to world evangelization and ecumenical unity.

Even before the Centenary Conference, A. T. Pierson had been restless in his role as pastor at Bethany. He had even tendered his resignation from Bethany in June 1888, but had withdrawn it at the congregation's urging. In his farewell letter to Helen and Fred, he had written that he was uncertain about his future, because as much as he liked Bethany Church, there was "little or no aggressive work." Feeling himself in the prime of life, Pierson longed to "take up a life of more faith and self-denial" in accordance with his spiritual convictions. "I think the more our dependence is wholly on the Lord even for daily bread, the greater the joy and blessing. . . . The secularized church makes life too easy. Self-sacrifice is evaded even by the ministry. We are living in too costly homes and spending too much money."

Pierson struggled against returning to a settled pastorate at a guaranteed salary. He undertook a promotional mission tour through Canada in the spring of 1889. The Piersons vacationed as usual at Northfield over the summer. After consultation with John Wanamaker, he penned a letter of resignation to the church: "I feel myself called to a somewhat peculiar work in behalf of world-wide missions." His "peculiar mission" was "to advance the speedy evangelization of the world. At present I have no definite plans save to hold myself open to divine leading and to go where God shows me the way."

Wanamaker was in Washington, D.C., serving as the new Postmaster General. He replied by offering to give Pierson an extended leave of absence, and to make him Bethany Church's "pastor-at-large with a missionary commission." In a letter to his pastor, Wanamaker expressed "actual pain" at the thought of Pierson's absence from his life. "I personally owe you more than I can ever tell — your uniform goodness and brotherliness to me will ever be a bright memory," he wrote. But loath to put the financial burden on the church, or an emotional burden on the next pastor, Arthur Pierson refused the offer of support. Despite four children at school, two at home, a dependent wife and elderly mother, on September 2, 1889, Arthur Pierson left Bethany Church. The Presbytery of Philadelphia commended him to the churches of Great Britain: "The Presbytery rejoices to believe that in other lands he may also be blessed of God in his earnest pleas on behalf of Christian Missions." Despite rumors in the secular press, Pierson's editorial associate J. M. Sherwood denied there was any scandal in his resignation from Bethany Church. Turning his face abroad and his eyes to heaven, A. T. Pierson never again held a regular pastoral appointment or position in a mainline denomination.

7 Living by Faith

In May 1889, the Young Men's Christian Association held its international meeting in Philadelphia. George S. Fisher, a leader in the Kansas YMCA, sought the advice of Dr. Pierson of Bethany Church while in town for the convention. Fisher had been born of missionary parents and was a strong believer in holiness doctrines. He believed that through the power of the Holy Spirit, Christians could live in total spiritual consecration to Christ. Under his leadership as evangelist, speaker, and administrator, the Kansas state YMCA was the fastest-growing in the country; and in 1890 the 34-year-old Fisher would be appointed its secretary, the leader of the Kansas branch. Fisher and three others visited Dr. Pierson in his Philadelphia home. Believers in the Second Coming, Pierson and the four younger men fervently prayed for God's guidance and asked that he would use them in the end-time task of world evangelization.

Over the next few months, deep in a spiritual struggle over God's direction for his life, A. T. Pierson reached the momentous decision to resign his pastorate. Feeling called to embody total reliance on God, he later wrote in his diary, "I purpose to separate all considerations of money, so far as is possible, from the interests of the kingdom of God. I record my confidence that all needful good will be

added to us according to God's promise. I do not desire a large income, as it is too often a hindrance to spirituality and endangers family life by many snares." Pierson aimed to live in intimate relationship
with God's will, dependent on God's grace for the support of his family. By living "on faith," he would reject the growing materialism of
modern western culture while working full time for the advancement
of world evangelization. He would follow the example of his father in
faith, George Müller of Bristol, for whom he prayed daily and had
visited in England the year before. He was also adopting the method
by which Hudson Taylor supported the China Inland Mission, the
first "faith mission" and largest Protestant mission in China. Taylor
and Pierson had met in 1885 at Moody's Northfield Conference for
Christian workers, and they became friends and correspondents.
Pierson wrote to Helen and Fred in 1890, "If I were going to a mission
field today I would go with Hudson Taylor sooner than any mission I
know. It seems to me he has built more nearly on Biblical principles
than any other."

Like Dr. Pierson, George Fisher was in the process of committing
himself full time to world evangelization, supported by the "faith
method." In June 1889, he held a summer Bible school at which
H. Grattan Guinness was invited speaker. As founder of two missions
in the Congo, and ardent believer in the necessity of evangelizing the
unreached parts of the world so that Jesus would return, Guinness
urged the young YMCA leaders to lead a movement for the
evangelization of the African interior. Through Guinness, Fisher
caught the vision of evangelizing what was called "the Sudan." The
vast area of Africa below the Sahara desert, extending from Senegal to
Ethiopia, the Sudan was dominated by a mixture of Islam and indigenous religions. With a hostile climate and political instability, it represented one of the great unevangelized portions of the globe, and thus
was an obstacle to end-time events. Since the early 1800s, Protestant
mission leaders had envisioned founding a chain of mission stations
across central Africa. These stations would not only stop the advance
of Islam into southern Africa, but would be radiating points for the
conversion of Africa to Christianity. In the 1880s, the Sudan was the
object of sustained intercessory prayer by British premillennialists.
Through the Guinnesses and their children, knowledge of its needs
spread to Germany, the United States, and South Africa.

Fisher began exploiting his YMCA connections to support his vision as he recruited participants for a mission to the Sudan. At the October meeting of the Interstate Convention of the YMCAs of Kansas, Oklahoma, and the Indian Territories, Guinness, Dwight Moody, and Robert Speer spoke in favor of the plan. Having been converted under Pierson's preaching while a student at Princeton, Speer was at that time serving as a recruiter for the Student Volunteer Movement. The collegiate YMCA ensured the movement's organizational survival by providing it staff support. For the first few years of the Student Volunteer Movement's existence, the boundaries between it and the sponsoring organization remained fluid. From the pages of *The Missionary Review*, Pierson supported the "Kansas-Sudan movement." Both he and George Fisher considered the prayer meeting at his house in Philadelphia an important milestone in their respective journeys toward "living by faith" in support of worldwide evangelization.

The Kansas-Sudan movement gained momentum during 1890. In a letter to Helen and Fred in Japan, Pierson wrote for a page and half in enthusiastic support. He described how fifty young men and women had volunteered for the Sudan and how God had met every need for eighteen young men to tour the United States on foot, speaking out for missions. Although he felt the group needed guidance to avoid the fanaticism of youthful exuberance, it was nonetheless a work of God.

But the powers-that-be at the YMCA were not so sure. Operating as a cooperative movement among evangelical Protestants, the YMCA was paying John Mott's salary to organize the fledgling SVM. As an ecumenical, evangelical mission organization directed toward young people, the YMCA policy of working through existing churches meant that it gladly channeled missionary volunteers into existing mission structures. But it balked at starting "faith missions" marked by controversial spirituality and visions of a literal Second Coming. C. Howard Hopkins, historian of the YMCA, described the Kansas-Sudan movement as the first serious tension between local and international units of the YMCA. In September 1890 the international organization sent John Mott to a meeting of the group that included Pierson, Robert Speer, George Fisher, and T. C. Horton, Pierson's associate at Bethany Church. As one of the Mount Hermon One Hundred, and a pious advocate of holiness theology himself, Mott wavered at the appeals of his friends. But in the end, his "inherent organizational sense" kept him from supporting the movement. He persuaded Robert Wilder not to join, and thus kept the young SVM leadership from being pulled wholesale into the nondenominational faith mission movement.

Unfortunately A. T. Pierson's cautions against "fanaticism" went unheeded, and three of the first Sudan missionaries to reach Sierra Leone died because they refused to take medicine. According to his report in *The Missionary Review,* the missionaries had met "faith healers" *en route* to Africa and had decided that they did not need the usual precautions of taking quinine against malaria. Citing their faith in God, they did not take precautions about their food and clothing — an important consideration for western missionaries in West Africa, which was widely known as the "white man's grave." Of the nine missionaries of the original Sudan party, five died of malaria within three months. By 1891, John Mott and the International YMCA had persuaded the Kansas YMCA to renounce the movement. The reason given for condemning it was the YMCA policy not to undertake missionary work unless previously called by a majority of missionaries in a given area. Given that the Sudan Party was en route to an area where there were no missionaries, the YMCA policy seemed designed to prevent its participation in pioneer missions to the unreached.

Dr. Pierson alluded to a deeper reason for the disapproval of the movement by the YMCA leadership in his editorial of December 1890. He hoped that the Kansas-Sudan movement would stop the YMCA from drifting toward "a sort of religious club, with athletic culture and good fellowship, but a lack of the evangelistic and missionary spirit." In their efforts to bolster the spiritual edge of the YMCA through supporting the Kansas-Sudan movement, Pierson and George Fisher were disappointed. While a man like John Mott remained centered on personal evangelism throughout his life, like a good Methodist he was more concerned about piety and ecumenical cooperation than about doctrines of the Second Coming. The YMCA refused to go down the road of premillennial faith missions, or of any doctrines not widely held by evangelical Christians. It operated from the middle rather than from the edge of the evangelical spectrum. By involving itself in the experimental Student Volunteer Movement, the YMCA was already incurring enough risks of alienating its more mainstream constituency.

In 1892, George Fisher resigned from the YMCA. Later that year, he founded the World's Gospel Mission, later called the Gospel Missionary Union. He led the GMU into four areas previously untouched by evangelical Protestantism — Morocco, Ecuador, Colombia, and Mali, and then died on the mission field. The GMU survived as one of the earliest American "faith missions," a nondenominational mission agency devoted to primary evangelism, whose early missionaries had to raise their support individually by "faith" rather than relying on the systematic work of a denominational mission board. A wave of faith missions came into being in the late 1880s and early 1890s in direct response to the ideas behind "the evangelization of the world in this generation." Supported by individual congregations, and recruiting lay personnel unable or unwilling to go under established missions, faith missions felt that the evangelization of non-Christians took precedence over all other missionary motives. Fueled by premillennial urgency, early faith missionaries overwhelmingly considered themselves part of the countdown toward the end times, when Jesus would return to gather believers into heaven, and the lost would descend into hell.

In his public support for the Sudan movement, A. T. Pierson took a stand as a founding father of the faith mission movement. Emerging simultaneously with his renouncing of his own salary and regular pastoral appointment, the Kansas-Sudan movement was a metaphor for Pierson's own walk of faith. It represented his revolt against materialism and prosperity, his affirmation of supernaturalism in theology and history, his reliance on God's daily leading, and his support for world evangelization in light of fulfilling biblical prophecies. Yet it also represented walking the fine lines of his own existence, carrying with it the potential of alienating friends of many years, breaking with institutions that had nurtured him since childhood, and risking the extremism that often accompanied finely tuned spiritual perfectionism. During the early 1890s, A. T. Pierson embarked on a new walk of faith. The risks that he took made possible great success at promoting the cause of world evangelization. But they also marked him as a key bridge figure between the denominational evangelicalism of the post–Civil War period and the independent evangelicalism of the early 1900s. In his personal search, he was unwittingly helping to redefine evangelicalism for the twentieth century.

THE RISE OF THE FAITH MISSION MOVEMENT

Following his resignation from Bethany Church, A. T. Pierson launched a second speaking tour of Scotland in November 1889. His first tour with A. J. Gordon had been a wonderful success. Six months later, the secretary of the tour committee wrote that intensified interest in missions could be felt throughout the churches. People were giving money to missions in such amounts that it "bids fair to place the good old Kirk of Scotland in the forefront of the Evangelical army." A committee of leading churchmen asked Gordon and Pierson to return for another round, but Gordon's pastoral responsibilities kept him in Boston. For seven months Dr. and Mrs. Pierson traversed the United Kingdom. As many as six thousand people attended his speeches at one time. Refusing to collect offerings lest people be offended, Pierson was supported by the churches who sponsored him. The chief object of the speaking tour was to get people fired up about world evangelization. Local committees hosted the Piersons and planned the ecumenical engagements in each city, as well as prayed for their success. Pronounced a great triumph, Pierson's second Scottish tour accelerated popular interest in missions and inspired almost three hundred people to volunteer for missionary service. In addition to receiving an invitation to speak at the General Assembly of the Church of Scotland, he was invited to return in 1892 and deliver the quadrennial Duff Lectures in Missions at Scottish universities — probably the most prestigious lectureship in missions in the English-speaking world.

It is tempting to speculate that Dr. Pierson looked toward Scotland to escape the tensions building at home. With his resignation from Bethany Church and the spectacular failure of the Kansas-Sudan movement, he was struggling over the future of the missionary renaissance he had himself spearheaded. Now that the missionary flame was burning in the hearts of thousands of young people, what was the best way to channel their enthusiasm? What were the appropriate boundaries between the walk of faith and organizational structures? The established denominational mission societies simply did not have the financial resources or the flexibility to accommodate the range of people feeling called to missionary service. The heightened holiness spirituality of the youth, combined in many cases with their expectations of seeing God's kingdom fulfilled in their own lifetimes, made them impatient with denominational structures. An additional problem was that denominational missions in many cases required highly educated personnel to run the schools and hospitals they were founding in Asia in the late 1800s. What could be done with less educated missionary candidates who longed to serve the Lord in cross-cultural evangelism, but who could not meet the increasingly high qualifications required by the denominational missions?

A. T. Pierson was at the center of a network of people, who while being educated, well-established pastors of large churches, recognized that the ground swell of support for foreign missions required innovative methods of missionary training, the founding of experimental missions, new means of missionary support, and different rationales justifying the involvement of lay people in the mission of the church. Yet the new mission movement did not mean repudiating the hard work of the denominations. It was not intended to compete with mainstream theological seminaries, established mission boards, and the like, but rather to supplement them in response to the pressing "crisis of missions." Since denominational missions had their hands full with the "older" mission fields of India, the Middle East, and the coastal areas of East Asia, a whole new wave of missions needed to reach the unevangelized interiors of Asia, Africa, and Latin America. But of course not everyone saw the new mission movement as compatible with the old. Where Pierson saw nondenominationalism, others saw competition. Where Pierson and Moody saw "gap men," others saw a lowering of standards. Where Pierson, Moody, and Gordon saw premillennial urgency, others saw extremism. A. T. Pierson was trying to support new movements without alienating the older denominational missions.

During the early 1890s, Dr. Pierson found himself advising a burgeoning faith mission movement. The Kansas-Sudan movement was only one of many new enterprises that sought him out in their need for advice and bid for legitimacy. Despite his lack of foreign mission experience, Pierson was the most senior, influential American pastor willing to run interference for the new movements through the pages of his journal and in his public addresses. In numerous articles, he praised the experimentation possible under faith missions. His own attempt to live without a stated salary put him on the same spiritual wavelength of risk-taking as the young faith missionaries. It is impossible to reconstruct a history of all the young people with whom Dr. Pierson met privately to encourage in their desire for missionary service, particularly in the United Kingdom on his hundreds of speaking engagements. But a rundown of the faith missions of the 1890s shows contact between Pierson and the leaders of many of the important ones.

The China Inland Mission, begun in 1865 by J. Hudson Taylor, was of course the archetype for faith missions. Modeling his mission on the example of George Müller of Bristol, who supported thousands of orphans on faith, Taylor felt called to evangelize among the millions of Chinese inaccessible by ordinary mission societies. He embarked for China without treaty protection at a time when foreigners were not permitted in the interior. One of his innovations was that he wore Chinese dress. He sent lay missionaries, often women, two by two into the interior. In 1885, seven popular and athletic Cambridge University students garnered wide publicity for the China Inland Mission when they volunteered as missionaries with Hudson Taylor. The group included England's leading cricket player, C. T. Studd, and they caused a huge stir when they toured British universities speaking on behalf of the mission cause. The example of the "Cambridge Seven" attracted university-educated young people, the elite of British youth, to missions as nothing had done before. When in 1887 Taylor prayed in faith for one hundred new missionaries, they reached China with full support by the end of the year.

According to YMCA leader C. K. Ober, the deputation of the Cambridge Seven to British universities was "the germ thought of the SVM." The existence of the Cambridge Seven sparked interest in faith missions in general, and the China Inland Mission in particular, among the earliest signers of the Student Volunteer pledge. Yet Hudson Taylor himself, overburdened with responsibility for the CIM, was hesitant to spread his movement to North America. Long an admirer of Taylor, Arthur Pierson was a link in the chain by which the CIM was drawn into North America. In 1886, Presbyterian minister and Princeton graduate Henry Frost became converted to the cause of missions while listening to Pierson's address at the Niagara Bible Conference. From a wealthy family that supported evangelical and philanthropic causes, Frost traveled to England in December 1887 and sought a meeting with Hudson Taylor. John Forman and Robert Wilder, the first two traveling recruiters for the Student Volunteer Movement, were in Glasgow at the time and also desired to link the emerging American student movement with the China Inland Mission. Unsure at first of the reception they would get from established denominational missions, the nascent student movement was exploring all possibilities for missionary appointments.

Although Hudson Taylor refused Henry Frost's initial request to begin a North American branch of the China Inland Mission, Frost attracted Taylor to the idea of visiting North America on his way back to China. Notifying the Niagara Bible study and Dwight Moody at Northfield that Taylor might agree to visit if asked, the Niagara and Northfield Conference movements agreed to invite Taylor and underwrite his visit to the United States. The momentous visit of Hudson Taylor to North America in 1888 changed the history of faith missions. When he came, he had no thought of allowing the CIM to expand into North America. When he departed for China three months later, he took with him money, prayer support from hundreds of followers, and a band of chosen workers hand-picked from over forty volunteers.

Speaking to four hundred YMCA college men at the Northfield Conference in 1888, Taylor fanned into flame the sparks struck by mission speakers Pierson and Gordon. From Northfield Taylor moved on to the Niagara Bible Conference. The response there was so favorable that after Taylor left, Pierson and other missionary enthusiasts generated pledges for a year's support for eight new missionaries in China. Henry Frost collected the money as it came in, even though no North American volunteers for the CIM had as yet come forward. Returning to Northfield for another speaking engagement, Taylor was encouraged by Dwight Moody to appeal for missionary volunteers at the General Conference for Christian Workers. But the most decisive speaking engagement in persuading Hudson Taylor to open an American branch of the China Inland Mission was the response he received when he spoke to YMCA gatherings in Toronto, Canada. The outpouring of support was so huge, that after the Toronto YMCA held a farewell communion service for Taylor, between 500 and 1000 people accompanied Taylor to the train station. The spiritual energy was overwhelming, as the crowd prayed and sang. Recalled one of the leaders of the meeting, "Slowly the train moved away. As we returned the members of the Y.M.C.A. walked four abreast, singing hymns, up the streets of Toronto." When he sailed to China, Taylor took with him seven volunteers from the Hamilton, Ontario, YMCA.

Pierson's protégé, Henry Frost, became the founding home director of the American Council of the China Inland Mission. Because of the response in Toronto, it was decided to place the North American headquarters there. Under Frost's leadership, by the 1930s one-third of the missionaries of the China Inland Mission were volunteers from North America. Frost always credited Pierson as his inspiration in the cause of missions. Having seen each other at Niagara and Northfield, Hudson Taylor and Arthur Pierson maintained a close friendship and correspondence from the late 1880s onward. Besides writing many favorable articles about Taylor and the CIM, Pierson spent weeks off and on at the CIM Mission Home in London, enjoying prayer and spiritual fellowship with new missionary recruits. In the late 1890s, Taylor requested that Pierson come to China to lead a spiritual awakening among his missionaries, a plan that never materialized.

The most significant faith mission that began in North America was the Christian and Missionary Alliance, founded by Canadian A. B. Simpson. Pierson and Simpson had much in common and had known each other for decades. Both were Presbyterian ministers with large congregations, though Simpson left the denomination to form an independent church. Both were premillennialists, ran extensive lay training programs from their urban congregations, and maintained interests in holiness theology. During the 1870s, Simpson was pastor of the church where Pierson had been ordained — the Thirteenth Street Presbyterian in New York City. In imitation of Moody's Northfield conferences, Simpson held annual summer Bible conferences at Old Orchard Beach, Maine, at which Pierson frequently spoke during the 1890s. Simpson's combination of urban social and rescue work, with foreign missions emphasis, paralleled Pierson's own commitments. With a "four-fold Gospel" of conversion, entire sanctification, divine healing, and the Second Coming of Jesus Christ, Simpson founded both the Christian Alliance and the Evangelical Missionary Alliance in 1887. They later merged, creating the Christian and Missionary Alliance. By 1897, the organization was fielding 300 missionaries in numerous overseas locations. As the first well-known American faith mission, the Christian and Missionary Alliance attracted a number of experienced faith missionaries who were already on the mission field as free-lance workers.

But in 1897, Pierson began criticizing the Christian and Missionary Alliance for its methods. Pierson was not always comfortable with what he considered to be Simpson's extremism. Apparently a number of his missionaries had gone overseas on faith, and had been left stranded on the mission field, ill and without financial support. Pierson noted in *The Missionary Review* that he had frequently urged Simpson to reorganize the Alliance under a responsible committee. He urged Simpson and his wife, who acted as financial secretary and secretary of missionary appointment, to step down from the mission because they were mishandling its funds and the work had grown too large for them to handle. Pierson publicly withdrew his name from a circular endorsing the work of hundreds of faith missionaries who had gone out under the banner of the Alliance. At the same time, Pierson and Simpson were friends, and in the same year, Pierson published fourteen articles in Simpson's mission magazine.

Pierson's uneven relationship with the Christian and Missionary Alliance indicated that he was not an uncritical admirer of the new faith missions. He was wary of any faith mission that began developing a cult of personality. As he stated in *The Missionary Review*, "It is the arbitrary and often tyrannical mode of carrying on independent missions that brings them into disfavor." While encouraging the formation of faith missions at every point he could, Pierson called for improvements when he felt them justified. On his second Scottish tour, he had visited the McCall Mission in Paris, an urban faith mission that was a radiating center for evangelicalism in that largely Catholic and secular country. While praising the faithfulness of the work, he criticized McCall's tendency to drive his workers and neglect the laws of health.

Although he cheered the entrepreneurial spirit of the faith missions as both biblical and efficient, from a theological perspective Pierson believed that missions were the function of all the church's members. In his view, the ideal situation would be when the church and the mission society were seen as one, with every Christian personally responsible for world evangelization. The answer to the theological question of the nature of the church's responsibility for missions was what he called "individual links." Individual congregations and families should support their own missionaries in the field, while at the same time relating responsibly to the larger church. The idea of "individual links" was what he had proposed to the Presbytery of Philadelphia in 1885. He speculated in 1898 that if the Presbyterian denomination could persuade five hundred congregations to support their own missionaries at a rate of two thousand dollars a year, keeping in touch with them by prayer, letters, and study, then the Presbyterian Church would have a million dollars for its mission work instead of always lagging behind. "To allow the missionary agency to be crippled by an empty treasury and half wreckt by debt, is something for which, therefore, every church-member is responsible." The idea of "individual links" would solve the problems of both denominational support for the mission of the church, and that of faith missions becoming the fiefdom of powerful individuals. Implicit in Pierson's theology of the church was that it was a gathered community of believers who had been saved by their individual relationships with Jesus Christ. Coming from a revivalistic spiritual tradition, Pierson emphasized an individualistic theology of both the church and its mission.

The faith mission in which Pierson was the most intimately involved was the Africa Inland Mission. Through the Kansas-Sudan movement and the influence of both Grattan Guinness and A. J. Gordon, Pierson had become aware that the African interior was a vital area needing missionary outreach. In 1895, he helped found the Africa Inland Mission. Pierson's involvement came about through a young Scot, Peter Cameron Scott, who had emigrated with his family to Philadelphia in 1879. Training under A. B. Simpson, Scott went to West Africa under the Missionary Alliance in 1890. His brother John joined him, but died of fever. While in England recovering from parasites, Peter Scott got the idea of approaching Africa from the eastern side so as to escape malaria. As had David Livingstone, Ludwig Krapf, William Taylor, and other famous missionaries before him, Scott envisioned a chain of mission stations across Africa that would both block the spread of Islam and facilitate the evangelization of Africa. Approaching Dr. Pierson for advice, Scott was persuaded to form a committee that would provide stability for the movement.

In 1895, Peter Scott, Pierson, C. E. Hurlburt, and others formed the home committee of the Africa Inland Mission. Hurlburt and Pierson were friends, for Hurlburt was state secretary of the YMCA for Pennsylvania and the two had prayed together while Pierson was still at Bethany Church. With Hurlburt as the elected chairman, the Philadelphia Mission Council founded the Africa Inland Mission to focus on evangelism by lay people: "If the world is to be evangelized in this generation there must be a vast increase in the army of messengers, but there cannot be any vast increase save by the enlistment of thousands of lay workers. It is from such that the African [sic] Inland Mission expects its material to come." The Africa Inland Mission drew many of its early missionaries from the new Pennsylvania Bible Institute, a lay training enterprise that shared quarters with the mission. The first party of eight AIM missionaries departed on August 9, 1895, for Zanzibar.

It soon appeared that the AIM would follow the tragic course of the Kansas-Sudan movement. Despite a promising beginning of four mission stations stretching from the coast into what came to be called Kenya, Peter Scott died of blackwater fever in 1896. Fever, lack of food, and exhaustion felled other members of the pioneer party, and the mission council asked Pierson whether the mission should continue. After prayer, Pierson concluded that the difficulties through which the mission had passed were caused by satanic opposition. He urged it to lay hold of God's promises and move forward. In 1901, Charles Hurlburt took his family and moved to Kenya to direct the Africa Inland Mission on site. Under his leadership, the faith mission recovered its equilibrium and expanded into Tanganyika and the Congo.

Pierson encouraged other young faith missionaries from around the world, many of whose names have been lost to history. While dozens of faith missions were founded between 1889 and 1895, not all of them survived as independent entities, and some merged into others of similar aim. A few of the leaders who are known to have been guided by Pierson, however, include Samuel Zwemer, an early student volunteer converted to missions by Pierson's preaching. Unable to find a mission that would take him and his classmate James Cantine, Zwemer founded the American Arabian Mission in 1889. Five years later, the Reformed Church of America adopted the mission, and Zwemer became one of its most beloved missionaries. Another important faith mission advised by Pierson was the South African Cape General Mission, founded in 1889. Its founder, Spencer Walton, was referred to Pierson for advice by the great South African spiritual writer Andrew Murray, whom Pierson had met in England. Walton visited Pierson in 1903. Dr. Pierson was also the means of inspiring a group of seven young men from Belfast, Ireland, to found the Egypt Mission Band. After hearing him speak on April 30, 1897, at the YMCA hall in Belfast on the current crisis of mission, the men spent the night in prayer. They opened a faith mission in Egypt the following year, which by 1910 was fielding twenty-seven missionaries.

Charles and Lettie Burd Cowman, founders of the Oriental Missionary Society, were indebted to Pierson's advice and quoted his books frequently. After her conversion in 1893, Mrs. Cowman carried around a booklet by Pierson entitled "Answered Prayer." While seeking their way to the mission field, they consulted with Pierson in the mid-1890s. Although Charles Cowman felt called to India, his wife did not. In the words of Mrs. Cowman about her husband's spiritual journey to the mission field, "In the providence of God, he at this time met Dr. Arthur T. Pierson, who had heard of his work in the telegraph office, and of the influence he was exerting in his own church among the young people. He said to him with much emphasis, 'Wait, young man, wait God's hour.'" Pierson's advice to Charles Cowman was key to his decision to wait until God opened the proper mission field — Japan, and then Korea. Committed throughout their lives to "the evangelization of the world in this generation," the Cowmans heeded Pierson's advice and started a holiness mission that grew into the third largest denomination in Korea. They also endorsed Pierson's views that "facts are the fingers of God" when founding their mission periodical, *Electric Messages.* Mrs. Cowman wrote of her husband, "He greatly loved his friend Dr. Arthur T. Pierson and his books were eagerly read." In the Cowmans' "Great Village Campaign" to reach every household in Japan with the gospel, their purpose was to follow Jesus' command to preach the gospel to all the world, so that the end would come. The men the Cowmans admired as being the most committed to the evangelization of the world in their own generation were A. T. Pierson, John Mott, Dwight Moody, A. J. Gordon, Hudson Taylor, A. B. Simpson, and William Blackstone.

The creative tension between faith missions and denominational missions was evident at the First International Convention of the Student Volunteer Movement, held at the new YMCA building in Cleveland in late February 1891. Under John Mott's skillful leadership as head of the executive committee, and with the hard work of traveling secretaries, branches of the SVM had been founded in colleges throughout the United States. Six thousand young people had joined the movement as prospective missionaries. Taking the phrase "the evangelization of the world in this generation" as its keynote, the conference sought to make connections among individual student volunteers, mission boards, and experienced missionaries. Among the practical results of the conference was to prevent the SVM from being pulled wholesale into the faith mission movement by bringing together denominational loyalists, some of whom were critics of the student movement, and student volunteers themselves. Representatives from 32 mission boards or societies attended the conference, of which half represented women's societies. Returned missionaries also numbered 32, most of whom were connected with denominations but a few with the new faith missions. With 558 students from 151 educational institutions in attendance, the First International Convention made it clear to the participating mission boards that student mobilization for world evangelization was a vision whose time had come — and they had better get on the bandwagon.

The conference was a watershed for the student mission movement. Even as the YMCA was unwittingly providing the founding leaders for new faith missions, in particular the China Inland Mission (North America), the Kansas-Sudan movement, and the Africa Inland Mission, John Mott knew that linkage with established denominations would determine the success or failure of the Student Volunteer Movement. The conference program reflected a skillful balance between inspirational speeches by advisory board members A. J. Gordon and A. T. Pierson and their protégés Robert Wilder and Robert Speer; and practical presentations on medical, educational, literary, evangelistic, and women's missions by experienced mission personnel. While the exciting vision that drew the students was world evangelization, the subtext of the conference was the necessity of pragmatic reflection as well as dependence on prayer under the guidance of the Holy Spirit.

As the acknowledged author of the official Student Volunteer Watchword "the evangelization of the world in this generation," A. T. Pierson gave a major address the second evening. He was preceded by Robert Speer, who spoke of the real possibilities of successful world evangelization based on the idea that missionaries were responsible for spreading the gospel, not converting the world. Pierson spoke on how to make world evangelization a fact. With echoes of the optimistic passion characteristic of his Civil War generation, he began, "This is a council of war. In the tent of the Commander we are gathered, and the Commander-in-chief is here. . . . And the question for consideration is, How can the marching orders of this invisible Captain be carried out promptly and energetically?"

Among the features of the day making possible the successful fulfillment of the Commander's orders, the Great Commission, was the openness of the world to the gospel message. Not only was it politically possible in the age of European imperialism to reach the peoples of the world, but the means of technology, inventions, and modern science made it technically possible: "Science is the handmaid to piety in these days. She offers us every facility that even the imagination of man could have suggested to accomplish this warfare of the ages." Pierson continued in prophetic voice, "It may be that twenty-five years hence we shall be navigating the air as now the waters." Relying on the men, money, and methods to make world evangelization succeed, he advocated the biblical policy of "diffusion" — "scattering the seed of the kingdom over the whole field."

Yet, in the final analysis, Pierson continued, only the coming of the Holy Spirit would make possible the evangelization of the world in this generation. Only reliance on the supernatural power of God, confirmed by Christ's authority and the witness of the Holy Ghost, could make the work succeed. Urging the students to do their part in spreading the gospel throughout the world, Pierson pleaded that the year should not pass before every hundred square miles on the earth would have its witness. The result of such diffusion of the mission force "would be an outpouring of the Holy Ghost to which even Pentecost would be simply the first drops of a coming latter rain." Without world evangelization, he concluded, the church at home would die. "I say to you the hope of the Church of God is missions. It is not simply how we shall save the world, but how we shall save ourselves."

In the context of the First International Convention of the Student Volunteer Movement, A. T. Pierson's speech on world evangelization represented a plea for as wide a mobilization as possible for world evangelization. In urging missions to "scatter the force," he was implicitly calling for the missionary innovation and rapid deployment made possible by faith missions. Rather than pouring volunteers into established mission centers, world evangelization required risk-taking dependence on the supernatural power of God. To use the terminology of a later century, Pierson was calling for the student volunteers to devote themselves to "pioneer missions" among the "unreached peoples" of the world. Even as John Mott and the YMCA officials were ensuring the respectability of the student movement by linking it to denominational missions, A. T. Pierson was promoting a Spirit-powered vision that could not be contained within the clerical establishment. It was the exploitation of the creative tension between vision and organization that ultimately guaranteed the success of the Student Volunteer Movement in providing thousands of missionaries for denominational and faith missions alike.

Disputes over how to support the new wave of missionaries in the 1890s were both public and painful for A. T. Pierson. The worst event in the struggle over mission support occurred at the Northfield Conference of 1897, and between Pierson and his friend Dwight Moody. Moody had backed Pierson during the Kansas-Sudan movement crisis in the YMCA. As old YMCA men whose piety was deepened in the revivals of 1857-58, they both opposed trends toward secularization in Protestant organizations. During a meeting conducted by the head of missions for the American Baptists, sentiments arose in favor of doing something for young men rejected by mission boards because of a lack of funds. Pierson moved to collect money at Northfield to help mission boards send out such men. Even though $5000 was pledged in half an hour, Moody opposed the plan. He feared it would establish a de facto mission board at Northfield that would compete with denominational boards. Upon learning of Moody's hesitation, Pierson withdrew the motion. Moody reiterated his confidence in the established channels and asked that people send their money directly to their denominational mission boards.

The press turned the situation into the "croaker" incident — one that painted Pierson and his supporters as "croakers" who lacked faith in their denominations. Pierson defended himself in *The Missionary Review* by tacitly accusing Moody of hypocrisy. Moody, he complained, opposed collecting money "outside of regular channels," yet he ran independent ministries that had provoked the same criticism from others: "Our dear brother, Mr. Moody, however fully in sympathy with the Boards, no doubt believes there are many organizations 'outside of regular channels' that God is greatly using, and he is not the man to hint that all who differ from the established methods, or encourage these outside agencies, are to be put down as croakers." The evangelist's fear of offending the denominations that provided much of his support contrasted oddly with the reality of his educational enterprises — especially with Moody Bible Institute, most of whose graduate missionaries served under faith missions.

In the final analysis, the struggle over whether missions should be funded the "normal" way — through denominational agencies and set budgets, or by "faith" — through individual dependence on God's will for sustenance, were symptomatic of the tensions in evangelicalism at the turn of the century. Moody's awkward position was actually the norm for many senior supporters of the new faith missions. Men like Pierson and Gordon saw themselves both as faithful, lifelong members of denominations, and as innovators for the sake of world evangelization. In the 1890s, leaders of faith missions were loath to cut themselves off from their denominations, even if they found them inflexible and stodgy. Faith missions represented interdenominational unity, not the creation of new denominations to replace the old ones. At one level, the conflict between denominational budgeting and faith missions was a rejection of the increasingly middle-class "establishment" mentality of the older Protestant denominations. Increased prosperity from the 1870s onward was accompanied by the development of denominational bureaucracies, and of professional attitudes toward the funding of institutions. Yet the spirituality of the faith mission movement rejected such middle-class assumptions as unfaithful and materialistic. At another level, the faith mission movement represented sustained belief in the supernatural providence of God, as opposed to the increasingly naturalistic theological outlook of many middle-class Protestants. To live "on faith" was to reject the materialistic secularizing of American churches in the late 1800s, as much as it represented an effective method through which to deploy additional workers for the evangelization of the world.

By the end of the century, it was perhaps inevitable that a widening gap separated denominational missions from the faith missions. Even though A. T. Pierson made periodic speaking tours on behalf of Presbyterian missions in the early 1890s, his support for faith methods irritated leaders in his own denomination. He resigned from one Presbyterian mission tour on principle because there was no money to pay him except by diverting funds collected for missionaries. His stance was tantamount to questioning the legitimacy of church agencies. Presbyterian leaders attacked the "faith method" of missionary support. Some denominational officials worried that faith missions threatened their collections by making the denominational boards seem unnecessary or unspiritual because they made budgetary projections before hiring new missionaries.

A leader of the Presbyterian mission board, Dr. Frank Ellinwood, singled out the Kansas-Sudan movement as an example of the danger of faith missions. Its missionaries had died from lack of support, he argued. George Müller and Hudson Taylor were successful because they were well organized and their faith methods were a novelty. But the proliferation of faith movements in the 1890s meant that the novelty had worn off, and support for them inevitably would drop. While encouraging prayer, Ellinwood argued that the Bible nevertheless taught the use of means when they were available. In his book *Questions and Phases of Modern Missions*, published in 1899, Ellinwood argued that "prayer without the use of means, where means can be employed, is a new doctrine." Faith missions idolized money acquired through "faith" while they disintegrated from failure to employ "means." Criticisms of faith missions kept growing among denominational mission executives, who blamed their lack of financial receipts to competition from independent groups. Beginning in 1898, and finalized in 1911, the Foreign Missions Conference of North America adopted rules that effectively excluded faith missions from participating in the ecumenical body of mission societies.

THE CASE FOR LAY MISSIONARIES

While he disagreed with the Presbyterian Board of Missions over methods of financial support for missions, the most serious problem Pierson had with denominational structures was his eventual rejection of what he believed was a nonbiblical distinction between ordained and lay church workers. In a striking contrast to his early pursuit of clerical authority, Pierson rejected a clerical "caste system" in the mission of the church and came to believe that the concept of ordination was not biblical. Missions were the responsibility of every believer rather than the privilege of a few seminary-educated ministers. By the 1890s, his views on the "priesthood of all believers" had moved him in a revolutionary direction. Despite being an ordained minister in the Protestant denomination that historically required the highest standard of education for its clergy, A. T. Pierson threw his support behind a lay training movement that promised to turn out large numbers of mission workers. With the "fields ripe for the harvest," what was needed were "eleventh hour" workers who could gather in the souls before the coming of the kingdom. While Pierson did not go around insulting the ordained ministry, his expectations of the imminent Second Coming meant that there simply was not time to send all mission workers through a full course of seminary training. The mission of the church was the responsibility of every believer — male or female, lay or ordained, rich or poor, educated or illiterate.

From his years in Detroit, Pierson had dedicated much of his time to lay Bible training. In each city where he worked, he ran weekly Bible studies for the Sunday School teachers of the city, often held in the YMCA building. While at Bethany Church, he taught the Bible in the night school for workingmen run by the church. Even after resigning from the regular pastorate, he continued teaching a large Bible class in Philadelphia. His work as Bible expositor was the basis for his reputation.

A. T. Pierson's devotion to equipping the laity for active ministry was shared by a network of like-minded urban pastors, who found that educational ministries grew out of their parish work. In the 1880s, a number of pastors of large churches in northern cities started Bible training programs on the side. Perhaps like Dwight Moody, they sensed that American society was turning away from the simple faith of an earlier day. Only study of God's Word could ground people sufficiently to help them navigate a society ever more hostile to evangelical Protestantism. Increasing acceptance of higher criticism and Darwinian science confused ordinary people in the pews, who wished to know what the Bible said on such matters. With the conversion of immigrants to evangelical Protestantism, pastors could not assume a high level of biblical literacy in their congregations. What seems safe to conclude is that those pastors who felt a strong need for lay Bible study programs were also those who preached a message that attracted newcomers into the church. Perhaps church growth itself made clear the necessity for Bible training. Or it could be that Bible training caused church growth by equipping the membership for evangelism. Sunday School teachers who went into urban slums to teach poor children felt a keen need for background study in the Bible and in evangelistic methods. City mission workers holding English classes for immigrants requested Bible classes to ground their work. In an age of intellectual change and social turmoil, the Bible was a bulwark in the storm.

For mission supporters like Pierson, the founding of Bible training programs had the added purpose of preparing workers for world evangelization. It was not enough to convert people and bring them into the church. Once converted, they needed to be equipped and sent back into the world for mission. After all, the church was a "rallying and radiating point" for world evangelization. The faith mission movement and the Bible training school movement operated like hand in glove. As lay people awakened to the cause of foreign missions, they sought short courses of Bible study that would qualify them for evangelistic work in a faith mission. In the United States, over sixty "religious training schools" opened between the years 1880 and 1915 to train evangelical social workers, foreign missionaries, and Christian educators. These Bible and training schools experienced great popularity until after World War I when the professionalization of city mission work put many of them out of business. As Bible study and social work grew apart, some training schools made the transition into being full Bible colleges with strong mission departments. Others that survived were absorbed into professional schools for social work.

Even as Arthur Pierson counseled young faith missionaries, he became involved on the ground floor of at least nine different Bible and missionary training schools, most of which followed premillennial interpretations of the Bible. His work as a Bible teacher rode the wave of an explosion of urban lay people clamoring for English-language Bible training. His own work in Philadelphia fed into what became the Pennsylvania Bible Institute, the feeder school for the Africa Inland Mission. By 1958 it had become the Philadelphia College of the Bible. The oldest school in which Pierson gave Bible lectures was the New York Missionary Training College, founded by A. B. Simpson in the early 1880s out of his independent Gospel Tabernacle. The purpose of Simpson's school, which developed into Nyack College, was to give lay missionaries a firm foundation in the Scriptures and in aggressive evangelistic methods.

In 1885, one of the committee members on Pierson's Northfield plan for world evangelization was Emma Dryer, who the next year founded with Dwight Moody's support a Bible Institute in Chicago. Later renamed the Moody Bible Institute, the school trained lay missionaries, the "gap men" of Moody's famous speech. Bible Institute students took to the garrets and alleys of Chicago, spreading the Good News, passing out tracts, and ministering to the poor. Located in mid-Chicago, it became a model for evangelistic outreach. As an occasional lecturer there over a twenty-year period, Pierson taught courses in Genesis, Acts, Psalms, the Gospel and Epistles of John, the Believer's Union with Christ, the Oracles of God, and missionary biography. Pierson had close relationships with both R. A. Torrey and James M. Gray, who each headed the Bible Institute during his lifetime. As of 1978, one in every eighteen North American missionaries was a graduate of Moody Bible Institute.

The Centenary Conference of 1888 was a turning point not only for A. T. Pierson, but for his companion A. J. Gordon, who returned to Boston determined to do more for the cause of world evangelization. Inspired by the missionary training school of Grattan and Lucy Guinness, in 1889 Gordon opened the Boston Missionary Training School in his church building. Although the American Baptists had accepted the transfer of Guinness's Livingstone Inland Mission, they still had not provided any reinforcements. Guinness was disturbed about the situation and urged Gordon to remedy it. Like Pierson, Gordon was frustrated at the long training period required for missionaries, and he opened his school on faith, without funds. With the Bible as its textbook, its purpose was to provide free or inexpensive Bible training to those who felt called to evangelistic and mission work. The Baptist press attacked the establishment of Gordon's school as a move to reverse educational qualifications for Baptist ministers. Its existence accused seminary education of incompetence. Gordon was castigated by other Baptist leaders as a premillennial fanatic and accused of aiding "short-cut" routes to the ministry. Gordon defended himself by saying that his school was a command from God for providing "eleventh hour" workers and was not intended to compete with theological seminaries. Arthur Pierson supported Gordon in his school and taught short Bible courses there. Pierson would play a major role in its operation after 1895.

Other Bible and missionary training schools at which Pierson gave lectures on the Bible and missions included the Toronto Bible Institute and the Bible Institute of Los Angeles. Pierson spoke in Toronto whenever he undertook speaking tours through Canada. He was friends with Toronto pastor Henry Parsons, one of the Niagara network and key sponsor of Hudson Taylor's Toronto speaking tour. BIOLA was founded in 1908 by Pierson's convert, associate minister at Bethany and partner in urban evangelism, T. C. Horton. In New York City, Pierson lectured at the Bible Teachers' Training School, later renamed Biblical Seminary. Dr. Wilbert White, brother of J. Campbell White of the Student Volunteer Movement and of Leila White Mott, John R. Mott's wife, founded Biblical Seminary in 1900. White had received a Ph.D. from Yale in Semitic Languages, and served two years as a Bible teacher in India. The curriculum revolved around the study of the English Bible. White employed methods of "inductive" Bible study promoted by Pierson and also copied at Moody Bible Institute by its president, James M. Gray. The purpose of inductive Bible study was to help the student get a picture of the Bible as an integral whole.

The founding of missionary training schools was to critics yet another danger imbedded in the idea of "the evangelization of the world in this generation." Short-term training for thousands of evangelistic missionaries, who were then unleashed under experimental faith missions, threatened to destabilize long-term aspects of Protestant missions such as upper-level schools, hospitals, and the production of Christian literature. Part of the criticism of premillennialism was that it undercut Christian institutions. And Pierson's sustained focus on immediate evangelization certainly gave the impression that he cared little for Christian institutions. In an essay "The Great Call of God to His Church," printed in the June 1892 issue of *The Missionary Review*, Pierson defined evangelization as making people acquainted with the gospel tidings without waiting for results: "To stop or linger anywhere, even to repeat the rejected message, so long as there are souls beyond that have never heard it, is at least unjust to those who are still in absolute darkness. Instead of creating a few centres of intense light, God would have us scatter the lamps until all darkness is at least relieved, if not removed." Pierson's rhetoric alarmed mission leaders, and in the November issue of *The Missionary Review,* he found himself having to clarify that his premillennial urgency did not exclude Christian institutions from the tasks of Christian mission. He was merely emphasizing that Christians must not loiter in any particular mission field, waiting for full results, before opening new missions. "Dr. Gordon and myself firmly believe that 'preaching the Gospel as a witness among all nations' means setting up churches, schools, a sanctified press, medical missions, and, in fact, all the institutions which are the fruit of Christianity and constitute *part of its witness.* . . . Missions begin in evangelization, but have *everything* to do with Christian education, and the printing press, and the organization of churches, and the training of a native pastorate." In terms of mission strategy, *The Missionary Review* was merely prioritizing evangelistic contact as the first duty of missions, not the only duty. Both Arthur Pierson and Judson Gordon preferred a strategy of "diffusion" in missions over that of "centralization."

A. T. Pierson's rejection of ordination as necessary for missionaries, and his accompanying support for lay training schools, upset many people. But the revolutionary edge of his message became even sharper when it became clear that by "lay missionaries," A. T. Pierson and others included "lay women." In the 1880s and 1890s, "lay" was a code word for "female." The advent of women's missionary societies in the 1870s, followed by the student mission movement of the 1880s and the faith missions and Bible training schools of the 1890s, led to the greatest expansion in the percentage of women missionaries in the history of the church. The rationales given for the ministry of lay people were in many respects arguments for the ministry of women. The great majority of Sunday School teachers and city mission workers were women. The majority of people excluded from colleges and theological seminaries were women. Therefore, in many training schools, like that of A. J. Gordon, the overwhelming majority of students were women. Women were the majority of people spiritually able and willing to live on the uncertainties of the "faith basis," and they crowded into faith missions to such an extent that they came to outnumber men by two to one. To erase the distinction between lay and ordained meant eliminating the barriers to women in ministry, for had not women been the last at the cross, and the first at the tomb? To define the church as mission, and to give every believer the responsibility for mission, meant empowering women.

In his early years of ministry, Pierson expressed limited support for women's active participation in church life. He encouraged women to speak in prayer meetings in the mid-1860s. At that time, he agreed that the Bible forbade women to speak in church, but he argued based on women's presence in the upper room that they were permitted to speak in home-like prayer meetings. By the 1870s, Pierson was delivering public lectures on Mary Lyon, the founder of Mt. Holyoke Female Seminary, to raise money for women's education in Michigan. As his system of reading Scripture developed in the late 1870s, his interpretation of passages on women's right to speak in church broadened. In sermon notes entitled "The Song of Mary," dated January 9, 1881, Pierson argued that when Mary bore Christ, the curse of Eve was erased. The motherhood of Mary was the "type" that marked the end of the Genesis restrictions on women: "From that hour *Woman* [has] been rising. Must *rise* wherever Christianity goes. Gospel *begins* by exalting womanhood, and, mark, *virginity*. Mary the Mother. No Man the Father of Messiah." In his jottings, Pierson made a point made much later by feminist theologians: that Christ's conception out of wedlock exalted woman in a way that would not have happened had Jesus been Joseph's son.

During the 1870s, as women's missionary societies took hold in Presbyterianism and other mainstream denominations, Pierson became convinced not only from the Bible but from experience that God was blessing women's missionary work. By the 1880s, he had absorbed the arguments put forth by women's missionary societies that women were uniquely gifted to shape the structures of society because of their influence on children. Echoing the woman's missionary slogan "woman's work for woman," Pierson underscored the importance of women's influence in the home as decisive for world evangelization. His views on women's ministry were fairly progressive. Not everyone in the denominations approved of the women's missionary movement, and in their early decades the women's missionary societies possessed the same "outsider" status as did the faith missions of the 1890s. Particularly in the South, women's missionary societies faced lengthy struggles for acceptance even of "auxiliary" status. Yet A. T. Pierson staunchly defended the right of women to have their own missionary societies and to be missionaries, and his wife remained active in women's mission circles. As Pierson's premillennial system of biblical interpretation grew more set in the 1880s, he expanded the scope of women's work beyond the home. It is not clear exactly when he crossed the line into believing that women had a right to preach, but his first article written for *The Missionary Review of the World* was on how the recruitment of women, as evidenced by the women's missionary societies, would solve the missionary problem of lack of personnel.

By around 1890, Pierson's views on women and ministry had grown radical for Presbyterians of his day. He began defending the right of women to preach, and by the middle of the decade, *The Missionary Review* carried a favorable article on women as pastors. The journal remarked on the significance of the Salvation Army's Maud Booth receiving a nondenominational ordination in 1897. As Pierson's biblical studies convinced him that there was no fixed line between clergy and laity in the early church, and that the Lord's Supper was a household ordinance that succeeded Passover, objections to women's ministry on sacramental grounds dropped away. The impact of being father to five daughters should not be underestimated. By the mid-1890s, Arthur Pierson was not only the father of a missionary wife in Japan, but one of his unmarried daughters was a home missionary in Vermont where she acted as pastor and conducted church services among the poor. The influence of A. J. Gordon was also important for Pierson's views. Not only did Mrs. Maria Gordon preach to mixed crowds in Scotland, and the Gordons support women's suffrage, but Gordon explicitly defended the role of unmarried women as missionary evangelists and the use of "Bible women" as mission agents in China.

The decisive arguments for Pierson in support of the full participation of women in missions were his dispensational reading of the Bible, and the argument from "facts" — the indisputable effectiveness of women preachers down through history. In Bible notes from the 1890s on "Woman's mission and ministry," Pierson stated that the entire question of woman's role needed to be "reconstructed." There was a danger in clinging to the past, even as there was a danger in abandoning it completely. The Bible showed four periods in the history of women: the Edenic, or ideal period; the Fall and consequent degradation; the age of Christ, and his redemption of women from the Fall; and the age of Missions, when women's role was returned to the original, Edenic ideal. And what was the role of woman in the Garden of Eden? That of duality in humanity, and of mutuality and joint authority with man. Since the time of the Fall, woman had been kept down by ignorance and domestic "slavery." But the original intent of God's creation was that human nature was dual. Pierson's reading of the Bible in the original Hebrew showed him that, rather than meaning "servant of Adam," "helpmate" meant "counterpart" — a relationship of partnership with man.

The issue of women's ministry in relation to equipping lay people for missions blew wide open in 1894 when *The Missionary Review* carried both a major editorial on women's rights to preach, and a ground-breaking article by A. J. Gordon entitled "The Ministry of Women." In the editorial, Pierson argued that "woman has a missionary apostolate." Responding to interpretations of Paul's words that forbade women to speak in church, Pierson noted that his words merely regulated women's speaking. While women were not to "usurp authority" over men,

> the idea that any Scripture forbids woman to tell the Gospel story, or to teach the unsaved great saving truths, is a strange perversion of the Word of God. While Christ Himself owned the Samaritan woman's preaching, and made Mary of Magdala His first witness of His resurrection; so long as Priscilla taught Apollos and Phoebe was a deaconess who labored with Paul in the Gospel; so long as the sixteenth chapter of Romans stands to qualify the apparent teaching of the Epistles to Corinth, can we have any real doubt that woman is man's authorized co-worker in missions? And if such false exegesis needs any other corrective, is not mission history enough?

Following up the historical argument for woman in mission, Pierson addressed the 25th Anniversary of the Woman's Foreign Missionary Society of the Presbyterian Churches of Philadelphia in a speech entitled "Woman as a Factor in the World's Evangelization." He also wrote a major article on women's work as one of the great spiritual movements of the century. His book on the subject, *Catherine of Siena: An Ancient Lay Preacher*, appeared in 1898. In writing a book on the great fourteenth-century preacher, Dominican sister, prayer warrior, and reformer of church and society, Pierson was arguing through Catherine's biography that women should be allowed to preach. He stated in the introduction, "The elements of true testimony are independent of sex; and there is an especial fitness in bringing to the front such a woman preacher in the day when godly women are first coming into real prominence as workers in the mission field at home and abroad, and when the sisterhood of the race seems to be for the first time mounting to the true throne of woman's influence and kingdom."

A. J. Gordon's defense of women's ministry was made necessary by criticism of the number of women enrolled at the Boston Missionary Training School. So many women attended Gordon's school that there was talk at one point of making it into a female school only. Not only were mainline denominations generally uncomfortable with women preachers, but not all premillennialists agreed either. Even if the temperance ministry of Mrs. Gordon had not been enough to convince her husband of the importance of women preachers, then the success of Baptist women missionaries like Adele Fielde, who trained Chinese "Bible women" as evangelists, was decisive. Like Pierson, Gordon's reading of the Bible gave him a rationale for defending women's ministry on the basis of "end times" prophecies. The prophet Joel clearly stated that in the latter days of waiting for Christ's Second Coming, "Your sons and your daughters shall prophesy." The current dispensation of the Holy Spirit gave women "equal warrant with man's for telling out the Gospel of the grace of God." Reviewing the Greek for various Pauline passages that had been used against women's ministry, Gordon pointed to places where Scripture had been deliberately mistranslated in order to limit women's sphere. The Bible clearly showed that women in the New Testament church acted as deacons, teachers, and even apostles.

The huge expansion of the lay missionary force that began in the 1880s was made possible in part by the defense of women's right to preach by premillennialists like A. T. Pierson and A. J. Gordon. Encouragement of women's ministry through Bible and missionary training schools gave faith missions the personnel they needed to open missions all over the world. "The evangelization of the world in this generation" may have started among the Mount Hermon 100, all men, but its prosecution was made possible by the thousands of women who became independent and faith missionaries. While the Student Volunteer Movement was aimed toward the college-educated, who tended to be males attracted to denominational mission societies, the faith mission movement drew the "rejects" of those same societies — women who had been denied advanced education by their poverty or gender, and who were thus unable to secure appointments in the established missions.

Exploration into the early history of faith missions shows a large number of mission fields opened by unmarried women. Hudson Taylor's reliance on women missionaries, sent two by two into China's interior, was legendary. In the Christian and Missionary Alliance, unmarried women opened the missions in India, Japan, Palestine, and Venezuela; and its Congo mission was opened by two men and two women. Throughout the 1890s, two-thirds of Alliance missionaries were women. The openness of the Christian and Missionary Alliance to women's ministry was a key to its head start in attracting missionaries from North America. As early as 1881, founder A. B. Simpson argued in his mission periodical *The Gospel in All Lands* that the Bible had been mistranslated to exclude women as evangelists in Psalm 68:11. The proper translation about spreading the Good News was "great was the company of women that published it."

For A. T. Pierson, A. J. Gordon, A. B. Simpson, and other fathers of the faith mission movement, the Scriptures permitted the ministry of women. Because of their lack of concern about ordination, the sacramental ministry of women was not an issue for them. Also, partnership in world evangelization did not mean that women and men brought identical gifts to mission work, as in some twentieth-century views of gender equality. Pierson continued to believe that the natures of men and women differed in essential ways. Nevertheless, the expansion of evangelization movements in the 1890s was made possible by equipping the laity in Bible and missionary training programs, and placing them in faith missions. And in two out of three cases, the laity were women.

THE METROPOLITAN TABERNACLE

A. T. Pierson's decision to leave the pastoral ministry and become a campaigner for world evangelization coincided with a burst of literary productivity. Always a prolific writer, he had published hundreds of sermons, lectures, and articles in the religious press. As editor of an eighty-page monthly mission magazine, and frequent contributor to other journals, the number of articles he published was in the thousands by the end of his life. From the mid-1880s into the twentieth century, his literary output was staggering, ranging from small books of sermons, advice on homiletics, and reflections on spirituality, to large books on missions or Bible study. In the late 1880s appeared *The Crisis of Missions; Evangelistic Work in Principle and Practice;* "God's Hand in Missions" (bound with a new edition of the *Memoirs of Rev. David Brainerd); Keys to the Word; Many Infallible Proofs;* "Our Lord's Second Coming a Motive to World-Wide Evangelization"; and *The Inspired Word.* His most significant books published in the 1890s included *The Acts of the Holy Spirit; The Divine Art of Preaching; The Divine Enterprise of Missions; George Müller of Bristol; The Greatest Work in the World; The Miracles of Missions* (4 volumes); *The New Acts of the Apostles; Seven Years in Sierra Leone; Shall We Continue in Sin?;* and *The Coronation Hymnal* (with A. J. Gordon). In an age before radio and television, with an evangelical audience from the United Kingdom to North America eager for mission studies, Bible studies, and aids to prayer life, Pierson's books spread all over the world and inspired multiple generations. His books on spiritual life and Bible study were still being reprinted a century later.

If he had not shaken free from regular pastoral ministry, it is unlikely that A. T. Pierson's literary productivity would have been so high in the last twenty-five years of his life. Undoubtedly Pierson's writings provided income that supported his family. Pierson's publications kept his ideas circulating and his bank account open. Prominent faith missionaries relied on publications to attract support: George Müller and Hudson Taylor both relied on annual reports of their work to stimulate donations. The famous Methodist missionary evangelist William Taylor, the apostle of "self-support," paid for his itinerant, globe-trotting lifestyle through book sales. Pierson's ability to support his family on a "faith basis" attests to his prominence in mission circles. Many of the books consisted of lectures and sermons delivered on the mission or Bible study circuit. Another way of supporting his family was through acting as supply preacher. Pierson preached in the First, Fourth Avenue, and Fifth Avenue Presbyterian Churches in New York City, First Baptist in New York City, and other leading pulpits.

On his Scottish tour of 1890, Pierson also deepened his network of contacts in England. In London, he addressed a meeting convened by the mission secretaries of the Congregationalists, Baptists, Presbyterians, and Wesleyans. He gave the closing prayer at the farewell meeting of the Church Missionary Society on January 20 for Bishop Crowther's return to West Africa, accompanied by a group of new English recruits who shared Pierson's commitment to rapid world evangelization. The group of missionaries would soon be embroiled in "firing" Crowther, the first African Anglican bishop, in events that have gone down in mission history as an example of missionary racism and arrogance. Together with the revivalist Major Whittle, who had been so important to Pierson's spiritual development in Detroit, the Piersons made a tour of Europe during which he spoke to Protestant groups in Catholic-dominated Italy and France. British evangelicals maintained a tradition of holding annual public meetings to showcase the accomplishments and needs of various benevolent societies. Pierson gave the keynote address at the annual May meetings of the China Inland Mission, the Baptist Missionary Society, and the London Missionary Society. It is likely that he received at least token payment for giving major addresses. A packed speaking schedule not only furthered his goal of promoting world evangelization, but it became a partial means of financial support during the 1890s.

For Dr. Pierson the most exciting moment of his time in England was when he preached at the Metropolitan Tabernacle of Charles H. Spurgeon in December 1889. Pierson had never forgotten the impressions made by the youthful preacher on that first trip to England in 1866. By 1890, Spurgeon had been leading the largest Baptist church in the world for thirty years. Before his sermon, the officers of the Tabernacle prayed with Dr. Pierson for fifteen minutes. Buoyed by the prayer support, Pierson went into the huge assembly and preached a powerful message. Spurgeon penned his thanks in an exuberant letter. "Our people have had nothing to compare with your sermon," he wrote. "It fired the whole mass." The great "prince of the pulpit" then requested that Pierson give additional addresses to men at the Pastors' College that Spurgeon ran out of the Tabernacle.

One of the key points of agreement between Spurgeon and Pierson concerned the infallibility of the Bible. Spurgeon's theology was essentially Calvinistic, and he believed in the Bible as the infallible Word of God. In 1888, he had taken his church out of the Baptist Union over the "Down-Grade Controversy" concerning theological ortho- doxy. Spurgeon had begun to feel that the Baptists were losing their moorings in the plain truths of the Bible and were sliding into heresy. When he took the Metropolitan Tabernacle out of the Union, his con- gregation stuck with him. The Down-Grade Controversy was one of the few public fights over biblical criticism that occurred in Victorian England. Pierson sympathized with his fellow biblicist during the public controversy, and they exchanged correspondence over Spur- geon's struggles. In March 1890, Spurgeon wrote to Pierson, "I touched on Smith's Isaiah some months ago, and set the ball rolling. I rejoice that you are in for that business: it is as bad as bad can be. It was in June 89 that I spoke of it. I will send you a copy." Spurgeon's letter was referring to the book by George Adam Smith that postulated the existence of two authors for the Book of Isaiah. Smith was a friend of Moody's and was a basically conservative scholar, but his defense of the dual authorship of Isaiah caused heated debate, instigated by even more conservative scholars. Pierson condemned Smith's views in the *New York Observer*, and Smith wrote him a ten-page letter of protest. Although Smith and Pierson were friendly acquaintances, the begin- ning of a public rift over higher criticism bode ill for the future of the evangelical unity they both supported.

In the spring of 1891, Charles Spurgeon was stricken with Bright's Disease, an incurable kidney condition. He had long suffered from gout and other health problems associated with his large size. While at the Niagara Bible Conference in July, Pierson and the other participants heard that Spurgeon was dying. A group of men prayed for an hour that he might be spared for further work in the Lord's vineyard. When a cablegram the next day brought news of the mighty preacher's improvement, the men gave thanks. Since he knew Spurgeon personally, Pierson was delegated to send a letter of prayer and support from the conference.

In response, Spurgeon's private secretary wrote to Dr. Pierson saying that even before his letter had arrived, Charles Spurgeon had been wondering if Pierson could come to London for six months to help out at the Tabernacle. To be called as supply preacher at the Met- ropolitan Tabernacle was a great honor. Pierson's style of preaching, with its combination of erudition, mastery of the Bible, rhetorical beauty, and emotion, was probably better received in the United Kingdom than in the United States, with its less intellectual tradition of revival preaching. And in his fifties, Pierson was at the peak of both his knowledge and his form. After prayerful consideration of the request, Pierson cabled to Spurgeon the text of Acts 16:9-10, "And a vision appeared to Paul in the night: There stood a man of Macedonia, and prayed him, saying, Come over into Macedonia, and help us. And after he had seen the vision, immediately we endeavored to go into Macedonia, assuredly gathering that the Lord had called us for to preach the Gospel unto them." Providentially, Pierson had kept his calendar clear of engagements after October 1. The deacons and then elders of the Metropolitan Tabernacle met and extended him a formal call. Dr. and Mrs. Pierson rose at 4:00 A.M. on September 25 to pray that God would arrange for care of their house, Pierson's elderly mother, and their children if the trip be his will. Unexpected funds arrived as an answer to prayer, and on October 23, 1891, the Piersons arrived in London.

Arthur Pierson was not the first American to take a pulpit in Victorian England, but he was unusual in being called as supply pastor to the foremost pulpit in the land. Preachers had gone back and forth across the Atlantic since the 1700s, with English revivalist George Whitefield having conducted spectacularly successful preaching tours through the thirteen colonies during the First Great Awakening. During the 1800s the direction was reversed, with American preachers finding great success in England. The revivals of 1857-58 were transatlantic in nature, and Phoebe Palmer and Charles Finney were well-received ambassadors of American holiness ideas. During the late 1800s, such American revival teams as Moody-Sankey and Torrey-Alexander were engaged by British evangelicals to help revivify Christianity among the working classes.

During the mid-1800s, churches were the major voluntary social institution in England. They conducted considerable outreach and charitable work in the slums and industrial centers. But in the 1880s, the number of active Christians began declining in the United Kingdom. The ecumenical appeals by Scottish churches for Pierson's assistance reflected the concern of churchmen about a feared loss of fervor. In 1890, however, the Baptists of England were in good shape and were picking up members. For thirty years, Charles Spurgeon had preached twice on Sundays to a packed house of five to six thousand people, mostly lower middle class and artisans. Pierson's experience at the working-class Bethany Church made him particularly suitable for the challenge of keeping together the Tabernacle congregation that had grown around the force of Charles Spurgeon's gigantic personality.

The Metropolitan Tabernacle was of Open Baptist convictions. While practicing total immersion of converted believers, it had a policy of open communion and a tradition of ecumenicity among evangelicals. Thus Spurgeon was free to call a Presbyterian to the pulpit. After Pierson arrived, Spurgeon made it clear to the congregation that he had personally chosen him for the Tabernacle ministry and that they should support him fully. Then Spurgeon departed for the South of France for a rest cure, hoping to return improved in February 1892. In frequent letters to his flock and to the interim pastor, he expressed gratitude for Pierson's timely assistance: "Dear Dr. Pierson," he wrote. "The Lord's name be praised that I ever knew you. He planned to set me aside and at the same time He made you ready to fill the vacancy. Every word about you makes me praise God for sending you. I feel that I can rest in you as one sent by my faithful Lord to do faithfully His work."

The night before his first Sunday sermon at the Tabernacle, Pierson could not sleep. His heart was beating so fast that he awakened his wife Sarah at 3:00 A.M. and asked her to help him pray for strength. After all, he was following into the pulpit the man considered by historians of Victorian England to be the "preeminent preacher of the century," the "High Priest of Noncomformity," and a man of almost unparalleled influence. Historians have compared Spurgeon's influence as a preacher in the nineteenth century to that of George Whitefield in the eighteenth. A child prodigy with a magnificent voice, he was first called to the Park Street Baptist Church in London at age 19. His success was so great that the congregation built him the Metropolitan Tabernacle in 1861. Spurgeon's sermons were published regularly, and the bound, multivolume set of his sermons remained a treasured possession by twentieth-century preachers on both sides of the Atlantic. Into the twenty-first century, pictures of Spurgeon continued to grace advertisements for homiletical instruction in popular evangelical magazines.

Pierson preached his opening sermon at the Tabernacle on Acts 10:29. *The Christian* reported that his pastorate began well. The crowd was heard praising Pierson's sermon and inquiring into each other's salvation. The magazine noted,

> Three young fellows of the artisan class foregathered, and one said to the others, "It was good, wasn't it?" "Yes, he didn't speak nothing but the truth; he didn't paint no pictures." The third remarked, "He gave a nasty rub to those aristocrats as look down upon the poor." "Yes, and he trod on the corns of some of the Christians, too." "Sure enough, those who don't love souls won't love him." Probably Dr. Pierson would not ask for a better testimonial that his opening sermons drew from these humble hearers.

Despite his scholarly predisposition, Pierson's identification with the urban working classes brought out his prophetic fervor and commitment to the simple, evangelical gospel message. His own insistence on a reduced salary during the 1880s, followed by renunciation of salary altogether in 1889, was part of his own spiritual discipline in identifying with the urban masses rather than with either the white-collar bosses in the U.S., or the hereditary aristocratic classes in the U.K.

Spurgeon's biographers commented that Pierson was much-loved by the people and that they continued filling the Tabernacle during his months in their midst. Commented a writer in *The Christian*, "In undiminished crowds the people flocked to the house of God, and the joy of reaping gladdened the heart of the preacher from over the sea." In comparing Pierson and Spurgeon, an observer described Pierson as a tall and thin "Puritan risen from his grave." His sermons appeared in a weekly magazine, and were collected into three volumes entitled *The Heights of the Gospel, The Heart of the Gospel,* and *The Hopes of the Gospel.* The straightforward titles of the sermon collections reflected a simple focus on the gospel. They symbolized the complete transformation of a preacher who began his career with "literary ambitions," but who ultimately fulfilled his calling by standing on the Word of God in rejection of worldliness, financial upward mobility, and a class-ridden intellectualism.

Generally, studies of late nineteenth-century "princes of the pulpit" have focused on the sophisticated rhetoric and middle-class appeal of such men as Phillips Brooks in Boston's Trinity Church, Henry Ward Beecher in Brooklyn, and Russell Conwell of Philadelphia. The great preachers of the day were men who could mediate the changing currents of American thought to their upwardly mobile, increasingly sophisticated audiences. Yet Pierson's success at the Tabernacle shows that the transatlantic "Gospel" movement of late nineteenth-century evangelicalism, represented in hymnody, architecture, and sermon style, attracted men like Moody, Spurgeon, Pierson, A. B. Simpson, and others who were concerned with the salvation and improvement of the urban poor. Part of Spurgeon and Pierson's rejection of the dual authorship of Isaiah was their intentional decision to identify with working people, for whom faith in the plain truths of the gospel trans- formed their lives one by one. Rejection of a materialistic, consumer- oriented church and rejection of higher criticism went together for those preachers who identified themselves with the poor. Victorian evangelicalism was not only a matter of theology, but could also be a matter of social class.

On January 31, 1892, Charles Spurgeon died in the South of France. When news of his death broke, newspapers quickly sold out across England. On February 4, his body was carried across the En- glish Channel, and sixty thousand mourners passed his coffin the day before the funeral. The bereaved Metropolitan Tabernacle held ser- vices from February 1 until his funeral on Thursday, February 11. Even in death, Spurgeon was a vehicle for urban revivalism. On the day be- fore the funeral, four memorial services were held at which the mourn- ers heard an account of Spurgeon's last days and listened to the mov- ing voice of hymnodist Ira D. Sankey. The next day, forty carriages drove in the funeral procession to the cemetery while the people of London lined the streets. Pierson conducted the graveside service and preached five major sermons in eight days, despite having been ill for the last half of January with a severe cold — brought on, no doubt, by the famous bone-chilling dampness of the London winters. A newspa- per noted that on the day of Spurgeon's funeral, there could not be found three women in London who were not wearing black.

At the evening service on February 14, Dr. Pierson preached on "Remember Your Leader," a text from Hebrews 13. He eulogized Spurgeon as a spiritual leader and as the greatest preacher he had ever heard. Pierson recalled that when he first heard him preach, twenty-six years before, Spurgeon's simple gospel preaching had "revolution-ized" his ministry. Spurgeon preached the crucified Christ, rejecting all doubt and fashionable cynicism. And Pierson strikingly concluded, "In the face of all infidels of all ages, and of the abounding infidelity of the present age, I boldly affirm that one man, who has recently gone from us into the eternal glory, is the standing refutation of infidelity."

At the conclusion of the evening service on February 7, the church officers read a statement requesting that Pierson remain as offi-ciating minister and that the Reverend James Spurgeon remain as pastor-in-charge. James Spurgeon had been assistant pastor under his brother and had become interim pastor when Charles Spurgeon went to France. Pierson agreed to remain at the Tabernacle until June 1892. The split of responsibilities between Pierson and Spurgeon's brother was consistent with Nonconformist and Puritan tradition that saw the teaching ministry and the pastoral ministry as separate roles. The preacher was the elder who gave people biblical and theological in-struction, while the pastor took care of the parishioners.

As preacher at the Tabernacle, Pierson's responsibilities included more than just Sunday services. He taught homiletics at Spurgeon's Pastors' College, which by the end of the century had trained over a thousand Baptist ministers. Pierson met with its Evangelical Associa-tion, spoke to associations of colporteurs, presided at college confer-ences and various city mission meetings, and preached at meetings of Spurgeon's Stockwell Orphanage. The best way for friends to keep track of Pierson's busy schedule was through the pages of the evangel-ical weekly, *The Christian*. Begun by R. C. Morgan to support revivals, *The Christian* covered all the evangelical activities of Victorian Britain — revivals, May meetings of charitable associations, Mildmay and Keswick conferences for reviving spiritual life, evangelical philanthro-pies, and the major evangelical pulpits.

Pierson was an accomplished preacher and a systematic thinker, and some of his lectures on preaching were published. His published works on homiletics or public speaking included *The Public Reading of the Word of God, The Making of a Sermon, The Divine Art of Preaching, Seed Thoughts for Public Speakers,* and "The Secrets of the Effective Treatment of Pulpit Themes." His basic theory of preaching was that sermons were to discover what was in the Bible, not to expound human philos-ophy. For each sermon, he made a full outline. Eventually the outlines filled thirty volumes. He frequently used biography to illustrate points about preaching, especially examples from the lives and work of George Whitefield, John Wesley, Charles Finney, Dwight Moody, and Charles Spurgeon. Many people were brought to a personal knowledge of Jesus Christ through Pierson's Tabernacle sermons. His best products were inspiring and full of clever, weighty observations on biblical texts. His weaker sermons were made boring by excessive systematization of the material. Since the annual sermons of the May meetings were seen as endurance tests for preacher and audience alike, the publication of Pierson's lengthy sermons enhanced his reputation, although critics found them too long and full of "Piersonian" hyperbole. He scorned "worldly" or excessively humorous anecdotes, preferring to rely upon an exposition of the gospel tinctured by a dry wit. One of his joys in preaching at the Tabernacle was that the congregation followed along in their own Bibles, flipping from text to text.

A. T. Pierson's position at the Metropolitan Tabernacle led to countless invitations for speaking across England. His editorship of *The Missionary Review* and mentoring of the movement for world evangelization made him especially popular among British missionary societies. Apart from his work at the Tabernacle and its related school, orphanage, colporteurs' association, and so forth, the most significant speaking he undertook while in England was at the series of events connected with the centenary of Baptist missions in 1892. The centennial celebration commemorated William Carey's *Enquiry* and the founding of the Baptist Missionary Society as the first major foreign-mission sending agency in Europe or America. Pierson even dedicated the 1892 volume of *The Missionary Review* to Carey's memory.

Three hundred international delegates attended the centenary celebration, and crowds of observers attended the festivities and heard the speeches. Pierson's address on June 1, "Lengthened Cords and Strengthened Stakes," based on Isaiah 54:2-3, was one of the best inspirational addresses of his life. Commentators considered it one of the finest missionary deliverances of the year in Great Britain. The audience sat enrapt as Pierson preached on the same text as had William Carey on May 30, 1792: "Enlarge the place of your tent, and let the curtains of your habitations be stretched out; hold not back, lengthen your cords and strengthen your stakes. For you will speak abroad to the right and to the left, and your descendants will possess the nations and will people the desolate cities." Pierson called for total dedication to missions, to lengthen the cords and strengthen the stakes holding the tent of God until Christianity covered the world. The sermon was one of Pierson's most powerful promotions of western missionary activity as the means of spreading Christian civilization and institutions.

At the end of June, Pierson preached his farewell sermon at the Metropolitan Tabernacle to an audience of six thousand congregants. The younger of Charles Spurgeon's twin sons, Thomas Spurgeon, had agreed to serve as the preacher over the summer. Thomas Spurgeon lived in New Zealand for his health and so refused to be considered for the permanent pastorate. James Spurgeon and the deacons invited Dr. Pierson to return in October for another interim year of preaching at the Tabernacle, and he happily accepted.

With great joy, Dr. Pierson returned to his family in America and to his aged mother. During the summer, he served as pulpit supply at the prestigious Fifth Avenue Presbyterian Church in New York City, probably the grandest and most socially prominent Presbyterian congregation in the United States. He continued receiving and turning down offers for both temporary and permanent positions at prominent churches in both the U.S. and the U.K. In August, the Pierson family made their annual trek to beautiful Northfield, Massachusetts, for the Northfield convention. When he looked back over a year and a half of living according to faith principles, relying on God to supply the needs of his family, A. T. Pierson was well satisfied.

8 The Parting of the Ways

A fter completing a highly successful eight months as preacher in one of England's most distinguished pulpits, Arthur T. Pierson was at the top of his game. With an international reputation as homiletician and Bible expositor, as senior statesman to the burgeoning student mission movement, as editor of the leading missions periodical in the English-speaking world, and author of popular books on missions and Bible study, A. T. Pierson by 1892 was one of the most prominent evangelical ministers on both sides of the Atlantic. The decision to leave the permanent pastorate and live by faith as a full-time missions promoter seemed fully justified: invitations poured in from North America and the United Kingdom. Because it mobilized young people, Pierson's vision for evangelizing the world "in this generation" had become the most exciting evangelical cause of the decade. Not only did his vision launch an ecumenical student movement on both sides of the Atlantic, but his biblically centered spirituality made him a valued advisor and supporter to a host of new evangelistic movements that were mobilizing the laity — faith missions, Bible and missionary training schools, the production of mission literature, and Bible conferences.

During the early 1890s, Arthur Pierson carried his vision for world evangelization beyond the confines of the United States — into the United Kingdom, Canada, and continental Europe. With the success of the Student Volunteer Movement in linking its fate to the denominational mission boards at its Cleveland convention in 1891, the North American movement for world evangelization was silencing its detractors among the older generation. The SVM was poised to play a major role within mainline Protestantism over the next few decades. Relying on the model of the "traveling secretary" to keep in touch with different branches of the movement, the SVM sent Robert Wilder, leader of the Mount Hermon 100, to tour British colleges on behalf of missions. In April 1892, British students founded the Student Volunteer Missionary Union and established links with the American movement. Their adoption of the motto "the evangelization of the world in this generation" rendered A. T. Pierson a visionary father of the British student movement as well as the American one. With *The Missionary Review* the recommended periodical of choice by both American and British student volunteers, Dr. Pierson's reputation spread further. For the next five years, A. T. Pierson's central role would be as senior ambassador for a North Atlantic movement to evangelize the world.

Part of Pierson's success in the 1890s was that he voiced the aspirations of young evangelicals during the high imperial period. Historian William Hutchison has called the missionary rhetoric of the high imperial period a "moral equivalent for imperialism," because it framed the missionary task in terms of the "occupation" of the world by western Christian powers. By the 1890s, British imperialism was in full swing in the Middle East, South Asia, and Africa. China, Japan, and Korea had all opened to western trade. In 1885, at the insistence of a unified Germany determined to have its own colonies, the Berlin Conference split Africa into spheres of European influence. In 1898, the United States joined the European nations' colonial adventures by annexing the Philippines, Cuba, and Puerto Rico after a brief war against Spain. By the turn of the century, more of the world was under the control of ostensibly Protestant nations than at any previous time in history. Part of the "crisis of missions" flagged by Pierson in 1886 was the unprecedented opportunity for missionaries to be admitted into previously closed parts of the world. In the tradition of his Puritan forebears, Pierson read the "signs of the times" — one of the features that made *The Missionary Review* and his many books on missions find such a ready market among ambitious youth.

While A. T. Pierson's popularity in the early 1890s can be situated in a particular historical moment, his own views were not a blanket endorsement of western culture and politics. The military rhetoric he sometimes employed was inherited from the Yankee postmillennialism of the Civil War generation, and combined with a conviction that spiritual life was an ongoing struggle against the forces of darkness. To Pierson and other evangelicals, the movement for world evangelization was preeminently a spiritual struggle, not a worldly one. Even as he inspired and mobilized young missionaries, he was scathing in his indictment of western materialism, which he saw even in the church. While living in Britain, he attended meetings opposing the British-sponsored opium trade. He castigated the United States for passing restrictive legislation against Chinese immigration. He condemned ostensibly Christian governments for not acting in a Christian manner, and for obstructing missions. Despite his optimistic missionary rhetoric, deep down he did not believe in the march of progress toward a world that would be converted to Christianity. According to his "biblical realism," the world would only be saved by the power of the Holy Spirit and the supernatural Second Coming of Jesus Christ. In the end, imperialism was not a goal of missions — it was rather an instrument in God's hands for opening the world to the penetration of the gospel during the last days. Yet perhaps naïvely, in seeing the hand of God in world events, Pierson had little interest in criticizing Euro-American imperialism itself.

The consistency of Pierson's call for world evangelization ultimately foundered on the contradiction between the biblical mandate for mission and his increasingly negative reading of modern western culture. Even as he inspired college students to see themselves as part of God's plan for world conquest, he was alarmed by theological developments in the western church that questioned the truthfulness of the Bible. He pleaded for missions as a means of saving the church from its own sin. The very years that his missionary vision took on international importance were a time of personal psychological trauma and then physical collapse. The era of his greatest success for missions was also probably the most difficult period of his life, as his personal loss of control mirrored the apparent decline of evangelical values in American Protestantism itself.

RETURN TO ENGLAND

Over the summer of 1892, Charles Spurgeon's son Thomas served as preacher at the Tabernacle. There were many for whom the Spurgeon name was so important that they pressed him to remain permanently. The September 29 issue of *The Christian* reported that a party was attempting to call a church meeting to consider the matter. Dr. Pierson immediately sent a letter to the Tabernacle saying that the members should decide what they wanted without reference to him. He considered his own position to be temporary and subject to change should the church find a suitable permanent minister. Pierson's denial of ambition toward the pulpit of the Metropolitan Tabernacle did little to quiet the controversy, which made its way into secular papers on both sides of the Atlantic. Reports of spurious interviews with Pierson circulated in the press. The Baptist papers in London became hostile when Pierson's popularity seemed to threaten the Baptist occupation of the Tabernacle pulpit. Arthur Pierson was discovering the down side of having become famous.

After a few weeks of controversy, the church met and decided to sustain the agreement made with Dr. Pierson and not select a permanent pastor for another six months. The church issued a letter saying that no person who was not an immersed believer and practicing Baptist would be considered for the permanent post. *The Christian,* ever Pierson's friend, commented that had this condition been made public sooner, the affair would not have gotten out of hand.

The unfortunate controversy at the Tabernacle was extremely painful to Arthur and Sarah Pierson. They endured the publicity the best that they could, realizing that only the force of Spurgeon's personality had kept such a large church together. Without the Spurgeon name, some feared that the congregation and the Pastors' College would collapse. Expressions of support came by post from many of their new friends in London, including the Reverend Joseph Angus, principal of the Baptist Theological College. Lord Radstock, famous evangelist of the upper classes, wrote inviting the Piersons to visit him overnight in Southampton. He regretted that "Spurgeon worship" was hurting Pierson and demonstrating that many were baptized in water but not in Christ.

In late October, the Piersons returned to London for another nine months while Arthur preached at the Metropolitan Tabernacle and lectured weekly at the Pastors' College. Charles Spurgeon's brother James remained as a supportive partner, covering the pastoral visitation side of ministry. But the strain of the situation took a toll on the couple's health and morale, and Mrs. Pierson found it difficult to part from the children again. Added pressure came from James Spurgeon and other friends who tried to convince Arthur Pierson to submit to immersion in order to be eligible for the permanent pastorate. For many years, the mode of baptism had been of little importance to A. T. Pierson, who considered there to be more than one possible interpretation of Scripture on that point. As a lifelong Presbyterian, he accepted his church's tradition that the baptism of children was covered by the idea of being incorporated into the church family, under God's covenant with Abraham. The mode of baptism, whether by sprinkling or full immersion, was also ambiguous in Scripture. Yet as an experiential Christian, he was drawn to the idea of believer's baptism because it signified a person's conscious turning toward God, and it was biblical. In a letter written in February 1893, he nevertheless indicated his refusal to be immersed in order to join the Baptists. For in his view, the Baptist position of denying the legitimacy of infant baptism was a bigoted one. "I hate bigotry, even when it goes by the name of 'positive conviction.' On some matters the Word of God admits of more than one interpretation. . . . I can never submit to immersion, if by so doing I am making a concession to those who would unchurch everybody who does not interpret the Scripture just as they do." At the same time, serving as pastor in a Baptist church meant that his position on baptism was being challenged constantly.

As he reached his late fifties, Dr. Pierson's spiritual walk was admired by others, and he bore a reputation for ascetic self-denial and simplicity of daily habits. He viewed the world through the pages of his Bible. Stated one of the admiring deacons of Spurgeon's Tabernacle,

> The ordinary, daily life of the dear man of God was so unworldly as to be well-nigh ascetic. His countenance reflected the purity of his soul. . . . He ate sparingly, his conversation was almost invariably concerning the Word and work of his Saviour. No one could be in his company for long without recognizing in him the image of his Lord. . . . His love for the Bible was extraordinary. . . . His

pulpit utterances gave him extraordinary popularity in London. Christian workers were drawn from many other places of worship to sit at his feet as he dispensed from Sabbath to Sabbath in the Tabernacle the result of his Spirit-taught discoveries in Divine Truth.

The very qualities that made Pierson so spiritual, however, also made him acutely sensitive to criticism and easily hurt. He was a highly strung man who drove himself very hard. With a relentless workload of daily Bible study, writing, speaking, and pastoral work, the stress of public controversy began affecting his health.

In early 1893, Pierson took two months off from the Tabernacle to deliver the Duff Lectures, to which he had been previously elected on his second missionary tour of Scotland. Endowed by Alexander Duff, pioneer Scottish Presbyterian educational missionary to India, the Duff Lectures were administered by a Board of Trustees consisting of eight leading Scottish Christians. Elected quadrennially, each Duff Lecturer had two years to prepare the lectures, and two years in which to deliver and publish them. As required by the lectureship, Pierson delivered them at the academic centers of Scotland — Edinburgh, Glasgow, Aberdeen, and Dundee. Coincidentally, his opening lecture on February 12, 1893, was delivered on the fifteenth anniversary of Duff's death.

With the surge of interest in missions among college-educated audiences in the 1880s, the popular demand for mission literature grew rapidly. Since few seminaries or colleges offered regular courses in mission studies, mission lectureships attracted large crowds of students interested in both factual and inspirational material on current events from around the world. Missionary lectureships, the predecessors of modern chairs of missiology, were started when the missionary movement realized the need for self-reflection and sound scholarship. Another reason for the establishment of mission lectureships in the late 1800s was to couple mission study with the "evidences of Christianity" as a form of apologetics. Culling information from his network of missionary correspondents for *The Missionary Review*, Arthur Pierson was able to relate the latest happenings in the mission fields, and place the information in a theological framework. From his biblical perspective, the thrilling events of modern missions were to

Pierson like a repetition of events in the early church as recorded in the book of Acts.

In January and February of 1891, Dr. Pierson had delivered the Graves Lectures at the Theological Seminary of the Reformed Church of America in New Brunswick, New Jersey. Published in 1891 as *The Divine Enterprise of Missions*, the Graves Lectures introduced themes to which Pierson returned for the Duff Lectures. Pierson saw Scripture and history as the two guides to reading God's plan for the world. Unless missions were based on both, they would not be in accordance with God's plan. Conflicts between the seemingly negative march of history and the hopefulness of Scriptures could only be apparent, not real. Pierson's approach to the basis for missions clearly reflected his own tension between living in the world of the late nineteenth century, with its heightened consciousness of historical processes, and remaining a biblical Christian rooted in the promises of God. Pierson saw the missionary enterprise as a movement subject to historical development. In this view, he was a modern man.

The point at which human history and biblical truth were reconciled was in human cooperation with God — partnership to fulfill God's plan. Pierson argued in *The Divine Enterprise of Missions* that the book of Acts represented the fullest embodiment of the divine plan in its role for the church. Acts showed that the purpose of the church was to evangelize the world, with the result being the outgathering of an elect church drawn from all nations. The order of evangelization in Acts was the Jew first and then the Gentile. In terms reminiscent of ecumenical mission theory of the mid-twentieth century, Pierson argued that the scope of the witness was that of the whole church to the whole world. Mission method should be to divide and scatter: different denominations should not compete with each other, but should cooperate to distribute missionaries around the globe.

Reconciling human history with the Bible was one of the major philosophical issues that occupied Pierson as a late nineteenth-century Christian intellectual. In *The Divine Enterprise of Missions*, it was clear that despite Pierson's historical consciousness, he continued to judge human history through the lens of Scripture. History was to him primarily a series of supernatural events put into motion by God's plan outlined in the Bible. History was thus not a random set of occurrences, but a process guided by God's plan that would conclude with the coming kingdom of God. That Pierson tightly imposed a biblical system on history modified his use of the new historical consciousness, in a sense taking back with one hand what he gave with the other.

In his Duff Lectures, published in 1894 as *The New Acts of the Apostles,* Pierson continued the theme that the model for modern missionary work was to be found in the Acts of the Apostles. He explored the book of Acts in light of its lesson for missions, for example comparing the labors of Paul and other apostolic missionaries with those of modern missionaries like Robert Morrison, Allen Gardiner, and David Livingstone — "the new apostolic succession." He treated the "age of modern missions" as continuous with the Acts of the Apostles, and compared and contrasted the two. In the modern era, worldwide communication, the dropping of barriers among different peoples, the decline of war, new technologies, and efficient organization were all marks of the new age. The Acts of the Apostles both judged and inspired the mission efforts of the nineteenth century. In terms of divine significance, according to Pierson, the late nineteenth century was a period of opportunity for missionary progress unparalleled since the days of the early church. The most interesting part of the *The New Acts of the Apostles* was Pierson's focus on "native" converts and their leadership in the evangelization of their own people. The real continuity with the biblical Pentecost lay with new converts and martyrs — for example, Kayarnak the Eskimo; Kapiolani the Hawaiian chieftess; Kho-Thah-Byu the Karen evangelist of Burma; and Ling-Ching-Ting, the Chinese opium smoker turned witness for the power of Christ.

The theme that mission history reflected the unfolding plan of God was continued in a series of four books entitled *The Miracles of Missions* that Pierson published from 1891 to 1901. As the title indicated, Pierson viewed the missionary enterprise as a continuation of the miracles of the Bible, specifically those of the early church. As he stated in *The Missionary Review* in 1891, "The thing that, more than anything else, has led the writer to devote himself to the advocacy of missions has been that he has recognized in the working of missions the nearest approach to the repetition of all the supernatural occurrences of the Old Testament and of the period of the Acts of the Apostles." At one level, then, publishing the series was an act of piety and spiritual inspiration. The series consisted of a string of popular narratives that told of exciting happenings on the mission field — the conversion of tribes, of faith under persecution, of individuals whose lives were changed by the gospel, of the transformation of communities. It was just the sort of compilation that mission speakers and preachers could mine to illustrate their talks on missions. Many of the vignettes first appeared as articles in *The Missionary Review*.

At another level, *The Miracles of Missions* demonstrated Pierson's philosophies of science and history, and marked him as a nineteenth-century thinker. The books drew upon history for illustrations of the unfolding plan of God as evidenced in modern missions. With Americans acutely conscious of their own perceived special "mission" in world history as bringers of both the gospel and democracy, the series appealed to the popular sensibilities of the "imperial" generation. *The Miracles of Missions* also demonstrated Pierson's continued reliance on "inductive" and "Baconian" traditions of scientific inquiry. The supernatural interventions of God in mission history were seen as "proofs" that missions represented the will of God. For "facts" fanned the flame of the "missionary crusade." The facts of mission history were new evidence for God's guiding providence in world history.

Even as *The Miracles of Missions* bore the unmistakable stamp of nineteenth-century assumptions about science and historical consciousness, the series continued the venerable American Puritan genre of seeing the hand of God in the "signs of the times." Just as eighteenth-century theologian Jonathan Edwards wrote of God's working through all the ages, including the events of the Great Awakening, in his *History of the Work of Redemption,* and American theologians saw the hand of God in the success of both the American Revolution and the Union cause during the Civil War, so did A. T. Pierson see the divine workings of God through the historical events of the modern missionary movement. Although Pierson saw the global power of the English-speaking world as part of God's plan for world evangelization, he did not locate God's activity in North America. Rather, the "miracles of missions" were occurring all over the world, among missionaries and people of many different nationalities and ethnicities. The evangelical vision of God's work in history was no longer centered in North America, but in calling the elect from all nations. Pierson's shift of focus to the world arena made his writings popular both in Europe and the United States, and they promoted an international and multicultural, rather than national or monocultural, image of God's kingdom. By emphasizing the transforming power of Christ among many peoples, Pierson's work also implicitly rejected the social Darwinism that argued for the innate superiority of some people over others.

In addition to giving the Duff Lectures, Dr. Pierson addressed a number of the usual May meetings of evangelical societies in 1893 — the Sunday School Union, the British and Foreign Sailors' Society, the Christian Colportage Association, the Railway Mission, the YMCA, the Baptist Total Abstinence Association, Moravian Missions, the Zenana Bible and Medical Mission, the Metropolitan Tabernacle Colporteurs. On May 10 he gave the annual sermon for the London Missionary Society, the pioneer Nonconformist missionary society in the South Pacific and southern Africa. In June he spoke at a meeting honoring the founder of the Christian Endeavor Movement and delivered a talk at the fiftieth anniversary meeting of the British Society for the Propagation of the Gospel Among Jews. His last speaking engagement before departing for America was when he gave the opening address to several thousand people at the annual Mildmay Conference for spiritual renewal. A few months earlier, the congregation of the Metropolitan Tabernacle had decided to hire Thomas Spurgeon as its permanent minister. James Spurgeon retired as pastor, and A. T. Pierson left in late June to great fanfare. The second nine months at the Tabernacle had been just as successful as the first. In gratitude for his nearly two years as preacher at the Metropolitan Tabernacle and its associated Pastors' College, the congregation presented him with an oil painting of Charles Spurgeon and gave Mrs. Pierson a cathedral chime clock. The greatest accomplishment of his tenure was that attendance at the Tabernacle remained just as high as when Charles Spurgeon had been alive.

THE CHICAGO WORLD'S FAIR
AND THE PARLIAMENT OF RELIGIONS

The Piersons returned to a United States that was focusing all its attention on the Chicago World's Fair of 1893. The "Columbian Exposition" commemorated the fourth centennial of Christopher Columbus's discovery of America. Spreading over 686 acres at lakeside Chicago, the pavilions attracted over twenty-one million visitors. People came from all over the country to gaze at the technology of the future: powered by the dynamo, electricity was introduced for the first time in the United States. Another invention unveiled at the Chicago World's Fair was the Ferris wheel, the staple of the modern amusement park.

One of the most significant features of the 1893 fair was the series of religious meetings held in conjunction with it. For one week various churches held denominational "congresses." A Congress of Missions, including a meeting of the World's Committee of Women's Missionary Societies, took up a second week, followed by a week-long international meeting of the Evangelical Alliance. The most innovative of the religious meetings was the World's Parliament of Religions, at which the representatives of various living faiths addressed the audience, followed by a Parliament of Christendom. The World's Parliament of Religions has gone down in history as a watershed event. It was the first time in the history of the United States that different religions were presented on a relatively equal basis to the public. It was also the first event in which Roman Catholic cardinals, bishops and priests, Eastern Orthodox leaders, and Protestant ministers — both male and female — shared a common platform. For seventeen days the Parliament met in the Hall of Columbus, with a seating capacity of 3000. It held three daily meetings that totaled seven to eight hours a day. While Christians dominated the proceedings, and each day was opened by a silent prayer followed by the Lord's prayer, for the first time representatives of the Baha'i faith, Vedanta, and theosophy made public presentations of their views.

For evangelical Christians, who believed that salvation occurred only through the death of Jesus Christ, the Chicago World's Fair caused an agonizing struggle over whether and how to participate. The Parliament was endorsed by hundreds of religious leaders, including many foreign missionaries, who saw an opportunity both to emphasize what religions had in common, and to present the claims of Jesus Christ as the fulfillment of all religions. On the other hand, many felt that participating on an equal basis with other religions represented a betrayal of their Christian faith. Many churches participated in the Congress of Missions or the Evangelical Alliance meeting, but others boycotted the Parliament of Religions. The General Assembly of the Presbyterian Church USA condemned the Parliament, even though the Board of Missions endorsed it. Baptists refused to hold a denominational congress because the World's Fair remained open on Sundays. Some Methodist bishops refused to participate by claiming they were too busy, and the Archbishop of Canterbury condemned the gathering. Dwight Moody rose to the challenge by holding evangelistic meetings and church services for visitors to the World's Fair, using his Chicago Bible Institute as a base. He held over 100 meetings every Sunday, with over 70,000 persons attending during the month of October. Moody appealed for funds, since he had to hire five or six theaters and other meeting halls to hold all the worshipers.

The debate among Protestants over whether to participate in the religious meetings at the Chicago World's Fair created a split along "liberal" and "conservative" lines. Church historian Philip Schaff, founder of the American Society of Church History, viewed the Parliament as a positive, ecumenical venture. Liberal theologians Lyman Abbott, Charles Briggs, Theodore T. Munger, and Washington Gladden participated, as did the founder of Christian Science, Mary Baker Eddy. Liberal Catholics and Jews, including Isaac Mayer Wise, founder of Reform Judaism; James Cardinal Gibbons, the head of the American church; and Bishop John J. Keane, the rector of Catholic University, presented papers or explained their beliefs. British Presbyterian George F. Pentecost spoke at the Parliament in order to set the Christian faith above other religions. He lamented in *The Christian* that few evangelicals had participated, for he believed the Parliament was an opportunity to witness publicly to the truths of Christianity.

During the summer of 1893, A. T. Pierson and A. J. Gordon remained busy running the various Northfield conferences, as Dwight Moody was fully engaged in Chicago. Pierson nearly refused to participate in any of the Chicago congresses because of the variety of theologies among the speakers. He wrote to his son Delavan, "[I] fear the basis is broader than I can fellowship." His months among the Baptists in England had deepened rather than lessened the unease he felt toward theology not firmly grounded in the Bible. After corresponding with Judson Gordon, he decided to follow his friend's lead and speak to the Congress of Missions, but to boycott the Parliament of Religions. Pierson also agreed to speak at the International Christian Conference of the Evangelical Alliance, despite his concerns. By the 1890s, the

American branch of the Evangelical Alliance was moving toward a social agenda that some hoped would usher in the kingdom of God. Arguing for "federation at the bottom," Secretary Josiah Strong believed that the future of church union lay in organizing such progressive community services as settlement houses, kindergartens, political reforms, fresh air funds, and the like. The conference leaders believed that practical cooperation between churches would not only save individual souls, but would help transform society. The pragmatic vision of church unity promoted by the Chicago meeting of the Evangelical Alliance foreshadowed the basis for the founding of the Federal Council of Churches fifteen years later.

Although the International Conference of the Evangelical Alliance considered four major subjects — the religious condition of Protestant countries, Christian liberty, Christian union and cooperation, and the church and social problems — over half the proceedings dealt with the church and social problems. The evangelical British evolutionist Henry Drummond claimed that the 1893 meeting marked "an entirely new departure in the work of this Alliance. . . . Now we see from this programme that the object of evangelical Christianity, at all events, is to leaven society in every direction — moral, social, and even political." The burning social issues for the conference were the problems of the cities — overpopulation, poverty, and the lack of evangelical vigor. Unity would follow as a matter of course once the social mission of the church was accomplished.

Speaking in the section on Christian cooperation, Dr. Pierson addressed "Christian Co-operation and the Social Mission of the Church." He agreed that the social mission was the *raison d'être* of the church, which should tolerate differences in nonessentials — modes of baptism, polity, etc. — in the interest of cooperation for social service. The social mission of the church justified its existence; and it failed when it did not oppose the control of the rich over the church, the failure by the church to reach the masses, and the sweatshops that oppressed the poor.

> That abominable "sweating system" that is to-day grinding the poor to powder finds its mainstay in the unwillingness even of the rich to pay a fair price for what they buy. . . . Should wealth complain of poverty, that it will not pay for religious care and culture,

while affluence is clothed with robes stitched by the hands of the starving? We invite the poor to our assemblies only to insult them with invidious distinctions when they come. While we write essays and make appeals in behalf of the "evangelization of the masses," we move our churches to aristocratic sites, hire for them costly preachers and singers, encumber them with heavy debts; then, if we approach the poor at all, we do it through a missionary, a "ragged school," a mission chapel . . . and make the impression that we regard all our approach to them as a condescension and a patronage! . . . If greed governs a man of God, common man will find it out.

Pierson made a scathing attack on the captivity of American Protestantism to upper middle-class values. He warned that "modern notions of culture" endangered not only the church's mission, but its faith. The social mission of the church was necessary to avert disaster brought about by unassimilated immigrants, crowded tenements, class conflict, social congestion, and the plague of crime. "While we boast of our great empires and republics, our institutions and liberties stand on a crater." The social mission of the church must be fulfilled, or else "social deterioration and decay" would continue unchecked. To meet the needs of the day, all disciples of Christ must cooperate, for the task was bigger than could be met by individuals.

"Let us thunder away on that truth — that the church is called out of the world for separation from it, and then sent back into the world for service in it. Its mission specific, salt, to savor and save; light to witness and illumine; to displace ignorance and idleness . . . but to do it by, first of all, giving men the Gospel." The essential force for Christian work in the world was not race or class or neighborhood, but love. Just as Jesus emptied himself on the cross for mankind, so must Christians empty themselves for the sake of the lowest in society. "And as Jesus thought not His 'equality with God something to be held fast to' as His right, surrendered it, emptying Himself that He might fill man, we are so to love man as man, that our social equality with the highest is freely surrendered, emptying ourselves for the sake of the lowest!"

What is fascinating about Pierson's view of the church's social mission is that it shared a radical vision of Christian civilization with social gospel liberals. He shared the socially engaged view that Christian unity should emerge from cooperative action for improving society. Along with advocates of a social gospel, he also critiqued the evils of capitalism. His differences with theological liberals were not over the needs of society. In fact, in an article published in 1893, he argued for a holistic view of evangelism that included Christian education, service, and founding institutions like schools that would further "the highest and truest Christian civilization." Where A. T. Pierson differed from the unfolding modernist agenda was in his view of Scripture and history. To the "progressive" theologian of the 1890s, committed to the march of human capabilities toward God's kingdom, the problem with "conservatives" like A. T. Pierson was that they still believed in supernaturalism — that divine intervention was necessary in human history, which left to itself was incapable of attaining the kingdom of God. Because of his close reading of the Bible, and his refusal to consider it anything less than the Word of God, A. T. Pierson insisted on reading the world through the Bible, rather than the Bible through the world.

In his paper for the Congress of Missions, delivered on October 5, Dr. Pierson struck a very different note from his paper on the church's social relationship to American society. Throwing down the gauntlet to those who anticipated the coming of God's kingdom on earth, brought about through human effort and peaceful means, Pierson read a provocative paper entitled "Thy Kingdom Come." Instead of the popular, optimistic view of a humanly obtainable kingdom, Pierson spoke against the notion of attaining God's kingdom on earth. With biblical authority at stake in the context of the World's Parliament of Religions, he was no longer willing to avoid theological controversy for the sake of Christian unity. By delivering a strongly millenarian speech in a public forum, he was upping the ante.

He began his speech with a challenge to the theological liberals who thought their own experiences were more important than the Bible: since experience provided no data on the kingdom of God, only an inductive reading of the Bible could provide a blueprint for the future. Starting with the premise that God created history and its different eras, Pierson laid out five ages distinguished in the Epistle to the Ephesians: "before the foundation of the world" (pre-creation), "from the beginning of the world" (creation to Christ's ascension), "this age"

(Christ's ascension to his second advent), the "coming age" (second advent to the kingdom), and "unto all the generations of the age of the ages." In the present age, which began at Christ's ascent into heaven, Satan still retained control of the world. The church was being separated out from the world during the present age. Since the present age was evil, the only kingdom that existed was in the heart of each believer touched by the Holy Spirit. The visible church was not the kingdom of God, for in the present evil age, the kingdom was secret.

In the fourth and coming age, Pierson argued, Jesus will return and rule over the earth. Israel will be saved, and holy war will mark the beginning and end of Christ's reign. Satan will be bound and the first resurrection of living and dead saints will occur. In the fifth and final era, according to 1 Corinthians 15:24-28, the Father will rule the kingdom and will conquer death. This final age and not the present is the kingdom of God. Pierson's view of the kingdom meant that the goal of missions in world evangelization was the identification and gathering of the saints, not the perpetuation of false hopes about a world conquered for Christ.

A. T. Pierson's two major addresses during the Chicago World's Fair were five days apart, with work for Dwight Moody occupying his time between them. Most of his hearers probably admired the ethical stances he took in his speech on Christian cooperation, but the view of human history he presented in "Thy Kingdom Come" was markedly against the optimistic spirit of the times. Because he believed Satan ruled the modern age, Pierson did not believe that the biblical witness permitted a theology of a progressive kingdom of God. What kept Christians in hopeful communion and social action was not faith in their own progress, but a strong sense of duty, sacrificial Christ-like love, and millennial hope. The social programs of premillennialists and modernists might look similar, but the theologies behind them diverged radically.

A subsequent printing of "Thy Kingdom Come" in *The Missionary Review* led to an outpouring of negative mail that condemned Pierson's premillennial assumptions as "cutting the nerve" of missions. In the January 1894 issue of *The Missionary Review*, Pierson both wrote a scathingly negative review of "The Columbian Exposition at Chicago" and defended his own views on the kingdom of God. As with Augustine, Pierson believed in unity on essentials and then charity in all things. But without unity, charity was misplaced. Since Jesus Christ was the only Savior, all the other religions presented at the World's Fair were false. In the editorial, Pierson defended his premillennial views by saying that he and A. J. Gordon, an associate editor of the journal since 1890, were in agreement. Their views on the kingdom and on Christ's Second Coming were shared by the majority of missionaries on the foreign field, he claimed. In addition, most of the leading evangelical Christians of the age were premillennialists. Pierson listed the names of leaders who not only believed in the Second Coming, but "the writer himself has heard most of them affirm that their zeal for missions *dates from their acceptance of these often ridiculed views*. . . . May not the common views of the kingdom be largely traditional and historical, rather than scriptural and spiritual?" Counting those who agreed with him, he listed Hudson Taylor, Spencer Walton, A. J. Gordon, C. H. Spurgeon, Dean Alford, S. H. Kellogg, W. G. Moorehead; E. P. Goodwin, D. L. Moody, D. W. Whittle, J. H. Brookes, T. C. Horton, H. N. Frost, James E. Mathieson, Bishop Baldwin, H. M. Parsons, Robert E. Speer, Robert P. Wilder, Sir Arthur Blackwood, F. S. Curtis, A. B. Simpson, George Müller and James Wright, Andrew and Horatius Bonar, George E. Pentecost, Henry Varley, Lord Radstock, F. B. Meyer, and others. On his list were mission leaders, revivalists, hymn writers, prominent pastors and churchmen, and leaders in spirituality. Most of the men listed were Baptists or Presbyterians. Pierson concluded the editorial by confessing that his views on the kingdom of God "were not the sentiments of his earlier ministry." But they had been revealed through diligent Bible study. "Hence he holds these views not as tentative nor theoretical, but as final, and unassailable on scriptural grounds. He therefore once more affectionately commends this discussion to those who love the Word of God and wait for the kingdom of God."

The Chicago World's Fair in 1893 forced A. T. Pierson to take a stand against religious pluralism, to reveal his premillennialism in a popular forum, to condemn the materialism of western Protestantism, and to publicly stake out a high view of biblical authority. His stand signaled that the mainstream Protestant consensus of the 1880s had vanished, even within presumably united groups like the Evangelical Alliance. For those with premillennial readings of the Bible, active struggle in defense of biblical Christianity was beginning. Both materially and spiritually, the church was to be "salt" in the world rather than part of the world. To be a Christian was to take a counter-cultural stand against materialism and relativism. From 1894, the premillennial views of the editors began appearing in *The Missionary Review.*

In a review of the Parliament of Religions he published in late 1894, A. T. Pierson summed up why in his opinion it had been a disaster. Not only had Christianity been badly represented, but the conference left misleading impressions on hundreds of listeners. The Parliament built a basis for the propaganda of "false faiths" — for example, by Swami Vivekananda — and it implied that salvation was not through Christ alone. In substituting laxity for liberality, the organizers of the Parliament had made a big mistake. Sensitivity to the danger posed by the Parliament of Religions was heightened by A. T. Pierson's concern for the mission of the church. Even as most Americans probably viewed the Parliament as a benign curiosity, or a chance to gaze upon the exotic, Pierson quickly grasped that popular acceptance of religious pluralism would undercut belief in the Bible and in the divinity and uniqueness of Jesus Christ. Along with scholarly criticism of the Bible, the Parliament of Religions was a force that leveled all religions by "lowering the Word to a human level" and "lifting all religions to a Divine level." Writing in *The Missionary Review* in 1896, he said,

> Let us boldly confront the dilemma which modern criticism and miscalled liberalism force upon us. . . . Once concede that the Bible is a fallible guide, and that the Christ it presents is not the solitary hope of a lost world, and we may as well recall our missionaries. Why should we send thousands of our best men and women to the ends of the earth, at a cost of millions of dollars annually and a dearer cost of priceless lives, if a Divine command does not both justify and sanctify implicit obedience? And if all religions are stages in the evolution of a Divine faith and life, differing only in the degree of their development toward perfection, why intrude Christian ideas and dogmas upon people who have the same Divine upward tendency, and some of whom regard themselves at a higher level than ourselves?

In answer to critics of his own premillennialism, he argued that a leveling of religions would be the real way to "cut the nerve of missions."

For "the Word of God makes no doubtful testimony. It acknowledges that men hold lords many and gods many, but affirms one only Name whereby men must be saved; and it sends disciples forth to proclaim in unwilling ears the Christ who led the way in a mission to a revolted world."

While the Parliament of Religions has been seen by historians of American religion as a decisive turning point in the development of religious pluralism in America, it was also a turning point for alarmed evangelicals like A. T. Pierson. Not only were Christian missionaries going from the West into the world to spread the gospel, but non-Christian missionaries had been given a platform from which to spread their views in America. The Parliament of Religions was a startling illustration of a changing America — and in the mind of premillennialists, not changing for the better.

A. J. GORDON: SOULMATE

Since their tour of Scotland in 1888, Arthur Pierson and Judson Gordon had been best friends. On their outlooks toward life, holiness piety, and essential matters of theological interpretation, they agreed with each other. They both balanced premillennial belief with broader, ecumenical cooperation. As highly respected pastors of large urban churches, they advocated social ministries while stressing the primacy of evangelism in the city. When they spoke together on foreign missions, their one-two punch made them the most effective promotional team on both sides of the Atlantic. When Pierson's co-editor of *The Missionary Review* had died in 1890, Gordon stepped in as associate editor. Each summer they worked together at Moody's Northfield conferences, and they both served as advisors and mentors to the Student Volunteer Movement. They began collaborating on writing projects, including co-editing *The Coronation Hymnal*, a collection of gospel songs many of which they wrote themselves. Pierson wrote the introduction to Gordon's spiritual autobiography, *How Christ Came to the Church, the Pastor's Dream.* Although Pierson was a Presbyterian and Gordon was a Baptist, Pierson's sympathy for believer's baptism and Gordon's admiration for Pierson's life of faith meant that their denominational differences were irrelevant.

Both men endured their share of public controversy. After returning from Scotland, in 1889 Gordon founded the Boston Missionary Training School in the old Bowdoin Square Church on the "faith" principle. After joining *The Missionary Review,* he put his entire salary as an editor, plus much of his church salary and book royalties into the Boston Missionary Training School. The Baptist denominational press attacked the school as a move to reverse educational qualifications for Baptist missionaries and as an accusation of incompetence against seminary education. Despite being the new chairman of the American Baptist Missionary Union, Gordon was establishing a dangerous precedent by acting as a maverick. Many accused him of being a premillennial fanatic. From its early days, the school attracted mostly women. Thus Pierson and Gordon's vigorous defenses of lay and women's participation in mission work had a concrete reference point in the Boston Missionary Training School.

A. J. Gordon's most important writing on missions was *The Holy Spirit in Missions,* published in 1893. He and Pierson were in complete agreement that the present age, or "dispensation," called for gathering elect believers from all nations through missionary activity. Similar to Pierson's proposal to the Philadelphia Presbytery in the mid-1880s, Gordon also called for "individual links" between missionaries and churches. In his address to the American Baptist Missionary Union in Philadelphia, 1893, he stated that the greatest missionary problem of the new century was the overcentralization of missionary responsibility. He favored having a central denominational administration as a financial and literary clearinghouse, but he felt that each congregation should support its own missionaries. His views on missionary support paralleled A. T. Pierson's. Thus they stood in the position of supporting both the denominational missions in which they had been long involved, and the new faith missions that allowed more flexibility and greater responsiveness to the movement of the Holy Spirit.

Of the two men, Gordon had the more winning and popular personality. But each man was a superb preacher in his own way. In February 1894, they set off for Canada on a speaking tour for missions. In the space of two weeks, they spoke in Toronto, Hamilton, Brantford, and London, Ontario. Rather than giving a straight promotional discourse on missions, they "sought to lay a foundation for a true and deep apprehension of the evangelization of the world, by calling attention first to the Holy Spirit, His personality, work, and manifold activity as the Spirit of truth, of life, of order, of power; then to the blessed hope of the Lord's coming and the true character of the present age as preparatory to His advent, and as the age of outgathering of God's people from all nations." One reason for going to Toronto was to attend the inaugural meeting of the Foreign Missions Conference of North America. This meeting of all the denominational mission board leaders in North America became an annual event in which the mission boards decided matters of common policy.

After collecting over $1470 in voluntary offerings in Canada, they crossed the border into Michigan to attend the second Student Volunteer Convention from February 28 to March 4. The Detroit SVM Convention of 1894 was the largest missionary meeting held in the United States to date. Twelve hundred student volunteers attended, in addition to seminary professors, missionaries on furlough, and denominational officials. John Mott once again demonstrated his superior organizational instincts in assembling the gathering, as it provided a perfect balance between spiritual excitement and businesslike efficiency. The chief inspirational and spiritual speakers were the "old men" of the mission movement — notably J. Hudson Taylor, en route from England to China. Luther Wishard, who was serving as senior mentor to the student mission movement from within the YMCA, and author of a forthcoming book on mission strategy, gave an address. Among the speakers from the younger generation were Robert E. Speer, now secretary of the Presbyterian Board of Foreign Missions; Donald Fraser, founder of the SVMU in Britain; and Geraldine Guinness, one of the daughters of Grattan Guinness, who was on her way to China to marry the son of Hudson Taylor, Dr. Howard Taylor. Returned China missionary Harlan Page Beach played an active role, and following the conference he became the first educational secretary of the SVM, responsible for producing educational curricula for the student missionary movement. Beach's unfolding role in mission education culminated in important works of scholarship and his appointment as Yale Divinity School's first professor of missions in 1906. At the Detroit convention, the full-blown organizational structure of the SVM was in evidence, with declaration cards to register the volunteers' commitment, news from the missionary bands in colleges, and so forth.

During 1894, A. T. Pierson slowed his pace somewhat because the strain of constant travel was beginning to affect his family. Mrs. Pierson became seriously ill, and the lack of a salary was creating significant financial worries. In June after speaking at the Eleventh Annual Meeting of the International Missionary Union, attended by 141 missionaries, Pierson worked as summer pulpit supply at Salem Street Congregational Church in Worcester, Massachusetts. August saw him supplying A. J. Gordon's pulpit in Boston, and in September he filled the pulpit of the Fourth Avenue Presbyterian Church in New York City.

Much of the year was spent on his writing and editorial work. *The Missionary Review* had added a department on women's mission work to those of international issues, statistics, editorials, and so forth. Each year the editors summarized the mission outlook for the world, commenting on the political and spiritual contexts for the pursuit of world evangelization. The summary of important issues for 1894 included attempts to overthrow the Irish political machine of Tammany Hall in New York City, the French invasion of Madagascar, war between Japan and China, the death of Tsar Alexander III of Russia and the persecution of religious and ethnic minorities, the first missionary opening of Tibet, the rising anti-opium movement, the movement for arbitration as a means of settling international disputes, and the massacre of Christian Armenians by the Ottoman Turks. *The Missionary Review* not only focused on the spiritual dimension of missions, but Pierson's fascination with the "signs of the times" was reflected by its active coverage of current events that potentially impacted Christian missions around the world.

In December 1894, A. J. Gordon celebrated the twenty-fifth anniversary of his pastorate at Clarendon Street Baptist Church. His congregation and many guest clergy graced the occasion. Pierson proposed that a collection be raised to free Gordon from his pastorate for a year so that he could tour the world's mission fields. Plans were laid for the two friends to visit many of the places around the world about which they had dreamed, written, and raised missionary support. The next morning Gordon's family gathered around the breakfast table. As his son Ernest recalled, "With him, too, was his close friend, Dr. A. T. Pierson, whose presence ever was as flint to steel. What raillery, what wit, what flow of anecdote that morning! Retort and repartee coruscated and sparkled. Twenty-seven admirable stories were jotted down afterward by an interested listener." 1895 dawned brightly with the exciting possibility of world travel ahead. Finally, it seemed, the two mission advocates would get to visit the mission fields that lay so close to their hearts.

But on the morning of February 2, 1895, shortly after midnight, Judson Gordon died after a brief but painful illness. Arthur Pierson had awakened at midnight with a "strange impression of his presence." The Piersons received a telegram at 3:00 A.M. informing them of his death. In his diary for February 2, Pierson wrote, "Gordon died today (February 2d) at midnight and the change it makes in my life is unutterable. Of all the men on this side he was dearest to me, my counsellor in everything — no difference of opinion in anything important and perfect sympathy of heart and action." In the April issue of *The Missionary Review*, Pierson said of the telegram, "That message of nine words meant, to the writer of these lines, the departure of one of the dearest of friends and the most sympathetic and helpful of co-workers — a man who seemed as part of himself."

For three hours before Gordon's funeral, weeping mourners passed his casket. After singing four songs Gordon had chosen, four men addressed the crowd. Dr. Henry C. Mabie of the American Baptist Missionary Union spoke of Gordon's commitment to missions. President Andrews of Baptist-related Brown University spoke, and Christian lecturer Joseph Cook. Then Arthur Pierson concluded with a final tribute. He expressed gratitude to God for taking Judson in his prime at age 58. "Is not that better than for him to have grown old, to have decayed in intellectual power, to have declined in social influence, to have dimmed the majesty of his imperial scepter? He will be remembered as the full-statured man."

A. J. Gordon's death shattered Arthur Pierson, breaking his spirit. It was as if he wished to die himself, rather than to live beyond his own prime, and to watch his own intellect and social stature decline with the ravages of age. He plunged into a deep depression that letters of sympathy from James Spurgeon and many other friends did little to allay. At age 57, he was left to fight alone — and battles for the foundations of the faith were looming on the horizon. With higher criticism and the Parliament of Religions showing just how far the church had slipped from the old doctrines of sin and redemption, with violence and militarism on the rise around the world, and with old age around the corner, Pierson's dearest ally and friend had been taken from him. To add to his burden, within two months of Gordon's death, Pierson's mother died in her mid-nineties.

Arthur Pierson's immediate concern was to ensure the survival of Gordon's school. In the month following his death, the executive committee of the Boston Missionary Training School changed its name to the Gordon Missionary Training School. By unanimous vote, they asked Pierson to succeed Gordon in the presidency of the school. Pierson accepted the position with the stipulation that his other responsibilities would keep him from devoting much time to it. He accepted the presidency to make sure that Gordon's vision lived on, even though he knew he could not be a hands-on leader in the way that was needed. Pierson's first public responsibility as president of the Gordon Missionary Training School was to give the sermon and address at the term's closing exercises in May 1895.

A. T. Pierson served as president until 1901. Over six years, he attended board meetings, spoke at commencements, publicized the school in *The Missionary Review,* and taught short courses on the Bible. He searched for an appropriate successor for himself. Retiring in 1901 and succeeded by Emory Hunt, Dr. Pierson remained an "advisory counselor" to the school and a special lecturer. While essentially a caretaker rather than hands-on president, Pierson's leadership helped the missionary training institute survive the transition from its founder's death. Its purpose remained to provide free or inexpensive Bible training to those who felt called to evangelistic and mission work. Men did not outnumber women in the student body until 1911. In 1908, it tried an experiment of merging with Newton Divinity School, where Gordon had attended seminary, for several years. The union of a mostly female missionary training school with a male-dominated theological seminary was a strategy being tried by similar schools around the country. But loath to lose its distinctive identity, the Gordon Missionary Training School re-emerged as Gordon College, an undergraduate Christian college with a strong department of Bible and missions.

The year of 1895 dragged on, and the editorial pages of *The Missionary Review* took on a distinctly depressed tone. Presbyterian missionaries faced retrenchment for lack of funds. Higher criticism undercut the biblical basis of missions. As anti-foreign sentiments grew in the Far East, assaults on missionaries were reported in China. Pierson demanded that anyone who massacred American or British citizens be treated as "an enemy of humanity" by western governments. He nevertheless felt that the many attacks on missionaries had been provoked by the imperialistic western governments who broke treaties and forbade Chinese immigration into the United States. He worried for the safety of his many friends in the China Inland Mission — far inland and out of reach from the protective arm of western governments. The massacre by Turks of 25,000 Armenians, the first nation to have embraced Christianity, prompted him to ask for troops to intervene in the decaying Ottoman Empire. He urged the Christian nations of the United Kingdom and the United States to defend the ancient Christian churches under persecution. Missionaries tried to defend and support the beleaguered Armenians, Nestorians, and other Christian minorities in the Near East. In 1896, founder of the American Red Cross Clara Barton chose to publish her report on relief to the Armenians in *The Missionary Review* because she felt that missionaries loved and valued the Armenian Christians even though most Europeans were apathetic toward their plight.

Another stark reality to face by 1895 was the lack of success of Pierson's statistical plan for world evangelization. Despite over 700 student volunteers having made it to the mission fields since 1886, there were clearly not enough volunteers or funds to evangelize the world in the immediate future, not to mention by the year 1900. A new strategy needed to be tried. In reviewing Luther Wishard's book *A New Programme of Missions,* Pierson praised his suggestion that instead of concentrating on sending western missionaries, perhaps the solution to the problem of missionary personnel was to make foreign mission colleges in non-western lands the radiating center for a new evangelistic force. The recruitment of "native missionaries" could very well fill the gap left by the lack of western personnel. Pierson asked, "Is God leading us to the master stroke of modern missions, the raising up and enlisting and equipping of a native agency in the educated young men of the Orient, who shall constitute a special home missionary contingent on foreign missionary fields to carry Christ's banner among their own countrymen and take possession of these Oriental empires in His name?" While the idea of raising up non-western missionaries was not new, it became a more active part of strategies for world evangelization as the year 1900 approached and the world had still not been evangelized. By 1896, Pierson's disappointment was palpable at what he considered the failure of the western church to respond adequately to the "crisis of missions":

> We believe, if the Son of God can feel vicarious shame, He is ashamed of His Church in this century; and that He whose omniscient eye pierces through all the glitter and tinsel of a deceptive enthusiasm and self-congratulation sees our mission work to be superficial, often artificial, utterly inadequate to the wants of a world field, and utterly unworthy of His Church, with her intelligence, numbers, wealth, opportunities, and resources.

Still depressed and missing his friend, Pierson attended the usual Northfield conferences in the summer of 1895. Northfield was the port in the storm for the Pierson family. With all their traveling, it was the one constant from year to year — the one place in which A. T. Pierson could truly relax. As the Piersons spent most of their time in large cities, they especially enjoyed the rolling hills, forests, and river valley of western Massachusetts. At some point in the 1890s or early 1900s, they purchased a small farm near the Moodys' that became their summer home.

While attending the Northfield Conference of Christian Workers in August, A. T. Pierson had a life-changing experience that helped him begin the process of healing from the devastation caused by the deaths of Gordon and of his mother. Two famous speakers had come from the Keswick Convention to Northfield. The Keswick Convention was an annual meeting to promote a higher Christian spiritual life that had been gathering in the Lake District of northern England since 1874. In 1895, the featured speaker was the South African mission leader and writer on spiritual life, Andrew Murray, Jr., a Dutch Reformed minister who was leading an evangelical renaissance among South Africans of Dutch descent, as well as spearheading the involvement of Afrikaners in cross-cultural missions. The Anglican Prebendary Webb-Peploe was a regular leader at the Keswick Conventions.

After hearing Murray and Webb-Peploe address the conference, Pierson rose, trembling, and confessed publicly that his life was un-

241

consecrated, prideful, and selfish. Onlookers were shocked that such a visibly spiritual and famous Christian leader, who served God without regular salary, could stand and make such a confession. Pierson's confession had spilled over from a tormented soul that always sought spiritual perfection, but it also reflected his depressed state of mind after the death of A. J. Gordon. After all, Northfield was the place in which the two friends had spent many happy days together. His confession of spiritual failure in the summer of 1895 was a cathartic experience that helped him refocus his life after having suffered deep psychological and spiritual trauma. As he wrote in his private journal on August 17,

> Praise God no blessing so rich ever came into my life. D. L. Moody consulted me about inviting Andrew Murray and Webb-Peploe to Northfield and I advised him to cable them to come. They came and closed their ten days of joint labours day before yesterday. Never have I heard such teaching and been so blessed. . . . Two addresses moved me beyond anything I ever heard — Webb-Peploe and Andrew Murray spoke on "Faith." Never did I see so clearly my privilege of resting moment by moment on the Word of God. I entered that day into the consciousness of the rest of faith and Thursday night sealed my new consecration in the farewell meeting. Henceforth my motto is "That God may be all in all."

In 1895, Arthur Pierson suffered a spiritual death and then rebirth. The loss of his partner in ministry had left him uncertain, and ill health was taking its toll on his family. All he could do to be healed was to throw himself on God's mercy, and claim the right to rest. His experience liberated him from carrying burdens too heavy for one man. In the process, he reconsecrated himself to God's purposes for the next phase of his life.

REBAPTISM

With his reputation as one of the most popular American religious speakers in Great Britain, Dr. Pierson sailed at the end of 1895 to attend the first convention of the Student Volunteer Missionary Union, held

January 1-5 in Liverpool. Addressing the SVMU was something Pierson and Gordon had planned to do together. After Gordon's death, Pierson persuaded the English Baptist pastor F. B. Meyer, minister at Christ Church, Westminster, to take his place as associate editor of *The Missionary Review*. Following attendance at the SVMU, Pierson planned to conduct with Meyer a series of four-day meetings in England, Wales, Ireland, and Scotland "upon subjects connected with the Inspired Word, Prayer, the Holy Spirit, Spiritual Life, the Lord's Coming, and Missions." Each four-day conference would consist of two sessions a day. The first day Pierson would speak on the Inspiration and Authority of the Bible; day two on the Personality and Power of the Holy Spirit; day three on the Culture of the Inner Life, and day four on Christian Missions. The conference schedule was projected to keep Pierson in Great Britain for the first six months of 1896. While promotion of world evangelization remained at the top of Pierson's priorities, he increasingly sought to incorporate missions commitment into an emphasis on the whole spiritual life of the believer. The events of 1895, beginning with Gordon's death in February and culminating in his experience at Northfield in August, were moving him in a more introspective direction. As the student missionary movement he had launched took on momentum, life, and organization of its own, led by a generation of active and committed young leaders in their twenties and thirties, A. T. Pierson began concentrating more on the spiritual and inner rather than public aspects of commitment to foreign missions.

Pierson arrived in England to find British students even more committed to missions than they had been during his last speaking tour. Their conference, "Make Jesus King," would be the first major student missionary convention in the British Isles. Although British students founded the SVMU in 1892, they faced more obstacles than had the Americans: financial difficulties, an innate British suspicion of innovation, and bias among the upper classes against evangelical enthusiasm. American student leaders assisted their British counterparts with organizational know-how and practical advice. By May 1, 1893, the Student Volunteer Missionary Union had enrolled nearly five hundred members, the largest group being medical students. In an innovation more startling in old-world England than in North America, women joined the movement. It adopted as its motto "the evangelization of the world in this generation."

The "International Students' Missionary Conference" was largely the work of chairman Donald Fraser of Glasgow University, who in 1892 had become traveling secretary of the British Student Volunteer Movement. During 1896, Fraser toured both Europe and South Africa to encourage the formation of student missionary bands and to raise interest in the forthcoming gathering. The conference committee chose Christmas vacation as the date and Liverpool as the site in order to maximize the student attendance. They recruited Continental and American students, ending up with 717 students from Great Britain and twenty other nations. The largest contingent of students was from Cambridge University, with 111 present. Seventy-four colleges from Great Britain and Ireland were represented, and forty-four missionary societies. As in the American conferences, one of the major purposes was to enable student volunteers to make direct contact with representatives of the various mission societies. The conference was remarkable in being the first British conference of any kind to provide private housing in the American style: the citizens of Liverpool housed 927 delegates. It drew so much public interest that its bound report sold out within a year. Inspired by the British example, and the steady work of recruiters like Fraser and American Robert Wilder, student volunteer movements jelled in Scandinavia, France, Switzerland, Germany, and Holland. By 1896, 212 British volunteers had sailed to the mission fields, and Fraser himself soon departed for Nyasaland (Malawi) as a missionary with the Free Church of Scotland.

Devotional meetings began each day, followed by sectional meetings on different mission fields and types of mission work. A. T. Pierson and Scottish biblical scholar George Adam Smith were two of the major speakers at "Make Jesus King," so named after the words in a cable sent from Japanese to American student leaders in 1889. Pierson spoke at four plenary sessions, including giving the keynote address at the opening meeting on January 1, 1896. With Robert Wilder absent and A. J. Gordon having died, he was the leading American speaker. One of his memorable addresses was on "The Evangelization of the World in This Generation," the inspirational theme of the conference. A high degree of spiritual dedication pervaded the meetings, with Pierson emphasizing prayer as the foundation for missions. Participants were optimistic that international organizations of students could evangelize the world — perhaps even within their own lifetimes. Pierson himself pointed to the telegraph, rapid boats, and other inventions as means by which missionaries could gain access to "heathen communities." By the end of the conference, the students had decided officially to adopt the American watchword as their own. Anglo-American unity was another theme that emerged from Pierson's presence during the conference. When the Anglican Bishop of Liverpool introduced Pierson for his speech, "The Plan of the Ages," the bishop expressed hope for eternal peace between Bible-reading nations. Pierson reciprocated by remarking that "if two such closely-related nations should be found embroiled in warlike conflict, there would be a jubilee nowhere but in hell." As the two men impulsively shook hands, the crowd cheered.

Following the conference, Pierson began his tour of the British Isles, with F. B. Meyer. While in London briefly visiting friends between lectures, A. T. Pierson was rebaptized. James A. Spurgeon, Arthur's coworker at the Tabernacle, immersed him in a leaky baptismal font at West Croyden Chapel in front of a few friends. The ordinance took place on February 1, 1896, nearly a year to the day of A. J. Gordon's death. From a spiritual perspective, the decision represented Pierson's struggle over many years to understand the meaning of Scripture and God's will for his life. From a psychological perspective, rebaptism represented the culmination of a grieving process for his Baptist soulmate, Judson Gordon. From a public relations perspective, it was a nightmare. The end result of rebaptism was widespread public criticism and dismissal from the Presbytery of Philadelphia.

For several years, Pierson had been struggling with the biblical validity of infant baptism. He held the opinion that Christians could disagree on both the mode of baptism and whether it should be administered to infants or to believers only. But during his two years at the Metropolitan Tabernacle, he was beset by inquirers who had been baptized as infants yet desired to be rebaptized at the Tabernacle. Although he may have provided the means of their heartfelt conversions to Jesus Christ, Pierson could not rebaptize them without departing from Presbyterian standards upholding the efficacy of infant baptism.

In his struggle with biblical texts and pastoral issues, Pierson had turned for advice to his friend A. J. Gordon. He wavered toward the Baptist position of believer's baptism by immersion, but Gordon died before the issue was resolved. Upon departing for England, Pierson was considering asking his old friend, Plymouth Brethren spiritual leader George Müller, to baptize him when he arrived in Bristol. But while speaking to students in Wales, Pierson was struck with his own disobedience to what he now believed was the biblical position that mandated believer's baptism. Unable to wait until he got to Bristol, he asked his friend James Spurgeon to perform the ceremony in front of a small group. As he explained to the press, the baptism was "needful on my part in order to fulfil all righteousness."

The public outcry nearly destroyed his speaking tour, and it had profound implications for his career. *The Christian, The Missionary Review,* and close personal friends treated it as a private affair between Pierson and his conscience. But *The Christian Pictorial,* a British paper edited by the Reverend David Davies, attacked. Davies accused Pierson of having plotted to take over the Metropolitan Tabernacle since his first offer of help to Charles Spurgeon in 1889. Davies described fond statements Pierson had made about the Tabernacle at his baptism as "unctuous," made with "characteristic indelicacy and effrontery," and "couched in that elliptical, flippant, and lower type of Transatlantic style that comes upon English reticence with a sense of outrage and indecency."

The British outcry over Pierson's rebaptism was summarized in a question raised by a subscriber to the *British Weekly.* "What would be the state of our churches if every man who has had a minority vote for a pastorate came into the neighbourhood, told this section that he loved them, and followed this 'extraordinary precedent'?" British Baptists objected especially to the semi-secrecy of the baptism, which was usually a public ordinance performed in the context of a regular church service. After much adverse publicity, Pierson felt compelled to deny in *The Christian* any intent to try for the Tabernacle pastorate, or indeed for any pastorate ever again. Any misspoken words uttered at his baptism were "informal and unstudied" and shared only with friends. In answer to the Baptist criticisms, Pierson explained that the baptism was arranged before a few people so as to avoid both extremes of high publicity and accusations of secrecy. An article in *The Presbyterian* carried Pierson's response to accusations in *The Belfast Witness* that he was trying to gain the Metropolitan Tabernacle pulpit: "After nearly forty years of public life, I have for the first time been accused of conduct and intentions which are worthy only of the most consummate hypocrite. I am sure such accusations could have had little influence, except where I am a stranger in a strange land."

At first, the scandal affected Pierson's speaking tour because clergy noticeably absented themselves from it. But he persevered with the tour until June despite the bad publicity and a severe bronchial infection. Mrs. Pierson remained ill from the strain of travel and controversy. In June 1896, Dr. Pierson returned home to face an even more unpleasant experience — that of being dismissed from his presbytery at age 59 after thirty-six years in the ministry.

In the fall of 1895, the Piersons had purchased a home in Brooklyn, New York, that became their permanent address. Upon moving there, Pierson had requested and received a certificate of dismission from the Philadelphia Presbytery, with a commendation to the Congregational Association of New York and Brooklyn. As an old Plan of Union man whose first parish had been a Congregational church, his request of transfer to the Congregationalists was not a big step. By and large, Congregationalists tended to be more liberal and less strict on points of doctrine than were Presbyterians. He did not request dismission to the Baptists because he disapproved of their exclusivism in denying fellowship to non-immersed Christians. Because Pierson had not yet presented the certificate of dismission, on April 6, 1896, while he was still in Britain, the presbytery revoked the certificate and told him to go join the Baptists. But Pierson refused. He wanted to be part of a Christian fellowship that cooperated freely with others — not a church that ostracized people over their personal views of baptism.

Through the spring of 1896, Pierson corresponded with his presbytery. He endorsed the belief that Presbyterian doctrine conformed to the Word of God and that presbyterial polity was the closest thing to the New Testament model. He affirmed his belief in the Abrahamic and parental covenant through which children could be consecrated and introduced into the church family. But, he argued,

> I hold strongly to a *regenerate church membership* exclusively; and yet even in this I do not differ from the great majority of my Presbyterian brethren; for, while our standards *nominally* encourage the idea that infants are "born within the pale of the visible church" and as such are baptized, such "membership" is practically construed by all the most spiritually minded brethren I have ever

known, as simply an external and covenant relation; and I have never known even a person "baptized" in infancy to be received into full communion without careful inquiry as to the evidence of a *new birth.*

Pierson perceived a conflict between traditional Reformed covenant theology and revivalistic practice that did not permit membership to those who could not recount an experience of saving faith. This tension between infant baptism and adult experiences of conversion was a classic sacramental problem that had haunted American Protestantism since the days of the Puritans. Pierson's decision to be rebaptized was followed in the twentieth century by other evangelicals who joined nondenominational Bible churches that practiced adult baptism.

In the months after its April 6, 1896, meeting, the Presbytery of Philadelphia dropped Arthur Pierson from its rolls. The presbytery testified to his piety, zeal, and ability as a minister, but it interpreted his rebaptism as a change of denomination — even if he did not. Pierson chose not to appear in person to oppose the decision because he felt it would be fruitless, and he desired no public controversy with former colleagues and friends. While the heresy trials of famous biblical critics Charles A. Briggs and Henry P. Smith were appealed all the way to the General Assembly in the 1890s, Pierson did not appeal the decision of the presbytery to a higher judicatory. Yet he was asking for the same kind of tolerance to differ in biblical interpretation that Briggs and Smith were asking for — though Pierson's deviation from Presbyterian norms was on the "conservative" rather than "liberal" side of the doctrinal spectrum.

The staid denominational periodical *The Presbyterian* believed that Pierson could not remain in good standing. It recognized the "peculiarly Piersonian ring about his [baptismal] address and conduct," implying that his immersion was just one more thing in a long line of typical enthusiasm, zealotry, and even extremism. *The Methodist Protestant* called Pierson the "denominational anomaly of the present generation" because he claimed to remain a Presbyterian. *The Watchman* of Boston argued that Pierson was still a Presbyterian minister since the presbytery had unjustly revoked his letter of dismission to the Congregationalists. But the final conclusion of Presbyterian authorities was that the Presbyterian Church had no room for the twice baptized.

The fallout from A. T. Pierson's rebaptism was that his possibilities for speaking engagements and pulpit supply in the United States dried up. Close friends continued supporting him. George Pentecost, then pastor of the largest Presbyterian church in the United Kingdom, showed his defiance of the Philadelphia Presbytery's action by writing him in July and asking Pierson to take his pulpit from October 1896 for six months. But the largely negative response in the United States made it exceedingly difficult to continue supporting his family "on faith," and it forced Pierson to spend more time in Great Britain in order to make ends meet. The financial implications of his immersion were profound.

Although Dr. Pierson did not fight the presbytery's decision, he considered himself a Presbyterian for the rest of his life. He began worshiping regularly at Bedford Presbyterian Church when home in Brooklyn. Yet at a deeper level, his immersion marked a parting of the ways with mainstream, denominational Christianity. His own reading of the Bible over many decades of daily study had become more important to him than his ministerial vows. His obedience to God's commands for his life required that he follow God's voice wherever it called him — even if it meant in effect renouncing his ordination. After all, the thrust of his writing for a decade, and his support for faith missions and parachurch movements, were an extended argument for the validity of lay leadership in the church. He had come a long way since he demanded obedience from the laity in his first pastorate. His work for world evangelization, for faith missions and Bible schools, and for cooperative Christian social movements to serve the poor, all pointed beyond the limitations of denominational structures. In the end, the believer's experience of the new birth was a more important indicator of evangelical commitment than his denominational affiliation. Following the Bible was more important than one's reputation or association with the comfortable and well educated. While A. T. Pierson's immersion was essentially an act of individual conscience, it nevertheless anticipated the future — the emergence of nondenominational evangelicalism in the early twentieth century.

9 The Spirit and the Word

The years 1895 and 1896 marked the transition to a new phase of life for A. T. Pierson. The death of his best friend, Pierson's experience of spiritual healing, and finally his immersion in February 1896 were all signposts of a deepening devotional life. While he remained completely devoted to the evangelization of the world, A. T. Pierson shifted the emphasis of his ministry from mobilizing young people for world evangelization to deepening the spiritual basis of the missionary movement. As he entered his sixties, he turned from the human and organizational to the divine and supernatural aspects of obedience to Christ's commands. From a psychological perspective, he was moving into old age. Beset with ill health and beginning to experience the deaths of his generational cohorts, he turned toward a deeper relationship with Christ. Yet far from retiring and losing his influence, A. T. Pierson through his writings and teachings in the last phase of his life had a profound impact on the spirituality of the twentieth-century missionary movement. His books reflected the maturation of decades of daily Bible study, and its testing in sermons, Bible and prophecy conferences, and missionary meetings.

The most enduring of Arthur Pierson's works were not the early books that launched the student missionary movement, like *The Crisis of Missions,* published in 1886. Rather, his reputation among subsequent generations came from his later writings on the relationship of the believer to Christ, and on Bible study. At least seventeen of his later books on spiritual life and the Bible were reprinted, some in multiple editions and languages, from the 1960s through the 1990s. A century after publication in English, his biography of George Müller was translated into Korean, following previous translations into many European languages including German, French, Dutch, Danish, Swedish, and also Japanese. The slim volume *In Christ Jesus* is considered by some to be the classic study of spiritual union with Christ in the Pauline epistles. In addition to his own writings, he served as advisor to an annotated version of the Bible that became the best-selling annotated Bible in the twentieth century. *The Scofield Reference Bible* was originally promoted as a one-volume aid for conservative missionaries without access to a set of Bible commentaries.

The shift in A. T. Pierson's writings toward the spiritual basis for missions became apparent in 1896. In August, *The Missionary Review* carried his article on "George Müller, Patriarch and Prophet of Bristol." During his six-month speaking tour of Great Britain in the first half of 1896, Pierson heard his 91-year-old friend speak on prayer as the basis for missions at the YMCA Hall in Bristol. Deeply moved by his mentor's seventy-year walk of faith, Pierson commented that Müller's exposition of Psalm 77 was the most eloquent address on missions he had ever heard. Pierson was moved to write to his readers, that "the *one grand key to all the problems of world-wide missions is an alliance by faith and obedience and believing prayer with the God whose work it is to evangelize and redeem this world through the instrumentality of his believing people.*" By the end of the year, even as Arthur Pierson was telling his readers that the world outlook for missions looked gloomy on both political and ecclesiastical fronts, he had decided to return to "basics" in his missionary writings. He announced in January 1897 that he would write a series of sketches of the "spiritual movements of the last half century" to show that all advances in missions were due to prayer. From now on, he would support the cause of missions by emphasizing the source of their spiritual power, namely, the believer's life in Christ.

SALVATION, SANCTIFICATION, SERVICE:
SPIRITUALITY FOR MISSIONS

Throughout his ministry, A. T. Pierson promoted the spiritual life of the believer. His formative experiences during the Businessmen's Revival in 1858 had opened him to God's ongoing presence in his life. By the late 1870s, the Fort Street Church had burned down in apparent answer to prayer; and during the months at the opera house, he felt new power surge through his simple gospel preaching. Following the example of Charles Finney and other "New School" Presbyterians who embraced holiness theology, by the late 1870s he was writing about the importance of sanctification in the life of the believer. Although he adhered to classic Reformed ideas about the gradual growth in grace that occurred after one's conversion, Pierson argued that sudden spiritual experiences were compatible with doctrines about sanctification as a gradual process. He wrote in 1878, "It is possible and practicable for most disciples to have a far more *vivid view* of *Christ's work as a sanctifier.* . . . Another marked stage in sanctification may be found in the *actual experience* of divine power in overcoming sin. It is one thing to come to clearness of *conception;* it is quite another to prove Christ's power by actual *reception.*" Sounding as if he were speaking from personal experience, Pierson noted that the rush of joy one felt at the new experience could almost justify the term "new conversion." "Sometimes a disciple is conscious of a *mighty movement of will* in the direction of God, which seems more marked than even his conversion." After such a powerful emotional experience, the believer was then "sealed" by the Holy Spirit — made conscious of God's constant presence in his or her life. By 1878, Pierson was also writing on the "enduement of power" given by the Holy Spirit, through which the believer could live a "higher Christian life."

Although an experiential definition of sanctification was a typically Methodist concept, Pierson shared his interests in sanctification with other Presbyterians and Baptists who experienced similar, postconversion emotional growth spurts in grace. A. B. Simpson, founder of the Christian and Missionary Alliance, embraced the idea of Christ as sanctifier. A. J. Gordon wrote extensively on the work of the Holy Spirit in the life of the believer. Dwight Moody encouraged postconversion religious experience in the annual Northfield summer con-

ferences he held for Christian workers. The work of holiness, or sanctification, was never an end in itself. Rather, it should culminate in service. And what was the most prayerful, self-denying form of service to
God and humanity? Becoming a missionary! During the early 1890s,
Pierson frequently characterized the path from salvation, through
sanctification, to service, as the spiritual trajectory of the missionary
life. In motivating young people to support world evangelization in
their own generation, A. T. Pierson stressed the importance of prayerful spiritual experience as the path to missionary service.

While Pierson's ongoing struggles with his own sense of sinfulness meant that he never embraced the possibility of "sinless perfection" in one's earthly life, he nevertheless was steeped in the piety of
nineteenth-century holiness theology. His positive response to Andrew Murray at the Northfield Conference of 1895 was therefore not a
surprise. What appeared to be new about Pierson's holiness theology
from 1895 onward was the experience of "the rest of faith." Author of
Abide in Christ and other spiritual classics, South African Andrew
Murray, Jr., made a big impact on the Keswick Conference of 1895 with
his views of the believer's union with Christ. To abide in Christ meant
to rest in him, giving over one's anxieties and inadequacies to Jesus,
who was big enough to handle them all. Murray's subsequent talks at
Northfield were later published as *The Master's Indwelling,* in which
Murray guided the seeker into spiritual rest, and complete surrender
to Christ. The fulfillment of both the individual believer's life, and of
the march of history, was "that God may be all in all," a phrase that
Pierson took as his goal in 1895. For God to "be all in all" meant to accept everything in one's life as coming from God, and to yield to him.
While A. T. Pierson was already an advocate of holiness spirituality
before 1895, his frame of mind after Gordon's death made him peculiarly receptive to the idea of resting in Christ's sufficiency, and sub-
mitting to God's will. He obtained a powerful emotional release by
standing and confessing his sinfulness, and claiming the right to rest
in faith.

As Pierson began writing about the "spiritual movements of the
last half century," he turned first to the Oxford-Brighton movement, a
series of conferences that in 1873 marked the beginning of the doctrine
of sanctification's impact on British Christianity, both in the established Church of England and other Protestant denominations, and in

the parachurch YMCA. The visits of American holiness advocates Mr. and Mrs. William Boardman, and Hannah and Robert Pearsall Smith brought holiness methods of obtaining spiritual peace to England in 1873. From small gatherings of a few seekers, to larger conferences modeled on American camp meetings, the meetings proliferated. Hannah Whitall Smith, author of the devotional classic *The Christian's Secret of a Happy Life,* was especially influential in helping seekers learn to yield themselves to the Holy Spirit, and experience the power through Christ over sin, anxiety, and depression. Then in 1874, the Anglican minister T. D. Harford-Battersby, an Oxford graduate, suggested to pious layman Robert Wilson that they hold a convention for Anglicans with the purpose of helping them attain an experience of sanctification. Erecting a tent near Derwentwater, amidst the beautiful mountains of England's Lake District, they began a series of gatherings known as the "Keswick Movement." The format consisted of a week-long series of prayer meetings, Bible studies, and addresses on the Christian walk by acknowledged spiritual leaders. By the 1880s, the Keswick Movement was having a profound impact on missions; the spiritual process it promoted was a source of missionary piety for at least forty years. Particularly in the Church of England, which saw a threefold increase of missionaries in the 1890s, the Keswick doctrine of holiness influenced thousands. One of the most famous of the Keswick-inspired missionaries was the adopted daughter of Robert Wilson, Amy Wilson-Carmichael, rescuer of Hindu temple girls in India and a devotional writer. Keswick piety played a major role in missionary revivals in China in the 1920s, and in the famous East African revivals that began around 1930. Both these revivals have gone down in history as foundational to the formation of indigenous Christianity in the twentieth century.

While A. T. Pierson had received an invitation to attend a Keswick convention as early as the mid-1880s, it was not until 1897 that he managed to attend. After communing with Andrew Murray and the Reverend Webb-Peploe in 1895, Pierson attended a series of preparatory meetings in London in 1896. His article on the Keswick Movement as a "spiritual movement of the last half century" appeared in the February 1897 issue of *The Missionary Review.* Although Pierson was a famous Bible expositor and preacher, and had expressed strong sympathy with holiness doctrines for decades, it was not until his 1895 experience of resting in faith that he planned to address the convention — part of the Keswick policy of allowing only the initiated to lead the prayer and Bible sessions. Accounts of the 1897 conference stress the importance of Dr. Pierson's presence to the movement and compared his influence to that of Andrew Murray in 1895. He and Mrs. Pierson had delayed their departure for the United States in order to attend the July conference. As the week unfolded and participants were led step by step into deeper surrender to Christ, the Piersons were deeply moved.

Over the next decade, A. T. Pierson was the most important and consistent American participant in the annual Keswick conventions. The spiritual fellowship he found there surpassed even what he had enjoyed at the Niagara Bible Conferences in the 1880s. The last year that he attended the Niagara Conference seems to have been 1890, even though the Niagara gatherings continued for another decade. Whether from lack of time, or in reaction against the doctrinal infighting that came to characterize the Niagara group, he stopped attending. Another possible reason for his lack of attendance at Niagara meetings was that A. J. Gordon apparently had a falling out with some of its leaders over interpretation of end-time events. As Pierson stood with Gordon on most matters, the death of Gordon may have necessitated that Pierson find a new spiritual home, in addition to the family summer place in Northfield. The more experiential as opposed to doctrinal focus of the Keswick Movement was more to his liking from the mid-1890s. Not only did A. T. Pierson participate in the Keswick conventions as prayer meeting leader, Bible study teacher, and missions advocate, but he wrote one of the few histories of the movement, *The Keswick Movement in Precept and Practice*, published in 1903.

After 1895, A. T. Pierson wrote many volumes on Christian spiritual life. He examined the life of holiness from biblical, theological, historical, and biographical perspectives. Publications such as *In Christ Jesus, The Acts of the Holy Spirit, Shall We Continue in Sin?, Foundation Truths, The Hand on the Plow,* and others reflected his preoccupation with the three progressive "departments of Christian experience": salvation from sin; sanctification, or growth in grace; and service. The Keswick emphasis on service as the fruit of holiness intersected with Pierson's commitment to the mission movement. Many Keswick-oriented missionaries took his books on spirituality with them to the mission field. During the first years of the Keswick Movement, mission advocates had not been permitted to speak or to collect funds, for the leadership feared that missionary meetings would be divisive. But in 1883, J. Hudson Taylor spoke at Keswick with great effect. The Cambridge Seven volunteered shortly afterward to join the China Inland Mission. By 1887, Keswick conventions included regularly scheduled missionary meetings. In 1888, after an anonymous donor sent ten pounds to the platform, conference participants collected money both for missionaries of Keswick convictions under appointment to the various mission boards, and for Keswick missioners to travel to the mission fields and speak to missionaries on the higher spiritual life. The Keswick missioners provided in-service training to missionaries around the world by leading them in conferences for the deepening of their spiritual lives. In 1897, Hudson Taylor sought the assistance of Keswick leaders to help refresh the spiritual energy of missionaries in the China Inland Mission. A delegation had helped revive both missionaries and native Christians in India the year before, and Taylor envisioned that a "fresh anointing" of spiritual power would help guide both missionary and native Christian evangelists. He proposed that A. T. Pierson be part of the new delegation.

One group that became important participants in Keswick theology by the 1890s were British university students, many of whom attended the conference to confirm their missionary callings. With Eugene Stock, secretary of the Church Missionary Society, as the regular chairman of the missionary meetings, Anglican students could also use the conference to make direct contact with the mission society. The spirituality of Keswick was embraced by many evangelicals in the upper classes — a group that included university students. Robert Wilder of the Student Volunteer Movement spoke on behalf of student mission work in 1891. Donald Fraser of Glasgow University heard him speak and determined to found a British counterpart, the Student Volunteer Missionary Union, that met for a few years in connection with Keswick. The emphasis on sanctification for service dovetailed perfectly with the motivational slogan "the evangelization of the world in this generation" to produce a new generation of pietistic, university-educated young British missionaries in the two decades before World War I. Keswick spirituality also dominated the British YMCA and its founder, Sir George Williams, in the late Victorian period.

Unknown to A. T. Pierson as he became involved in promoting the spiritual basis for missions through Keswick piety, his health was on the verge of collapse. Each year in London he had suffered severe colds and bronchial infections. He also continued having digestive troubles that drove him toward a light diet devoid of the fatty meats, gravies, and lard-ridden pie crusts that typified nineteenth-century cuisine. By the end of 1896, despite keeping speaking engagements such as opening the term at the Boston Missionary Training School, and the annual meeting of the Inter-Seminary Missionary Alliance in Chicago, he was having significant problems with his upper respiratory system. He suffered with a lingering "catarrhal headache," fever, and an inner ear problem that damaged his hearing — probably something like a sinus infection that today would be treated by antibiotics. In his determination to seek the spiritual causes of things, he wondered if his continued illness was a rebuke from God, or was a case of Satan at war with the Spirit. During February 1897 he filled a set of speaking engagements at the Berkeley Temple of the Boston Alliance. On February 25, after praying about the problem, he felt healed while walking near the Park Street Church along the Boston Common. After checking his ears and finding no infection, his doctor announced that God had healed him: his ears were clear. Every year following, Pierson remembered February 25 as the anniversary of his miraculous healing.

But later in 1897, he came down with an illness that nearly killed him. A severe kidney infection put him in bed for six months, with little hope that he would survive to return to active ministry. He had to cancel his plans to travel as a Keswick missioner to China. Struggling with his own age-related health problems, Hudson Taylor wrote to him sympathetically in April 1898,

> Ah, how much pains the Lord takes to empty us and to show us He can do without us! My experience has not been yours, of suffering pain for any long periods, but of great prostration and weakness, so that I have had to decline all public work since reaching China. . . . Sometimes God can carry on His work better without us than with us. . . . Then, again, the best work is not always done with large numbers. Our Lord fed the five thousand on the mountain-side, and eternity may show results we shall not know of till that day, but the record does not tell of much immediate out-

come. On the other hand, He fed one woman at the well of Samaria, and immediately, through her, brought multitudes to His feet. So, do you not think, the Lord may see fit to call us away from the thousands, and do perhaps His best work through us to tens or even units, whom we may meet by the way?

Despite continuing to plan for future usefulness, A. T. Pierson spent much of 1897 and 1898 in pain from his kidneys, bladder, lungs, arm, and digestive tract. He suffered attacks of gout. He was also developing severe arthritis in his writing hand — a sore trial for someone who wrote constantly and did not use a stenographer. He kept pushing himself by speaking at the Mildmay and Northfield conferences, chairing events at the Boston Missionary Training School, and so forth, but his 1898 itinerary was curtailed.

In July 1898, his prayer partner of over twenty years, George Müller, died. Müller's son-in-law and successor at the orphanages, James Wright, agreed that Dr. Pierson would be the best person to write the authorized biography. While flat on his back in Liverpool in September, Pierson began assembling the material on the life of his friend. He also providentially received money by October that allowed him to publish the book himself. In 1899, *George Müller of Bristol and His Witness to a Prayer-Hearing God* was printed, with an introduction by James Wright. Pierson distributed it free of charge to thousands of missionaries within a couple of years of Müller's death. In telling the moving story of Müller's direct reliance on prayer for supporting thousands of orphans, as well as his later travels on behalf of premillennial biblical interpretation, *George Müller of Bristol* strengthened missionaries' faith in the power of prayer to meet every need. Pierson's Müller biography circulated throughout the Keswick network on the mission field, including among non-English-speaking missionaries. One missionary influenced by the Müller biography was Marie Monsen of the Norwegian Lutheran Mission in China. Arriving in China in 1900, by the 1920s Monsen had become an important revivalist who sparked the famous Shantung revival among both Chinese Christians and missionaries of different denominations. Her meetings were marked by powerful workings of the Holy Spirit for healing, dreams, and visions. Monsen attributed her strong prayer life partly to the example she found through Pierson's biography of George Müller Unfortunately, A. T.

Pierson never received adequate recognition for the importance of the biography in stimulating missionary spirituality, for twentieth-century writers widely plagiarized it. After the death of James Wright, Pierson wrote his official biography as well.

After the turn of the century, the air of Keswick was thick with spiritual anticipation. As people waited and hoped for signs of the Second Coming of Jesus Christ, they prayed for a revival of the Holy Spirit that would sweep across the world. Advocates of Keswick theology set up conferences across the British Isles for the deepening of spiritual life, in hopes that an outpouring of the Holy Spirit would occur at the beginning of the new century. The Keswick Convention of 1902 started an "Upon All Flesh" prayer circle for the worldwide effusion of the Holy Spirit. Dr. Pierson was one of the four secretaries of this prayer circle, which organized Keswick-style meetings that helped spark revival in Wales. A regular convention for spiritual deepening, the Llandrindod Convention, was organized in Wales. By 1903, "Upon All Flesh" prayer circles were active in England, Wales, India, Canada, and the United States. At the May Meetings of Christian benevolent organizations in 1904, Pierson addressed the "Pentecostal League," a group organized both in Los Angeles and the United Kingdom to pray that every believer in the world would be filled by the Holy Ghost. Clearly by the time the Welsh Revival broke out in 1904, spiritual expectations had reached a fevered pitch in holiness circles both in the United Kingdom and North America. A. T. Pierson was in demand as Bible study leader at the various conferences for deepening spiritual life, ranging from the venerable Mildmay Conventions to the Llandrindod Convention, the Tunbridge Wells Convention, the Bristol Convention, the Brighton Conference, the Mundesley Conference, the Bath Convention, and others.

During the Keswick Convention of 1904, Pierson gave a series of Bible readings on the relationship of Christ to believers. It seemed that the older Pierson got, the more attuned he became to the processes of helping people deepen their spiritual lives. He recalled, "I was enabled, in coming to this conference, more completely than ever before, to lay aside all dependence upon human scholarship and intellect and learning; to take the position of a babe, and to ask for a new revelation of God and His truth. And in my life I have never had such revelations as since I have been here." With suppressed emotion and broken voice, he gave the last of his four readings. Commentators noted how moved was the assembly as Pierson "led them farther and higher and deeper than they had ever been led before into the sublime and transcendent revelations of the glory that shall be revealed."

The year that A. T. Pierson played his most important role at Keswick was in 1905, during an uncharacteristically volatile Keswick Convention. The 1905 gathering was the largest to date, with thousands in attendance inspired by the Torrey-Alexander revival meetings and the Welsh Revival. One of the most powerful spiritual movements in the history of Wales, the Welsh Revival was characterized by all-night, lay-led prayer meetings and spontaneous singing. An estimated 100,000 persons experienced conversion. Engaged in a speaking tour of Wales in February and March of that year, A. T. Pierson observed the Welsh Revival first-hand, and became caught up in its powerful currents. As he described for *The Missionary Review,*

> The writer was speaking at a convention in Pontypridd, and a simple reference to the overcoming power of Christ set the whole audience to singing in Welsh, "March on, O conquering Christ!" and the "interruption" lasted ten minutes, nor would we have checked it if we could. At another time the speaker was slightly altering a familiar chorus to suit his theme — the power of Christ to give deliverance from bondage to sin — "I do believe, I will believe/that He prevails for me,/And, seated on the throne of God,/Gives me the victory!" when again the whole audience took up this new version of the chorus at once of their own accord, and for perhaps fifteen minutes continued to sing it, rising to their feet *en masse;* and again the speaker waited till this outburst of song subsided before he could complete his address. . . . In no meeting have we yet seen any need of human leadership. At Rhos, where we attended three meetings, the pastor of the church sat quietly at the table before a crowded house, doing nothing but listening. Not a moment passed in silence; there were successive outbursts of song, or prayer, or testimony, but no one was called on.

The apparent presence of supernatural guidance has caused the Welsh Revival to be remembered as the most dramatic in the history of British evangelicalism.

Spilling over from the revival, more than three hundred Welsh-men attended the Keswick Convention in 1905. The atmosphere vibrated with energy, as everyone expected a powerful manifestation of the Holy Spirit and prayed that God would use the convention to revive all of England. A. T. Pierson and another speaker had just come from South Wales, and their opening addresses at Keswick centered on the revival. At the separate ladies' meeting, a German deaconess felt led to give her deaconess ring and the clasp off her Bible, her only possessions of value, for foreign missions. Sixty-eight women followed her example and donated their jewelry for missions.

On Wednesday evening, three to four hundred people gathered for an unapproved all-night prayer meeting at the Skiddaw Street tent. The meeting surged out of control. Dr. Pierson mounted the platform and calmed the crowd, saying that many people needed sleep but that he would be willing to lead an orderly prayer meeting until 3:00 A.M. Three hundred sixty-eight written prayer requests deluged the platform. Praying through the requests, personal confessions, and praise to God lasted until the appointed time. In describing the meeting to the convention the next day, Pierson noted,

> When we proposed to gather in the tent for prayer it was obvious that there was some disturbing anarchy, and causing distress amongst those jealous for our harmony here. But a few prayed that God would overrule what was felt to be a Satanic disturbance. Feeling that the Spirit would have me speak, I ascended the platform. . . .

Persuading the crowd to proceed in an orderly manner, Pierson guided the meeting. Just before adjournment, with around eight hundred persons present, "every man and woman stood to claim God's fidelity to His promise." In the words of one of the convention organizers, "Friends at the Convention cannot be too thankful to God for putting it into Dr. Pierson's heart, in spite of weariness to go to this meeting, and then for giving him grace to pour oil upon the troubled waters . . . the torrent from the Welsh hills meeting the sluggish stream of English propriety threatened tumult." Keswick conventions were usually characterized by quiet waiting on God, and the English organizers who favored a quiet approach felt uncomfortable at the spiritual exuberance of the Welsh presence.

By Friday, revival had spread throughout the convention. Once again, Pierson led a prayer meeting at which all three thousand people in the Skiddaw Street tent rose to show their consecration to God. He had planned to speak on "Praying in the Holy Ghost," but spontaneously, people began confessing their sins one by one. Prayer and confession continued for two and a half hours. The great emotion that attended the events of 1905 included signs of pentecostal "speaking in tongues," to which Pierson was possibly referring when he spoke of anarchy and Satanic disturbances at the all-night prayer meeting.

In 1905, Pierson's friend and associate editor of *The Missionary Review*, F. B. Meyer, visited Los Angeles and shared with holiness supporters news of the wonders in Wales. As holiness leaders prayed and worked to bring about a Holy Ghost revival in Southern California, "speaking in tongues" broke out among believers waiting for the new Pentecost. The tongue speakers, called pentecostals, rented a church at 312 Azusa Street from where the movement spread. The San Francisco earthquake of April 1906 provided energy for the movement, as many Christians believed that Jesus' return would be heralded not only by the Holy Spirit poured out "upon all flesh," but by earthquakes and other natural disasters as well. Tongue speaking broke out at a woman's holiness mission in India, in Wales, and in Los Angeles at roughly the same time. Those who held holiness doctrines and were waiting for the Holy Spirit to be poured out were the most affected by pentecostalism. In the spirit of the Welsh Revival, pentecostals sang and prayed spontaneously and audibly. But even more than in the Welsh Revival, "signs" such as instantaneous healings, babbling and tongue speaking, jumping and shouting, and prophetic revelations broke out. Since the evangelization of the world was part of the end-times countdown, the earliest pentecostals believed they had been given the spiritual gift of foreign languages with which to spread the gospel. Missionaries streamed out from Azusa Street, inspired by the new evidence of spiritual power. Segments of the holiness movement, such as that of blacks in the American South, were swept wholesale into pentecostalism.

Reaction of the official Keswick Movement to the early tongue speaking was largely negative. Although Keswick theology had fed the expectations of Holy Spirit revival that opened the door to pentecostalism, the English Keswick leaders considered the outbreaks of tongues and disorder in worship to be of Satanic rather than of divine inspiration. As a Bible expositor who was encouraging a worldwide spiritual awakening, had helped carry the Welsh Revival into the Keswick Movement, and spoke widely across the British Isles in spiritual life conferences, Pierson found it necessary to address the new, controversial practice of speaking in tongues. After all, he had written much about Holy Spirit baptism and the need for a new Pentecost. In 1907 his series of articles on "Speaking with Tongues" appeared in *The Christian* in England, and an abridged version in the American *Missionary Review*. First Pierson explicated the scriptural witness on speaking in tongues in 1 Corinthians 14. He argued that the Bible ranked tongues as the least among the spiritual gifts, and that without the gift of interpretation, tongues were not edifying in worship. The gift of tongues must be judged by its fruits, and the fruits would be whether tongue speaking was helping to spread the gospel. Pierson concluded that when gifts of prophecy and interpretation were absent, then tongues were worth little. He decided that the modern manifestations of tongues were accompanied by indecencies, especially committed by hysterical women. On the basis of eyewitness reports on tongue speaking at Pandita Ramabai's school for child widows in India, and elsewhere, Pierson deplored that pentecostals exalted tongues above the other spiritual gifts and thereby encouraged self-display, schism, and fanaticism. Nowhere were tongues being used in a scriptural fashion to preach the gospel or to unify the church. From a biblical perspective, unless tongues led to the unity of believers, then they were false.

In none of his articles on "Speaking in Tongues" did A. T. Pierson deny that the gift of tongues was possible, or claim that it belonged to the bygone apostolic age. But comparing the news he heard with Scripture, and evaluating its fruits, led him to conclude in the final article that the modern manifestations of tongues were imitations by the Devil of true tongue speaking. After all, if God is working hard to impact the world, then so is the Devil. While not condemning tongues per se, Pierson believed that none of the cases he had researched were consistent with Scripture. Pierson agreed that the age of miracles had not declined with the passing of the first generations of the church. Even as he condemned the "disorder" of early pentecostalism, he remained open to the movement of the Holy Spirit. As a consistent supernaturalist, Pierson believed in the possibility of miracles such as divine healing and revelations, as long as such experiences occurred in good order and humility, as in the Bible.

While A. T. Pierson stopped short of endorsing speaking in tongues, he did connect the Keswick views with divine healing. In a letter to a "sister in Christ," Pierson drew parallels between empowerment for holy living and divine healing. If a believer dwelled "in Christ," and the Holy Spirit lived in him or her, then Satan had little power over the believer. Prayer by a believer in whom the Holy Spirit dwelled should successfully dissolve Satan's power over sickness. While Pierson hoped and prayed for faith healing, he also believed in the use of "means" such as doctors, medicine, dietary control, exercise, and good hygiene. A. J. Gordon, A. B. Simpson, and R. A. Torrey, other Reformed advocates of the Spirit-filled life, all approved of the use of "means" in addition to faith healing. Along with a Swiss faith healer, Dorothea Trudell, Pierson wrote a booklet published in Toronto, called "Is Divine Healing for Us — NOW? or Have Supernatural Signs Ceased During This Church Age?" In it, he affirmed the reality of divine healing, but he labeled those who disapproved of the use of doctors and human knowledge as "fanatics." By his promotion of Keswick theology, the Welsh Revival, and even faith healing, A. T. Pierson made an important contribution to the origins of pentecostalism, even as he repudiated the pentecostals' claim that tongue speaking was the "sign" of Holy Spirit baptism.

Through linking spiritual power for service with missions, and believing that the world was experiencing a mighty movement of the Holy Spirit in anticipation of Christ's return, the writings of A. T. Pierson had a strong impact on missionaries around the world in the early twentieth century. Keswick itself was an international event, with frequent visits by missionaries and indigenous Christians. Pierson met and inspired hundreds of missionaries at various conferences. He also addressed groups of outgoing missionaries for the China Inland Mission, the Regions Beyond Missionary Union, and other British faith missions. As Keswick missioners spread the experience of sanctification for service throughout the mission field, missionaries shared information on the higher Christian life with their converts. For example, Pierson's spiritual writings influenced leaders of revival movements in 1920s China. One missionary revivalist in China, YWCA worker Ruth Paxson, was inspired by a series of articles on spiritual life by Keswick authors, including Arthur Pierson. Paxson herself was a major spiritual influence on the first generation of indigenous Chinese church leaders. Through the Keswick network, A. T. Pierson probably was at the height of his influence during the last years of his life. Despite their overlap, if the various student missionary movements and the Keswick Movement are added together, then it can be assumed that A. T. Pierson and his writings influenced the majority of English-speaking missionaries who departed for the mission field in the 1890s and early 1900s.

KEYS TO THE WORD

By the 1890s, after decades of daily Bible study, A. T. Pierson felt that he had discovered the keys with which to unlock the meaning of the Bible. From his early ministry, his primary reputation was based on his skill as a Bible teacher. While a full exploration of A. T. Pierson's biblical theories demand a separate study, a brief summary of their main contours helps illuminate the basis for his missionary commitments. After the turn of the century, the YMCA in Great Britain commissioned him to give the venerable Exeter Hall Lectures on Bible study. Built in 1831 in London, Exeter Hall was at the center of English evangelical life for fifty years. In its auditorium for three thousand people were held anti-slavery rallies, the annual May meetings of charitable organizations, and musical and cultural events. For twenty years more, it was the headquarters of the London YMCA. The YMCA sponsored the first Exeter Hall Lectures on Bible study in 1845 as part of its program of self-improvement for young workingmen.

A charter member of the New York City YMCA, A. T. Pierson had met the founder of the Association, Sir George Williams, on one of his trips to England. Pierson had given the main address at the jubilee of Williams's St. Paul's Missionary Society in 1893. In 1897, Queen Victoria celebrated the diamond jubilee of her reign. Hosted by Sir George, A. T. Pierson observed the diamond jubilee pageant from a window overlooking the steps of St. Paul's Cathedral where the ceremony was performed. As part of the jubilee activities, he addressed nearly ten thousand people at a philanthropic exhibit of youth work and women's mission work for women. With Williams in the chair,

Pierson also addressed the diamond jubilee celebration of the YMCA in 1904 along with the Archbishop of Canterbury. Williams introduced A. T. Pierson during his first course of Bible lectures in 1903. Pierson also delivered the Exeter Hall Lectures for 1904; and after the death of Sir George, A. T. Pierson gave a third series of Exeter Hall Lectures in 1907.

The Exeter Hall Lectures represented A. T. Pierson's mature thinking on the Bible. They were printed as *God's Living Oracles, The Bible and Spiritual Criticism,* and *The Bible and Spiritual Life.* His final major work, which summed up fifty years of Bible study, was published in 1910 as *Knowing the Scriptures: Rules and Methods of Bible Study.* Taken together, these four substantial books represented the heart of A. T. Pierson's contribution to the international Bible study movement. Published at a time when higher criticism and modernist theology were sweeping through theological seminaries, Pierson's work on the Bible provided a counterargument to works that emphasized the human and historical aspects of the Bible. All the books were marked by Pierson's pastoral concern for the Christian life. He stated that the purpose of the Bible was to reveal Jesus Christ and to supply Christians with "a divine standard of both doctrine and duty." Since the purpose of the Word of God was preeminently spiritual, then higher critics were missing the point. Rather, "Insight into the scriptures . . . is conditioned upon actual conformity to their precepts and sympathy with their spirit. True biblical learning is not so much mental as experimental."

Dr. Pierson's first set of Exeter Hall Lectures filled the auditorium of three thousand. When published, *God's Living Oracles* became a classic exposition of the organic unity of the Bible. Pierson's views of organic unity became standard fare at the various Bible and missionary training schools in the early twentieth century — Moody Bible Institute, Gordon Missionary Training Institute, Toronto Bible Institute, Bible Institute of Los Angeles, and the like. The unity of the Bible was an important apologetical tool for conservatives because it stressed the internal coherence of the Scriptures vis-à-vis the tendency of higher criticism to fragment the Bible into various documents and sources that did not necessarily have continuity or doctrinal parallels with each other. Around the turn of the century, a yawning gap opened between the kind of biblical training given in mainline theological seminaries and that provided in Bible schools. A. T. Pierson's works on biblical unity were so foundational to the emergence of twentieth-century conservative biblical interpretation that evangelical scholar Wilbur M. Smith in 1960 recommended Pierson as one of three key authors on the unity of the Bible. Theologian J. I. Packer in 1982 recommended A. T. Pierson as one of the three key writers on biblical unity, along with Adolph Saphir's *The Divine Unity of Scripture* and A. M. Hodgkin's *Christ in All the Scriptures.*

Pierson began exploring the organic unity of the Bible in the 1880s, and gave his first major lecture on the topic at the 1887 Bible Conference in Philadelphia. His arguments for the unity of Scripture were a form of "Christian evidences," or arguments from design applied to Scripture. Since natural law could not explain the unity of the sixty-six diverse books of the Bible, written by different authors over the centuries, Pierson believed that their unity must be due to supernatural foresight and divine origin. Conversely, therefore, to prove the unity of the Bible would be to substantiate its divine origin and thus silence critics who denied its authority. Because the Bible was the revelation of Jesus Christ and as such was vital to Christian faith, anti-Christian skeptics attacked the Bible as their central target.

The concept of organicism was a metaphor common to nineteenth-century romanticism. By analogy with living beings, organic unity implied that parts could not be removed without damaging the whole. Just as a body cannot lose a limb or organ without taking away its unity or destroying its completeness, Pierson argued that parts of the Bible could not be removed or replaced without maiming the truth. Each part of the Bible had a divine purpose for existing, and each part was necessary to the whole body. One life principle pervaded all the parts. The concept of organic unity had biblical origins in Paul's motif in 1 Corinthians 12 about each part of the church being a necessary member of the Body of Christ.

In Pierson's logic, the organic unity of Scripture entailed other kinds of unity: structural, didactic, ethical, historical, prophetic, mathematic, and especially personal and Messianic unity. By structural unity, Pierson meant that the Bible appeared to be built on a plan of symmetry, even in details. Each Testament had historical, ethical, and prophetic elements, and the very arrangement of the books followed a plan. One of the "laws" of biblical interpretation upon which Pierson hung his theories of unity was that "the first mention of a number, person, place, or subject usually, if not uniformly, determines its general usage afterward, and its relation to the entire remainder of the book." For example, the number seven at first usage stood for completed work and subsequent rest, and it represented those concepts throughout the Bible. The "law of first mention" proved organic unity. For how could the writer of Genesis have predicted that his use of a word would be appropriate for subsequent biblical authors?

Pierson's second "law" that demonstrated organic unity was that of "full mention." With his divine authorship of the Bible, God ensured that each subject important for human spiritual life would be fully explained without repetition. Apparent repetition of themes in the Bible denoted that a different spiritual truth was to be gained from the subject. It took years of scrutiny of the most minute details of the Bible for Pierson to discover the laws of first and full mention.

In Pierson's theories, the didactic and ethical unity of the Scripture referred to the idea that "there is no inconsistency in the moral teaching from beginning to end." An example of consistent moral teaching on which all biblical ethics hinged was the universal fatherhood of God and the brotherhood of man, lost through human sin but restored to believers through Jesus Christ. A second important law of didactic unity was that of the progress of doctrine: one biblical doctrine leads to the next in a progressive unfolding of God's will through history. This progress of doctrine for Pierson furnished additional proof of divine authorship, for biblical progress occurred through canonical order, the order in which the books were placed, not the order in which the books of the Bible were written. In *The Bible and Spiritual Criticism*, Dr. Pierson demonstrated the progress of doctrine in single verses, paragraphs, chapters, books, groups of books, the Testaments, and then the entire Bible.

Pierson postulated the historic unity of the Bible through its consistent concern with the kingdom of God, centered upon the chosen nation of Israel. He believed that whenever Israel was apostate or in captivity, historical narrative was suspended. Prophetic unity also concentrated on the kingdom of God, but especially on the coming of the King and head of the Adamic race, Jesus Christ. All prophecy rotated around the first and second comings of Jesus. Pierson was fond of noting that of the 666 prophecies in the Old Testament, 333 referred to the coming Messiah. Study of biblical numerology also led Pierson to conclude that the Bible displayed mathematical unity — another proof of divine authorship. Numerical significance echoed that of science, thereby proving that a divine mind was behind the Bible just as it was behind nature. For example, the number of completeness in the Bible, seven, was the same number of notes in an octave and colors in the spectrum.

The major principle of biblical unity outlined by Pierson in *God's Living Oracles* was the personal and Messianic. In other words, the central theme of the Bible was the Messiah and Son of God, Jesus Christ. Jesus was the key to the structure of the whole Bible, unlocking God's plan for the ages, of the creation, fall, and ultimate redemption of humankind. The prophecies, life, and coming reign of Jesus Christ revealed the mind of God as no other discussion of biblical unity could do. The Bible is the first and the last book, "God's living oracles," alive and life-giving. Pierson concluded *God's Living Oracles* with a powerful statement of faith:

> When one has lived in the atmosphere of certain conviction, under the power of a deep persuasion that this book is the Word of God, that Jesus Christ is the Son of God and the Saviour of men, amid all the disturbing doubts and perplexities of this age of negation and opposition, he calmly sings, like a lark in the midst of the storm: "Let all the forms that men devise/Assault my faith with treacherous art,/I'll call them vanity and lies,/and bind Thy Gospel to my heart."

The third set of Exeter Hall Lectures, *The Bible and Spiritual Life*, sought to prove that the Bible was the perfect guide for human life, a divine book for a divine creation. The lectures dealt with the church, the family, suffering, service, prayer, faith, and other aspects of the Christian life. Pierson introduced each theme with selected Bible verses and then discussed them with special application for daily Christian life. All three sets of lectures underscored that for A. T. Pierson, the end result of Bible study was faith in Jesus Christ and growth in the life of faith, not a dry or systematic theology. In some ways, under the impact of deepened spiritual life, Pierson had moved away from the Enlightenment rationality of trying to prove through

"Baconianism" that the Bible was consistent with modern science. His focus on "organic unity" was a partial shift to a Romantic model of biblical interpretation, with various systems of unity revealing the totality of spiritual truths found in the Bible.

In *Knowing the Scriptures: Rules and Methods of Bible Study,* his last published book on the subject, Pierson shared the fruit of fifty years' work as a student of the Bible. The key purpose of Bible study was to reveal the Living Word, Jesus Christ. Early in his career, he had warned against making the Scriptures a legalistic substitute for Jesus Christ. Rather, the "main mission of the Written Word is to lead to the Living Word." But since the Bible was the witness to Jesus Christ, its inspiration and authority must be upheld, or else people could deny his divinity. Pierson wrote in 1890, "The more we see of Christian life the more do we feel confident that *every step away from a full faith in the plenary inspiration of the Word of God* is a step away from the Cross of Christ and from all which that Cross represents in the believer's life of devotion to the spread of the kingdom."

Inspiration of the Bible did not mean that every word had God's approval; the Bible also contained the words of Satan and of fallible humans. Verbal inspiration merely ensured the accuracy of the language used to convey divine meaning. There were several levels of authority in the inspired Word, the highest being when words and deeds were controlled by the Spirit of God, as for example in sentences preceded by "thus saith the Lord." While he believed that God guided translators of Scripture so as to avoid errors in doctrine, Pierson claimed inspiration only for the original documents of the Bible. He thus urged the use of commentaries and original languages to get back to the original texts. Pierson allowed for different philosophies of biblical inspiration as long as the Bible remained the true Word of God, infallible for doctrine and duty.

As an advocate of lay Bible study, Pierson believed in the "perspicuity" of the Scriptures. Since Scriptures are self-interpreting, anyone can study and understand them, but Scriptures must be taken as a whole to teach truth. Isolated passages only communicate partial truths, thus Scripture must be compared with itself. To get around the tendency of seeing half truths in the Bible, Pierson advocated several different methods of Bible study. First was topical study, by which laymen could compare various themes. Another method was the "scientific" or Baconian method of classifying and arranging facts to infer general laws from them. Through classification, Scriptures could be put into a consistent system of teaching. A third method was the "structural," developed by B. W. Newton, a Plymouth Brethren Bible expositor. The structural method entailed examining the first and last reference to a topic to grasp the character of what lay between.

A. T. Pierson was not hostile to all biblical criticism, for he believed that the Word of God could defend itself. He longed for more knowledge about the authors of the various books — where they lived, their context, and why they spoke as they did. Biblical events might not have followed immediately as written, depending on the perspective of the observer. He urged literary and philological criticism, as well as limited redaction criticism. Poetry should be read as poetry, especially noting Hebrew parallelism; and figures of speech should not be taken literally. Parables should be studied as a unit, as narratives of "either fact or fiction, used to convey moral and spiritual truth." While biblical criticism was to be affirmed, all criticism must be conducted with a spiritual attitude since the Bible was preeminently a spiritual book. Higher criticism was thus illegitimate not because it was critical, but because it denied the spiritual truths of the Bible.

One of Pierson's most important methods of Bible study was the typological. Perhaps because of his poetic bent, he loved compiling lists of "types" — concrete objects, persons, colors, emotions, cities, illnesses, and even animals, that when used, represented deeper spiritual truths. The use of types was subject to difficult interpretive questions that had vexed the Protestant reformers and his Puritan forebears. Pierson was therefore cautious in their use and recommended that doctrinal truth not be determined from typology unless such doctrine was clearly taught elsewhere in the Scriptures. Typology, like prophecy, could only be understood after its fulfillment in Scripture or history. Another feature in proving the unity of the Bible, typology bound the Old Testament to the New Testament and proved that Jesus Christ was Lord. Types were prophetic elements fulfilled.

Ever the poet, Pierson loved symbols, literary images, and biblical poetry. His Bible lectures were famous for their illustrative diagrams. The Gospel Publishing House even printed a pamphlet entitled "Charts Used in Dr. Arthur T. Pierson's Lectures on the Bible Delivered Before the National Bible Institute" (1908). At an Exeter Hall Lecture on "The Power of the Bible" delivered in April 1904, he gave utterance to the imaginative power of biblical symbolism for his own faith:

> You can find fault with the Church, but let me state that there stands One Supreme, and that is the Son of God. . . . Every time I see a rock I remember that He is the Rock of Ages. I walk out under the stars and remember that He is the Morning Star of Eternal Day. I walk in the sunlight, and I remember that He is the Light of the World. When I sit down to my table, I remember that He is the Bread of Life. When I come into one of God's temples, I remember that He is the Chief Corner Stone. When I walk the streets, I remember that He is the Way, the Truth, and the Life. When I see the birds of the air, I remember that he said, "Not one sparrow shall fall to the ground, etc." The flowers tell me that He is the Rose of Sharon, the Lily of the Valley. Wherever I go and wherever I look, in every land and in every city, the name of Jesus is wonderful. No man ever lived as he did, and His name shall be called Wonderful.

As part of Pierson's work as Bible teacher, he provided leadership in what came to be called "dispensationalism," a system of biblical interpretation codified in the *Scofield Reference Bible* and recognized by scholars as foundational for the twentieth-century fundamentalist movement. The Niagara Bible study was a network of pastors and church leaders who were developing the dispensationalist system through their Bible and prophecy conferences. Seven of the leading premillennialist Bible teachers became consulting editors to C. I. Scofield, who in 1909 published his annotated Bible. The *Scofield Reference Bible* was the first independent publishing venture of the American branch of Oxford University Press. After initially slow sales, it experienced phenomenal popularity and became the best-selling reference Bible in the English language. An updated version published in 1967 sold over a million copies in about ten years. The success of the *Scofield Reference Bible* was key to the financial stability of the American branch of the press.

A lawyer who became a Christian in 1879, Cyrus Ingerson Scofield had studied Scripture under the tutelage of James H. Brookes of St. Louis, organizer of the Niagara Bible studies. After pastoral work in Dallas and founding the Central American Mission, the first faith mission directed toward Latin America, Scofield moved to Northfield, where he served as pastor of Dwight Moody's home church and as president of the Northfield Training School. Pierson and Scofield became friends, and sometimes Pierson acted as pulpit supply for him. While running a Bible correspondence course, Scofield had a vision for a chain reference edition of the Bible that would incorporate all the exciting new insights being plumbed by the network of premillennial Bible expositors. In 1902, Scofield received financial backing and began full-time work on the Bible in Dallas. The editing of the Bible — supplying headings, notes, references — was a tedious job that took seven years. Scofield corresponded with the editors, especially about the definitions of terms such as justification, atonement, and kingdom. All the editors were noted for their premillennialism and dedication to lay Bible study: Henry G. Weston, president of Crozer Theological Seminary; James M. Gray, dean of Moody Bible Institute and friend of Pierson's; W. J. Erdman, Bible teacher and Pierson's old college and seminary classmate; W. G. Moorehead, president of Xenia Theological Seminary; Elmore Harris, president of Toronto Bible Institute, where Pierson sometimes lectured; Arno C. Gaebelein, editor of *Our Hope;* and A. T. Pierson. The editors met as a group three times, the last time for several days in Princeton, New Jersey, so that they could have access to the seminary library.

When the Bible appeared, *The Missionary Review* carried a favorable review, commending it as a handbook for missionaries who lacked ready access to commentaries. The theory underlying it was that the Bible was a self-interpreting book, hence the extensive cross references. At each mention of a subject, Scofield listed the first and last reference to it, with a chain of references showing development between. The most controversial features of the Bible were its extensive typology and dispensational division of Scripture. Some of Scofield's notes were also criticized for being extreme. Nevertheless, *The Scofield Reference Bible* attained such dominance in the twentieth century that it achieved the status of fundamentalist orthodoxy. While Arno Gaebelein's son was adamant that Scofield would not have wanted his system to be equated with ultimate truth, it became so analyzed and systematized by later generations of Bible students that it now seems

difficult to believe that Scofield's system was not the only dispensational scheme available at the turn of the century.

While the editors advised Scofield, he wrote all the notes and had
the final say on all matters of interpretation. Pierson's own system of
interpretation did not coincide entirely with Scofield's. But on most
basic hallmarks of dispensationalism, namely the dispensations and
the separation of Israel from the church, they were in agreement.
Dispensationalism rests on the assumption that God dealt differently
throughout history with Israel than with the church, and nothing in
the Bible that refers to Israel can be applied to the church, and vice-
versa. Dispensationalism takes the division between Israel and the
church to be key to understanding the whole Bible. God is believed to
have dealt with human beings in different ways during different ages
or dispensations, hence the term "dispensationalism." "Rightly dividing the word of truth" into its dispensations is both an axiom of the
system and the title of Scofield's most important monograph. As
quoted in the introduction to the reference Bible, St. Augustine said,
"Distinguish the ages, and the Scriptures harmonize."

Most modern dispensational systems, including Scofield's, lay
out seven distinct periods of time under which God dealt differently
with humanity. As humans failed the test of obedience each time, God
set up another dispensation with a new set of rules. For example, the
first dispensation of innocence failed because Adam ate the apple. So
God set up a new dispensation of conscience with a new set of rules for
dealing with Adam's descendants. The final dispensation will be that
of the kingdom, in which Israel and the church will be reunited in a
Messianic kingdom under Jesus Christ. While A. T. Pierson employed
dispensations as useful divisions of Scripture, he was not rigid about
their number. He found them important because they helped prove
the unity of the Bible. He used a variety of prophetic charts for references, from a chart showing seven dispensations by Henry M. Parsons
to a map by A. J. Gordon outlining the present and coming age in more
general terms. In his own writings, he generally spoke of five great
ages into which history falls. For Pierson, the progress of doctrine in
the Bible was more important than the number of dispensations. But
he believed that each dispensation was marked by the same distinguishing marks: first would occur a new revelation from God; human
disobedience to the revelation would follow; a parallel development of

"wheat" and "tares" would occur in the church; and ultimate human apostasy would cause a catastrophic end to the dispensation. The sequence of dispensations was a way to permit historical development within the Bible while upholding God's divine guidance over history.

The present dispensation was the Church Age, which dispensationalists agreed was evil. Pierson argued that after the apostle John wrote his last works, new revelation to the church ceased, and it began to decline. The evidence Pierson gave for the decline of the church not surprisingly paralleled his own ministerial concerns — loss of church unity and the rise of sectarianism, barriers to the poor by a worldly church, loss of lay power, formalism and ritualism, costly buildings and choirs, and lack of missionary zeal. Pierson also cited the decay of doctrine and the denial of Christ through rationalistic criticism as other "signs of the times."

A second basic aspect of dispensationalism, the split between the church and Israel, was another means of "rightly dividing the word of truth." For example, when Jesus appeared to be handing down laws in the Sermon on the Mount, he was speaking to Israel, not to the church. Since Israel was under the "law" and the church was under "grace," any laws handed down by Jesus must therefore apply to Israel and not to the church. The real implications of dividing Israel from the church became clear when one accepted another principle of dispensationalism, namely that of literal interpretation of all prophecy. In dispensationalism, the church could not be "spiritualized" to be a continuation of Israel as was common in traditional Christianity. Rather, there was radical disjunction between Israel and the church once the Jews rejected Jesus. Because the Jews rejected him, the Church Age interrupted Jewish history as a "parenthesis," "intercalation," or postponement of the completion of Daniel's seventy weeks — the prophetic countdown to the end of the world.

Along with other Bible expositors, A. T. Pierson found the split between Israel and the church and their final reconciliation in a future kingdom to be keys to understanding the Bible. He decried "spiritualizing" Israel by seeing the New Testament church as its continuation. Rather, a literal Hebrew kingdom would be founded after Jesus' return. Jesus offered to fulfill God's kingdom for the Jews, but they rejected him and consequently God withdrew the offer of the kingdom until the age of the dominance of Gentiles had passed. Pierson believed that making an absolute distinction between Israel and the church solved his exegetical problems as to why Jesus did not return immediately after his resurrection as prophesied. Since the Jews had rejected Jesus, God's countdown to the end of time could not be continued. Instead, God called out the "parenthesis" church to replace Israel as the locus of salvation.

The dispensationalism of A. T. Pierson, in a few important respects, softened the radical split between Israel and the church. Over all the dispensations, ages, and covenants, he superimposed a three-fold division of the "mediatorial work of Jesus Christ." The prophetic age of Christ was from the fall of Adam to the cross; the priestly age was from Christ's incarnation to the Second Coming; the kingly age from the Second Coming forward. Christ's mediatorial work extended in some sense back to Adam. Since the Spirit of Christ spoke in the prophets, Christ's mediation extended to the Old Testament, although Jesus was not yet incarnate. Another way Pierson unified the radical split between Israel and the church was through typology. Types and shadows of Christ in the Old Testament were fulfilled in the New Testament. Therefore, Israel and the church remained united through Christ, be he in prophetic, priestly, or kingly mode. As in a Christian model of marriage where the two partners become one in Christ Jesus, so Israel and the church joined each other through him. Pierson was fond of quoting Augustine to the effect that the New Testament was latent in the Old, and the Old latent in the New.

A. T. Pierson's and other dispensationalists' fascination with the relationship between the church and the Jewish nation had practical implications. They believed that the return of the Jewish diaspora to Palestine would signal that Jesus' coming was near. In 1893, Pierson wrote a booklet "Israel, God's Olive Tree" in which he argued that God was preserving the Jews as a separate people in order to bring the entire nation of Israel to salvation. *The Missionary Review* reflected Pierson's interest in Jews and biblical prophecy. In 1891, Pierson wrote in support of the Blackstone "Memorial" to purchase Palestine for the resettlement of Russian Jews who suffered under persecutions and pogroms. W. E. Blackstone, author of *Jesus Is Coming*, published his "Memorial" six years before the first Zionist conference. Pierson and Blackstone had spent some time together in 1888 after the London Centenary Conference. *The Missionary Review* thus became a very early supporter of Zionism, the Jewish return to the Holy Land. In 1900, Pierson chaired the Hebrew Messianic Conference held in Boston; and in 1909, he was a leader of the Jewish Missions Conference in New York City. As a premillennialist, Pierson advocated both the restoration of Jews to Palestine and missions to the Jews. He believed that the biblical order for evangelization was to the Jews first, and then the Gentiles; and so like many other mission-minded Protestants, he remained keenly interested in Jewish evangelism.

While A. T. Pierson shared standard Scofield dispensationalism's interest in the dispensations, and in the biblical split between the church and Jews, in another key area he may not have agreed with Scofield's interpretation. A. T. Pierson did not dwell on the pretribulationist rapture of the saints. J. N. Darby, founder of the Plymouth Brethren, had first popularized the idea of the pretribulational rapture. According to Darby and Scofield, who used Darby's notes in editing the reference Bible, Jesus could come at any moment to take his saints to heaven, thus snatching them from earth before the tribulation — a final period of earthly human misery. While Darby's influence spread widely through the Niagara Believers' Meeting for Bible Study, by the late 1880s some of the participants began questioning the biblical and historical basis for a pretrib rapture. George Müller, B. W. Newton, and Samuel P. Tregelles were Plymouth Brothers who all wrote against the pretrib rapture, and their influence extended to North America. Men such as W. G. Moorehead, W. J. Erdman, Nathaniel West, and A. J. Gordon reversed themselves and rejected Darby's rapture of the saints. As someone who heavily quoted Müller, Newton, and Tregelles, and who counted Erdman and Gordon as his closest friends, A. T. Pierson was possibly in the group who rejected the rapture, though the evidence from his writings was mixed. His vision of the last days focused on Jesus' return, not on distinguishing between Jesus' pretribulational return for his saints, and then a kingly posttribulational return with his saints.

A. T. Pierson seemed to believe that Scofield's view of the church was too negative. Scofield followed Darby's view of the "ruin of the church" — that the organized church had apostatized and that true believers should separate themselves from it. The doctrine of the rapture argued that only the "true" church would be saved. The purpose of the church was not to save the world through conversions or Christian action, but merely to find the true believers and wait for the Lord's return. The men who rejected the pretribulational rapture believed that the church was composed of wheat and tares and had a task to witness to the world. To expect the church to be raptured before the tribulation would take the church out of the world when it needed the church the most. Anti-Darby premillennialists believed the church would be purified by tribulation, not exempted from it. While Pierson believed in the idea of a gathered church and in the inability of a worldly church to save the world, he also believed that Jesus' coming depended on the work of the church. The Christian had work to do in the world, not as a price for salvation, but as a condition of sanctification and service. Jesus commanded the church to "Occupy until I come." Pierson quoted British Congregationalist Campbell Morgan: "The race we are called to run is not in order that we might win heaven, but that God might win earth. . . . It is one thing to sit at home and sing 'Rescue the Perishing' and another to go down to the perishing and lift them up." In emphasizing that Jesus' return depended on a faithful church, Pierson was not a believer in its total ruin. He was too involved in movements of church unity, missions, and the "higher Christian life" to speculate on events for which there was little scriptural clarity, or to set exact dates for Christ's return.

REALIGNMENT IN AMERICAN PROTESTANTISM

During his late sixties and early seventies, A. T. Pierson encouraged Christian unity and cooperative mission work based on a common spirituality shared across denominational divisions. In his work as prayer leader and Bible teacher at the many conferences for attaining the higher spiritual life, he fellowshiped with Anglicans, Baptists, Methodists, Presbyterians, and Congregationalists. In most respects, he rejected a role as controversialist, preferring to emphasize the unity of the Holy Spirit for all evangelical believers. His commitment to holiness ideas, and his theories of the organic and dispensational unity of the Scriptures, were two sides of the same coin. In both his holiness piety and biblical work, he emphasized the preeminently spiritual and supernatural aspects of Christian life and work. Rejection of worldliness entailed rejection of the carnal by the individual Christian, and rejection of secular, rationalistic approaches to the Bible by the church. Especially as movements of the Holy Spirit swept across the world after the turn of the century, ranging from the Welsh Revival to spiritual awakenings in the mission fields of India and China, A. T. Pierson prayed hopefully for Christian unity based on common commitments to God's divine work. *The Missionary Review of the World* remained the leading ecumenical missions periodical, and was read by student volunteers in both Great Britain and North America. Throughout Pierson's life, he consistently supported a vision of evangelical unity that transcended denominational differences, even as he remained for the most part a loyal Presbyterian.

Yet toward the end of his life, it was becoming evident that major realignments in American Protestantism were underway. A broadly evangelical consensus no longer existed within the established denominations, or within denominational seminaries. A split had emerged in the late 1800s between those who accepted the higher criticism of the Bible as a logical consequence of modern reason and those who clung to the Bible as supernatural revelation. In 1881, conservative Presbyterian scholars A. A. Hodge and B. B. Warfield had postulated the doctrine of inerrancy — that the Scriptures are the Word of God and therefore without error, infallible in matters of divine truth. By 1892, in the midst of heresy trials of several prominent theologians who advocated higher criticism, the General Assembly of the Presbyterian Church adopted beliefs in the inspired, inerrant Scriptures. Union Theological Seminary, the New School seminary attended by Pierson, withdrew from the Presbyterian Church rather than submit to its control.

From 1889 to 1903, the Presbyterian Church was embroiled in a struggle over biblical inerrancy that resulted in momentary victory for the conservatives. In 1909, the conservative mainstream periodical *The Presbyterian* used the word "Modernism" to characterize theological liberalism, with its support of biblical criticism, denial of the innate sinfulness of humanity, and belief in Darwinian evolution. In 1910, in response to finding the theological views inadequate of three candidates for ministry from Union Seminary, the General Assembly approved what later became known as the "Five Points of Fundamentalism." Doctrines of the inerrant Holy Scriptures, the Virgin Birth of Jesus, the crucifixion of Jesus to "satisfy divine justice," the bodily resurrection, and the reality of miracles, were deemed "essential and necessary" doctrines. While not intended as a new creed, the five points represented a distillation of the minimum test for orthodoxy required in changing times.

During the 1890s, A. T. Pierson's premillennialism and holiness ideas had placed him on the emotional fringe of Presbyterianism. With his rebaptism in 1896, he became *persona non grata* in Presbyterian Church circles. He remained busy founding a nondenominational evangelicalism that expressed itself through independent faith missions and Bible training schools that offended the sensibilities of mainstream, conservative Presbyterians. What seemed like a movement of spiritual unity to A. T. Pierson appeared as a new sectarianism to denominational officials. Yet after the turn of the century, it became apparent that a greater danger loomed than divisions between premillennial supernaturalists and confessional conservatives. With mainline seminaries nearly all teaching the new higher critical views, the battle for the Bible as the inspired Word of God supplanted the old divisions within conservative ranks. A new gap had opened that even the higher Christian life could not bridge, despite its evangelical ecumenism and irenic spirit.

Despite his profound commitment to Christian unity, the last battle that A. T. Pierson fought was also the first, namely, the battle for the Bible. Early in his ministry he had written with confidence of the "evidences of Christianity." During the 1880s, he published his defense of the Bible, *Many Infallible Proofs,* an extended refutation of atheist orator Robert Ingersoll. In 1893, he criticized the Parliament of Religions as putting Christianity on an equal basis with other religions. In the years after 1900, however, the firm foothold gained by higher criticism and the increasing popularity of modernist theology caused him to dust off his armor as defender of the Word of God. By the time he entered his seventies, he had become very alarmed at the new trends in Protestant theology.

> I feel as did Mary Magdalene at the sepulchre, "They have taken away my Lord." The apostasy of the present day has gone beyond the Word written, and has assailed the Incarnate Word. When you come to the denial of the virgin birth of Jesus, his resurrection, and the infallibility of his teaching, one is led to ask: "If the foundations

be destroyed, what can the righteous do?" During the whole of my ministry, covering over half a century, I have never seen a more appalling thing. What we now need are not negations but positions.

The purpose of Pierson's biblical work in the last years of his life was to prove biblical infallibility and authority against rationalistic criticism. Though advanced in age, he worked feverishly both to rescue the Bible from skeptics and to provide logical alternatives to critical views. He seemed unaware that the distillations of right belief behind which conservatives were rallying were in some ways as much a product of nineteenth-century rationalism as were the views of so-called liberals.

In a November 1910 article in *The Missionary Review*, Arthur Pierson accused higher criticism of undercutting missions. To preach human brotherhood under divine fatherhood without a doctrine of sin negated the need for the new birth. Social Darwinism and evolution led to considering Jesus Christ a mere stage in the development of full human potential. Pierson had always believed that the claim of missions rested on salvation through Jesus Christ. But destructive critical views questioning humanity's need for Christ made evangelism not only unnecessary but impossible, because they gave people no reason to become Christians. The effect of higher criticism on sending churches was equally devastating, for "wherever the 'higher critical' views most strongly obtain there has been a *loss of spiritual power*."

In 1910, the doctrinally conservative journal *The Presbyterian* printed a twenty-one-week series by A. T. Pierson entitled "Modern Doubt." The series demonstrated how the fight against higher criticism was consolidating the ranks of biblical conservatives. As the bastion of confessional Presbyterianism, *The Presbyterian* had been hostile to Pierson's "enthusiasm" during his ministry and highly critical of his rebaptism. The journal disapproved of Pierson's holiness theology and his interest in faith healing and prophecy. Conservative Presbyterians also tended to see dispensationalism as a kind of heresy, a perversion of traditional Reformed covenant theology. Yet fourteen years after his rebaptism, the journal depended on someone of known holiness and premillennial sympathies to unleash a major offensive against the common enemy. A realignment of conservatives versus liberals was taking place across the denominational spectrum.

In the series "Modern Doubt," A. T. Pierson attacked "literary and historical criticism" for undermining the trustworthiness of the Word of God. Denying the "plenary and verbal inspiration of the Scriptures" would lead to the denial of the divinity of Christ.

> Upon the Inspiration and Infallibility of the Holy Scriptures rest, also, the Divinity and Redemptive work of the Lord Jesus. They stand and fall together. And it is very noticeable that one is never assaulted without involving the other. The Written Word and the Living Word are so inseparable that whatever impugns the former necessarily affects the latter. What we know of the Christ we know primarily from the Scriptures; and his appeal was constantly to the Word of God; so that if one is untrustworthy, so must be the other.

Pierson believed that assaults on the Bible and on the church by "nihilists," "atheists," "skeptics," "traffickers in souls," and others meant that the Battle of Armageddon was drawing near. In "The Harm Done by Higher Criticism," one of the articles in the "Modern Doubt" series, he cited authorities who claimed that higher criticism was taking over seminaries, journals, denominations, and ministers.

Pierson's attacks on higher criticism showed thorough familiarity with the doctrines of the "New Theology." Those which he found most objectionable included: the theory that the first five books of the Old Testament were a compilation of several different documents (the documentary hypothesis), the indebtedness of the Israelites to "heathen" religions, the postexilic invention of the levitical system, the referral of "messianic" prediction to Israel the servant rather than to Christ, kenotic theory, miracles as the result of natural causes, and the idea that all religions are simply equal attempts by people to find God. Arthur Pierson attacked higher criticism both by defending the Bible with his own apologetics and by attempting to discredit the conclusions of higher criticism itself.

At the very end of A. T. Pierson's life, he joined together with other conservative ministers and theologians into a self-conscious movement defending the essentials of evangelical Protestantism as it had developed during the late nineteenth century. Some of his last articles appeared in a series of books entitled *The Fundamentals*, published in 1909-1911. Two businessmen from Los Angeles, Lyman and Milton

Stewart, who were active supporters of evangelistic missions and founders of the Bible Institute of Los Angeles, donated the money to issue twelve volumes of *The Fundamentals* and to send them free to three hundred thousand Christian workers, including missionaries, throughout the world. The purpose of the volumes was to set out the basic doctrines deemed "fundamental" to trinitarian, evangelical Christian faith. In their efforts to appeal across the conservative spectrum, the controversial tenets of premillennialism were not strongly evident in the books.

Pierson's contribution of five articles to *The Fundamentals* marked him as a father of "fundamentalism," a movement that coalesced in the 1920s and took its name from the books. He wrote articles on the organic unity and inspiration of the Bible, the divine efficacy of prayer, George Müller, stewardship, and God's providence in foreign missions. With A. T. Pierson as elder statesman of the late nineteenth-century Bible study movement, the division between modernism and fundamentalism had begun. The realignment in American Protestantism in the early twentieth century showed just how far things had changed from his youth, when the Old School Presbyterians split from the New School, and the northern branches of churches split from the southern branches over slavery.

Perhaps the ultimate symbol of the changing religious scene was the *Scofield Reference Bible*. Scofield himself had fought on the Confederate side during the Civil War, and he joined the Southern Presbyterian Church — the old voice of pro-slavery theology — while working on his reference Bible. He founded a Bible school in Dallas, Texas, that continued his legacy. Even though the northern and southern branches of Presbyterianism had never reunited after the Civil War, Pierson and Scofield's common premillennialism and supernatural approach to biblical revelation unified them forty years later. The New York Yankee and the Confederate Rebel made peace — and joined forces in the twentieth-century battle for the Bible.

10 Occupy Until I Come

A s someone who spent the final decade of his life promoting the spiritual life of the believer and leading Bible studies in lay Bible-training institutes on two continents, the elderly A. T. Pierson could have retreated into an entirely spiritual world. After all, chronic ill health dogged him from 1897 onward. The death of A. J. Gordon in 1895 was followed by the death of Dwight Moody in 1899, of Hudson Taylor in 1905, and other dear friends during the first decade of the twentieth century. The Piersons' daughter Louise died of typhoid fever in 1904 while working among women and girls in India. Although Dr. Pierson clearly grew more preoccupied with prayer in his old age, his interest in international and political events never waned. Even as *The Missionary Review* contained more articles by Pierson on spiritual issues, it also became more sharply political. Especially in the new century, evaluating the "world outlook" for missions became a defining feature of the journal. Under the managing editorship of Pierson's son Delavan since 1891, *The Missionary Review* nevertheless felt the guiding hand of its editor-in-chief as it analyzed the "signs of the times." As someone who since the Civil War had been fascinated with God's workings through human history, Pierson's premillennialism made him even more interested in social and political issues. While recapping the important events of 1898, he remarked, "Even such a hurried resumé of the chief events of the past year indicates the close connection between politics and missions. Every war and rumor of war, every reform and attempt at reform, every famine, massacre, riot, and earthquake has a bearing upon the missionary outlook. Moreover the purpose of God for the nations is wrought out in political as well as in missionary movements, and all co-work for the final consummation of the Divine plan." In 1905, he stated, "One must fall in love with the world to be possessed with the missionary spirit. Christ's dream was of universal empire, and should our vision be less extended?"

The Missionary Review remained at the top of its field because it was the only general-interest journal that combined popular and scholarly articles on missions, set in a context of active curiosity about God's work in the world. While some of the preoccupations of Pierson's final decade seem predictable, others reveal that the journal fit the progressive politics of the early twentieth century. A typical issue of the journal was likely to have an article on a Zionist conference — clearly of interest to dispensationalists looking for Israel to reoccupy Palestine in advance of Christ's Second Coming — and an article on the progress of international talks about arbitration of national disputes. The mixture of the prophetic with the sociopolitical might have seemed peculiar for a mission periodical in a later era, but under A. T. Pierson's and his son's leadership, the journal never lost its interest in social justice issues. Its conservative progressivism, combined with practical features like book reviews and statistical surveys, and predictable interests like missionary biography, meant that it kept the loyalty of a wide readership. During Pierson's lifetime it remained the preeminent missionary periodical of the day.

The Missionary Review is the best historical source for studying the varied concerns of evangelical Protestantism in the late nineteenth and early twentieth centuries. While full discussion of its range is not possible here, it is instructive to see how a number of Arthur Pierson's lifelong interests filled its pages in addition to more predictable articles on missions. One recurring interest that reflected Pierson's formation in the anti-slavery milieu of early nineteenth-century New York was the journal's continued reporting on "the caste spirit," or racism and oppression of ethnic minorities. Articles on the Anglo-Boer War, for example, condemned the treatment of black South Africans by the Dutch settlers, and compared the Boer attitudes to those of Southerners in the United States. Pierson decried race prejudice and the lynching of southern blacks during what was the solidification of the segregationist "Jim Crow" era. In the September 1901 issue, the journal carried an article by the young black sociologist W. E. B. DuBois, "The Spawn of Slavery. The Convict-Lease System in the South." Published four years before his classic work *The Souls of Black Folk*, the article reviewed the history of the chain gang system in the segregated South, and justified crimes by African-Americans as part of a revolt against social injustice. An editorial praised the DuBois article and called upon preachers to advocate reform of the system "by tongue and pen." The journal carried a glowing review of DuBois's book when it appeared. In 1905, an article called favorable attention to the new Negro Niagara Movement led by DuBois, the forerunner of the National Association for the Advancement of Colored People (NAACP).

Even as *The Missionary Review* supported the rights of black Americans, Pierson supported the rise of "Ethiopianism" in South Africa, namely the forming by black South Africans of independent churches that rejected the racism of the white churches. He strongly condemned human rights abuses by colonial powers in Africa, and editorialized against forced labor in the Belgian Congo, under the administration of King Leopold. The journal contained the first exposés of the atrocities committed against rubber workers by the colonial agents of King Leopold, replete with photographs of armless and earless natives who had been tortured by Belgian soldiers for not collecting their full quota of rubber. With Presbyterian missionaries being the ones who blew the whistle on the atrocities, it is not surprising that *The Missionary Review* carried information on their discoveries to a broad audience. An editorial in 1907 lamented that colonial powers were turning Africa red with the blood of its people. Pierson relied on missionary informants to reveal the human rights abuses against minority peoples. He commented on the anti-Semitism of the Dreyfus affair, pogroms against Jews in Russia, and the massacre of Armenians by the Turks.

The treatment of Native Americans was another aspect of race prejudice covered by *The Missionary Review*. Pierson's interest in American Indians increased in 1889 when his daughter Laura went to Tucson, Arizona, as a missionary. Pierson denounced the United States government for breaking past treaties and sending Indians to smaller reservations. Because of severe water shortages among the Pima and Navajo, Pierson got a friend in Brooklyn to pay for an artesian well. Dr. and Mrs. Pierson, and son Delavan and his wife belonged to the Lake Mohonk Conference of Friends of the Indian. Pierson promoted the annual Mohonk conferences as one of the few places where people regularly worked for justice for Native Americans, supporting legislation to secure land and education for them. In 1904, in light of the take-over of the Philippines, Cuba, and Puerto Rico by the United States, the Mohonk gathering changed its name to "Friends of the Indians and Other Dependent Peoples." *The Missionary Review* reported conference proceedings, and in 1904 A. T. Pierson gave a short address. While Mohonk policies promoted citizenship and assimilation for American Indians, and had little interest in maintaining Indian cultures, the conferences were nevertheless among the few voices for Indian rights at the turn of the century. In general, A. T. Pierson's attitude toward ethnic minorities remained focused on "uplift" and strategies of "civilization" through conversion to Christianity. The overt focus of *The Missionary Review* on racial prejudice, however, was a voice crying in the wilderness at the turn of the century, the nadir of race relations in the United States.

One issue that deeply concerned A. T. Pierson was the arms race between England and Germany that was heating up in the late 1890s, and led to the outbreak of World War I. As someone who spent much of his time in the United Kingdom, he was probably more aware of European saber-rattling than most Americans. In an article "The Menace of Militarism," the journal decried the building of weapons "disguised in the cloak of a peace measure." It argued that the cost of battleships, obsolete before they were finished, could be used to exterminate tuberculosis or give every family a dollar a week. Pierson worried that the kinds of weapons being built were more destructive than anything previously known to humankind, and he frequently advocated arbitration in disputes among nations. He reported on peace conferences held in the Hague, in New York City, and on the international peace conference held in Boston in 1904. Supporting a "Prayer Union for International Peace," an editorial urged that readers pray that the church might realize her calling as a peacemaker.

A. T. Pierson believed that God would judge the nations for their sins, including the United States.

The Missionary Review reported on wars and signs of wars, especially when political violence threatened the church. It also reported extensively on the massacre of Chinese Christians and missionaries during the Boxer Rebellion of 1900. It was concerned with the rising military prowess of Japan, and its aggression against China, Russia, and Korea. The journal thoroughly discussed the Spanish-American War and urged a united approach toward sending Protestant missionaries to the Philippines.

Besides militarism, materialism came in for condemnation as a particular sin of the West. The journal urged tithing and financial sacrifice by Christians as an antidote to the materialism of Christians. Pierson's hostility to materialism was a consistent feature of his urban ministry, and he deliberately sought downward mobility as an action against it. The editorial discussing the outlook for 1905 commented that a gigantic money power threatened the United States: "Ten men in America hold an amount of wealth so enormous that practically it throws even the scales of justice out of balance, and threatens to control the government of the country, legislative, judicial, and executive." In 1908, the editor warned that concentration of wealth was a peril that led to autocracy and domination by the rich. Through criticizing massive wealth, *The Missionary Review* was implicitly supporting the trust-busting and other attempts at regulating wealth by progressive Republican President Theodore Roosevelt, who challenged the monopolistic practices of businessmen in the railroad, beef, oil, and tobacco industries. The journal continued Pierson's interest in questions of labor and capital, and poverty. One of the "signs of the times" noted in 1906 was the rise of a "sociological gospel" that addressed the Christian responsibility for society.

> Another marked indication of our day is the recognition of a human brotherhood and of our obligations to man as man. Of course this may easily lapse into mere humanitarianism without spiritual significance, but there is a deep truth which it recognizes, that the gospel is not only for the individual, but for the home and for the nation, that its principle is to remold and regenerate, that its ultimate object is a new city of God, a community in which nothing

enters that defiles, or works abomination, or makes a lie. Every church should interest itself in reorganizing society on Christian principles, and all work is essentially defective which leaves out of view man's domestic and social conditions.

While supporting Christian responsibility for all of society, *The Missionary Review* worried at the same time that sociology might crowd out theology, or sentimentalism replace deep conviction.

The social commentary in *The Missionary Review* under A. T. Pierson's editorship represented a theologically conservative form of progressivism consistent with mainstream American politics at the turn of the century. Some historians of the era have argued that scholars have ignored the conservative contribution to progressive social reform by making a radical separation between those interested in social Christianity and those interested in individual conversion. While showing steady interest in revivalism, dispensational prophecy, prayer, and the Bible, *The Missionary Review* demonstrates that there was not necessarily a connection between conservative theology and conservative politics among early twentieth-century evangelicals. On the contrary, Pierson's roots in the anti-slavery movement and years in urban ministry among the poor made his political agenda compatible with Theodore Roosevelt's progressivism. His assumption that God worked through secular history meant that striving to Christianize society, both in the West and in the mission field, remained an important part of the missionary agenda. Writing in support of legislation to secure shorter working hours, equitable wage scales, and safe working conditions, he commented that pro-labor legislation represented "a legitimate sphere for mission work on Scriptural principles."

An issue that received sustained attention from A. T. Pierson in *The Missionary Review* was that of church unity movements. As long-term member of the Evangelical Alliance, Pierson continued to believe that the Bible demanded Christian unity across denominational barriers. The last international meeting of the Evangelical Alliance he attended was in London in 1907. Among a heavily British rostrum of speakers, A. T. Pierson stood out as an American. Promoting the meeting, he stated that "The Evangelical Alliance — whose motto is 'Unum corpus sumus in Christo' — maintains universal testimony to a great truth in the oneness of the Church which is the Body of Christ, and

seeks to promote love and union between Christians in various lands."
As someone who had been promoting the creation of ecumenical fed-
erations since at least the 1880s, he reported with great approval the
meetings that led to the formation of the Federal Council of Churches
in 1908, though he always urged that church federation be based on
shared belief in salvation through Jesus Christ. But Pierson saved his
greatest enthusiasm for ecumenical meetings promoting the mission
of the church.

After the Centenary Conference of 1888, organizers planned the
next large Anglo-American missionary conference for New York City
in 1900 — a development praised and publicized along the way by *The
Missionary Review*. During the year 1900, the journal carried detailed
reporting on the Ecumenical Missionary Conference, the first modern
conference to use the term "ecumenical," meaning the entire inhabited
world. Held from April 21 to May 1, 1900, with headquarters at Carnegie Hall, the conference attracted up to 200,000 people, making it the
best-attended mission conference in history. Twenty-five hundred official delegates hailed from 162 mission boards, not including women's
mission societies. Three United States presidents participated, including Benjamin Harrison, sitting president William McKinley, and future
president Theodore Roosevelt, then governor of New York. Occurring
after the end of the Spanish-American War, and the acquisition of the
Philippines as a colony, the conference demonstrated a convergence of
religious and nationalistic interests among ordinary Christians, who
attended the many concurrent sessions held at churches around town
and visited the groundbreaking exhibit of cultural artifacts collected
by missionaries. On a popular level, the conference celebrated how
missions were leading to "progress" by spreading Christian ideas (and
western civilization) around the world. Backed by a 25-by-50-foot
world map, distinguished politicians, businessmen, and churchmen
took the stage. When the opening hymn "Jesus Shall Reign Where E'er
the Sun" was sung by thousands, the proceedings inspired even the
most jaded onlookers. In addition to regular coverage by the major
newspapers, the *New York Tribune* issued a sixteen-page extra edition
on the conference.

In his opening address, former president Harrison declared that
the brotherhood of all under the fatherhood of God was the goal of
Christianity, and that Christians should unite to spread these ideals

around the world as the highest form of altruism. Speaker after speaker called for linking the gospel with "acts of benevolence and human progress." In the words of the two-volume conference report, "Christianity was shown to be connected with everything best and most beautiful on earth." Probably nothing captured the optimism of the American people as they headed into the twentieth century as well as the Ecumenical Missionary Conference.

At a more technical level, the Ecumenical Conference permitted six hundred missionaries and many mission executives to strategize and to map out ways in which they could cooperate with each other. The Foreign Missions Conference of North America, the annual meeting of denominational mission boards, ran the event. A series of committees met on different missionary topics. The consensus among the delegates was that regional strategic planning among different mission societies should occur, so that needless duplication and rivalry would cease. Missions should collaborate in higher education, medical work, publishing, and other areas of mutual concern. While the conversations allowed a valuable exchange of ideas, the delegates were not permitted to vote officially on behalf of their sending churches. The day after the conference ended, two hundred delegates met and resolved to establish a permanent international missions committee, a project near to the heart of A. T. Pierson. The Executive Committee of the conference sent letters of inquiry to mission board secretaries, but in 1901 the Foreign Missions Conference of North America met and decided that the time was not ripe to establish an international organization. The founding of a "continuation committee" to provide coordination of Protestant foreign missions would have to wait for its establishment until the next international missionary conference at Edinburgh. In the meantime, the Foreign Missions Conference of North America authorized a "Bureau of Missions" as a clearinghouse for research and information. The Bureau of Missions, it was hoped, would inspire other countries to form similar research units and thus hasten the establishment of an international committee.

Given that *The Missionary Review of the World* had been promoting ecumenical mission cooperation for years, it is no surprise that it took the Bureau of Missions under its wing. In January 1905, the journal carried a major article on the Bureau of Missions, describing its literary work, library collection, and museum, and asking for donations. It urged the public to borrow materials collected by the Bureau and to send inquiries for needed information to them. The responsibilities of the Bureau included completing the ethnographic missions exhibit and donating it to the Museum of Natural History, and collecting all published works on missions. Because the aims of the journal and the Bureau of Missions were compatible, three leaders of the Bureau became consulting editors for *The Missionary Review,* an affiliation they maintained on an experimental basis for two years.

In his numerous articles on the Ecumenical Conference, A. T. Pierson lauded the spirit of harmony that pervaded the assembly. He saw in it the hand of God, who controlled the world according to his purposes. Pierson had special praise for the high visibility of women and youth. Many of his protégés from the Student Volunteer Movement took leading roles, with John Mott in the chair. During the middle of the conference, four hundred female missionaries appeared in Carnegie Hall, organized by the widow of A. J. Gordon. The presence of so many female missionaries inspired the audience to applaud and wave thousands of handkerchiefs. Young Christian women from different countries were introduced in native costume. Miss Lilavati Singh of India, protégé of educational missionary Isabella Thoburn, was widely agreed to have delivered the most inspiring address of the entire conference. Pierson commented on the high quality of women's participation, stating that "the epiphany of woman has come — her emergence out of the obscurity of the ages into her true and rightful sphere of influence."

A. T. Pierson himself was hailed as one of the father figures of the modern mission movement — author of the Student Volunteer watchword, tireless promoter of world evangelization, and editor of the movement's leading periodical. He delivered an address on "The Superintending Providence of God in Foreign Missions" at a plenary session in Carnegie Hall on April 23. Relying on military metaphors that compared different units of the mission force to regiments, he sounded the familiar theme of God's working through history. With the "Church Army" now complete, only one thing more was needed, namely "to recognize the invisible Captain of the Lord's Hosts, as on the field, to hear his clarion call summoning us to the front, to echo His Word of command; and in the firm faith of His leadership, pierce the very center of the foe, turn his staggering wings, and move forward as one united host in one overwhelming charge." Pierson's speech vibrated with millennial fervor as he envisioned the final war of Christ and the church against the Devil and his cohorts. A unified mission movement for world evangelization was itself part of God's plan for the ages.

While A. T. Pierson praised the Ecumenical Conference in public, in private he jotted his reservations in his diary. At the beginning of the conference he confided, "Thus far little or no *spiritual* impression on conference. Word of God not read. The whole air post millennial, undue stress on culture. Fatherhood of God. Brotherhood of Man. Education, etc. Too much like Congress of Religions." Thus even as Pierson promoted the ecumenical cause in *The Missionary Review,* he worried privately about the spiritual basis of the enterprise. He reacted against the optimism and easy association of western culture with the gospel. He worried if he heard too much of liberal theology's phrase "the brotherhood of man under the fatherhood of God," without a corresponding emphasis on the divine and supernatural aspects of Christian faith. He had moved long ago from believing in postmillennialism, that the kingdom of God could be attained gradually through human effort.

The irony of Pierson's concern about the Ecumenical Conference was that the Student Volunteer watchword, associated in the public mind with his own views, was the lightning rod for German critics who thought it smacked of Anglo-American self-importance and optimism. In 1897, the leading German mission theologian, Gustav Warneck, had attacked the watchword as superficial because it dealt with verbal proclamation rather than the upbuilding of national churches. By 1900, however, with the world clearly not yet evangelized, the idea of "the evangelization of the world in this generation" was undergoing modifications. While to committed premillennialists it still had the ring of hastening the Second Coming, the leaders of the Student Volunteer Movement were retreating from an idea of the watchword as predicting immediate success. John Mott cleared up Warneck's objections to the watchword in his book, *The Evangelization of the World in This Generation* by defining it to mean giving all people "an adequate opportunity to know Jesus Christ as their Saviour and to become his real disciples." To evangelize did not mean hasty preaching, or converting the world, or a particular prophecy or eschatology.

Rather, it meant preaching the gospel to all the living people of "this generation" by the people now alive, also of "this generation." The watchword was a motivation, a source of strength, and a source of spiritual power for those who answered its call.

As the years passed and time came for the great missionary meeting at Edinburgh in 1910, the watchword "the evangelization of the world in this generation" was still very much in evidence. Like all great slogans, it meant different things to different people. Above all, it came to characterize the activistic optimism of the pre–World War I missionary generation. *The Missionary Review* continued to promote the watchword and the ecumenical causes with which it became associated, but by 1910, A. T. Pierson himself was 73 years old. His son Delavan went in his place to the historic meeting that finally represented the fulfillment of A. T. Pierson's dreams for a permanent, international missionary organization. The meeting at Edinburgh in 1910 marked the beginning of the twentieth-century ecumenical movement, which culminated in the founding of the International Missionary Council in 1921 and the World Council of Churches in 1948. While the "old guard" — Pierson, A. J. Gordon, Dwight Moody, J. Hudson Taylor, H. Grattan Guinness — were not present in person, their spirit lived on in their followers. Although they modified aspects of their mentors' dreams to fit the needs of their own day, the younger generation took their places as the visionary leaders of a groundbreaking twentieth-century ecumenical missionary movement. John Mott, Robert Speer, Donald Fraser, and others never forgot the legacy they had received from their fathers in the faith.

THE FINAL MISSIONARY JOURNEY

In 1910, Dr. Pierson celebrated the fiftieth anniversary of his ordination to the ministry. In fifty years, he had delivered over thirteen thousand sermons and addresses, and had written over fifty books and innumerable tracts, poems, songs, articles, and pamphlets. At Northfield, where he enjoyed encouraging the high school students and leading Bible studies for conferences, the summer crowd held a meeting in his honor. The Piersons also celebrated their golden wedding anniversary there in July. The Reverend J. Stuart Holden came from Keswick to bring the greetings of friends in the United Kingdom. Mr. and Mrs. W. R. Moody joined the family for the occasion. After the death of his father, Dwight Moody's son William had continued to rely on A. T. Pierson for assistance in the summer conferences, and the families were close friends.

One of the most gratifying events of Pierson's "jubilee year" was receiving a message from the General Assembly of the Presbyterian Church — the denomination that had thrown him out of the ministry over his immersion fifteen years before: "The General Assembly of the Presbyterian Church in the United States of America, at the close of a session devoted to Foreign Missions, sends you affectionate greetings, and expresses its gratitude to God for the service you have been enabled to render by voice and pen towards the world-wide extension of the Redeemer's Kingdom." Following passage of the resolution, Robert E. Speer, secretary of the Board of Missions, offered a prayer of thanksgiving for the life of his mentor A. T. Pierson, and prayed that God would either restore his health, or raise up others who could share and even enlarge his vision. The act of reconciliation on the part of the Presbyterian Church in 1910 showed how time could shift the ground, and reshape alliances among evangelical believers. Not only was Pierson's protégé, Robert Speer, the head of the mission board, but the convergence of conservative forces against modernism meant that Pierson's controversial views on baptism, spirituality, and prophecy had become less important to the denomination than his spirited and consistent defense of an infallible Bible, and his promotion of foreign missions. Passage of the "five points of fundamentalism" occurred at the same General Assembly that held out an olive branch to the elderly Bible teacher.

By 1910, A. T. Pierson had spent over twenty years "on the road." In his extensive travels, he had endured a train wreck, a ship collision that caused fatalities, and being struck by an electric car on lower Broadway in New York City. He had traveled, preached, taught, written, and prayed tirelessly in the cause of missions. All seven of his children had become involved in the mission movement. The oldest daughter, Helen, remained in Japan and Korea with her husband as a lifetime missionary of the Presbyterian Church. Laura spent her life as a home missionary among American Indians and Appalachian mountaineers. Louise died in India while working under a woman's missionary society. Daughters Anna and Edith worked in settlement houses in New York City and Philadelphia, and later Anna spent a year working in Papua New Guinea. Devoting their lives to mission work, two of the Pierson daughters never married. Older son Delavan took over *The Missionary Review of the World* and some of his father's other responsibilities, and the younger son Farrand became a medical doctor and missionary in Central America until forced to return because of impaired health. Yet A. T. Pierson had never visited the missions himself. While on the verge of going to China in 1897, he had become seriously ill and had to cancel the trip.

The greatest gift of Pierson's anniversary celebration was that friends collected money to send him and his wife on a tour of the mission fields, starting in East Asia. Plans were laid for youngest daughter Anna to accompany her elderly parents to visit their daughter Helen in Japan. Despite precarious health, the Piersons with Anna and two friends from England departed for Japan in October 1910. Dr. Pierson carried with him a questionnaire for each mission station they visited in order to survey the field and publish the results in a study volume. He planned to write regular letters to *The Missionary Review* for publication. The itinerary included Japan, Korea, China, Siam, India, Burma, Ceylon, and Egypt. By the time he reached Japan, Pierson was ill, for the sea voyage had been cold and rough. But he rallied enough to give several addresses, insisting against doctor's orders that he speak on behalf of his friend John Wanamaker, who had donated the funds to build the YMCA building in Kyoto, Japan. Because of his limited strength, he refused to play the tourist so that he would have the energy to visit missions and religious sites.

Writing to *The Missionary Review* from Japan, Pierson told of how Wanamaker, working with Bethany Church, had paid for YMCA buildings and schools in several locations in India, as well as provided YMCA buildings for Peking, China, and Seoul, Korea. While in Kyoto, Pierson was extremely impressed by the social work of Japanese Christians among the poor and criminals. He visited Doshisha University, and the outreach work of a Japanese minister he had known at Bethany Church. In Hiroshima, he enjoyed visiting a missionary girls' school. He conducted Bible studies for resident missionaries in Hiroshima, and visited evangelistic work in Yamaguchi. A. T. Pierson's impression of the mission field was even more moving than a lifetime of dreams had pictured. "What we have seen and heard surpasses all we have known or imagined. . . . It requires personal contact to understand both the problems of missions and the adequacy of the gospel to solve them. The more we see of missionary work the more we believe it to be God's work."

After a month in Japan, the Piersons traveled to Korea and remained in Seoul for six weeks. He began holding daily Bible readings with missionaries, but his health gave way and he was hospitalized. Refusing to give up now that he had finally reached the mission field, Pierson gave two addresses a week — all that he could manage without collapsing. It is probable that his illness was related to the kidney and bladder problems he had suffered since 1897, and he was in intense pain. When it became clear that he would have to abandon his tour of mission fields and return to the United States, he fought against it. Having met Korean Christians who were experiencing deep spiritual conversions to Christianity as they struggled against Japanese imperialism, he decided to ask friends to contribute to the founding of Bible schools in Korea. Korean Christians showed intense desires to study the Bible, which was providing them with spiritual resources for their resistance to the Japanese. Protestant missionaries had first entered Korea only in 1884, and the need for training institutions was large because of the great interest in the gospel.

After three months, the Piersons and their daughter Helen and her husband sailed for the United States. Because of a loss of equilibrium, Pierson had to remain for two months with T. C. Horton in Los Angeles, his old associate pastor at Bethany Church and founder of the Bible Institute of Los Angeles. In March 1911, he celebrated his seventy-fourth birthday with a Japanese meal. He wrote verses for family members and gave away seventy-four dollars in gold pieces. Collapsing after supper, he wrote sadly in his diary, "If ever better, only Divine power can secure it. At present no abler to go East than two weeks ago."

He managed to make the train trip to Brooklyn about three weeks before he died on June 3, 1911. Despite the many places in which he had ministered, he was born and he died as a New Yorker. He worked right up to the end, preparing editorials for *The Missionary Review* and writing Bible studies for the *Record of Christian Work*. His funeral was held at Bedford Presbyterian Church, where he had worshiped. Speakers included a lifelong friend, the Reverend Wilson Phraner; Dr. John Carson, moderator of the General Assembly of the Presbyterian Church; Robert E. Speer; and Dr. John Jowett, English friend and new pastor of Fifth Avenue Presbyterian Church in Manhattan. The presence of so many highly placed Presbyterians reemphasized the reconciliation that had occurred between A. T. Pierson and the denomination of his birth. The congregation sang "Jesus, Lover of My Soul" and "When I Survey the Wondrous Cross." Mrs. W. R. Moody sang two solos. Pallbearers included William Moody and Charles Erdman of Princeton Seminary, both the sons of dear friends; and Henry Frost, director of the China Inland Mission's North American home council. On Pierson's grave, his family and friends erected a monument on which stood a globe of the world, with an open Bible beneath it. On the Bible were engraved two verses that summed up his priorities in life. The first was from his favorite book of the Bible, 1 John: "God hath given to us Eternal Life and this life is in His Son." The second was the Great Commission of Matthew 28, Jesus' post-resurrection words to his disciples, and the verse that more than any other characterized the Protestant missionary movement: "Go ye into all the world and preach the Gospel to every creature."

AFTERWORD

In reflecting on his impending death, Arthur Tappan Pierson had expected to be freed from his labors, but to carry all "joyous activities" with him to Jesus Christ. "I expect to go to more active service. I have a desire to depart and be with Christ but I also have a desire to abide in the flesh because of the needs I see for work in God's kingdom." Preparing to "die in the Lord," A. T. Pierson did not live to see the hoped-for Second Coming. Nor did his spiritually intense, theologically conservative, socially progressive evangelicalism survive his generation in one piece. But working until the end, never with passive resignation to his fate, and never giving up his belief that God was moving through human history, he followed his Master's command to "occupy until I come."

The question remains as to what "active service" the legacy of A. T. Pierson performed after his death. What was the lasting significance of the life of this man who never stopped working, and who even approached death in a spirit of activism? His ministry stretched roughly from the period of the Civil War to World War I, a time of momentous change in American society. He spent his life in northern cities, where he saw firsthand the effects of industrialization and the immigration of millions of Irish, Germans, Eastern Europeans, and Italians. With the advent of Darwinian science and biblical higher criticism, and the increasing wealth of the northern middle classes, the simple certainties of revivalistic evangelicalism lost ground within Protestantism. But having been spiritually and emotionally formed during the struggle against slavery, he retained a vision of a united, evangelical Protestantism that would prosecute God's purposes in the world. With his generational cohorts Dwight L. Moody, A. J. Gordon, and others, he embraced missions as a cause that united his concerns both for the future of American society, and the spread of the gospel throughout the world. Those who launched the missionary movement of the 1880s and 1890s were the activistic generation of Yankee evangelicals who had come of age during the Civil War. They shared their vision with like-minded English speakers from the United Kingdom and its colonies, building on a tradition of transatlantic revivalism that had flourished since the eighteenth century. Despite the changes in Protestantism itself, the men of Pierson's generation never completely lost their faith in the power of united evangelicalism to transform society. A. T. Pierson was thus a grandfather of the twentieth-century ecumenical movement, an international movement of church cooperation that led to the formation of the World Council of Churches. His promotion of "world evangelization" inspired young people because it combined personal responsibility with a grand vision of a united, faithful church at work in the world.

Yet, the grand vision came up against the hard realities of the shrinking evangelical base for American society after the Civil War. Despair over inability to reach the masses, combined with anxiety over the middle-class pursuit of wealth and consumerism rather than God's causes, meant that discovering premillennial interpretations of Scripture was a profound relief to A. T. Pierson and his cohorts. A pessimistic reading of the future of western society seemed confirmed by biblical "facts." With the Bible and history in agreement, it became clear that just as the righteous crusade against slavery had not brought in

God's kingdom, neither would the missionary movement. Neverthe-less, the emphasis remained on obedience and doing one's duty. De-spite its grounding in the supernatural, belief in the Second Coming represented a kind of "realism" with regard to western society, a "chastening" of the postmillennial optimism of Civil War–era northern evangelicals. The crusade for world evangelization was part of God's plan, even if the conversion of the world was not. In short, the mis-sionary movement gave divine sanction to the existence of evangelical Christianity, even if it seemed to be losing ground to skepticism, mate-rialism, and an increasingly pluralistic American society. Thus A. T. Pierson was also grandfather to the faith mission and Bible training school movements, the scaffolding for the building of a separatist, nondenominational evangelical subculture in the twentieth century.

The grand ecumenical vision, and the willingness to build sepa-ratist, parachurch organizations, were two sides of the same coin. Dur-ing his lifetime, A. T. Pierson held a world-changing "churchly" vision in creative tension with a purity-seeking "sectarian" one. The synergy between the two visions empowered a missionary movement that sought both to spread the spiritual gospel and to encourage schools, modern medicine, and other signs of western Christian progress. The missionary movement was successful in capturing the imagination of the younger generation because it held together the spiritual and emo-tive with the intellectual sides of Christian faith. Pierson succeeded as a missions promoter among college students because he absolutely re-fused to separate the spiritual from the intellectual. As a product of New School Presbyterianism, with a first-class education in both a lib-eral arts college and a theological seminary, he insisted on keeping the American revivalistic tradition connected to a rational exposition of biblically based Christian doctrine. To the end of his life, he believed that mastery of the "facts" was essential to creating support for mission work in the world. At the same time, he repeatedly sought spiritual ex-periences, and used Bible study to deepen the spiritual lives of believ-ers. The mission movement thrived on its emotional appeal to personal spiritual instincts toward holiness, combined with logical analysis of the world's needs and of the church's responsibilities to meet those needs. Missions drew upon both the latent emotion of American popu-lar religion and a system of rationality that valued certainty and the classification of historical facts as the "fingers of God."

The mission movement of the late nineteenth century was a primary source of both the ecumenical and the fundamentalist movements of the twentieth century. During Pierson's lifetime, the two contradictory elements shared a common holiness piety, evangelical belief system, Anglo-American activism, and international focus. But the changing context after World War I caused the nineteenth-century synthesis to collapse. By the 1920s, as variations of new theologies swept through the mainline denominations, those who held to more traditional formulations about sin, redemption, and salvation exclusively through Jesus Christ found themselves at odds with so-called "modernists." Bitter fights for control over denominations and theological seminaries led to a separatist fundamentalism that rejected many of the things A. T. Pierson had stood for — ecumenical cooperation, social progressivism, and the ministry of women. Even the holiness piety that had fueled much evangelistic activity was discarded by the early 1930s for a more rigid, propositional approach to Christian belief, or else transformed into an even more emotional pentecostalism. Fundamentalists elevated the dispensational system in the *Scofield Reference Bible* to an authority unintended by its original editors.

In the 1940s, a "new evangelicalism" was born that most closely represented the continuation of A. T. Pierson's ideals. Emerging from the fundamentalist subculture, evangelicalism moved toward the cooperative breadth that had characterized Pierson's life and ministry. The lifeblood of mid-twentieth-century evangelicalism remained foreign missions, including a rediscovery in the 1960s of the old Student Volunteer watchword, "the evangelization of the world in this generation." In 1974, evangelicals from around the world met in Lausanne, Switzerland, to formulate a covenant that became the basic statement of belief for self-consciously evangelical missions. The Lausanne Covenant, with its affirmation of classic Protestant doctrines, the centrality of missions, its affirmation of work for social justice, and its anticipation of the Second Coming of Jesus Christ, most closely continued the vision for which A. T. Pierson had lived. With the Lausanne Covenant as the basis for belief and cooperation, self-consciously evangelical missionaries, both from independent and denominational missions, became by far the largest family of missionaries during the late twentieth century.

But the longest-lasting aspect of A. T. Pierson's legacy was in the exponential growth of non-western Christianity during the twentieth century. The missionary vision that he fostered among the youth of the late nineteenth century led to the sending of missionaries into previously non-Christian parts of the world. By the end of the twentieth century, in one of the most remarkable demographic shifts in the history of the faith, Christianity had become primarily a non-western religion. After A. T. Pierson's death, contributions poured in to fulfill his last dream of starting a Bible teacher training school in Seoul, Korea. With $27,000 raised initially, the Pierson Memorial Bible School opened in October 1912. Under the initial control of the Presbyterians, it also received the endorsement of various denominations that worked in Seoul. The training it offered was seen as preparatory to entering a denominational seminary. During the twentieth century, Pierson Memorial Bible School evolved into a university and theological seminary under Korean control. In 1996, it changed its name to Pyongtaek University. Korean Christianity had by the late twentieth century become one of the most dynamic and mission-oriented forms of Christianity in the world. The "active service" that A. T. Pierson anticipated on his deathbed continues to live in the missionary visions of a multicultural, global, evangelical Christianity.

A Note on Sources

By far the most important sources on the life and thought of A. T. Pierson are his own writings. Given that Pierson had published a hundred articles by age 21, the impossibility of tracking down all of his writings becomes apparent. Throughout his lifetime, he was a daily, disciplined writer. He wrote fifty books, edited a major journal, published articles in dozens of periodicals, corresponded with the leading evangelicals of the day, and kept voluminous notes from his daily Bible studies. Fortunately for the researcher, he had a beautiful handwriting. He kept a daily journal from his childhood until his death, of which only fragments appear to exist today. His sermons were usually published by the churches he served, but only a small number of the sermon pamphlets have survived. A few collections of sermons, Bible readings, and articles also appeared as books. The quantity and importance of A. T. Pierson's publications mark him as a major Christian intellectual in the late nineteenth century, and his books continue to be reprinted. Yet until my doctoral dissertation on him appeared in 1984, there had been no major scholarly study of his work. The lack of research on A. T. Pierson demonstrates the poor state of scholarship on conservative evangelical leaders as recently as the 1980s.

After Pierson's death, his son and successor at the *Missionary Re-*

view of the World, Delavan Pierson, went through his papers and published a fine biography entitled *Arthur T. Pierson* (New York: Fleming H. Revell, 1912). Delavan had access to his father's private journal, and many quotations from it found their way into the biography. While Delavan's study is a superb example of a comprehensive, early twentieth-century biography, it has limitations. Arthur's son was not entirely comfortable with his father's holiness and mystical leanings and so downplays them. The biography also lacks a scholarly overview of the larger context in which Pierson worked. Delavan Pierson organized his father's papers and must have thrown out many before donating some of them to the Speer Library at Princeton Theological Seminary. By far the best source of Pierson papers is the Speer Library, as it holds scrapbooks of his early articles, Bible notes, and a correspondence file with letters to Pierson from famous people. Other Pierson collections are held by Gordon College in Wenham, Massachusetts; the Presbyterian Historical Society in Philadelphia; and Moody Bible Institute in Chicago. Since Pierson corresponded with so many people, and contributed to the beginnings of so many Bible schools, many libraries undoubtedly hold bits of his writings in other collections. For example, the American Baptist Historical Society has one of his letters. Insights into Pierson's work can be gained from the papers of those whom he influenced, most notably from the John R. Mott Papers and the Student Volunteer Movement Archives at Yale Divinity School in New Haven, Connecticut.

A. T. Pierson's major publications on missions and evangelism included *The Missionary Review of the World* (from 1888 until his death in 1911); *The Acts of the Holy Spirit* (New York: Fleming H. Revell, 1895); *The Crisis of Missions* (New York: Robert Carter & Bros., 1886); *The Divine Enterprise of Missions* (New York: Baker & Taylor, 1891); *Evangelistic Work in Principle and Practice* (New York: Baker & Taylor, 1887); *The Greatest Work in the World: The Evangelization of All Peoples in the Present Century* (New York: Fleming H. Revell, 1891); *The Miracles of Missions* (4 volumes) (New York: Funk & Wagnalls, 1891-1901); *The Modern Mission Century Viewed as a Cycle of Divine Working* (New York: Baker & Taylor, 1901); and *The New Acts of the Apostles* (New York: Baker & Taylor, 1894). The paper he presented in 1885 to the Philadelphia presbytery was published that year as "The Problem of Missions and Its Solution." The personal testimony that recounted his "conversion" to a ministry of soul-saving was printed in 1880 as a pamphlet entitled "The Pillar of Fire. To the Brethren in the Minstry [sic] of Christ." Pierson's many writings on missions included promotional, theoretical, and historical treatments of the subject.

Bible study was a second major area of publication. Books included *The Bible and Spiritual Criticism* (New York: Baker & Taylor, 1905); *The Bible and Spiritual Life* (New York: Gospel Publishing House, 1908); *God's Living Oracles* (London: James Nisbet & Co., 1904); *Keys to the Word* (St. Paul: Asher Publishing Co., 1887); *Knowing the Scriptures* (New York: Hodder & Stoughton, 1910); *Stumbling Stones Removed from the Word of God* (New York: Baker & Taylor, 1891); and *The Inspired Word* (New York: Anson D. F. Randolph & Co., 1888). Of the books on Bible study, the most important is *Knowing the Scriptures*, as it summarizes the insights of decades of study and fully develops Pierson's "organic" view of biblical interpretation. An influential aspect of Pierson's biblical work in the twentieth century was his contribution as one of the original editorial consultants for the *Scofield Reference Bible* (New York: Oxford University Press, 1909). The *Scofield Reference Bible* became a bestseller and laid down the system of interpretation known as dispensationalism. Its history was written by Arno Gaebelein, *The History of the Scofield Reference Bible* (New York: Our Hope Publications, 1943).

A third area in which Pierson published, especially in the latter part of his life, was that of holiness and Keswick spirituality. Unlike the works on missions, these books tended to be short, as they originated as meditations, sermons, and Bible readings. They included *The Believer's Life* (London: Morgan & Scott, 1905); *The Dove in the Heart* (New York: Fleming H. Revell, 1892); *The Hand on the Plow* (New York: Fleming H. Revell, 1892); *In Christ Jesus* (New York: Funk & Wagnalls, 1898); *In Full Armour* (London: Passmore & Alabaster, n.d.); *The Keswick Movement in Precept and Practice* (New York: Funk & Wagnalls, 1903); *Lessons in the School of Prayer as Taught by the Lord Jesus Christ Himself* (New York: Anson D. F. Randolph & Co., 1895); *Love in Wrath* (New York: Baker & Taylor, 1892); *Shall We Continue in Sin?* (New York: Baker & Taylor, 1897); and *A Spiritual Clinique: Four Bible Readings Given at Keswick in 1907* (New York: Gospel Publishing House, n.d.). Of his books on spirituality, my personal favorite is *In Christ Jesus*, a marvelous exposition of the believer's relationship with Christ, that has been reprinted numerous times. *The Keswick Movement in Precept and Practice* was one of the few overviews made of Keswick thought. While purists disliked the "typical" American systematization that Pierson brought to the material, the book has proved valuable to historians.

As a great preacher on both sides of the Atlantic, and as a teacher of preaching both at Spurgeon's college and in less formal settings, Pierson published a number of sermon collections and studies of homiletics. These included *The Divine Art of Preaching* (New York: Baker & Taylor, 1892); *The Heart of the Gospel* (New York: Baker & Taylor, 1892); *The Making of a Sermon* (New York: Gospel Publishing House, 1907); and *Seed Thoughts for Public Speakers* (New York: Funk & Wagnalls, 1900). Hundreds of his sermons and lectures on preaching were published individually. His major work on apologetics was his early book, *Many Infallible Proofs: The Evidences of Christianity* (New York: Fleming H. Revell, n.d.). Another pastoral aid was the hymnal he edited with A. J. Gordon, *The Coronation Hymnal* (New York: Fleming H. Revell, 1894).

While Pierson's life and later ministry were suffused with faith in the Second Coming of Jesus Christ, his work on explicitly premillennial themes tended to be in the form of sermons and lectures rather than book-length treatments. The most notable publications on the Second Coming were *The Coming of the Lord* (London: Passmore & Alabaster, 1896); *Our Lord's Second Coming a Motive to World-Wide Evangelization* (Philadelphia: John Wanamaker, 1886); and *The Second Coming of the Lord* (Philadelphia: H. Altemus, 1896). Pierson also attained a modest reputation as a biographer and eulogist, with such works as *Catherine of Siena* (New York: Funk & Wagnalls, 1898); *From the Pulpit to the Palm-Branch: A Memorial of C. H. Spurgeon* (New York: A. C. Armstrong & Son, 1892); *George Müller of Bristol and His Witness to a Prayer-Hearing God* (New York: Loizeaux Bros., 1899); *James Wright of Bristol England* (New York: Gospel Publishing House, 1906); and *Seven Years in Sierra Leone: The Story of the Work of William A. B. Johnson* (New York: Fleming H. Revell, 1897). Of all his books, the one that has probably been the most widely distributed is his biography of George Müller. Later Müller biographies were heavily dependent on Pierson's treatment, even to the point of plagiarizing his work.

One book that stands alone is *Forward Movements of the Last Half Century* (New York: Funk & Wagnalls, 1905), a historical overview of major evangelical, spiritual, and mission movements of the late nineteenth and early twentieth centuries. This book has been a valuable guide for historians and was reprinted in a documentary series on the holiness, pentecostal, and Keswick movements. Other works of historical importance included the series of articles he wrote near the end of his life that defended emerging fundamentalist views of biblical authority. He also participated in the historic collection of articles in *The Fundamentals* (1910-), the series of books that gave the movement its name. Journals to which he contributed are too numerous to name, as they ranged from popular Christian magazines, to denominational publications, to mission periodicals.

Tracing the life of such a busy man as A. T. Pierson required far more than tracking down and reading as many of his writings as possible. The biography by Delavan Pierson was helpful in many matters of chronology, as was a systematic reading of *The Missionary Review of the World*, in which Pierson often reported on his travels to major conferences. Reports of major conferences of the Evangelical Alliance, the Centenary Conference in London (1888), the Ecumenical Missionary Conference in New York (1900), the World's Parliament of Religions, and the Student Volunteer Movement quadrennial conferences, as well as the reports of such groups as Conventions of Christian Workers, YMCA summer conferences, and minutes of General Assemblies and state synods of the Presbyterian Church, helped to locate Pierson and identify his contributions to these groups. For Pierson's years in the United Kingdom, the most helpful way to reconstruct his speaking schedule was by reading the periodical *The Christian* (London: Morgan & Scott), the evangelical paper that reported on all events of note, including conferences on spirituality, the May meetings of Christian philanthropic and mission societies, and Keswick meetings. *The Christian* is an indispensable source for following the activities of leading Victorian British evangelicals. It also covered lectures in Exeter Hall and events at leading churches. *The Journal of Our Journey* (Wenham: Gordon College Archives, 1989), by Maria and A. J. Gordon, edited by Gordon College archivist John Beauregard, provided insight into the European tour of the Piersons and Gordons in 1888.

Another way to gain insight into the life and times of A. T. Pierson was through biographies of his contemporaries, especially the old-fashioned kind that often contained anecdotal details not considered important in scholarly biographies. Helpful biographical studies included Ernest Bacon, *Spurgeon: Heir of the Puritans* (Grand Rapids: Eerdmans, 1968, reprint edition); Clyde Binfield, *George Williams and the Y.M.C.A.* (London: Heinemann, 1973); Ruth Wilder Braisted, *In This Generation: The Story of Robert P. Wilder* (New York: Friendship Press, 1941); Lettie B. Cowman, *Charles E. Cowman* (Los Angeles: OMS, 1928); W. M. Douglas, *Andrew Murray and His Message* (Grand Rapids: Baker Book House, 1981, reprint edition); Mary Ellinwood, *Frank Field Ellinwood* (New York: Fleming H. Revell, 1911); James Findlay, Jr., *Dwight L. Moody* (Chicago: University of Chicago Press, 1969); W. Y. Fullerton, *C. H. Spurgeon* (London: Williams & Norgate, 1920); W. Y. Fullerton, *F. B. Meyer* (London: Marshall, Morgan & Scott, n.d.); Herbert Gibbons, *John Wanamaker*, 2 vols. (New York: Harper & Bros., 1926); Ernest B. Gordon, *Adoniram Judson Gordon* (New York: Fleming H. Revell, 1906); Stanley N. Gundry, *Love Them In: The Life and Theology of D. L. Moody* (Grand Rapids: Baker Book House, 1976); Charles E. Hambrick-Stowe, *Charles G. Finney and the Spirit of American Evangelicalism* (Grand Rapids: Eerdmans, 1996); C. Howard Hopkins, *John R. Mott, 1865-1955* (Grand Rapids: Eerdmans, 1979); John F. Piper, Jr., *Robert E. Speer* (Louisville: Geneva Press, 2000); John C. Pollock, *The Cambridge Seven* (Chicago: Inter-Varsity Press, 1955); Dr. and Mrs. Howard Taylor, *Hudson Taylor and the China Inland Mission* (London: China Inland Mission, 1927); George Thompson, *Thompson in Africa* (New York: Privately printed, 1854); Charles Gallaudet Trumbull, *The Life Story of C. I. Scofield* (New York: Oxford University Press, 1920); and Bertram Wyatt-Brown, *Lewis Tappan and the Evangelical War Against Slavery* (New York: Atheneum, 1971).

One category of materials that needed to be consulted to put A. T. Pierson into his context were institutional histories, especially of organizations with which he was involved. Models in this regard were Philip D. Jordan, *The Evangelical Alliance for the United States of America, 1847-1900* (New York and Toronto: Edwin Mellen Press, 1982); and C. Howard Hopkins, *History of the YMCA in North America* (New York: Association Press, 1951). Since the churches he served in Detroit, Indianapolis, Philadelphia, and London were all major parishes, it was possible to get helpful information both from local church histories and from the Presbyterian Archives in Philadelphia. Pierson's childhood churches in the Third Presbytery were also mentioned in early histories of New York City. Another category of institutional history that was especially helpful was that of Presbyterian history, including overviews of Presbyterianism in the United States, as well as more focused studies like William A. McCorkle, *A History of the Presbytery of Detroit, 1828-1888* (n.p.); Alfred Nevin, *History of the Presbytery of Philadelphia* (Philadelphia: W. S. Fortescue & Co., 1883); Robert Hastings Nichols, *Presbyterianism in New York State* (Philadelphia: Westminster Press, 1963); and Lefferts A. Loetscher, *Presbyterianism in Philadelphia Since 1870* (Philadelphia: University of Pennsylvania, 1944). Understanding of theological controversies within Presbyterianism was also important background for the study, for example George Marsden, *The Evangelical Mind and the New School Presbyterian Experience* (New Haven: Yale University Press, 1970); and Lefferts A. Loetscher, *The Broadening Church* (Philadelphia: University of Pennsylvania, 1954).

Understanding A. T. Pierson's many contexts was a key part of writing this book, starting from the New York City of his youth to the spiritual movements of his mature years. The most important contexts to understand were those of the development of nineteenth-century evangelicalism, both in the United States and the United Kingdom, and the unfolding history of Protestant missions in the high imperial age. The first evangelical context of Pierson's youth was that of the New School movement in Presbyterianism, and of evangelical abolitionism. Joel Tyler Headley, *The Great Riots of New York, 1712-1873* (New York: E. B. Treat, 1873), was important to setting the context of Pierson's birth, as was Bertram Wyatt-Brown's study of the Tappans. Kathryn Long has ably described *The Revival of 1857-58* (New York: Oxford University Press, 1998). For the views of northern evangelicals during the Civil War, see the classic by James Moorhead, *American Apocalypse: Yankee Protestants and the Civil War, 1860-1869* (New Haven: Yale University Press, 1978). After the Civil War, Pierson's location in urban ministry and evangelical social reform meant that literature on that subject is essential, for example Aaron Abell, *The Urban Impact on American Protestantism, 1865-1900* (Cambridge, Mass.: Harvard University Press, 1943); Joseph Gusfield, *Symbolic Crusade: Status Politics and the American Temperance Movement* (Urbana: University of Illinois, 1963); Norris Magnuson, *Salvation in the Slums: Evangelical Social Work, 1865-1920* (Metuchen, N.J.: Scarecrow Press, 1977); Henry F. May, *Protestant Churches and Industrial America* (New York: Harper & Bros.,

1949); and Sandra Sizer, *Gospel Hymns and Social Religion* (Philadelphia: Temple University Press, 1978).

Pierson's leadership in the emerging premillennial dispensational network of the late nineteenth century required attention to key treatments of the intellectual origins of fundamentalism. The three most important books in this regard were George Marsden, *Fundamentalism and American Culture* (New York: Oxford University Press, 1980); Ernest R. Sandeen, *The Roots of Fundamentalism* (Chicago: University of Chicago Press, 1970); and Timothy Weber, *Living in the Shadow of the Second Coming* (New York: Oxford University Press, 1979). Older works that were helpful included Norman Kraus, *Dispensationalism in America* (Richmond: John Knox Press, 1958); and Clarence Bass, *Backgrounds to Dispensationalism* (Grand Rapids: Eerdmans, 1960). On Pierson's Baconian philosophical method, see Theodore Dwight Bozeman, *Protestants in an Age of Science* (Chapel Hill: University of North Carolina Press, 1977).

The overall context of British evangelicalism in the Victorian era was ably chronicled by David Bebbington, *Evangelicalism in Modern Britain* (Grand Rapids: Baker Book House, 1989); L. E. Elliott-Binns, *Religion in the Victorian Era* (London: Lutterworth Press, 1936); and John Kent, *Holding the Fort: Studies in Victorian Revivalism* (London: Epworth Press, 1978). Although they do not focus on Pierson, issues of transatlantic connections among evangelicals were raised by Richard Carwardine, *Transatlantic Revivalism* (Westport, Conn.: Greenwood Press, 1978); and George Rawlyk and Mark Noll, eds., *Amazing Grace: Evangelicalism in Australia, Britain, Canada, and the United States* (Grand Rapids: Baker Book House, 1993). On theological controversy among British evangelicals, see Willis B. Glover, *Evangelical Nonconformists and Higher Criticism in the Nineteenth Century* (London: Independent Press, 1954). The Keswick Movement played a large role in the last fifteen years of Pierson's life. Several works attempted an overview of Keswick, including John C. Pollock, *The Keswick Story* (London: Hodder & Stoughton, 1964); and J. B. Figgis, *Keswick from Within* (London: Marshall Brothers, 1914). Books and articles on British missionaries by Andrew Porter and Stewart Piggin provided good insight into the missionary context entered by Pierson when he spoke to British students and attended missionary departures.

The history of American Protestant missions provided an important backdrop to the study. Several key articles by William Hutchison were essential in analyzing trends in the high imperial period, including relationships between theological liberals and conservatives. His book *Errand to the World: American Protestant Thought and Foreign Missions* (Chicago: University of Chicago, 1987) will help readers put Pierson into the broader context of American mission theory. Research on the Student Volunteer Movement has been considerable. Classic studies included articles by Clifton J. Phillips, and a recent history by Michael Parker, *The Kingdom of Character: The Student Volunteer Movement for Foreign Missions, 1886-1926* (Lanham, Md.: University Press of America, 1998). A pioneer study of evangelical missions was edited by Joel Carpenter and Wilbert Shenk as *Earthen Vessels: American Evangelicals and Foreign Missions, 1880-1930* (Grand Rapids: Eerdmans, 1990), in which appeared my article "'The Crisis of Missions': Premillennial Mission Theory and the Origins of Independent Evangelical Missions." An overview of faith missions was provided by Klaus Fiedler, *The Story of Faith Missions* (Oxford: Regnum Books International, 1994). Since A. T. Pierson was involved at the start of so many faith missions, I consulted existing histories of the varied missions, including Kenneth Richardson, *Garden of Miracles: A History of the African Inland Mission* (London: Victory Press, 1968); and Robert D. Wood, *In These Mortal Hands: The Story of the Oriental Missionary Society* (Greenwood, Ind.: OMS International, 1983). The Billy Graham Center at Wheaton College is the major archive in the United States for faith missions, and its collections contain much interesting information on missions and Bible schools with which Pierson was involved.

Finally, there is a category of materials that did not contribute to the book, but that might attract readers who are interested in A. T. Pierson. As evangelical missions made the year 2000 their goal for planting a church in every people group, there was a rediscovery of Arthur Pierson's passion for systematic world evangelization. The July-August 1993 issue of *Mission Frontiers*, the Bulletin of the U.S. Center for World Mission, was entitled "Will We Fail Again?" A. T. Pierson's photograph graced the cover, and the authors asked whether efforts to evangelize the world by 2000 would fail just as Moody and Pierson's "Appeal to Disciples Everywhere" in 1885 did not succeed in completing the task of world evangelization. Pierson's mission theories and numerical scheme for world evangelization were highlighted in a publication by Todd M. Johnson, *Countdown to 1900: World Evangelization at the End of the Nineteenth Century* (Birmingham: New Hope, 1988). As the A.D. 2000 Movement targeted the year 2000, the visionary genius, enthusiasm, and numerical calculations of A. T. Pierson attracted new attention. In the twenty-first century, evangelical Christianity has spread around the world. Although Pierson did not live to see the harvest, his ideas continue to inspire leaders of evangelical missions today.

Index